SUPERVISORY STUDIES

PREFACE TO THE THIRD EDITION

This book has been written for individuals who are actively engaged in supervision and for those who wish to qualify in this subject. It covers in detail the syllabuses for the courses in supervision offered by the National Examinations Board for Supervisory Studies and the Institute of Supervisory Management. Numerous test questions and suggested projects are given for each section of the work. The work also covers the production aspects for subjects incorporated in the Certificate in Industrial Management offered by the Institution of Industrial Managers. It will be useful for those studying the appropriate syllabuses offered by colleges of further education as these have followed a pattern similar to that of the original scheme drawn up by the N.E.B.S.S. for external examinations.

Supervision permeates all levels of organisation from first line supervision up to the managing director, who also supervises a group of senior executives by very close contact, in addition to his managerial activities.

Furthermore, he should be using the same techniques and principles recommended to the lowest level of supervision. Most jobs involving the direction, co-ordination and control of individuals contain managerial and supervisory elements, the ratio mainly varying dependent upon the position in the organisation.

The book is divided into three parts. Part One discusses how to build and maintain an efficient organisation. The main topics are covered in seven chapters dealing with various aspects of supervision, selecting and training supervisors and introductions to organisation, growth, industry and management.

Part Two, on creating an effective working force, includes detailed discussion on human relations and motivation, various aspects of communication, and a number of personnel aspects.

Part Three deals with a range of topics under the general heading of "Controlling the Work". A chapter on the nature of control is followed by three chapters on work study and chapters on statistical method, production control, quality control, financial and costing aspects and cost reduction.

No attempt has been made to omit situations where a group such as management, supervision, trade unions, employees or the Government appear to be at fault. Where such topics and other situations are of a controversial nature, some information and remarks have been given with the intention of stimulating the reader to investigate further to form his own opinions.

Often there is no best way of solving many of the problems seen in industry. Students are reminded, therefore, that many questions involving human beings demand something more than a stereotyped approach. The importance is stressed of presenting a *balanced* answer in an examination, indicating the extent of knowledge on the subject. Very few topics of supervision may be satisfactorily considered in terms of a concise list of points, but often an author is forced to resort to such methods to illustrate distinctly the main aspects in written form.

In addition, some important topics appear in more than one aspect of supervision. Where this occurs, I have intentionally repeated the various points as a reminder and then stressed the importance of the topic from the particular aspects under discussion.

Since the second edition of this book, published in 1973, the main areas of change in the industrial scene have been new industrial relations and health and safety legislation, and the increase in acceptance of new motivation theories. The work has been updated to include these features.

My sincere appreciation is given to Dr. Joseph Batty, for his encouragement and help in the preparation of the manuscript. I should also like to thank my colleagues at Harrow College of Higher Education, who kindly offered their assistance.

A list of professional bodies and Government departments who kindly helped me is given on the opposite page. Lastly my personal thanks go to my wife for her advice during the preparation of the manuscript and for her help in typing the draft.

P.W.B.

October 1979

ACKNOWLEDGMENTS

I GRATEFULLY acknowledge the assistance given me by the following:

The British Institute of Management, for details of the Foremanship Certificate which has now been superseded by the Certificate in Supervisory Studies controlled by The National Examinations Board for Supervisory Studies.

British Standards Institution, for extracts from *The Glossary of Terms in Work Study*, BS 3138, 1959, reproduced by kind permission. Copies of the complete Standard may be obtained from the British Standards Institution, 2 Park Street, London W1Y 4AA.

The Department of Employment, for details of the Training Within Industry programmes (now run by the Manpower Services Commission). Full details are available on application to The Manager, at any local Employment Office or Jobcentre.

National Examinations Board for Supervisory Studies, for kind permission to quote extracts from their publication on the scheme of examinations and qualifications in the field of foremanship and supervision.

National Institute of Industrial Psychology, for kind permission to reproduce "The Seven-Point Plan" from the *N.I.I.P. Paper*, Number 1.

Macdonald & Evans Ltd., publishers, for kind permission to reproduce the "five-fold framework" extracted from John Munro Fraser's book, *Employment Interviewing*.

Controller of Her Majesty's Stationery Office, for permission to reproduce tables from the *Annual Abstract of Statistics*, the *Department of Employment Gazette* and *Britain 1979: An Official Handbook*.

The Institute of Supervisory Management for kind permission to quote extracts from their examinations scheme.

CONTENTS

Part One

BUILDING AND MAINTAINING AN EFFICIENT ORGANISATION

Part Two

CREATING AN EFFECTIVE WORKING FORCE

Part Three

CONTROLLING THE WORK

BUILDING AND MAINTAINING AN EFFICIENT ORGANISATION

CHAPTER I

THE SUPERVISOR

The Changing Role of the Supervisor

SOME people say that the days of cheap labour and cheap gin, of the landed gentry, and the revolution in industry, saw the climax of the foreman's power in Britain. The right to engage and dismiss labour and to dictate on practically every function connected with production elevated his job to one of high status with little interference from management, as long as output satisfied the owners.

The accuracy of this view is unimportant for it holds no place in the modern supervisor's outlook and misleadingly assumes that foremanship has suffered a decline. The change towards a more civilised or human approach to supervision is not a decadent step; it forms another phase in the continuous drive towards effective supervision.

Any lengthy process of development involving people is subject to fluctuations. For several years after World War II, operators were in the limelight, receiving waves of pay increases and general attention, while foremen merged into the background and continued to play their important role at a critical stage in the organisation structure. Around 1950, the unique position of the foreman became obvious to industry in Britain, and many schemes to improve performance and status were introduced. This long chain of events can be roughly grouped into four phases, as follows.

1. Autocratic management

During the Middle Ages, supervision through force was commonplace, both for free and slave labour. Output was probably very low. This barbaric use of labour died slowly: slaves were still being used in the British Empire even as late as 1833.

2. Semi-autocratic management

The early modern period, from about 1500 to 1940, saw the introduction of a more subtle form of supervision through fear of dismissal, although driving and bullying continued. In an era of unemployment dismissal could mean near-starvation for the worker and his family. The foreman also faced similar treatment from management, with many operators standing by to take his place at a moment's notice. The supply of labour continued to outpace industrial growth owing to a huge increase in the population from three million in 1500, to forty-five million in 1935. Those who were employed submitted, at various times, to truck, cheating, and low wages. Underemployment also occurred through trade cycles.

The inevitable conflict between labour and capitalists first took on an organised form early in the nineteenth century. Local trade clubs were set up, followed by trade unions on a national level, towards the end of the century. By 1940 waves of amalgamations had strengthened the bargaining power of the trade unions considerably. Thus they remained, as technological advances continued to create new industries and an increasing demand for labour.

Most companies were small family concerns with only a few levels of management. The foreman possessed considerable power because he was performing a whole range of functions in keeping with the size of the business. As company size grew in the twentieth century, there was little change in management techniques in Britain. Most managers were technical men, wholly absorbed in the problems of technological advancement, which overshadowed labour troubles, though some pioneers such as Robert Owen, Wedgwood, Cortez, Cadbury, Boulton, and Watt, attempted improvements.

By 1900, F. W. Taylor, who is often known as the "Father of Scientific Management", developed new techniques in the U.S.A. which included ideas of fostering close co-operation between management and men, and functionalising many of the foreman's duties. His methods eventually "caught on" and were extensively used in the U.S.A. to speed up production.

In Britain, Taylor's teaching was ignored. Some articles on Taylorism appeared in the press about 1913–14 but, with the exception of a few large, progressive firms, little interest was shown until 1940.

3. Constitutional management

The critical war situation in 1940 demanded about four times the existing output in industry. Soon it became obvious that working overtime was not the complete answer to this problem. Attempts were made, therefore, to increase production in other ways.

Ernest Bevin transformed working conditions; welfare officers were introduced, and the unions and employers agreed to set up joint production committees. Although the effectiveness of these committees varied considerably, it began to be recognised that the first steps towards maximum efficiency were only possible when human relations and machine operations were considered to be of equal importance.

Close consultation between the Government and trade unions led to many trade union leaders and officials entering Government departments. Wages were guaranteed and claims were settled at a national level between the unions and employers' associations.

A new era had commenced, with the unions gathering strength

and consolidating, with Government co-operation and consultation, and with employers gradually changing their attitude towards employees.

In 1948 a new word appeared, *productivity*, introduced by the Anglo-American Council on Production. Productivity teams were introduced and employers were pressed to mechanise, support joint consultation, give more information to employees, improve amenities, and set up realistic wage structures. The unions agreed to help, and in 1952 the British Productivity Council replaced the Anglo-American Council. The framework for promoting higher productivity was firmly established.

At this time the problem of increasing exports became more urgent and, coupled with full employment, the only solution was the more efficient use of existing resources, i.e. machines, production techniques, and labour.

This does not necessarily mean harder work (unless output is already below a reasonable level). Some improvement can nearly always be made through better methods, more use of machinery, and the application of techniques in production organisation, in the same way that an experienced operator uses his greater skill and ingenuity to produce more with less effort than the learner. Productivity means balancing *all* the factors of production so that the highest output is obtained for lowest effort. It is achieved through proper attention to selection and training; human relations; motivation; communication; work study; and control; and the supervisor plays a major role in co-ordinating the resources of production and achieving co-operation at all levels.

Phase 3 is an interim period of rapid change and adjustment, continually checked by the unchanging attitudes towards each other of the State, management, employees, and trade unions.

Outdated autocratic attitudes still persist in some parts of Britain where the threat of dismissal is exercised by supervisors.

The confusion that must exist in many employees' minds will no doubt persist for many more years considering the opposing ideologies confronting them, the long-standing suspicion and distrust of management, and the never-ending clashes between unions, management, and the State.

Management in British industry seems reluctant to develop new techniques to increase productivity although, of course, some companies are making tremendous efforts. The Industrial Training Act 1964 illustrates the State's sense of urgency, the changing opinion of many people towards education and training, and the critical part these play in higher productivity.

Industrial friction is unavoidable in such a fluid situation, thus making life very difficult for the supervisor. But if the industrial climate is to change, much will depend upon the supervisor's ability to aim for higher ideals and clear objectives which he fully appreciates will not be reached in just a few years.

4. Combined democratic and constitutional management

In this future phase, it is hoped that efforts to use new techniques of supervision through persuasion, reasoning, and consideration, will lead eventually to a common understanding and a common purpose among all members of industrial society. Far-sighted and persevering supervisors will not bring about this revolution alone, but their help is essential during the period of industrial adjustment.

The process of supervision will be easier when industrial harmony is reached. Good relationships will allow more time for improving methods and developing new products. Close co-operation between management, trade unions, and employees, with complete freedom in exchange of information, will then become automatic.

It is most important that this objective should be quite clear in the mind of every supervisor. Any attempt to distort this aim, dismissing it as a Utopia which is impossible to achieve, or rejecting the idea that people *can* get on together, will upset the balanced outlook which is essential in order to achieve co-operation throughout all levels of industry.

Definition of a Supervisor

A supervisor is any person who is given authority and responsibility for planning and controlling the work of a group by close contact. Broadly speaking, this definition means that a supervisor may be delegated the authority to engage, transfer, suspend, reprimand or dismiss an employee under his control. He may deal with grievances and take appropriate action, be responsible for discipline, for quantity and quality of output, and make recommendations to management. The definition may also be interpreted in its narrow sense to include anyone who directs the work of others by giving instructions on production, by co-ordinating specialist departments and by recommending courses of action to management.

SUPERVISION AND MANAGEMENT

Supervision implies operating at close range by actually overseeing or controlling on the shop floor, dealing with situations on the spot as they arise, whereas management implies controlling remotely by using other administrative means. Supervision and management naturally overlap in practice, partly from necessity, where managers show a close personal interest in order to achieve co-operation, and partly from lack of management training.

It is essential to note the difference between the two functions. The supervisory function is concerned with the day-to-day running of the group, which will entail a certain amount of attention to detail depending upon the size of the section. If the section is large the supervisor will need to master the art of delegation, passing on the minor tasks to his subordinates, thus giving himself more time to plan and control the work effectively. The managerial function, on the other hand, should be concerned with thinking well ahead on questions of policy, programmes of expansion, new products, new markets and so on, thus leaving the detail and less important tasks to managers' subordinates. This distinction between a supervisor and a manager, although very clear in theory, is frequently obscured in practice when supervisors are inclined to skip essential detail and concentrate on forward planning, whereas managers are seen to be very keen on attending to detail, often in order to compensate for their lack of drive, vision and decision-making ability (*see* Chapter VI on Management).

SUPERVISION AND OPERATORS

In general terms, the difference between an operator and a supervisor is that the operator performs his own work, using technical knowledge manually, but the supervisor controls the work of others by using his technical knowledge theoretically, combined with supervisory techniques.

Basic Elements of Supervision

The supervisor will considerably improve his performance by using effectively the techniques of each of the basic elements of supervision to supplement his technical knowledge.

The basic elements are as follows.

   I. Building and maintaining an efficient organisation.
  II. Creating and maintaining an effective working force.
 III. Controlling the work.

This book is divided into three parts on the basis of these elements, and a breakdown is given shortly to indicate the main aspects which are discussed. Many of the techniques are used instinctively by supervisors, who simply apply sound common sense. To be really effective, however, the application of these principles must be sustained even during difficult circumstances, such as pressure of work or lack of information from management.

The ability to apply the right principles at the right time demands something more than knowledge alone. The three elements of supervision must interact closely although they are considered independently. For instance, no decision should be made on facts and theory alone; the human factor must also be given due consideration.

Training and a balanced outlook are essential for successful application of supervisory techniques.

BUILDING AND MAINTAINING AN EFFICIENT ORGANISATION

The supervisor must be able the appreciate the significance of the organisation structure and recognise relationships within it, in order to improve co-ordination with other groups in the concern. These aspects and the practical steps towards improving an organisation are described in Chapters III and IV. The importance of human groups and grouping, which is an essential part of organisation, is also discussed in Chapter IX (Improving Human Relations).

Within the sphere of organisation the supervisor should possess a knowledge of the general industrial background, the work of management, and the supervisor's place in the management team. These aspects are covered in Chapters V, VI, and VII.

The following list indicates the supervisor's part in maintaining a smooth-running organisation, but it should be clear that many of these duties have an important bearing on the other two basic elements. Hard and fast distinctions are unrealistic.

1. Organisation planning (using principles of organisation outlined in Chapter IV) to achieve the objective.
2. Keeping subordinates informed and conscious of objectives.
3. Establishing and maintaining organisation relationships between all subordinates.
4. Explaining, directing and controlling all the activities of the group and, in turn, of individuals.
5. Ensuring that the group is an integral part of the organisation.
6. Recommending changes in organisation where necessary.
7. Using specialists effectively.
8. Co-ordinating all the activities within the group to achieve the objective.

CREATING AND MAINTAINING AN EFFECTIVE WORKING FORCE

Any aspect of supervision has some bearing on employees and their attitude towards work. Probably this element of supervision, running an effective working force, involves the most controversial, misunderstood, and yet critical of topics within industry.

The effective supervisor must be able to understand and motivate individuals, develop and maintain good communication, and pay close attention to a number of personnel aspects. Part Two, therefore, includes chapters on human relations and motivation (VIII, IX, and X); and on communication (XI, XII, and XIII); personnel aspects covered are the personnel function (Chapter XIV), employment and remuneration (Chapter XV), training (Chapter XVI), industrial relations (Chapter XVII), health and safety (Chapter XVIII), and welfare (Chapter XIX).

A summary of duties concerning this second element of supervision now follows.

1. *Fostering good working relationships:* mediating between operatives and management; co-operating with fellow supervisors; and consulting shop stewards and convenors.

2. *Promoting good communication:* submitting reports to management on production; making special reports where necessary; and attending committees as directed.

3. *Providing information:* interpreting company policies and instructions and *informing* employees of their meaning to avoid ambiguity.

4. *Promoting and maintaining high morale:* keeping in constant touch with operatives; dealing with grievances as they arise; operating a suggestion scheme and encouraging participation.

5. *Maintaining general discipline,* and conducting disciplinary interviews.

6. *Keeping up to date on wages systems* in the company and rating employees accurately in this respect.

7. *Interviewing candidates* and introducing newcomers; giving induction interviews.

8. *Training new and transferred employees* in their jobs; these will include apprentices, adult workers, and deputies.

9. *Liaising with the Personnel Officer* on questions of transfers, promotions, and terminations.

CONTROLLING THE WORK

This element of supervision covers the wide field of control which begins at the planning stages of production and ends with the finished product. The field of control includes:

(*a*) Division and delegation of responsibility to individuals;
(*b*) decisions on the work content (e.g. how and when it should be done);
(*c*) budgeted costs of performing the work;
(*d*) regulation of work performance by such factors as human relations and motivation; cost reduction and progress;
(*e*) quality control.

The essential topics discussed in Part Three are the nature of control (Chapter XX); work study (Chapters XXI, XXII, and XXIII) and statistical method, production control, quality control, financial aspects, costing aspects, and cost reduction (in Chapters XXIV to XXX respectively).

The supervisor's duties in connection with control are as follows.

1. Planning production and setting up procedures which will include routeing, scheduling, controlling, despatching, and follow up.
2. Maintaining plant and equipment.
3. Using work study techniques and procedures to develop the department.
4. Achieving and maintaining quality, and keeping statistical records on quality control.
5. Recording and ensuring adequate supplies of materials in accordance with stores and material control.
6. Checking waste and establishing cost reduction controls where necessary.
7. Keeping adequate records and control costs as budgeted.
8. Promoting safety.

Range of Supervisory Jobs: Levels of Supervision

No two supervisory jobs are exactly alike. Two apparently similar supervisory jobs may in fact be very different, depending on such factors as status; company size; the product; the type of company and its structure; relationships between management, supervision, trade unions, and operators; production tempo; growth problems; staffing; and the use of specialists.

This variation in supervisory jobs depends mainly upon the range of duties, the complexity of each duty and the particular level of supervision. An understanding of the latter aspect is most important.

The many levels of supervision can be grouped in a number of ways according to factors such as titles, salary, number of employees controlled, or degree of authority and responsibility.

A typical example of grouping supervisors into levels, based on the last two factors, is given below.

1. Primary group supervision
Included in this level are operators, leading hands and charge-hands who are given additional responsibility for supervising small groups. Such a cluster of six to twelve operators forms a primary working group, and the person in control is known as the *primary group leader*. His position is important because he represents the vital link between operators and management. Weakness at this point is obviously dangerous, and often not fully appreciated by management, although this extremity of control can easily nullify the efforts of higher management levels.

2. Section supervision
This level includes all supervisors who are responsible for sections

consisting of about six primary groups. Various titles are used, such as *section supervisors*, junior foremen, and assistant foremen. They rarely do any manual work; instead their authority and responsibility is generally restricted to allocating duties, ensuring smooth work flow by co-ordinating the activities of the primary group leaders, and dealing with the day-to-day running of the section.

3. Department supervision

A control group, consisting of about six sections, is headed by a foreman. The group is also termed a department, and the foreman may be called department superintendent, or *department supervisor*. General responsibility for the department includes planning and controlling the work. This is the level most often thought of when considering what is meant by supervision. Procedures and policy normally originate from higher levels.

4. Works supervision

All senior supervisors come under this category. There are many titles used to describe this level, including general foreman, senior foreman, production foreman, *shop supervisor*, and shop superintendent. They have substantial authority and responsibility in order to control effectively the six to eight departments which generally make up the shop or works.

In most cases a supervisor will fit into one of these groups. Generally, all four levels are seen in the medium and large size companies, whereas in the small firm, levels two and four only would be apparent.

Responsibilities of a Supervisor

IMMEDIATE RESPONSIBILITIES

A supervisor is responsible for his subordinates, the activities and the workplace which he is given formal authority to control. Within this over-all definition, the finer points of responsibility should now emerge which make possible the performance of the job.

One way of thinking about these responsibilities is to examine again the list of duties given under each basic element and to summarise them in a list of responsibilities, as follows.

1. Staff—morale, consultation, discipline, welfare, safety, employment, induction, training.
2. Work—quantity, quality, and timeliness.
3. Cost—maximum economy.
4. Machines and equipment—maintenance, loading, operation.
5. Materials—supplies, waste, suitability.
6. Workplace—layout, tidiness, good housekeeping.

The above responsibilities can only be fulfilled by giving the supervisor the authority to forecast and plan in accordance with company policy; to organise and execute; and to co-ordinate and control. He, in turn, becomes responsible for these activities.

SOCIAL RESPONSIBILITIES

The wider field of social responsibilities covers indirect relationships with the shareholders, the customers, the State and the suppliers. Although these social groups appear remote from supervision, their interests must be considered if a supervisor is to realise his full responsibility.

The shareholders or proprietors have invested capital in the business, and they naturally expect it to earn interest in the form of dividend. The customers expect goods to be priced in relation to quality and delivered on time. Unfortunately, the latter point often is considered too lightly, bearing in mind the chaos late delivery can cause, especially with goods for industry. The question of better designs and a wider range of products for the community presents deeper problems of research, cost, and profitability.

The State relies upon industry and everyone connected with it to provide sufficient goods to export and to supply the home market. Economic stability is vital to everyone; success depends largely upon the best use of capital and the effectiveness of labour.

Finally, the supervisor's responsibility to suppliers means that promises should be kept whenever possible and wrong impressions carefully avoided. For example, the impression that regular supplies of a commodity will be needed is easily created, leading a supplier to plan accordingly, whereas a limited quantity only may be actually required. Any information of use to the supplier should be given freely, especially on the question of specifications which may be unnecessarily fine, such as tolerances, finish and packing.

QUESTIONS

1. Discuss the changing role of the supervisor.
2. Describe how you would increase productivity in your department.
3. Explain how the method of controlling employees has changed over the past few centuries and why the change has occurred.
4. Give a reasoned account of the connection between productivity and standard of living.
5. "The cost of labour depends upon the supply of labour." Discuss this proposition.
6. Give a detailed definition of a supervisor.
7. Outline the range of supervisory jobs under the headings of supervisory levels, range of duties and complexity of each duty.
8. List the typical duties of a supervisor.
9. What do you consider to be the basic elements of supervision?
10. How would you assess morale in a workshop?

11. What are the likely qualities to be seen in a successful supervisor?

12. Describe the problems faced by Britain after World War II.

13. Write a brief history of trade unions and their changing role since World War II.

14. Write an account of the various levels of supervision and the significance of each.

15. Discuss the social responsibilities of a supervisor.

CHAPTER II

SELECTING AND TRAINING SUPERVISORS

Qualities of a Good Supervisor

THE previous chapter on the duties of a supervisor outlined *what* he should be doing, particularly his part in the maintenance of an efficient organisation, an effective labour force, and controlled production. This chapter firstly describes the qualities of a good supervisor, which determine *how well* he supervises and secondly discusses the selection and training, which determine the effectiveness of the supervisory force.

The main problem when discussing personal qualities is the measurement of degree. For example, when people refer to intelligence as a quality, they use such terms as average, reasonable, high level, low level, and general level. Unfortunately there is no standardised method of dealing with these matters and each individual will naturally interpret these terms in a slightly different way.

It should be appreciated that a general foreman may possess no more qualities than a primary group leader, but he will possess them in greater degree. Moreover, a comprehensive list of an outstanding general foreman's qualities would correspond with specifications for general management. Nevertheless, the same qualities appear at the lower levels of supervision, but in a less intensive form.

The main differences in supervisory job specifications occur in the technical and administrative aspects, which vary considerably depending upon the industry, company size, or different circumstances within the same factory, e.g. special qualities may be desirable in supervising particular groups that contain an unusual feature.

The following five essential qualities of drive, leadership, intelligence, technical skill and knowledge, and character, are not discussed in order of importance. Each job demands a different proportion of all these requirements.

1. Drive

The basic need for vitality, energy, and enthusiasm, is good health. Physical and mental fatigue impair judgment and are demoralising for subordinates who need to be "caught up" by the supervisor's example and vigour. Making the best use of time and energy requires careful planning. Whenever possible, over-excitement and bursts of stop-gap measures should be avoided to conserve nervous energy. An even spread of effort sustained over long periods is desirable for good performance, which can then be expected from others. This sustained effort or drive demands self-discipline and conscientiousness in the face of outside distractions and the general pace of living.

2. Leadership

A good leader must be an outstanding member of the group who gets along easily with people and has above-average competence. Leadership is difficult to define accurately; its intangible qualities cannot be learned, yet they are easily recognisable.

Naturally, ability is not enough. Previous environment, which moulds personality and character, should provide a balanced background for an individual to feel at ease, mix easily with many types of people, and sense his ability to supervise well. Some people, of course, manage to overcome an unhappy past, while others who were more fortunate fail to make the grade.

A good leader sets a high standard of performance for himself, keeps to it, and expects a similar performance from others. He mixes easily with people by understanding them and using clear and constructive methods of handling everyday problems. He is not always more skilful or more intelligent than his subordinates, but he appreciates his own technical and human limitations. He recognises his responsibilities and uses his authority in a fair and impartial manner. This implies that he is temperamentally suited for the task of solving problems, is sufficiently far sighted to see potential ones before they arise, and can take appropriate early action.

An important management task is to create conditions under which leaders can become effective but, at the same time, avoiding the development of a situation where leaders struggle for power among each other. If the well known "rat-race" is allowed, subordinates suffer, and organisation is badly affected. Given the opportunity and the right conditions, the leader can push people beyond their normal capabilities towards a higher level of effectiveness, with greater work satisfaction.

3. Intelligence

Most supervisory posts require average intelligence, similar to the general level of intelligence found among skilled operators. Some people expect the supervisor to be more intelligent than his subordinates, which is naturally desirable. Whether there are sufficient people of this calibre to fill over half a million jobs among a working population of about twenty-three million is for the statisticians to decide.

A high level of intelligence is essential in some supervisory jobs, where technical and administrative problems are intricate and demanding. On the other hand, many supervisory jobs contain a large proportion of routine work which would soon frustrate the highly intelligent man.

In reality, the foreman needs shrewdness, judgment, and an acute mind with plenty of common sense. He must be quick-witted, able to distinguish between major and minor problems, apportioning sufficient time to deal with each problem. He must decide whether permanent or temporary arrangements are needed. He must understand clearly the many and varied written and spoken instructions and be able to pass on information clearly to a number of different types of subordinates.

4. Technical skill and knowledge

An inherent part of any supervisory job is technical competence. The supervisor needs a good knowledge of every operation or process under his control to be able to eliminate common faults, wastage, and any dangerous practices. Practical and theoretical knowledge plus varied experience are essential to command respect and help others. To train successfully, he must illustrate why, as well as how, a job should be done, and at the same time appreciate the trainee's problems. He does not necessarily have to be the best operator in the group, but certainly he should not be the worst.

A reasonable elementary education is necessary and in many supervisory jobs further education is essential. Practical experience is sometimes still sufficient, but technical education will most likely become imperative in many industries, as rapid technological advance continues.

5. Character

Nobody possesses all the qualities of character of the ideal supervisor. A compromise is inevitable, and the choice will be governed by the particular circumstances.

Some of the important qualities are honesty and trustworthiness, with a strict sense of fairness and justice. A stable personality is essential for an even temper, steadiness, and reliability. A direct, open, and positive approach is desirable, giving due consideration to all parties when dealing with problems and grievances. Cheerfulness and enthusiasm, coupled with a sense of humour, are essential to provide the right type of industrial atmosphere.

In brief, a good supervisor must possess something besides technical competence, clearly placing him above his particular group. Someone without higher intellect can still shine by having more drive, or inherent qualities of leadership. A person displaying strength of character who "bubbles over" with activity can make up for other faults.

Each particular combination of qualities would suit a certain group in a particular work situation. Thus, one person stands out in a group and, provided his outlook is reasonably aligned with management policy and not objectionable, he is a likely choice.

Selection of Supervisors

The importance of careful and fair selection of supervisors is often overlooked by management. Promotions from the shop floor and appointments in the lower levels of supervision are viewed very critically by operatives who are often directly affected.

Poor selection may destroy the efforts of previous supervisors who have managed to improve the industrial climate. Overlooked employees may feel frustrated and suspicious of management if the appointed individual is obviously unsuitable. The working harmony of the group or groups may be upset and resentment tends to spread like a disease—in all directions. The disgruntled individuals, who may have a legitimate complaint, mention the "injustice" to everyone and a sense of frustration may develop throughout the concern.

SOME OBSERVATIONS ON SELECTION
External influences
Before considering the methods of selection, some circumstances which can affect selection must be mentioned. A common fault among supervisors is to baulk the promotion of an individual because he is considered to be indispensable in his present position, although he is eminently suitable for promotion. Sometimes the supervisor cannot be bothered to train a replacement and the easiest remedy is deliberately to penalise the person's chances of promotion, often forcing the person to seek employment elsewhere.

It is not uncommon for superiors who are able to influence promotion, or who actually select the individual, to allow unimportant incidents (such as dancing out of turn with the works manager's daughter, or failing to recognise the general manager's wife in the High Street) to dominate their impressions or opinions of subordinates, sometimes holding a trivial misdemeanour against a person for years. In some cases, even the suspicion of wrongdoing is sufficient reason to by-pass an individual. A true understanding of reality makes due allowance for human errors, and it is wiser and fairer to give other people the benefit of the doubt.

Type to suit management
Managers' opinions on the type of supervisor required are diverse and also vary with company size. The manager in a small concern may demand a "Yes-man" who carries out his orders to the letter, while in a large establishment the opposite type may be required, who shows initiative, makes his own decisions, and has a powerful personality. Some prefer the outsider with new ideas, others favour

internal promotion. No two managers agree entirely on the qualities they seek for a particular position and usually compromise is necessary.

METHODS OF SELECTION

The methods of selection are divided into two groups to highlight the importance of using scientific methods.

1. Unsubstantiated methods

All methods that do not allow for systematic selection and result in the detrimental effects of poor selection upon employees and the company, come under this heading. These methods do not necessarily imply spontaneous selection; some are planned well in advance, but selection is based not on true grounds but on such grounds as:

(a) favouritism, promoting friends and relatives;
(b) length of service or age seniority;
(c) high standard of skill alone;
(d) haphazard recommendations by a supervisor;
(e) chance, through stop-gap arrangements, i.e. someone being at the right place at the right time.

2. Scientific methods

Any method that attempts to reduce the possibility of error comes under this heading. The aim is to find the best man available for each vacancy. All employees, therefore, initially have equal opportunity and those with ability have good prospects of promotion which will not depend upon influence and favouritism. The essential requirements for any scheme with these aims are as follows.

(a) Planning ahead by estimating the vacancies which are likely to occur.
(b) Preparation of a job specification listing all the main requirements of the vacancy.
(c) Advertisement internally and externally with the understanding that promotion from within will always take precedence where suitable internal applicants are available.
(d) Careful investigation of *all* employees as promotion prospects.
(e) Interviews of all candidates who are likely to be suitable. These must be conducted by skilled, objective interviewers and supplemented by appropriate tests.
(f) Final choice or approval by top management or a selected panel.

Scientific choice, although not perfect, has obvious advantages. Many factors which may have been omitted are now included in the job specification; there is less chance of potential supervisors being overlooked; better assessment of individuals is now assured; and unbiased selection is more likely.

Frankness and open dealings are needed to make the scheme acceptable. Any queries should be discussed openly. Every applicant should be fully informed of proceedings and the unsuccessful candidates must be told (in confidence) why they failed.

A fair scheme must be seen to be fair by everyone. This is essential to smooth the way for the new supervisor, who may have to face special problems if he comes from the group he is to supervise. This type of change can be a big wrench and it will help him to adjust quickly if everyone accepts the selection as fair.

Training of Supervisors

INFORMAL TRAINING

Most supervisors learn their jobs by actually doing them, making mistakes, and correcting them as they gain experience. Although this system of trial and error is considered to be an essential part of training, practical experience must be supplemented by formal training to form a sound working basis.

Working with an effective supervisor is an invaluable experience but, to gain full benefit, a knowledge of the basic elements of supervision helps considerably. Techniques, built up through the experiences of many supervisors and specialists who have spent years studying supervision, need ideally to be learned and integrated with informal training.

FORMAL TRAINING

Nearly half a century has passed since the Institute of Industrial Administration issued its first syllabus for the Foremanship Certificate in 1938. The Ministry of Labour and National Service launched "Training Within Industry for Supervisors" (T.W.I.) in 1944, after a study of the application and effects of the scheme in the U.S.A. Residential courses have developed since 1945 through local education authorities and independent organisations. Some companies operate their own internal courses.

Yet even after this long period, many of the half a million supervisors in this country still have not received any formal training.

THE TRAINING SCHEME

Any successful training scheme must have the following.
1. Suitable training facilities and the right syllabus.
2. Suitable lecturers and an appropriate body of knowledge.

3. Management support, including follow up and assessment of effectiveness.

These are dealt with in turn below.

1. Training facilities

Technical colleges, and similar institutions throughout the country, have offered part-time day and evening courses in foremanship and supervision for many years. Most establishments followed the syllabus (revised in 1948), issued by the British Institute of Management who awarded the Foremanship Certificate on successful completion of the two-year course.

In 1964 the British Institute of Management decided to give up its responsibility for foremanship examinations and a new body was formed in June 1964 called the National Examinations Board in Supervisory Studies.

Members of the Board include representatives from interested professional bodies such as the Institute of Supervisory Management, the Institution of Industrial Managers and the British Institute of Management, both sides of industry, technical colleges, the Department of Education and Science, the Training Services Division of the Manpower Services Commission, and the Business Education Council.

The Board provides examination schemes and qualifications in the field of foremanship and supervision. Its objectives are "to stimulate and co-ordinate the provision of suitable courses for supervisors at all levels over the whole range of industry, trade and commerce and, by the provision and control of nationally accepted examination standards, to establish a general recognition of the cardinal need for supervisors to be properly qualified to enable them to discharge their responsibilities with maximum effectiveness."

The Board established a flexible structure which provided a three-way approach to courses and examinations in supervisory studies, in view of the wide diversity of supervisory functions.

One of the approaches—the external examination—was abandoned in 1972 but the regulations continue to be used as a guide for the two remaining approaches: approved courses and approved colleges.

The main regulations are now outlined for each of the three course classifications: certificate, supplementary certificate, and diploma in supervisory studies. Other aspects of training are discussed afterwards.

The N.E.B.S.S. Certificate Scheme. A minimum of 240 hours of tuition and tutorials is required and not more than 40 hours of this time should be spent on project work. A residential period of at least two full days is essential in day release and part-time day and evening courses; this residential period is also strongly recommended for full-time, sandwich and block-release courses.

Students must carry out a project and submit a concise report which will form the basis for part of the oral examination. Recommended examinations are two written papers each of two hours' duration, an oral examination of about 30 minutes, project report assessment, and course work assessment.

The N.E.B.S.S. Supplementary Certificate Scheme. A minimum of 60 hours of tuition (not normally extending over more than one year) is required for each supplementary subject. Students should possess the Board's certificate and the examinations consist of an oral examination based on project and course work, a project report assessment, and course work assessment.

The N.E.B.S.S. Diploma Scheme. A minimum of 180 hours of study under the direction of a course tutor is recommended. Students should hold the Board's certificate. Similar regulations apply for the residential period and the project in the certificate course. There is no formal written examination but an interview is conducted by a panel of not more than three people, one of whom is the Board's assessor. The assessment is based upon the course tutor's report, the project report, the student's log-book, and the student's performance during the interview.

Approved courses and assessed internal examinations. Colleges and industrial or commercial organisations may operate their own integrated courses and assessed internal examinations, if the proposed schemes are submitted and approved by the Board. This approach is designed to meet specific local and industrial (or commercial) requirements and the schemes must be concerned with the application of general principles of supervision. Similar conditions for the duration of the course and examinations apply, as outlined above. The proposed syllabuses and other relevant information are submitted to the Board for approval.

Approved colleges. Approved colleges are empowered to develop suitable courses and to conduct their own internal examinations for the various schemes. The course content and the college facilities must be submitted to the Board for approval.

The I.S.M. Certificate Scheme. The Institute of Supervisory Management offers a Certificate in Supervisory Management Studies. This certificate is awarded to those students who, in the opinion of the course tutor, satisfactorily complete a sustained course of study, the syllabus and structure being approved by the Institute.

A minimum of 150 tutorial hours is required within a specified period, a typical programme being two evenings a week over an academic year plus a week-end period.

There are no formal written examinations. A continuous assessment scheme monitors each student's progress, taking into account attendance, homework, log-book, preparation and presentation of a paper, participation in exercises and case studies, and the degree of understanding of course content in relation to the job of the supervisor. The Institute monitors the tutor's continuous assessment, and a successful student is admitted to the Graduate grade of membership.

The I.S.M. Diploma Scheme. Entry is restricted to those students holding the I.S.M. certificate or the N.E.B.S.S. certificate. A minimum of 100 tutorial hours to be completed in one academic year is required. A typical programme would be one evening a week over the academic year plus one week-end period.

Students are given reading and writing assignments for homework and they are expected to keep a handwritten log-book of their course work. A project is undertaken which is relevant to the course. A continuous assessment scheme similar to the one operated under the certificate course is retained for the Diploma course, with the addition of a project assessment.

The award of a Diploma entitles the holder to apply for membership up-grading. In addition, the Diploma provides a basis for the third phase of the I.S.M. scheme: group projects on problems in supervisory management.

Training Within Industry. The Manpower Services Commission (Training Services Division) provides courses for supervisors which consist of three programmes:

(*i*) job instruction, for developing skill in training operators;
(*ii*) job relations, for developing skill in management; and
(*iii*) job methods, for improving methods of work.

Under this scheme the Commission also trains the instructors, most of whom are employees from firms wishing to introduce the course. The smaller concern may use instructors employed by the Commission. The course is ancillary to, and does not replace, other forms of education and training.

Residential courses. Short courses, varying from one to three weeks' duration, are offered by many "country house" establishments who charge a fee for their services. Outside speakers, who are specialists in their own particular fields, are often used in conjunction with a resident tutor. Some companies are now running their own residential courses, with the added advantage of relating the policies of the concern directly to the course syllabus.

Internal courses run by individual companies. These courses vary considerably in length from several months to a few days. Talks are given by managers of the company and the company training officer, with the object of explaining policies and plans, and promoting better communication.

2. Suitable lecturers and an appropriate body of knowledge

Successful presentation of the information is very important and this aspect depends upon the skill of the lecturer who needs sufficient experience in industry and a flair for teaching as well as the knowledge of his subject. Training lecturers is a fundamental problem which will continue to retard the expansion of supervisory training until it is solved.

A great deal of knowledge has accumulated over the past ten years, including opinion on the best content of training and the techniques of presentation. The resourceful supervisor will find a considerable amount of literature published on a wide range of topics which are considered to form part of supervisory training. A representative guide to further reading is given in the Bibliography.

3. Management support

Although many managers agree that some form of supervisory training is needed, and show enthusiasm when the matter is discussed, few seem prepared to take any practical steps towards improving the situation. The number attending T.W.I. courses fell after the introduction of fee-charging in 1962, but a recovery has now been made. Some managers say either that supervisors cannot be spared the time for training, or that they are too busy to make the arrangements. Others simply ignore the facilities offered, presumably because they think the subject is unimportant, or they are scared to be faced with the situation where a subordinate might know more than the superior. Such short-sighted policies may eventually be changed through pressure being applied by the Training Boards under the Industrial Training Act 1964 (*see* Chapter XVI).

(*a*) *Follow-up*. Enthusiasm to learn is essential and enthusiasm to practise is equally important. Management must provide the opportunity for supervisors to put the theory learned into practice. The general feeling among some supervisors is that they appreciate the course, but it is not practicable in their establishments. Some managers say that the effects of the course soon disappear. In both these circumstances it seems obvious that management has failed to create the right conditions for supervisory development through lack of encouragement and general sympathy. Managers themselves, therefore, need appropriate training before any supervisory training scheme can have a lasting effect.

(*b*) *Assessment of effectiveness*. The measurable components which indicate the effectiveness of supervisory training schemes are as follows:

(*i*) An improvement in output.
(*ii*) Less absenteeism and lateness.
(*iii*) A fall in labour turnover.
(*iv*) Lower costs per unit of production.
(*v*) A lower number of employees required to perform the same amount of work.
(*vi*) Fewer complaints and grievances.

(*vii*) More accurate appraisal of employees.
(*viii*) Smaller number of accidents.
(*ix*) Improved schedule keeping.
(*x*) Increased number of suggestions.

QUESTIONS

1. If you were asked to select a supervisor, what qualities would you look for in the candidates?
2. Outline a typical training programme for supervision.
3. How would you judge the effectiveness of a supervisory training course?
4. What do you understand by the term scientific selection of individuals for vacancies?
5. Outline some of the problems of selecting supervisors.
6. Would you expect a supervisor to be the best workman in the department? Explain your answer fully.
7. What are the responsibilities of a supervisor to his subordinates and to management?
8. Define leadership and its importance in supervision.
9. Outline the qualities of a superior for whom you would like to work.
10. What common faults are found in superiors? Explain how these faults affect subordinates and suggest possible causes for them.
11. Outline a suitable code of conduct for a new supervisor.

CHAPTER III

INTRODUCTION TO ORGANISATION

Elements of Organisation

ORGANISATION involves grouping people together in a stable yet flexible working pattern.

NATURAL GROUPING

People naturally tend to organise themselves into groups of about five or six. This phenomenon may be seen in all forms of social and business activity. A large party invariably divides itself into smaller groups of people who have something in common. This natural grouping together creates a friendlier atmosphere; each individual has more opportunity of making some contribution to the conversation, although after a short while, one member of the group will find himself leading the discussion.

This natural grouping forms the basis of organisation planning at all levels of supervision. The different levels are then coupled together by making a group of individuals responsible *to* one superior, and responsible *for* their subordinates; or, in the case of operators, responsible for performing allocated operations.

DEFINITION OF ORGANISATION

Organisation may be defined as the planned design of the company structure, showing the relationships between all employees, and the function each should perform to make the organisation work effectively towards given objectives.

Planning company organisation is an exacting task which involves finding out all the activities that are needed and allocating them first to groups and then to individuals. The work content of each activity must be assessed, together with its importance, and the capacity of each employee must be known. The difficulty of judging whether individuals will work well together makes the planning hazardous. It is now possible to plan scientifically, using principles, structures, and procedures that have been proved practicable by exhaustive studies of both successful and unsuccessful organisations.

A good organisation is essential in the long run, but it depends on its members for its effectiveness. A poor organisation, therefore, may run very smoothly, and a drastic change towards the ideal might cause disruption and poor operation. Design must allow for existing personalities, adjustments being made to the job rather than trying to adjust people.

Achieving the ideal is a long-term project and alterations should be made as opportunities occur. A useful analogy could be related to a composer, the conductor, and his orchestra, who respectively plan, interpret and direct, and perform. Successful performance depends on the skill and willing co-operation of all.

THE MODERN VIEW OF ORGANISATION

The traditional concept of organisation assumes that an industrial environment is similar to military practice. This concept largely ignores political, social, economic, and human factors, which partly accounts for the slow improvement in management's effectiveness.

The aim of organisation is to establish a structure which enables managers to utilise fully each employee's potential. Unfortunately traditional methods of influencing employees tend to stifle initiative and creativeness. Authority, for example, has limited effectiveness because it depends upon applying a penalty (punishment) if rejected, it is open to retaliation or counter-measures, and it cannot successfully deal with indifference, poor performance and general hostility.

Although direct authority is indispensable for over-all control there are other forms which produce better results during normal daily industrial activity. These forms use persuasion through advice: authority is exercised by adapting it to the idea of offering professional help to subordinates who feel they can seek the knowledge and experience of the superior whenever they need it.

Subordinates' mistakes traditionally demand criticism and punishment, whereas the modern approach is to ignore them on the assumption that learning occurs through experience or to use the mistake as an educational exercise to demonstrate a better way of performing a task. It is claimed that more time spent on training and taking a personal interest achieves a higher performance from subordinates.

Recent surveys in the U.S.A. show that the most effective managers use this sophisticated approach towards subordinates. An atmosphere of interdependence between superior and subordinate is fostered which tends to reduce formal authority and to encourage the freedom to develop and improve performance. This approach is in conflict with traditional views that people inherently are lazy and dislike work, and that they must be forced, threatened with punishment, and closely directed and controlled towards stated targets. It assumes that people are ambitious and will work naturally, employing self-direction and self-control when they are committed to objectives. Moreover, it relies upon the subordinate's desire to seek responsibility, to be creative and to release intellectual potential, under the right conditions.

Achieving integration (aligning each person's efforts towards common objectives) requires a slower and more sensitive approach by superiors towards subordinates, but the results are worth while.

ORGANISATION AND THE SUPERVISOR

The supervisor is responsible for organisation within his group and, to be effective, he must possess a clear idea of organisation structure, its characteristics, and the principles upon which the structure is built. He should recognise the futility of operating in isolation instead of being an integral part of the organisation. He must face up to his responsibilities not only within his group, but to the concern as a whole.

Studying organisation, trying out changes, and analysing the results, are an essential part of a supervisory development programme.

In order to recommend changes the supervisor must substantiate his case with sound reasoning, based upon established principles. When he wishes to advance to higher levels, this knowledge of principles becomes essential.

The effectiveness of supervision depends more and more on using specialists effectively, understanding the organisation structure, and co-operating closely with others.

Building the Organisation

SUPERVISORY GROUPS

Any organisation is built up of smaller parts—departments or groups —often in a pyramidal structure (*see* Fig. 1). The following examination of the different levels of supervision in a factory illustrates this basic organisation structure.

1. The primary group

A leader, appointed by management, is needed to supervise each small group of six to twelve operators. If no appointment is made, an informal or unofficial leader will emerge within each group. His aims and outlook might be aligned with management, but it is more likely that he will associate himself with the group as its protector and representative.

If a large group of about thirty is placed under one formal supervisor on so-called grounds of economy, it will splinter into smaller groups each under an informal leader. The formal supervisor is now confronted with, say, four unofficial leaders, through whom he must operate to gain support. If their views cannot be reconciled with the supervisor's, then conflict, compromise, or capitulation will result. The formation of primary groups, under *charge-hands* or leading hands, is essential to ensure that management control reaches down to the shop floor.

The size of the group varies dependent upon the work situation. Operators clustered around a machine, operating similar machines in a unit, assembling similar components, or those who are engaged on any similar function, are some examples.

2. The section

The next logical step is to form a secondary group, or *section*, consisting of five or six primary groups. Figure 1 illustrates this building process. The section supervisor's job is to co-ordinate the work of his subordinate supervisors who must work closely with him if he is to be effective as a problem solver, smoothing out production difficulties and promoting harmony in the section.

3. The department

Forming a department is simply a repetition of the same grouping process (*see* Fig. 1). Linking about six sections under a foreman is

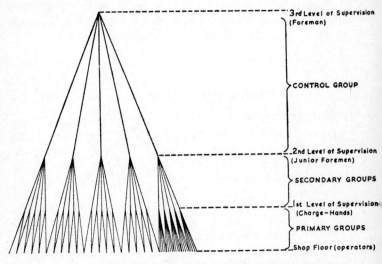

Fig. 1.—*Organisation Pyramid of a Department.*
This diagram shows the build-up of a department based on natural grouping at the primary level. The pyramidal structure reveals quite clearly the closeness of the lower working groups, the increase in distance between the groups at higher levels, and the increasing remoteness of each higher level from the level beneath.

done by coupling those sections which group naturally together, such as all sheet metal forming, metal casting, assembly, or electrical wiring sections.

4. The works

The next stage is to place about six departments under a shop superintendent, the whole now being termed the factory or the works.

PRODUCTION, DISTRIBUTION AND FINANCE

The factory workshop is only part of the organisation. Production must be financed and the finished goods must be sold. This three-fold division is the basis of a concern's organisation.

1. The production function

Continuing upwards from the production shops (the works), arrangements must be made to co-ordinate and control the specialist services which aid production. The main service departments are inspection, work study, plant maintenance, stores and materials handling, production planning and control, research and development, and the drawing office. The importance and use of these services is discussed under the heading of Functional Relationships later in this chapter.

A scheme showing some of the functional specialists who assist production and a breakdown of production departments under the shop superintendent is given in Figure 2.

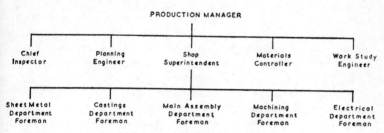

Fig. 2.—*The Production Function.*

This breakdown into production departments shows the use of functional specialists.

2. The distribution function

Distribution normally takes over at the packaging stage of the product, and covers the sale and after-sales service. Those concerned with production should appreciate the problems of distribution, otherwise they will lack sympathetic understanding when abnormal demands are made.

Obtaining sales orders, in the face of competition, may mean that the salesman has to commit himself to offering an earlier delivery date, a cheaper price, or a modified product. The burden of satisfying these demands falls on production and those concerned may feel antagonistic towards a sales policy which has committed them to difficult, or sometimes impossible, tasks. Distribution on its part must be aware of the problems of production. The need for co-ordination and close co-operation between distribution and production is obvious, as they are dependent upon each other. The Managing Director's role of co-ordinating these two functions (and the third, finance) is clearly vital.

Fig. 3.—*The Distribution Function.*
This breakdown shows the various departments involved in marketing
the product.

Figure 3 gives an indication of the organisation structure of this
function, called variously Distribution, Marketing or Sales.

3. The financial function

Effective financial control of any undertaking is essential for it to
pay its way, to improve and to expand. Management decisions
involving finance hinge upon presentation of information, accuracy
and timeliness. A qualified accountant holding this responsible position must control all financial transactions which are recorded
through the accounting and costing systems.

Much depends upon individuals outside those departments directly
connected with finance. Without conscientious support from everyone
who is involved in completing financial returns, effective presentation
is impossible and the probability of incorrect management decisions

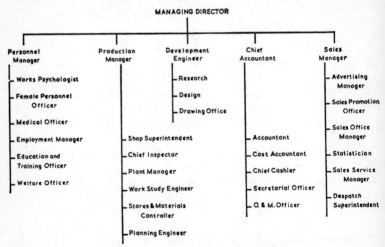

Fig. 4.—*A Medium-size Undertaking.*
Ancillary functions such as personnel and development are added
to the production, distribution and financial functions.

is increased. These decisions affect the prosperity of the company, the employees and the community. The chief accountant may be assisted by other specialists in costing, law, company secretarial, and office services (*see* Fig. 4).

4. Completing the organisation

To complete the structure a number of activities appear either as functions, or sub-functions, dependent upon the peculiarities, circumstances, and particular trade of the company. Such activities as personnel, buying, development, office services, public relations, legal matters, and transport, are typical examples.

Similarly, some of the ancillary functions, already mentioned as under the control of main functions, emerge as main functions in their own right in some companies (e.g. Buying in a timber company). The example in Figure 4 shows the organisation of a medium-size undertaking where personnel and development have emerged as main functions. A breakdown into sub-functions is given under each main function.

Organisation Relationships

Each individual in an organisation will be involved in a number of formal and informal relationships with other members of the company. The complexity of organisation relationships increases with size, and unless each type of relationship is clearly understood by everyone, misunderstandings can develop, which help to destroy their usefulness.

To achieve co-ordination, all relationships (informal as well as formal) must be fully appreciated and used properly by everyone. In this way each member is allowed to develop fully and become effective. Communication will improve, and control is simplified, through smoother running. Official combinations of these relationships produce various types of business organisation which are outlined in the early part of the next chapter (Chapter IV, Growth of Organisation).

FORMAL RELATIONSHIPS

The three formal relationships are *line*, *functional*, and *staff*. They are often termed *authority* relationships, as the type of authority exercised in each case reveals their true significance. This is shown in Figure 5.

1. Line relationship

Easily recognisable through its strong connection with military practice, this formal relationship of direct authority and general

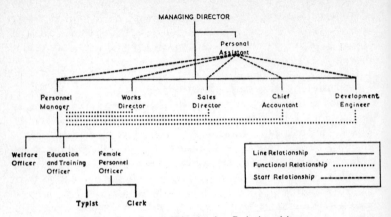

Fig. 5.—*Formal Authority Relationships.*
This diagram shows the interaction of the three formal authority relationships. The line relationship or scalar chain of command runs directly
from the top, down through each level of authority to the lowest. The
functional relationship operates between line supervisors and functional
specialists. When a personal assistant is introduced to liaise between
the managing director and his executives, the staff relationship operates.

responsibility flows from the top executive, through the levels of
supervision in turn, to the operators.

This line of command is also known as the hierarchy, the scalar
chain, or scalar process. Each supervisor, or line commander, must
have complete responsibility for his subordinates, and sufficient
authority to direct their full range of activities so that the line of
command is clear. This relationship also provides the line of communication through which all information and instructions should
flow. Each person must be responsible to only *one* Line Supervisor.

The advantages of this relationship are that everyone easily understands it, and through its flexibility, the organisation can quickly
expand and contract. Discipline is normally strong and decisions are
easily obtainable as responsibility is fixed. The snag with line relationship lies in overloading senior executives, and at lower levels the
pressure of work makes co-ordination more difficult, because there
are no specialists who can concentrate on problems when they arise.

2. Functional relationship
This term is used to describe the relationship between the functional
specialist and the line supervisor. Both parties involved should be quite
clear as to the intention of this most important combination, which is
often misunderstood and misused through lack of proper introduction.

The specialist is appointed to help and advise the line supervisors.
He has spent a considerable time studying and gaining experience in

his specialised subject so that he can support the line supervisor, who cannot possibly be an expert in every function in which he is involved. To avoid upsetting the chain of command the specialist has no direct authority. He deals with people throughout the concern by exercising indirect authority through the line supervisors.

The idea of specialisation was originated by F. W. Taylor (1856–1915), who was an engineer in America. Early in his career he became a foreman and soon discovered that he had far too much work to do in the time available. Results were generally achieved by force and fear, with which he disagreed fundamentally.

He claimed that insufficient attention to detail, and lack of scientific method and planning, were the causes of low output and high costs. Work was commenced without adequate preparation, and with little supervision of method. The rates of pay were inadequate and unfair, and inspection was often neglected.

Taylor recommended that specialists should be appointed to cope with the many facets of the foreman's job which demanded expert knowledge and experience. The specialists were to be found among different foremen, resulting in eight being employed as *functionalised foremen*. Four were transferred from the shop floor to the office as planners, and given titles of (*a*) shop disciplinarian, (*b*) order of work, and route clerk, (*c*) instruction card clerk, and (*d*) time and cost clerk. The other four were used on the shop floor to assist the operators, but each in one particular function only: (*e*) speed boss, (*f*) gang boss, (*g*) inspection boss, and (*h*) repair boss. The result caused considerable chaos because the men were responsible to more than one superior, which led to confusion and the "playing off" of one supervisor against another. The idea was sound, however, and from this beginning emerged the line-and-function type of organisation which is discussed shortly.

Staff relationship

When an executive is overloaded with work, one method of helping to relieve the strain is to appoint a personal assistant, or staff officer, whose job is to represent his superior by ensuring that his policies and decisions are interpreted correctly.

The intention is *not* to create a further level of authority between the executive and his subordinates, although it is often interpreted this way because the staff officer's position is not carefully explained. He needs no direct authority as his function is plainly representative of his superior's authority, and his responsibility is *advisory* only. In this capacity he cannot give orders, except by issuing written instructions through his superior's authority.

When the relationship operates correctly, the subordinates use the staff officer as a source of information and advice centre, to avoid bothering the executive unnecessarily. The line is not blocked, but supplemented; if the problem cannot be solved through application to the staff officer, direct access to the executive is still open.

The executive must work closely with his assistant to ensure that both are of the same mind on matters of policy, views, and general feelings on particular topics. The good staff officer must be able to present his superior's image to other executives in such a way that they are quite clear about the intentions of the superior.

INFORMAL RELATIONSHIPS

The authority relationships already discussed would form a very rigid and impracticable organisation if it were not for the *horizontal*, *ad-hoc*, and *line by-pass* relationships, which bind the concern together to form a working unit (*see* Fig. 6).

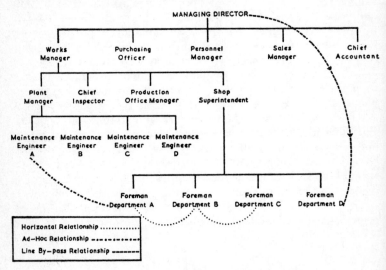

Fig. 6.—*Informal Authority Relationships*.

This diagram illustrates the three informal relationships which bind the concern together to form a working unit.

1. Horizontal relationship

The horizontal or lateral relationship describes the interaction between supervisors on similar levels of authority. Where supervisory duties interlock, the co-ordination necessary for smooth work flow and co-operation is only achieved by close horizontal exchange of information and planning.

If one awkward supervisor refuses to participate the working unit becomes a dislocated number of smaller units. This applies to any level of supervision, and the lack of concord sets a bad example to lower levels.

2. Ad-hoc relationship

This "time-saver" gives an excellent indication of whether an organisation works well.

Although in theory everything should pass up and down the line, if this were carried out in practice every supervisor would become a *bottleneck*, and the organisation would break down owing to the time-factor. The practical answer, when members are working in harmony, is to establish *ad-hoc relationships* with members of other groups for information and discussion, without bothering superiors for approval. This arrangement works well provided it is obvious to both parties that they are not committing their immediate superiors on questions of policy or decisions affecting other members or groups.

A supervisor may also instruct subordinates to contact others in this way, after discussion with the appropriate supervisor.

Although this sensible working arrangement cuts across the line principle, it forms the essential network that brings the organisation to life.

3. Line by-pass relationship

A "trouble-spot" often demands the use of *line by-pass*. The reason why managers seem reluctant to take obvious action at times is often that accurate information has not reached their levels.

Assuming firstly that the person who knows most about a situation is the one nearest to it and, secondly, that by the time information has passed through a number of intermediaries the facts are inevitably distorted to some degree, there is a clear need for line by-pass relationships.

In use, any manager or supervisor who feels that he is not satisfied with the way a situation is developing—when it does not respond to decisions as would normally be expected—should by-pass the supervisors between himself and the situation, and speak to the person who is in close contact. Every supervisor needs to understand that such action is often essential to avoid minor problems building up into upheavals, such as strikes, and need not feel slighted if he is the person by-passed.

Figure 6 illustrates horizontal, *ad-hoc*, and line by-pass relationships.

The Supervisor's Position

Because of his peculiar middle position between operatives and management, the supervisor can promote the smooth working of formal and informal relationships, or he can disrupt these lines of communication completely, whether through wilful lack of co-operation or through ignorance and misunderstanding.

His position in relation to management is discussed in detail in Chapter VI. At this point, however, consideration of the problems met by the first level of supervision, i.e. the chargehand, reveals the supervisor's critical part as the link between the different levels of organisation.

The chargehand must bond together primary and secondary groups, but as a superior in one group and a subordinate in the other, he will find that all his actions are viewed from two fronts, and it is frequently impossible to please both subordinates and management. Both "sides" expect him to support their view: subordinates think in terms of wages, stability of employment, conditions and participation; management thinks in terms of cost, flexibility, output, and productivity. While his task is to control and look after one group's interests as their superior, and at the same time to carry out orders which are frequently unpopular and pass on information for the other group as a subordinate, the chargehand must be master of conciliation and compromise.

STATUS OF SUPERVISORS

Every supervisor needs full support from management, particularly in the form of status. The status he is given governs the degree and quality of reaction by subordinates to the supervisor's instructions, requests, and suggestions. The supervisor, in turn, will mould his attitude towards responsibility, according to his status and degree of management support.

Most members of an organisation are "status conscious". They consider status symbols such as rank, position in the organisation chart, wages, bonus, social privileges, dress, size of office or desk, and use of own telephone, as important; but capability and personality provide the intangible aspect which also influences opinions of a particular supervisor's standing.

Titles such as manager, officer, superintendent, foreman, and supervisor, do not always convey the true status of executives who are on apparently similar levels.

Moreover, a supervisor may be held in high esteem by his group as possessing more knowledge, or participating in certain social activities within the company; but top management may be unaware of these factors. The potential status of the supervisor, in these circumstances, will remain unrealised until the facts are transmitted to top management.

CONTRIBUTING FACTORS

In recent times the problem of the supervisor's general position has been aggravated by a number of developments, which are discussed below.

Wages

The differential between supervisors' and workers' pay has decreased drastically as workers' pay has risen to a point where the worker can easily earn more than the supervisor. Such a poor situation must affect the supervisor's morale, produce ill-feeling towards management, and have an adverse effect on prospective foremen.

Management's attitude towards supervision

The attitude of managers towards supervisory jobs is never a secret, and it generates feelings appropriate to the situation.

Lack of management support cannot be concealed during the day-to-day running of a group. Having to "climb-down", or retract a statement through lack of support is humiliating to the supervisor and has a detrimental effect in the eyes of his subordinates. On the other hand, if management accepts him as being in a key position which demands adequate backing, and he receives it, he is elevated to his rightful place.

Communication

Being up to date on policy changes, and on current information, is another indication of status. If management does not realise the significance of this fact to the supervisor, he may well be the last one to hear of likely changes. For example, joint consultation meetings may be attended by a number of shop stewards and only one foreman. After the meeting the word passes rapidly round to operators and, if management does not notify supervisors quickly, they will receive the information first from either shop stewards or operators.

Use of specialists

The supervisor's ability to adjust to change and use specialist departments effectively is a factor of increasing importance. As more firms change over to the use of service or specialist departments, which directly affect the supervisor's duties, it is essential, if the company is to obtain full benefit, that the supervisor clearly understands the change and its implications. His job is enhanced to one of managing his department, with the assistance of specialists who act as advisors on personnel, planning and control, wage rates, costs, and work study. He can now spend more time on organising his department to make production more effective, but he must be able to adapt himself to this change otherwise the object will be defeated.

Apparently, in some cases managers are prepared to spend large sums of money on introducing specialists, but they draw the line at training supervisors to use the newcomers in the most effective way. If the supervisor merely tolerates specialists instead of using their knowledge, a difficult situation may develop. Subordinates will probably by-pass a supervisor who encourages them to deal directly with specialists. The specialists then become virtually line managers, which means giving direct orders to those particular subordinates. True control is lost, the supervisor loses face, and relationships are upset.

Shop stewards

Lastly, the shop stewards' increasing power has made a marked change in the supervisor's position. In some cases closer co-operation has been achieved between the supervisor and the shop steward, but in others antagonism has developed and relationships have deteriorated to a point where sensible control ceases.

"Whom you know"

The amount of power developed by any individual, which of course benefits status, goes deeper than personal qualities. Much depends upon friendships and relatives: "whom you know" is the term commonly used, and most people in industry and commerce are aware of its underlying significance. Similarly, if managers are seen to be friendly with some and completely ignore other supervisors, although perhaps unintentionally, they are influencing performance and status.

Conclusion

Individuals on all levels in the organisation are particularly sensitive to treatment by their superiors and automatically they maintain a watchful eye on how their superiors in turn are treated. Unfortunately, the lessons to be learned from seeing how others are treated, and noting their reactions, are not applied by many who fall into the same trap when dealing with subordinates. Lowering subordinates' status is an easy occupation; raising it is demanding on time and ingenuity, but it pays since people work much better when they feel important.

QUESTIONS

1. Compare and contrast the formal and informal organisation.
2. Carefully explain the staff principle in an organisation.
3. Describe fully the nature and purposes of functional and staff authority.
4. What is meant by natural grouping in the organisation?
5. Define organisation and discuss its importance.
6. Discuss the status of supervisors.
7. Give an account of the structure of organisation, indicating the main groups involved.
8. Describe the primary group and its function in the organisation.
9. Draw an organisation chart of your establishment. Indicate any aspects which might be improved according to the principles of organisation.
10. Give a brief description of the formal relationships of organisation and mention an example in each case.
11. Outline the informal relationships in organisation and comment on their value.
12. Define the *ad-hoc* relationship and illustrate its use by examples.
13. Give some practical examples of the line by-pass relationship.
14. Discuss the supervisor's position in relation to management and operatives.

CHAPTER IV

GROWTH OF ORGANISATION

The Progress of Expansion

THE following sections illustrate the growth of a business from a one-man to a large-scale concern, before analysing in detail the problems of size.

1. The one-man business

An examination of the small concern where one man performs all the activities provides a good insight into the organisation problems of growth. If every member in larger companies carried the operation of the one-man business in his mind, his true function and contribution would be obvious.

One way to study this initial form of business is to imagine the concern operating in one room where all the functions are clearly visible. Stocks can be seen on the shelves. Production processes and semi-finished goods are all on view. On the financial side, the desk top has a cash book showing the bank balance, a tray for bills to be paid and, on the sales side, an order book.

An assessment of the business is easily made if the owner turns slowly round in the centre of the room, visually making a mental note of the situation of each main function. If stocks are dangerously low or there is a hold up at one stage of production it is clearly seen. An immediate decision which will be based upon sufficient facts is now possible, regarding the allocation of time and money on each activity.

The following table illustrates this process of assessment. It seems very obvious but it shows the variety of situations which are met

Raw Materials:	Low	Low	High	Low
Finished Goods:	High	Low	Low	Low
Cash Balance:	High	High	High	Low
Action:	Buy raw materials Sell finished goods	Buy raw materials Produce more	Produce more	Borrow cash Buy raw materials Produce more

even in the simplest organisation. In a larger firm the greater number of variable factors to be considered and the greater sums of money involved indicate the importance of accurate assessment and the difficulty of making right decisions.

Provided the man, who is normally the owner, has reasonable intelligence and a knowledge of management, control is straight-forward. Automatic co-ordination is achieved through the ideal communication system of a single brain.

No co-operation problems appear until another person is employed. This major step is critical as the owner himself is probably a specialist, often on the technical side. He may be limited in management knowledge and will therefore have the familiar problem of a narrow viewpoint. Thus growth may suffer and development proceed on a "stop-gap" basis, splitting work as overloads occur. The question of whether specialists can be afforded, and the owner's personal problem of delegating some authority, also aggravate the problems.

2. The small business (line organisation)

In the absence of planning, and as the amount of work increases, a point is reached where the need to divide activities becomes so glaring that natural steps are taken and employees are allocated narrower fields of work.

Similarly, the strong pressure to delegate functions finally forces the owner to relinquish some of his authority. The appointments of a sales manager, a works manager, and possibly an accounts supervisor (distribution, production, and finance functions), follow in time, and more staff are engaged as people become overloaded with work. The result is the formation of a line type of organisation, which is illustrated in Figure 7.

This type of organisation is an excellent proving ground for executives. Everyone is aware of the objective. Each person's responsibility and authority are known and there is very little opportunity to "pass-the-buck".

The absence of specialists is felt as expansion continues: the

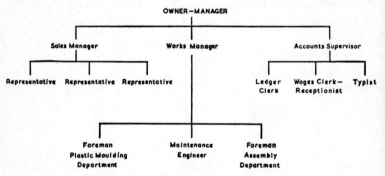

Fig. 7.—*Line Type of Organisation*.
This diagram shows the formation of a line type of organisation in the small business.

managers are expected to be good "all-rounders" with their responsibility increasing continually. These key men have to work at high pressure, and the organisation inevitably suffers until more specialists are introduced.

3. The medium-sized business (line/functional organisation)

The disadvantages of the line type of organisation become more noticeable and acute as growth continues. The situation leads eventually to the introduction of functional specialists to ease the burden of the line executives. Thus functional control may begin with, say, the engagement of a personnel manager, a transport manager, and a purchasing officer.

The authority and responsibility of the line commanders are unchanged, but they now have available the technical assistance of specialists. Sound relationships must exist between the line commanders and the specialists and each one must resist the temptation to dominate.

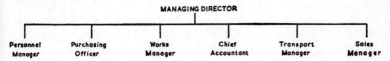

Fig. 8.—*The Introduction of Specialists*.

As a firm grows, it becomes necessary to introduce specialists, such as personnel and purchasing officers, to spread the work load more evenly.

The specialist, when giving advice, must have a true understanding of the line and, in turn, the line executives should understand that he is still responsible for his subordinates. Full use of the specialist must be made, and both should appreciate the basic idea of working together to achieve the objective more quickly and efficiently.

The specialist may have staff directly under his control, such as a secretary, records clerk, or assistant specialist. In these circumstances, he performs a dual role of line commander to his immediate staff, and functional commander to the rest of the organisation.

The line/functional type of organisation is shown in Figure 8 which gives the top line of executives who are responsible directly to the managing director.

4. Large-scale organisation

Continual growth of functional control soon reaches the stage where the number of executives reporting directly to the managing director is too great for him to control effectively.

An illustration of using staff officers to ease the situation is given in Figure 9, which shows the inevitable growing weight of senior

Fig. 9.—*The Introduction of Staff Officers*.
Marketing and production development staff officers have been introduced where the number of executives has grown too great for the managing director to control effectively.

executives responsible to the managing director in a large-scale organisation. In this example the emphasis lies in the marketing and production development functions. A large proportion of the managing director's time was spent on these two fields to the detriment of the other functions. To offset this situation two staff officers were introduced to bear the load, and relieve the pressure on the managing director, who could now balance his work more effectively.

Problems of Growth

1. The gyro analogy

Problems are magnified proportionately as an organisation expands. One way of thinking about large-scale organisation is to consider the *gyro analogy*. The concept of a gyroscope representing an organisation is shown in Figure 10.

Certain ideas may now be associated with conditions in a company, if a gyroscope is visualised spinning in space.

(*a*) *Centrifugal force:* The main driving force comes from the centre, the managing director.

(*b*) *Centripetal force:* Each member of the organisation must supply small trickles of energy to the centre, to be converted into driving power by the managing director. (Each member must be pointing in the right direction.)

(*c*) *Creep:* A business is never static for any length of time and has inherent creep, like a gyroscope. A company is either rising or declining, and the managing director's job is to control the direction of the "creep".

(*d*) *Periphery blur:* Operators on the surface of the gyro appear as blurred masses to observers and their importance and feelings are often overlooked. The surface must be smooth and well knit together to form a tough finish, otherwise the gyro speed will be affected by

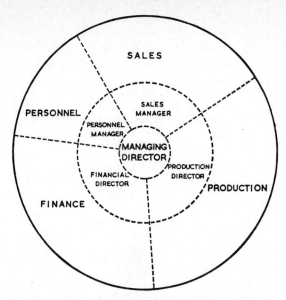

Fig. 10.—*The Gyro Analogy*.
This plan of a gyroscope, if visualised as spinning in space, illustrates many of the unavoidable problems of large-scale organisation.

ripples and protrusions. Constant attention to the outer limits is essential.

(*e*) *Surface cohesion:* The tendency for any object on the surface to fly off at a tangent, is a major problem. Making the operator feel an *integral* part of the organisation is a question of communication and able management.

(*f*) *Limited environment:* Any section of the gyroscope is completely immobile, relative to other sections, and strictly limited in awareness of its surroundings and the functions it performs. Similarly, operators feel isolated and ill at ease unless induction courses are introduced (*see* Chapter XV).

(*g*) *Pressure points:* Any pressure applied to a gyro at a particular point will eventually topple it, if allowed to develop sufficiently. If trouble spots are allowed to grow unchecked in an organisation, a similar problem arises.

(*h*) *Stability:* The essentials for stability are sufficient power, correct design, and even balance of each segment of the gyro. In a company balance is equally important but must be relative to the peculiarities of the business. For example, if a company's production process is simple, such as mixing a few solvents together and canning the mixture, but marketing is difficult and competitive, balance would be achieved with a small production and a large marketing staff.

(*i*) *Continuity:* In the event of power failure an emergency supply is necessary to maintain stability. In companies the application of this principle is often ignored when dealing with employees. To maintain continuity, there must be deputies who are capable of taking over at short notice.

These nine points are sufficient to indicate the host of problems that appear as company size increases. Feelings of remoteness and lack of interest must be overcome because they affect everyone's performance.

2. The organisation pyramid

In addition to the effects of large-scale organisation on employees, growth also frustrates unless it is based upon sound principles of organisation. A further examination of Figure 1, the organisation pyramid of a department, indicates a building technique that can accommodate any number of employees, and adjustments may be made within an existing framework. In the example given, growth could be absorbed in the following way:

	Existing organisation	*Future organisation*	
Primary Group	8	8	
No. of Groups	× 5	× 6	
Section	40	48	
No. of sections	× 5	× 6	
Department	200	288	
No. of departments	× 5	× 6	
	1000 Operators	1728 Operators	

Remoteness. From the operator's viewpoint, the impression of lengthening distance of communication between supervision levels as the top is approached indicates the remoteness of higher supervision. This feeling of being cut off as more levels are introduced indicates that levels should be kept to a minimum but, at the same time, without infringing natural grouping.

Co-ordination. The inverted triangles in Figure 1 represent the ground which is not covered adequately in the organisation. Every supervisor has the task of co-ordinating or covering these unidentified areas, by co-operating laterally with his fellow supervisors to close these "gaps" effectively. When this is achieved the team will be much stronger, compared with the total number of members on an individual basis. (Owners, management, trade unions, employees, and the State would similarly be much stronger if they were united.)

How a Good Organisation Works

A good organisation achieves its objectives in the shortest time, at lowest cost, and with the least disruption to its members. The dominant feature, however, is people and no organisation will be effective without their co-ordinated efforts.

The efficient supervisor must understand the reasoning that governs organisation structure and its operation. Subordinates have a sixth sense about the principles of organisation, many of which are common sense; they recognise immediately the lack of organisation or mis-management, for they are on the "receiving-end". It is essential to appreciate what effect management measures can have on subordinates. A good rule is to *treat people as you like to be treated yourself.*

The main principles of organisation are given below under six headings: objective; working plan; leadership; duties and responsibilities; delegation; and co-ordination.

OBJECTIVE

Knowing the direction in which a business is heading, with clearly stated aims, allows people to work along the right lines with less detailed instructions. Full advantage of stating the purposes or objectives is often not taken by managers, and yet the same people would think it dangerous to ask someone to fire a rifle without specifying the target. In private life most of us set our own targets and make plans, for people are usually happier with something to look forward to rather than being aimless.

Although the main aim of a business is to provide a service or goods to the community, with profitability in mind, the use of more immediate objectives is necessary. Producing a new model within six months, or completing a project at a certain cost, are much closer to individuals who can see short-term results more quickly.

At one time the objective was to maximise profits; many individuals, including managers, still cling to this narrow view. The modern outlook, which takes into account consumers, shareholders, the community and the country, is to provide adequate shares to each group by *optimising* profit. This means making the best use of all resources and creating sufficient surplus for the effective development of the concern, which is vital to the national economy. The question of profit is also discussed in Chapter XXVII.

WORKING PLAN

When the objective is decided, the organisation designed, and the staff established, there remains the plan that brings it to life. Effective planning of all factors is essential to achieve the objective. Feedback of information to planning points is necessary to achieve control and for revision of plans.

Within the working plan certain principles are essential to its operation; these are now discussed.

1. Stability
The quickest way to cause confusion and poor operation is by issuing instructions and routines, and then continually countermanding and changing them. The old army saying, "order, counter-order, disorder", applies equally in business. Careful thought is necessary before instructions are issued, otherwise they will carry little weight if altered within a short time, and the constant uncertainty is bad for morale.

2. Balance
The problem of balance is twofold. Firstly, there is the question of allocating time to each task within the supervisor's job. The natural tendency is to spend more time on those tasks that are interesting at the expense of the distasteful, mundane ones. Strong self-discipline is required in the supervisor to counter this noticeable habit, which has an adverse effect on those subordinates who work in the neglected sections. Secondly, is the wider problem of maintaining balance of functions, which has already been mentioned. For example, if "empire-building" is allowed to develop at the expense of other functions, the disrupting effect can be considerable and dangerous. This action highlights the weakness of the managing director and has a detrimental effect on the morale of executives and operators. His aim must be to ensure that each function is appropriate to the demands of the business and that proportionate effectiveness is achieved.

3. Orderliness
Order and organisation go together. The old adage, "a place for everything and everything in its place", shows the strength of organisation and the capacity to cope with situations effectively when they arise.

4. The Scalar process
Co-ordination of the working plan is made possible by operating a formal line of command, from top to bottom of the organisation. The line, or chain, is the channel through which information flows in both directions. These lines of authority are needed to prevent overlapping, or gaps, thus providing adequate coverage of the whole structure.

5. Reports
The proper use of reports means that only those serving some purpose are prepared, and appropriate action or record is made by a higher authority. Reports are part of the communication system which binds the organisation together, although supervisors often dislike com-

piling them. They must be conscientiously completed and contain the relevant information. Conciseness is important as executive time is expensive. Report writing is discussed in Chapter XIII.

6. Records
Like reports, records should serve a purpose and be regularly and accurately kept. The cost of making and maintaining records is expensive, and in most cases is justified, although some supervisors tend to ignore their usefulness. Supervisors should make full use of records from many departments rather than rely solely upon their memory and judgment.

7. Continuity
Most companies are committed to a continuing existence, and therefore replacements must be provided for, to meet termination, retirement and death among employees. Smooth change-over involves a planned training scheme which ensures that each supervisor has a deputy who is capable of taking over at short notice. When no scheme is in use, a supervisor has the advantage at promotion time if he has personally trained someone who can replace him effectively.

If management allows people to become indispensable, the company will be in jeopardy when they are no longer available. One person may work well if allowed to think he is indispensable whilst another may be tempted to take advantage of a situation which does not exist. One of the few definite courses of action for management is to provide a continuous supply of replacements.

LEADERSHIP
Making the organisation live and become dynamic depends upon leadership. Although providing supervisors with formal authority is important, they must foster group enthusiasm by their personality, inspiring subordinates to achieve higher levels of performance. The personal attributes of leadership were described in Chapter II. The following section discusses the principles of leadership in the wider concept of organisation.

1. Progressiveness
Good organisation coupled with forward-looking leadership provides the right working atmosphere where members are willing to contribute something over and above a normal day's work. They know that suggestions and ideas will be favourably received and adequately rewarded, when supervisors encourage the urge to progress.

2. Authority
Authority is conferred from superiors as a natural process of delegation. Unfortunately, the act of providing a person with official backing

to give instructions does not always mean that subordinates will carry them out. This question involves the degree of power developed by the supervisor. If he is strong, he will use power to ensure that his wishes are carried out. If he is weak, his subordinates soon find out and control is lost.

A very powerful superior who confers the authority, will find his influence permeating through the levels below, thus giving weight to the subordinate supervisor's position.

3. Discipline

The degree of discipline required by concerns varies considerably, either being accepted by tradition or by formal agreement. Discipline covers the obligations of individuals, such as complying with regulations, the amount of work considered acceptable, and general behaviour within the company's premises. The true strength of discipline, however, lies in the ability of managers to develop a sense of responsibility in all employees which, in fact, is self-discipline. Under conditions of self-discipline, employees conform to set patterns of behaviour and respond to situations in accordance with certain concepts when relieved of the direct influence of supervision.

The advantages are obvious, but achieving self-discipline is essentially a long-term project, which demands sincerity and perseverance from management. Appreciation of the recent changes which have affected discipline must come first. These changes include high unemployment, the growing strength of trade unions, higher State allowances, and the growth of an affluent society. The social revolution also is having a marked effect on people's attitudes through higher education.

The questioning approach to all changes is quite normal, and people are very critical of management's action. The key to self-discipline in these circumstances means that management's outlook must be pitched towards ensuring that all regulations and actions are fair and acceptable to employees, clearly understood, and sincerely applied. Discipline is also discussed in Chapter XII.

4. Justice

Justice is possibly the most misunderstood concept in industry, even by those who feel they are experienced in this difficult task and qualified to advise.

Three points of view must be considered. Firstly, the person administering justice. He must have full knowledge of the facts and of previous decisions. He must be able to weigh the case quite objectively and decide upon a punishment with strict fairness.

Secondly, the offender. He will not be prepared to accept the decision if he is given no reason for it, so that he can see that it is fair.

People usually feel that they have suffered an injustice when no adequate explanation is given.

Thirdly, the onlookers. It is not surprising that they form distorted impressions when they do not know all the facts of the case, and there is usually little time to explain the reasons for the decision either. Whenever possible, however, justice should be "seen to be done".

Other practices, such as "making an example" of an offender or "picking on" someone when one's patience has run out, although others have escaped punishment before, only complicate the problem. Haphazard and inconsistent applications of punishment are inevitable when a supervisor is harassed. If this fact is overlooked by a management which fails to appreciate the problem of justice and its effect on employees, much of the effort made in other directions towards goodwill will be nullified.

5. Policy, rules, and regulations

The true functioning of the organisation is impossible unless every employee is aware of, and interprets correctly, the policy, rules, and regulations of the company. Ambiguity must be avoided and departmental policies should be in harmony with each other.

A common understanding makes for a better appreciation of a person's authority, responsibilities, and duties. Leadership is made easier as a more sensitive awareness of the job develops, which assists the individual in taking intelligent action without bothering his superior.

DUTIES AND RESPONSIBILITIES

In addition to the two principles mentioned in the heading there are others, equally important, which must be considered. All are now discussed below.

1. Duties

Allocation of duties must be consistent with a person's capabilities. Clarity is essential, as an individual cannot be held responsible for activities he should be carrying out if he is unaware of them.

Vagueness in defining employees' duties is not uncommon, even in the large firm. Some managers think that if definition is vague, employees will automatically perform activities which may be overlooked if duties are *clearly defined*. This may be so, but if control is not efficient, some activities will be left unattended and unnoticed.

This situation is really a "cloak" for covering poor administration. Clarifying duties does not mean they must be narrowly defined within fine limits; a broader definition will often solve the problem of dealing with new tasks which arise. Defining duties should also be open to periodic revision as a control function.

2. Responsibility

A fair system demands that every supervisor possessing authority over others should be answerable to a superior for his actions. Furthermore, each person should be responsible to one superior only, and be responsible for either getting work done, or actually doing the work.

Shedding responsibility is not possible in these circumstances, yet various levels of responsibility are essential to accommodate the levels of supervision. The answer lies in understanding the concept of absorbing all lower levels of responsibility into the next level, and so on, until complete responsibility for the whole concern is reached at managing director level. Lower levels of responsibility do not affect the higher responsibility in any way. Thus, any supervisor's responsibility can be expanded downward and allocated to subordinates, but the original responsibility still remains.

This process continues downward until a particular task, involving manual or clerical work, is completed. Actually doing the work is termed operational responsibility, to distinguish it from responsibility for getting work done. An example of responsibility levels for a payroll is given below:

MANAGING DIRECTOR:	first rate responsibility	⎫ Getting the
CHIEF ACCOUNTANT:	second rate responsibility	⎬ work done
PAYROLL SUPERVISOR:	third rate responsibility	⎭
PAYROLL CLERKS:	operational responsibility	Doing the work

Responsibilities must be clearly defined and spread as far down the organisation as efficiency will allow.

3. Flexibility

One of the supervisor's duties is to ensure that working arrangements are such that any job, however unusual or unique, is always accepted by someone as his responsibility. This is true flexibility. This means that all the borders of responsibility always impinge on each other, thus making it impossible for a job to fall between two people.

If a situation arises where a job rests on *two* areas, intelligent discussion should arrive at the best arrangement. All routines should be sufficiently flexible to accommodate the unexpected situation, which implies that people involved must be adaptable and understanding.

Narrow interpretation of rules and regulations leads to a rigid, dogmatic organisation.

4. Personal capability

Each person's capabilities, status, and personality, must be considered when organising staff, making working arrangements and allocating duties. Some people work together easily while others have difficulty, and if this fact is not taken into account personal effectiveness suffers.

To overcome this problem, each supervisor must know his staff, not only on the practical side, but also from the personal aspect. Armed with sufficient knowledge of employees, it is possible to rearrange to meet new situations with a minimum of disruption, thus promoting the smooth working of the organisation.

5. Authority and responsibility must correspond

If a person is given authority without being answerable to a superior, lack of control from above is inclined to place the individual in a comfortable position where he can sit back and relax. Conversely, a person who is given responsibility without the requisite authority, either assumes the authority without official recognition, or does nothing.

Both situations are obviously unsatisfactory and cause considerable friction between individuals.

DELEGATION

The principle of delegation is often misunderstood because it can be abused and used as a means of shirking responsibility. The other extreme is also not unusual, where supervisors have great difficulty in delegating.

Balanced workload

The importance of delegation lies in ensuring that no one should be overloaded with work, otherwise his efficiency will drop. Successful delegation means that the supervisor is released from lower grade tasks, and can spend more time on more important activities. The load of work is spread more evenly and, as decisions are pushed lower down the line, people have the opportunity to develop their abilities quickly. Conferring some of the superior's authority to a subordinate in this way is true delegation.

Co-ordinated responsibility

Bearing in mind the principle of responsibility already mentioned, a form of shared or co-ordinated responsibility is practised: the subordinate is always responsible to his superior for doing the job, and the superior is responsible for seeing it done.

Inspection

As the superior remains responsible, the natural consequence of delegation is inspection. Control is lost without inspection of the work; hence the saying, "Inspection is the corollary of delegation."

IMPORTANCE OF DELEGATION IN PRACTICE

There is nothing complex in delegating. The common reasons for shirking it are as follows.

(a) People succumb to their natural laziness and spend their time on the simpler jobs which, of course, are the ones they should be delegating.

(b) Fear that they cannot cope with higher work compels people to become absorbed with detail to impress others, with the resulting shortage of time for anything else.

(c) Feelings of insecurity make people reluctant to pass on authority.

(d) They feel that subordinates are incapable of performing the tasks involved, and that they cannot be entrusted with the requisite authority.

A simple procedure to follow for delegating is given at the end of the chapter.

In a situation where all the subordinates are overloaded there is no alternative but to appeal to management. If no action is taken, it has the kind of organisation it deserves. Where the right type of subordinate is missing, planning ahead for change when the opportunity presents itself, or transferring internally, is the answer.

Successful delegation is involved with the deeper problem of aligning aims and fostering team spirit. Training and developing people is not complete without delegation, which acts as a continuous process of improvement and has a balancing effect as the company grows. There is continuity of purpose through the different levels of supervision when supervisors understand the frustration of overloading and the need to encourage people to take responsibility. Bottlenecks are dispensed with and smoother working is assured.

A word of caution is needed on the question of inspection. The object is to check on the work without destroying initiative and causing resentment. Initiative is a vital ingredient for expanding capability; how to inspect and encourage it requires experience and judgment.

A saying worth remembering during inspection is, "People with average intelligence are very sensitive whilst those above average are extremely sensitive."

When the superior shows an interest in the work, this can give much pleasure and satisfaction to the subordinate. In this manner the art of unobtrusive inspection is developed, where the checking comes to the normal course of contact. The object is to keep all operations running smoothly, therefore finding out any unsatisfactory work is only the half-way stage. Action is necessary, which is just as delicate an operation as finding out, since people's feelings are involved. Tactless treatment is likely to lead to repercussions later, although they may be disguised and seemingly unconnected.

Span of control
Most supervisors have difficulty in effectively controlling more than six subordinates, whose functions interlock. Each time an extra person

is added, relationships in the group increase geometrically through the various associations between members.

On the shop floor it is feasible to double this number as generally the work does not demand such a close working relationship; but on supervisory levels the number of supervisors in a group is critical, and the results of overloading are clearly seen. The supervisor in these circumstances works under great stress; there is not enough time to give due attention to all the activities under his control, which leads to ineffectiveness.

Centralisation and decentralisation

Part of the natural function of organisms is to transmit information or sensations to a central point and to divert instructions from this point to those parts which need attention. This natural process, called centralisation, seems to be in conflict with delegation. Centralisation, in its absolute form, means direct contact between manager and subordinate as seen in the small business. When levels of supervision appear, the direct line of control is distorted slightly with each degree of delegation.

In the large firm, considerable decentralisation is essential, every manager relying more upon the specialised knowledge of his colleagues. As decentralisation is practised, the subordinate's role increases in importance; and conversely, as centralisation is increased, the subordinate's role is accordingly reduced in importance.

Specialisation

The principle of specialisation means breaking down the activities into different tasks for each individual, so enabling everyone to concentrate his efforts in a narrower field. Performing a single leading function, or task, allows a person to develop high skills which result in less mental strain and better work with less effort. Output can more easily be increased under conditions of high skill and accuracy.

The small company is limited in the application of specialisation as there are insufficient employees to allow the principle to operate fully. Caution is also needed in applying the principle to the extreme, because of the danger of excessive boredom and monotony.

CO-ORDINATION

Co-ordination is an over-all term denoting the practice of gathering all the efforts of individuals together to ensure smooth operation. This process of aligning all effort in one direction must include all the principles of organisation to be effective.

Combining and building up economically, after applying specialisation, summarises co-ordination. The large number of short-cycle operations created by specialisation must be coupled in the best possible way, which means quick and economic transference from stage to stage, with minimum interruptions in work flow. The essentials of co-ordination are communication—avoidance of misunderstandings and friction between stages of work and operational departments—and co-operation—close understanding between all functional departments and a genuine interest in their objectives.

Practical Steps Towards Improving Organisation

RULES

The following rules, which have been discussed in this chapter, should be observed by the supervisor. Where appropriate, regular checks and action should be taken.

1. The over-all objective and the purpose of each part of the organisation must be known by everyone.
2. Know each person's capabilities.
3. Orders must be final and concise.
4. Do not spend, or allow subordinates to spend, too much time on enjoyable tasks at the expense of distasteful or mundane ones.
5. Always welcome suggestions and ideas.
6. Reports must be conscientiously completed.
7. Reports must be used and kept up to date.
8. Plan carefully with the objective in mind.
9. Policy, rules, and regulations should be known by every employee.
10. There should be a place for everything, and everything should be in its place.
11. Each employee's responsibilities must be clearly defined and known to him.
12. The authority conferred upon an employee must correspond with his responsibilities.
13. Any changes in responsibility should be made known to everyone concerned.
14. Each employee should be responsible to, and receive instructions from, only one superior.
15. All duties and instructions must be clearly defined and consistent with a person's capabilities.
16. The formal line of command must run from top to bottom of the organisation.
17. A supervisor should not control more than five or six subordinate supervisors, who in turn should not control more than twelve operators.
18. Excessive overloading of work will impair efficiency.
19. Delegate lower-grade work, and spread the workload evenly.

20. Provide a continuous supply of replacements to ensure continuity.
21. Full use of specialisation should be made of men, machines, equipment, and processes.
22. Encourage self-discipline.
23. Try to be scrupulously fair and just at all times.
24. Critical words to individuals must always be given in private.
25. Any query on organisation should be carefully investigated and settled quickly.

PROCEDURE

1. Organising

A sound practice is to write down information on the organisation under the supervisor's control, rather than to rely upon memory. The over-all position is often clearer on paper; the balance of work-load, possible improvements and any deficiencies can more easily be seen.

A simple method of assessing and improving organisation is outlined below.

(*a*) *Job specification:* note all the duties and responsibilities of each subordinate. This may be elaborated, if desired, to include skill required, mental effort, physical needs, working conditions, and any other relevant factors.

(*b*) *Process chart:* draw a diagram, in flow form, from the beginning to the end of each process or procedure, using information from the job specifications.

(*c*) *Organisation chart:* draw a diagram showing the lines of authority and responsibility, using titles instead of names. Remember to indicate status by using some form of code where misinterpretation otherwise may occur.

The above method may be supplemented to suit particular requirements. The important factor is to put something down on paper, which can be rearranged and improved as a continuous process.

This task is made easier by drawing up a functional analysis, and an ideal organisation chart.

(*d*) *Functional diagram:* draw up a form, listing the functions and sub-functions down the left-hand side, and the subordinates across the top in columns, so making a space available for each function to be allocated to an individual. Better grouping of functions is immediately apparent when the form is completed.

An outline of functional analysis and appropriate diagrams is given in Chapter XV in connection with Job Evaluation and the need to analyse jobs when a concern is growing rapidly.

(*e*) *Ideal organisation chart:* draw the chart with all the improvements which are considered desirable so that, as opportunities occur to make changes, they can be made with a definite plan in mind.

2. Delegating

The supervisor's most common organisation problem is delegation. The following procedure clarifies this problem.

(*a*) Make a list of all the tasks performed and include also those that are neglected or omitted through lack of time.

(*b*) Mark each one on an "importance" basis and rearrange in descending order of importance.

(*c*) Allocate time for each task. Accuracy is unimportant so long as an estimate is made to provide a rough basis.

(*d*) Decide how much can be coped with by oneself, starting from the top, and draw a line across the list at this point.

(*e*) Make sure that each subordinate is assessed for his capabilities, and give the benefit of the doubt where necessary.

(*f*) Allocate the tasks below the line to subordinates, as appropriate to their capabilities.

(*g*) Follow-up and inspect to ensure they are not in difficulties.

(*h*) Rearrange if vital, but remember that it takes people some time to expand and adjust. A fair trial is essential.

Methodical approaches such as those outlined above make the supervisor's task less harassing.

QUESTIONS

1. Explain why a one-man business is the easiest to manage.
2. Describe the line/functional type of organisation.
3. Discuss some of the problems which are associated with large-scale organisation.
4. Give an account of the characteristics of good organisation.
5. Why is the principle of the objective so important?
6. What is meant by the term *balance* in the organisation structure?
7. How is co-ordination achieved in an organisation?
8. What is meant by the term *specialisation*? Explain its purpose.
9. Carefully define authority and responsibility.
10. Describe the Scalar process and comment on its effectiveness.
11. Discuss span of control and comment on the problems of this topic.
12. Discuss the principle of delegation and its importance to the supervisor.
13. Outline and discuss a simple procedure for delegating.
14. As a supervisor, how would you ensure that successful delegation is achieved?
15. Consider the problem of continuity in an organisation.
16. How would you decide on the degree of discipline to adopt in a concern?
17. Consider the question of centralisation in an organisation.
18. What problems arise over the administration of justice in industry?
19. State some practical steps on how to improve organisation.
20. Outline a procedure for investigating an organisation with a view to its improvement.
21. Discuss the traditional and modern concepts of organisation.

CHAPTER V

INDUSTRY

General Outline

A VAST range of business firms exist in which a manager or supervisor may be expected to operate effectively. Movement from one job to another within the same industry soon convinces individuals that each concern is different in some respects. British industry is complex and difficult to portray in textbook form, it is possible to describe it in outline but only first-hand experience reveals the true situation.

POST-WAR HISTORY

The magnitude of the problems which managers in industry and successive Governments have had to face is often overlooked. The end of World War II in 1945 marked a drastic change in the financial position of the United Kingdom. Before the War a long reputation as a creditor nation had been enjoyed, mainly through flourishing export markets. Owing to the cost of the War, which meant selling many foreign investments, and severe restrictions of exports, Britain entered a precarious phase of financial instability.

Debts amounted to £3500 million and these were blocked by the Government. Aid from the U.S.A. included a loan of about £1000 million which was soon disposed of, and this was followed by a gift of goods, valued at nearly £1500 million under the Marshall Plan, as part of a scheme of assistance to many European nations, including West Germany and Italy.

The urgent need to increase exports was thrust upon industry under changed conditions where, (*a*) the labour force had become highly organised and fully employed; (*b*) greater spending power existed in the home market which tended to distract from exporting; and (*c*) extensive Government influence over many aspects of industry had increased. Such conditions, and the objective, could only be met by increasing output, raising quality, and reducing the price of products. These three vital factors, *output, quality and price*, mainly depend upon such factors as technical efficiency in all fields of production, higher productivity, adopting a new attitude towards employees, and effective management.

Today the problem is still unsolved, over thirty years after World War II, while other countries forge ahead and apparently leave Britain farther behind. This gloomy outlook does not, however, match entirely with obvious signs of material prosperity in Britain.

Table 1—Size of manufacturing units 1975—United Kingdom

	Total	Analysis by number of employees						
		11-19	20-49	50-99	100-199	200-499	500-999	1,000 or more
Number of units								
All manufacturing industries	58,241	17,804	18,002	9,093	6,121	4,637	1,566	1,018
Food, drink and tobacco .	4,777	1,237	1,342	778	540	558	214	108
Coal and petroleum products	169	44	38	26	14	32	8	7
Chemicals and allied industries	2,047	517	494	334	278	244	103	77
Metal manufacture .	2,180	470	602	384	281	262	95	86
Mechanical engineering .	8,466	2,966	2,572	1,202	787	589	221	129
Instrument engineering .	1,239	393	353	185	138	106	40	24
Electrical engineering .	3,282	899	792	486	381	366	194	164
Shipbuilding and marine engineering .	673	213	188	97	65	52	16	42
Vehicles .	2,131	528	560	293	261	218	101	170
Metal goods not elsewhere specified	6,920	2,555	2,325	1,038	508	333	124	37
Textiles .	4,285	930	1,154	797	723	540	101	40
Leather, leather goods and fur .	776	296	258	132	65	24	1	–
Clothing and footwear .	5,541	1,502	2,028	961	638	339	63	10
Bricks, pottery, glass, cement, etc. .	2,150	544	734	354	229	197	64	28
Timber, furniture, etc. .	4,713	1,840	1,700	657	352	133	28	3
Paper, printing and publishing .	5,761	1,976	1,849	811	543	407	120	55
Other manufacturing industries .	3,131	894	1,013	558	318	237	73	38

Number of employees (thousands)

All manufacturing industries	7,014,985	255,823	552,235	636,826	853,325	1,422,981	1,080,789	2,213,006
Food, drink and tobacco	719,702	17,888	41,831	54,859	76,213	174,138	150,848	203,925
Coal and petroleum products	35,427	653	1,150	1,725	1,957	10,598	5,764	13,580
Chemicals and allied industries	379,366	7,449	15,656	23,308	39,619	77,902	72,078	143,354
Metal manufacture	478,560	6,805	18,840	26,872	39,793	82,105	67,648	236,497
Mechanical engineering	866,093	42,775	78,259	83,756	108,701	183,261	149,925	219,416
Instrument engineering	148,267	5,633	11,241	13,081	19,313	32,103	28,508	38,388
Electrical engineering	707,748	12,989	24,216	34,456	53,085	114,787	134,571	333,644
Shipbuilding and marine engineering	177,728	3,089	5,556	6,775	8,940	17,581	11,723	124,064
Vehicles	770,057	7,554	16,841	21,013	36,758	67,432	71,450	549,009
Metal goods not elsewhere specified	486,638	36,646	70,625	71,929	68,505	99,892	85,508	53,533
Textiles	508,533	13,271	36,342	56,797	102,250	162,878	68,401	68,594
Leather, leather goods and fur	37,846	4,273	7,940	8,869	8,904	7,325	535	—
Clothing and footwear	391,321	21,557	62,134	66,671	89,100	96,144	40,780	14,935
Bricks, pottery, glass, cement, etc.	233,863	7,901	22,837	25,001	31,735	60,841	43,149	42,399
Timber, furniture, etc.	232,683	26,133	51,319	45,690	48,534	39,843	17,343	3,821
Paper, printing and publishing	518,562	28,412	56,508	57,022	75,641	125,430	81,758	93,791
Other manufacturing industries	322,591	12,795	30,940	39,002	44,277	70,721	50,800	74,056

Notes (i) The analysis follows the Orders of the Standard Industrial Classification 1968. (ii) Reliable figures for units employing 10 or less persons are not available at Business Statistics Office. It is estimated, however, that there were about 55,000 such units in 1975 with total employment of approximately 270 thousands.

Source: Central Statistical Office, Annual Abstract of Statistics 1979 by permission of the Controller of Her Majesty's Stationery Office.

An outline of industry is built up through this chapter by isolating a number of aspects and discussing each one in turn. Some of the aspects are dealt with in other chapters more fully, but it is necessary first to understand their essential part in industry. These aspects are: Management in Chapters VI and VII; Finance in Chapter XXVII; and Trade Unions in Chapter XVII. The aspects discussed in this chapter are: types of industry; business structure, location of industry, the national economy; international influence; and employment and the cost of living.

TYPES OF INDUSTRY

The emergence of particular industries in a country is the result of various factors: technical knowledge, availability of trained labour; raw materials and power; the climate; capital resources; stage of economic development; social climate; and political organisation.

In the United Kingdom during the eighteenth century conditions were favourable for industrial change and expansion. Natural advantages such as climate, geographical position, harbours, navigable rivers, and supplies of coal and iron, were supplemented by political and financial stability, and an accumulation of capital. A gradual development of industry occurred, which is known as the Industrial Revolution. The main industries that emerged were textiles, coal, iron, steel, and engineering, including railways. Agriculture continued to improve as demand increased.

The introduction of machinery, new techniques, and improved communication and transport, brought about large-scale production which considerably increased the range and quality of goods. Today the number of manufacturing establishments is about 115,000 and they employ just over 7 million individuals. The classification of factories, according to size and type of industry, is illustrated in Table I. The figures in the main table do not include establishments with fewer than eleven employees. These small factories tend to fluctuate in number but a footnote on the diagram gives an estimate of about 55,000.

Business Structure

The thousands of industrial concerns in Britain vary in structure as well as in size. The six main types of business range from the one-man firm to the nationalised industry.

1. Sole proprietor

The one-man concern is the oldest type of business and is still quite common, especially among retailers and farmers. The proprietor provides his own capital, raised either by savings or borrowed from his relations and friends. He is liable for all his debts, is responsible only to himself, and profits do not have to be shared.

2. Partnerships
The common form of partnership consists of two or more individuals who agree to establish a business and who generally share responsibilities and profits. The total number of partners is limited to twenty except solicitors, accountants and stockbrokers, under the Companies Acts 1948–76. The Limited Partnership Act 1907 allows individuals to form a partnership under which a partner's liability is limited, but such a partner is not allowed to participate in the concern's management.

3. Limited companies
The principle of limited liability means that investors are liable for the concern's debts only up to the amount invested in fully paid up shares in the company. Such a system, legalised in the original Companies Act 1856, has encouraged industry to develop at a phenomenal rate. Large amounts of capital can be raised and companies may expand more easily by raising further sums of money.

The two types of limited company are the private company and the public company. Limited companies and shares are discussed in the chapters on Management (VI and VII) and the Financial Function (XXVII). Briefly, the *private limited company* may consist of two members but not more than fifty. Only friends, relatives and past or present employees may be approached to buy shares. The consent of other shareholders is necessary before a shareholder can transfer his shares. The *public limited company* can have any number of shareholders, but the minimum is seven. The company may advertise for capital and usually the shares may be bought and sold freely through the Stock Exchange.

4. Co-operative societies
The co-operative movement *in production* has *not* grown, mainly because the employees provide the capital and elect their own managers from within. The restriction in raising capital and the problem of locating effective managers has resulted in the establishment of only twenty-seven concerns who are members of the Co-operative Production Federation. The main lines of production are footwear and clothing; the bulk of output is distributed to co-operative societies.

Consumers' co-operative societies are very popular, with a membership of about twelve million. Each member is a customer who may invest up to £1000 in the particular society, but he has only one vote. Interest on the investment is at a fixed rate and the profit for distribution is paid in the form of a dividend on purchases. Any individual may join or leave whenever he wishes and there is no maximum number of shareholders. Management is elected by members and the accounts must be published.

Recent attempts by Labour Governments to establish co-operatives following threatened closures have encountered many economic difficulties. Examples are the Kirkby Manufacturing and Engineering Company, Triumph Ltd. at Meriden, and the *Scottish Daily News*. These co-operatives have been severely criticised mainly on the grounds that practically all declining industries suffer from misguided enthusiasm caused by added strains on an already faltering spirit. The result is a further decline which tends to increase in speed. Other criticisms include the inference that backing—in various forms—is insufficient and too late.

Supporters of co-operatives claim that given a viable situation the principle of co-ownership avoids the innate conflict between the two sides: owner and employee, and provides a firm basis for operating industrial democracy successfully.

5. Municipal undertakings

Local services such as airfields, local transport, and water supply are provided by the local authority. Ratepayers are the owners, but the local council is responsible for management.

6. State undertakings

Within this group are the Post Office, the British Broadcasting Corporation, the London Passenger Transport Board, and the Port of London Authority. The nationalised industries also are included, consisting of the Bank of England, the gas, electricity, steel, shipbuilding and coal industries, and parts of transport which include British Railways, British Waterways and Roadline. A committee is appointed by the Minister who is responsible for the particular undertaking. He reports to Parliament, but the committee actually manages the concern in accordance with Parliament's policy. For example, a sudden cold spell in November 1965 caused electricity cuts and low gas pressures in some areas, which created chaotic conditions in certain industries. The Government ordered the coal, gas and electricity industries to stop all advertising in an attempt to stem a further increase in demand.

Location of Industry

Choice of position to build a factory naturally depends upon finding the most economical place, considering a large number of factors which are individually weighted, dependent upon the type of industry involved.

Such economical sites become congested because of their exceptional facilities. This congestion, on the one hand, may lead to certain disadvantages which force some concerns to move elsewhere;

while, on the other hand, such concentration of a particular industry leads to certain advantages which encourage *localisation of industry*. Changes in demand cause some industries to decline and, as a result, unemployment develops in areas which creates a national problem and invokes State planning to solve the difficulty.

The three main aspects of location are factors influencing selection of the site; localisation of industry; and planned location of industry. Each one is now discussed.

SOME FACTORS IN THE SELECTION OF A FACTORY SITE

1. Proximity to services

Proximity of power was a major consideration in the nineteenth century when coal was used to raise steam power; hence industry developed around the coalfields. As electricity, gas and oil were introduced in the twentieth century, the restricting effect of using coal was overcome. The need for services such as water and drainage also has to be considered.

2. Proximity to raw materials

The cost of shipping raw materials from the source of supply to the factory can be excessive if raw materials form a major part of the production cost. The tendency to concentrate around ports, if raw materials in bulk come from abroad, applies to oil refining and flour milling.

3. Proximity to the market

The trend towards large centres of population eventually became an inducement to concerns to locate premises near to such potential markets for their products. In addition, specialist service industries such as insurance and banking appeared in these areas, which increased the advantages to industry.

4. Transport

The rapid growth of road transport after World War I broadened the suitable areas of location considerably, thus reducing the importance of this factor so far as location was concerned.

5. Employees

Many people were drawn towards the new industries around the coalfields, and large towns developed in the nineteenth century. As some of these industries declined, the trend to set up new industries in the south-east and Midlands developed. The disadvantages of unsuitable labour and high rates at the old centres of industry encouraged the change. Some people moved to these new industrial areas, notably the Midlands, where the motor vehicle industry was growing rapidly, and London, where a large range of light industries was appearing.

6. Local facilities

A number of other considerations which must affect the owners' decisions to some extent are the attractiveness of the area as regards social and climatic conditions, educational and commercial facilities, the countryside, housing development, and established local skills. Both employees and owners like a pleasant environment for their families to live in.

7. Local government influence

The attitude of local government towards industry may affect the choice of site because of such restrictions as local zoning of areas where no development is allowed, the problem of waste disposal, the level of rates and method of assessment. Some authorities—in conjunction with national schemes—encourage industry to expand in the district by setting up factory sites in the form of trading estates or factory centres.

8. Financial factor

The cost of land and the additional area expenses are important. Mining rights, suitability of land, plans for extensions in the future, existing rights of way, and, in some cases, the prestige value of the site, must be considered. Whether the land is freehold or leasehold, and any building problems, such as the high cost of draining, must be investigated thoroughly. Actual building operations must be costed to include the proximity of a construction company, closeness of building materials, transport services to the site, and the joining of various services from the mains to the factory.

LOCALISATION OF INDUSTRY

When an industry concentrates in one area the effect is known as localisation of industry. Many industries in Britain are highly localised; the advantages of this concentration are organised markets, regional division of labour, a pool of skilled labour, and development of subsidiary industries.

Organised markets tend to appear in the locally-manufactured product. New concerns are attracted and established; a new form of economy emerges where each firm specialises in one process or one part of the product. Thus, regional division of labour—like the dividing up of labour within a company, so that each person performs a separate function towards manufacturing the product—is extended to the whole industry so that specialisation within each firm is achieved.

Full use of skilled labour is possible with localisation as companies will be attracted to areas where such labour is available. Subsidiary industries will also be attracted.

Localisation is not possible in some industries such as public utilities where the service must be near the consumption point because of high transportation costs.

PLANNED LOCATION OF INDUSTRY

Although high economic advantage is attained by localisation, the problem of rising and declining industries causes considerable misery through unemployment when a localised industry contracts. The decline in cotton and coal-mining in Britain in the 1950s and 1960s illustrates the problem of high local unemployment which existed even while most of the rest of the country was fully employed. Structural unemployment, as it is known, is a form of economic waste which Britain cannot afford.

Ignoring the question of mobility of labour, which is discussed under "Employment" below, this situation appears to call for State planning by encouraging industry to move to unemployment areas. Whether this policy is sound is debatable because companies localise on a basis of being able to operate more effectively. If freedom of movement is restricted these economies will be lost. A further consideration is that over 50 per cent of the companies who have been persuaded to move are subsidiaries or branches of large companies which produce consumer goods. If a depression developed, these would tend to contract quickly.

Government action may be summed up by mentioning the legislation there has been in this field. In 1945 the Distribution of Industries Act listed the development areas and gave the Board of Trade powers to extend this list. The Town and Country Planning Act 1947 assisted the scheme, as also did the New Towns Act 1946, which provided loans and established development corporations for each new town. A further New Towns Act in 1959 established a Commission to accept the liabilities of the development corporations, including the property involved which, by this time, was considerable and included sixteen towns.

The Local Employment Act 1960 dispensed with development areas and gave the Government the right to encourage industrial movement anywhere in the country where unemployment was above the average (development districts). The Industrial Development Act 1966 restored the development areas, and later intermediate (grey) areas were added to those areas receiving aid.

Under the Industry Acts 1972/1975 regional development grants are offered in assisted areas for helping to meet the costs of buildings and works engaged on specified activities. In the case of special development and development areas assistance is also given towards the cost of plant and machinery. Furthermore, selective financial assistance is given for projects which are likely to provide, maintain or safeguard employment in assisted areas.

Under separate legislation, the Industries Development Acts 1966 and 1971 provide the Northern Ireland Department of Commerce with facilities to offer a full range of incentives similar to those available in the assisted areas of Britain.

The National Economy

TRENDS

An industry is seldom stable for any length of time. Demands change for various reasons such as fashions, market saturation, new inventions, and competition from abroad. In Britain, some older industries such as textiles, mining, quarrying, and agriculture, are declining. Other industries are expanding; examples are paper and printing; chemicals; engineering and allied industries; construction; gas, electricity, and water supplies; and electronics. Since 1938, some typical expansion programmes have been seen in scientific instruments, aircraft, motor vehicles, man-made fibres, plastics, and electrical equipment.

IMPORTANCE OF GROWTH

If our standard of living is to be maintained and improved, industry must grow faster than the present rate. To increase total output, which is known as the *Gross National Product*, all resources must be fully and effectively utilised. The capacity to produce must be raised by modernising, replacing and expanding the productive machine. Britain's performance is low compared with other countries on a basis of growth per head. West Germany, Italy, the Netherlands, Sweden, France, and Denmark, all manage to achieve better results.

In the 1960s successive Governments attempted to hold down rises in incomes and prices as a means of encouraging growth. The devaluation of sterling in 1967 allowed exports to recover which led to a substantial surplus on visible trade and a record current account surplus in 1971. However, the energy crisis in 1973 caused the growth rate to slow down. In the following year the world economy entered a phase of recession due to accelerating inflation and the enormous increase in the price of oil.

In Britain manufacturing output fell and unemployment started rising. At the beginning of 1976 an improvement was apparent in world trade, which resulted in a rise in export volume, but unemployment continued to rise.

CONTROL OF INFLATION

The urgent need to regenerate British industry was recognised in 1976 and stronger measures were introduced to reduce inflation. The main steps taken were the introduction of certain limits on pay increases, further control of prices, and the restriction of dividend payments above a 10 per cent increase. Extensive use of cash limits on public expenditure was also introduced by the Government.

The £6 pay limit proved to be acceptable and, in general, successfully applied. The result was that retail price inflation dropped to about half the level of the previous year, 1975. Unfortunately the inflation rate still continued to be above that of major overseas competitors.

Talks between the Government, the T.U.C. and the C.B.I. resulted in a second round of wage restraint being agreed for another year (1977), namely a 5 per cent guideline along with a number of tax reliefs.

In 1978 the proposal for a third round of pay restraint, again limited to a 5 per cent guideline, met with opposition from various trade unions.

GOVERNMENT INFLUENCE

The extended government influence today really amounts to the State assuming in many respects the function of top management of industry. Through the Budgets, demand for goods and services can be varied, growth adjusted, inflation checked, and modernisation programmes can be encouraged. The Government's own investment schemes also play a very important part in the economy. Spending on educationand other services in the so-called *public sector*, and expenditure and increased efficiency in nationalised industries, must also be included. In addition, the Government has been pushing ahead with schemes to revise apprenticeships, management training, adult training generally, and industrial relations.

An expanding economy naturally needs more imports which means that Britain must export more goods—of the right type, at the right quality and price—to stabilise the balance of trade. Government concern over this general problem of growth has resulted in the introduction and abandonment of many schemes to improve the situation. These schemes are dealt with by various Government departments, each one usually being headed by a Minister. About 500,000 civil servants are employed, comprising about 2 per cent of the working population.

Some of the main activities, which are always subject to organisational change in line with any radical change in policy, are: finance; agriculture, fisheries and food; customs and excise; defence; education and science; employment; environment; foreign affairs; forestry; health and social security; home affairs; inland revenue; law; national savings; trade and industry; energy; prices; consumer protection; and transport.

The main ways that the Government can influence industrial activity are through the amount of public expenditure, fiscal and monetary policy, placing of government contracts, policies of publicly owned enterprises, physical controls, exhortation, inducements, provision of services, information and advice. Close association between the Government, managers and trade unions is maintained through various channels such as the National Economic Development Council and the Economic Development Committees.

About forty tripartite working parties have been established within the National Economic Development Council framework. Three sets of reports have been issued and these have been used to attempt to encourage improvements in the sectors' shares of home and overseas markets. In 1978 considerable emphasis was placed on the need to improve productivity, and the findings were communicated to individual companies.

Under the Industry Act 1975 the National Enterprise Board (N.E.B.) was established to assist the national economy, private industrial efficiency and international competitiveness, and provide productive employment. The N.E.B. has the power and facilities to provide finance for industrial investment and restructuring. It acts as a holding company and is expected to exercise commercial judgment and to look for an adequate return on its investments.

In 1975 and 1976 the Scottish, Welsh and Northern Ireland Development Agencies were set up. These are designed to stimulate industrial development by exercising powers similar to the N.E.B.

Investment is encouraged under the Finance Act 1972. A system of free depreciation is offered which enables the whole of capital expenditure to be written off against profits for tax purposes in the year in which it is incurred. Other benefits are also allowable.

Such a wealth of economic planning machinery is difficult to imagine and harder to visualise in operation. Unfortunately, providing the means—no matter how elaborate and expensive—does not solve the problem. Government decisions have so many side-effects that can throw out the most carefully laid plans.

A simple example is Value Added Tax (V.A.T.): the application of V.A.T. on a product may raise its price level to a point where it is worth while to repair rather than replace when it develops a fault. Accordingly, companies are formed and a new service industry throughout the country is established. Suddenly, V.A.T. is removed by the Government. The effect is to reduce the price level to a point where it is no longer economic to service the product. The inevitable disbanding of most of the service companies, who cannot find alternative work, follows soon after the move. Although obviously unintentional, the effect is economic attrition.

International Influence

Britain is very dependent upon her dealings with other countries throughout the world. The country cannot be self-sufficient because it has insufficient supplies of foodstuffs and raw materials internally to convert into products for home consumption and for exports to pay its debts. This situation places Britain in a vulnerable position, to some extent. The country must avoid running into financial difficulties abroad by ensuring that it is in a position to offer countries acceptable products. This market is also influenced by overseas competitors who are now capable of supplying up-to-date goods of reasonable quality at keen prices. The fight to maintain and increase Britain's markets abroad is becoming tougher, and the ingenuity of marketing specialists is not sufficient unless the products are competitive. Such important factors as availability of replacement parts and after-sales service must not be ignored.

THE BALANCE OF PAYMENTS

Business dealings with other countries are recorded, and the balance is calculated. It is known as the *balance of payments*, which may be adverse or favourable. These business dealings are divided into two groups. The first is called *visible* trade, which accounts for the importing and exporting of all goods. Generally, Britain imports more than she exports, therefore the country nearly always has an adverse balance of trade.

The second group deals with "*invisibles*", which cover all dealings in services such as insurance, shipping, and the tourist trade; these are more favourable as they also include investment interest and profits from abroad. Generally, the "invisibles" provide a favourable balance but, in combining the balances of "visibles" and "invisibles" to indicate the *balance of payments*, an adverse balance has appeared and grown in recent years. Another important factor which affects the balance of payments is Britain's capital dealings. These must be distinguished from "visibles" and "invisibles" which are known as current transactions. Capital dealings are investments abroad for building factories, expanding industry, or general loans to foreign governments. About £150 million a year *more* has been invested abroad for over ten years compared with investments by other countries in Britain.

Although British exports have doubled since 1938, the constant drive for more exports is necessary to pay for four main items. *Firstly*, rising imports through production growth and increasing prosperity; *secondly*, defence programmes abroad; *thirdly*, financial aid to underdeveloped countries; and, *fourthly*, a less favourable balance of "invisibles", owing to a fall in shipping services and other items such as interest and profit from investments abroad.

In 1971 the current balance of payments was a surplus of £1084 million. By 1975 the figure had fallen to a deficit of £1673 million due to the low level of domestic activity, substantial de-stocking and a set-back in world trade.

A sharp turnround occurred between 1976 and 1977 when North Sea oil production increased. In the first quarter of 1978 the current balance was a deficit of £317 million and in the second quarter a surplus of £198 million.

BARRIERS TO INTERNATIONAL TRADE

Foreign countries may decide to impose restrictions on the entry of British goods for various reasons such as political bias, to protect a home trade, or to balance their economy. The general effect of these policies among countries is to restrict the development of international trade.

An attempt to overcome this problem was made in 1947 when the *General Agreement on Tariffs and Trade* (GATT) was established by forty-four countries outside the Soviet bloc. The object is to reduce gradually *tariffs*, which restrict entry of goods, and *quotas*, which allow only a certain volume of goods to enter for each particular period.

Other organisations have also assisted in removing the barriers to trade. These are the *International Monetary Fund* (I.M.F.), which helps to stabilise currencies and assist countries who are in temporary financial difficulties; the *European Free Trade Association* (EFTA) which consists of five countries—Austria, Norway, Portugal, Sweden, and Switzerland (Finland is an associate member; Denmark and Britain left in 1972 to join the E.E.C.); finally, the *Organisation for Economic Co-operation and Development* (O.E.C.D.) was formed between eighteen countries to develop economic co-operation in Western Europe.

In addition, France, Germany, Italy, Belgium, Holland, and Luxembourg founded the *European Economic Community* in 1957. This community has improved its prosperity impressively and in 1961 and 1967 Britain applied to join, but was unsuccessful both times. In 1969 new attempts to reach an agreement were commenced in view of a favourable approach from France. Negotiations were completed in 1972, and on 1st January 1973, Britain, Denmark and the Irish Republic became new members of the Community. It is claimed that Britain's membership will mean that there will be better opportunities for British industry to sell more and produce more, thus eventually improving the standard of living.

The aim of the nine countries with about 255 million inhabitants which now make up the Community is to establish "an even closer union among the peoples of Europe and to ensure economic and social progress by common action".

To achieve this objective, a Common Market has gradually been established which permits the free movement of goods by abolishing customs barriers and other obstacles to trade. Workers seeking employment can move freely among member states. A Community policy which extends the Common Market to agriculture is being developed.

Common rules have been established to guarantee free competition among companies who apply a common policy in their trade with non-member countries.

The member countries are co-ordinating their economic, monetary, tax, scientific and energy policies. Social links are also being encouraged. Joint action is being undertaken in the fields of vocational training and retraining, employment, social security, migrant workers, and equal pay for men and women. Efforts are being combined to improve the environment and working conditions, and to help regions where industry is underdeveloped or facing structural change.

Foreign policies are being increasingly co-ordinated and numerous measures have been taken to further the development of the Third World.

Employment and the Cost of Living

SHORTAGE OF SKILLED WORKERS

Since World War II there has been, in certain occupations, a shortage of labour which has become chronic at times as economic activity has fluctuated and in spite of high unemployment levels. The wide diversity and dynamism of the labour market produces a variety of imbalances and shifts in demand for skills.

Typical factors which affect labour shortages are inadequate training programmes, legislation, industrial relations problems, organisation of work, the transition from school to employment, and structural changes in industry and commerce.

Skill imbalances seem to occur for a variety of reasons, according to a report published by the Manpower Services Commission, "Training for Skills". The M.S.C. undertook an Industrial Facts and Forecasting Survey which disclosed that most employers blamed the shortages on such factors as not enough good or experienced applicants, general shortage of labour, or low training levels. Other factors offered by employers and trade unions included employment legislation, pay relativities, increased fixed labour costs, reliance on subcontracting and overtime, poor employment policies, high incidence of redundancy or short-time working, and bad working conditions. Comments were also made on low productivity, the inflexible use of labour because of demarcation practices, other rigid manning practices, poor deployment and organisation of resources, and the mis-match between skill levels required of the individual and skills actually used.

Finally, it was thought that in some areas of the country there were too few young people at the age of 16 with sufficient basic education to enable them to commence long-term training programmes.

New industries are seeking a higher proportion of skilled workers. This demand can only be met by increasing training and retraining programmes, and improving the mobility of labour. An extensive scheme is already in operation for training under the Industrial Training Act 1964, which is discussed in Chapter XVI.

The Training Services Division of the Manpower Services Commission has expanded its training programmes considerably since it was set up in 1974. Under the Training Opportunities Scheme (TOPS) 15,500 people were trained in 1971, and in 1977 this number had risen to 94,200. The number of places in skillcentres (previously Government training centres) rose from 10,500 in 1971 to 18,000 in 1977, but the proportion of completions on skillcentre courses fell from 83 per cent to about 25 per cent.

The range of courses offered has also increased from 80 in 1971 to over 200 in 1978. Particularly rapid increases in training have been noted in clerical and commercial occupations, which in 1977 accounted for 36 per cent of completions, followed by manual craft occupations with 25 per cent, and higher level occupations with 9 per cent.

Redundancy and the need for alternative employment have been a national problem for many years. Unemployment benefit has been increased and legislation has been introduced to provide for redundancy pay as a form of compensation to long-service employees who lose their jobs. These redundancy provisions were originally laid down in the Redundancy Payments Act 1965 but are now contained in the Employment Protection (Consolidation) Act 1978.

To encourage mobility from area to area, grants and allowances have been increased by the Department of Employment, but serious areas of long-term unemployment persist and there has been excessive fluctuation in unemployment since 1945. From 1948 to 1967 the average unemployment rate was under 2 per cent in most years, but since 1967 it has been over 2 per cent and over 3 per cent at the beginning of 1971. In August 1971 3.7 per cent was recorded and by the end of that year over one million persons were unemployed. In 1977 unemployment (excluding school-leavers) had risen to 1,378,000 which represented about 5.8 per cent of all employees. Little change occurred in 1978. By April 1979 provisional figures (including school-leavers) were: 1,279,808.

MANPOWER

In 1977 the total working population in Britain was about 26.3 million, which represented about 46 per cent of the total population. About two million are employers or self-employed while the rest work for a wage or salary.

Up to 1966 the working population increased slowly; it declined between 1966 and 1971; since then it has been rising again. The industrial distribution of the working population is given in Table II. An

Table II—*Manpower in Britain 1970–7 (thousands[a])*

Year	Employees in employment[b]	Employers and self-employed	Unemployed[c]	Armed Forces[d]	Total working population[d]
1970	22,471	1,902	555	372	25,300
1971	22,122	1,909	724	368	25,123
1972	22,120	1,899	899	371	25,194
1973	22,662	1,947	575	361	25,545
1974	22,790	1,925	542	345	25,602
1975	22,707	1,886	866	336	25,795
1976	22,539	1,886	1,332	336	26,093
1977	22,661	1,886	1,450	327	26,367

Source: *Department of Employment Gazette*
[a] Discrepancies between totals and their constituent parts are due to rounding.
[b] Part-time workers are counted as units.
[c] Excluding adult students.
[d] The working population figures and the Forces figures include ex-Service personnel on leave after completing their service.
Reprinted from Britain 1979: An Official Handbook, *by permission of the Controller of Her Majesty's Stationery Office.*

analysis of civil employment shows that about 1.6 per cent are engaged in agriculture and fisheries, and 31.3 per cent in manufacturing and mining industries; detailed figures are given in Table III.

According to numerous assessments by independent research workers, a number of industries do not use manpower effectively. The endless stream of stories that circulate about labour wastage always seems to match accurately with employees' own experiences, which is surely significant.

Some of the factors involved are strikes, overmanning, unnecessary overtime, restrictions on the tempo of work, and labour deployment which is not suited to production techniques. Overtime, it seems, is a particular example where the practice has become a routine which is expected by employees, who adjust their output during normal working hours accordingly.

Management is responsible for improving the efficiency of employees. Improving the standards of management, therefore, should lead to an improvement in manpower effectiveness. The British Institute of Management has contributed a considerable amount of effort in the field of management training since the World War II, and two graduate business schools were established in London and Manchester in 1965, to be followed by many others throughout the U.K.

Table III—*Analysis of Civil Employment in Britain 1970 and 1977*

Industry or Service	1970		1977[a]	
	Thousands	Per cent	Thousands	Per cent
Agriculture, forestry and fishing	468	1.9	391	1.6
Mining and quarrying	410	1.7	349	1.4
Manufacturing industries	8,339	34.2	7,343	29.9
Chemicals and allied industries	491	2.0	466	1.9
Metals, engineering and vehicles	4,315	17.7	3,795	15.5
Textiles	678	2.8	516	2.1
Clothing and footwear	455	1.9	390	1.6
Food, drink and tobacco	792	3.2	723	2.9
Other manufactures	1,609	6.6	1,453	5.9
Construction	1,335	5.5	1,265	5.2
Gas, electricity and water	391	1.6	350	1.4
Transport and communications	1,573	6.5	1,449	5.9
Distributive trades	2,676	11.0	2,734	11.1
Professional, financial, scientific and miscellaneous services[a]	5,801	23.8	7,144	29.1
National and local government service	1,479	6.1	1,633	6.7
Total: employees	22,471	92.2	22,661	92.3
Employers and self-employed persons (all industries and services)	1,902	7.8	1,886	7.7
Total in Civil Employment	24,373	100.0	24,547	100.0

Sources: *Department of Employment and Northern Ireland Department of Manpower Services*
[a] Excludes private domestic service.
Discrepancies between totals and their constituent parts are due to rounding.

Reprinted from Britain 1979: An Official Handbook, *by permission of the Controller of Her Majesty's Stationery Office.*

The Government also circulates literature which encourages universities and establishments for further education to provide more and better management courses.

A continuous study of manpower resources and requirements for certain industries and occupations, and for the whole economy is undertaken by the Manpower Services Commission (M.S.C.). The Training Services Division of the M.S.C. also co-operates with Industrial Training Boards on technical problems associated with recruitment, training, careers and industrial and manpower planning.

The M.S.C. has a responsibility to assist employers in obtaining suitable employees and to assist people to select, train for, obtain and retain employment. It aims to fulfil this responsibility through a number of services, including the employment offices and jobcentres operated by the Employment Service Division, Professional and Executive Recruitment (P.E.R.), Occupational Guidance Units and other specialist employment services, and the Training Opportunities Scheme (TOPS).

WAGES AND PRICES

More employees now appreciate the significance of rising wage levels and their effect on prices as trends have become increasingly obvious since 1938. An upsurge in prices provides employees and trade unions with the opportunity to ask for more pay, but extra cash is not effective as further waves of price increases soon follow. Furthermore, the group that receives its share of wage increases last has been forced to pay for the rest in the form of increased prices for a much longer time.

The simple fact that increased wages are passed on to the community in higher prices for goods would appear to be inescapable. A second fact is that this process reduces the purchasing power of the pound each time wages are increased. Hence, the community receives more money but the real value of each pound falls. Another important fact is that when prices are increased in this fashion it becomes harder to sell goods abroad and easier for imported goods to be sold in Britain.

In view of these three proven facts it seems illogical to claim more pay, but far better to insist on stable wages and prices to enable Britain to compete abroad.

Underlying this problem is the deeper one of how to decide upon levels of income of all types including profit, rent, interest, and wages, and their equitable distribution among the community. For instance, which occupations should receive the same wages? Perhaps if this question could be solved to suit everyone, there would be less tendency to push wages up in individual trades towards the levels existing in other occupations.

Before considering production, it should be recognised that prices rise for reasons other than wage increases, although on average wage increases account for about 75 per cent of the price increases. Three other factors are involved.

(*a*) The effect of supply and demand. The *price mechanism*, as it is called, will operate when supplies are restricted, as in the case of foodstuffs which are affected by a poor summer, and when demand increases through, say, a change in fashion.

(*b*) A rise in the price of imports such as raw materials.

(*c*) Government controls such as increased V.A.T. and reduced subsidies.

One point is clear at this stage: employees claim rises because the cost of living has increased which is caused by rising prices which, in turn, are 75 per cent caused by increased wages. Such a farcical situation conjures up visions of an extrovert "Oozlum Bird" which flew in ever *increasing* circles until it disappeared off the face of the earth.

Rising prices cause considerable concern because of their adverse effect on the balance of payments. Industrialists naturally seek easy markets and, therefore, it becomes more profitable to sell at home than to sell in markets abroad. Many of these overseas markets have enjoyed relatively stable costs and some have even dropped, as in the case of West Germany. The conscientious exporter will have increasing difficulty in remaining competitive under such conditions of rising costs at home and stable costs abroad. Finally, rising prices in Britain provide a wonderful opportunity for countries like Japan to increase

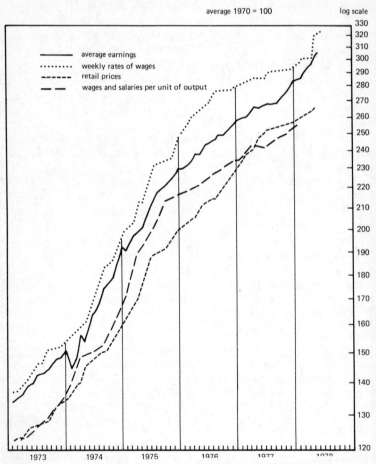

Fig. 11.—*Earnings Wage Rates, Retail Prices, Wages and Salaries, 1973–8.*

Reprinted from Britain 1979: An Official Handbook, *by permission of the Controller of Her Majesty's Stationery Office.*

exports because their goods become more competitive in price and quality. Britain can ill afford to open the door to rivals in this short-sighted way.

Figure 11 illustrates the main points so far discussed. For the period April 1970 to April 1977 the average weekly earnings of manual operatives increased by 167 per cent for males and 220 per cent for females, these percentages being calculated before deductions for tax and national insurance. Over the same period the increase was partly offset by a rise of about 140 per cent in retail prices, by larger national insurance contributions and by income tax. The burden on people with fixed incomes, particularly old folk, is particularly serious in these circumstances.

The question of output (not productivity, which in part relates output to the amount of labour employed) is now considered in relation to wages and prices. The fact that wages are only worth what they

WAGES AND PRICES			
Example	Wages/Prices	Details	Maximum Ratio
A	Wages ☐ Prices ☐☐☐☐	1. The exercise assumes that wages represent ¼ of the price. 2. £1 of wages: £4 of goods.	1 : 4
B	Wages ☐☐ Prices ☐☐☐☐☐	1. Wages are doubled 2. Price increased by 25%. 3. £2 of wages: £5 of goods	2 : 5
C	Wages ☐☐☐ Prices ☐☐☐☐☐☐	1. Wages increased by 50%. 2. Price increased by 20%. 3. £3 of wages: £6 of goods.	1 : 2
Note: The diagram ignores the fact that wage increases will also have an indirect effect on the cost of raw materials and expenses which will rise in sympathy. As the cost of some factors may be less effective it is true to say that wages will become a higher proportion of price but not to the extent indicated, hence the term maximum ratio is used.			

Fig. 12.—*Simplified Diagram of Wages and their Effect on Prices.*

The maximum ratios indicate that as wages increase they become a larger proportion of the total cost of the product and have a greater influence on price.

will buy indicates that they must be closely connected and move in sympathy with increases in output, otherwise the value of money will fall. On the basis of the Central Statistical Office's calculations for the Index of Retail Prices, all items of products and services costing £1 in 1962 cost £1.91 in 1974. The index for this calculation equalled 100 on 16th January 1962. On 15th January 1974 the index was revised to 100 again, and by December 1977, using a similar calculation, all items costing £1 had increased to £1.88. Considering these figures, the performance of management, trade unions and employees (individually or collectively) is questionable.

Real income, or the value of wages, depends mainly upon wages, prices, output, and productivity. Reference to the over-simplified diagrams on "Wages and Prices" (Fig. 12) and "Wages and Output" (Fig. 13) should indicate the importance of integrating these four factors to form a balanced economy.

Figure 12 shows the effect on prices of goods when wages (i.e. labour costs) are increased. The maximum ratios should be noted. They give an indication that as wages increase they become a larger proportion

WAGES AND OUTPUT		
Example	*Wages/Output*	*Details*
A	Wages / Output	The exercise assumes that £1 of wages = 1 unit of output.
B	Wages | Wages / Output	1. Wages are doubled. 2. Output is unchanged. 3. £1 of wages = ½ unit of output. 4. £1 of wages is now worth 50p.
C	Wages | Wages / Output | Output	1. Wages remain doubled. 2. Output is doubled. 3. £1 of wages = 1 unit of output. 4. £1 of wages is worth £1.
D	Wages / Output | Output	1. Wages remain unchanged. 2. Output is doubled. 3. £1 of wages = 2 units of output. 4. £1 of wages is now worth £2.

Fig. 13.—*Simplified Diagram of Wages and Output Relationships.*
This diagram is over-simplified since it ignores the fact that the cost of other factors of production may vary. Wages may be assumed to be the "national wage packet".

of the total cost of the product thus having a greater influence on the price. For the purpose of clear illustration, the fact that wage increases also have an indirect effect on the prices of raw materials and expenses has been ignored; the ratios given in these circumstances will be the maximum.

The behaviour of wages and output is indicated in Figure 13, which is an over-simplification because it ignores the fact that the cost of other factors of production may vary. Wages may be assumed to mean the "national wage packet".

Example C in Figure 13 reveals that where output doubles through higher productivity—despite the fact that wages have doubled—the purchasing power of the pound remains unchanged. The production units have increased, which has a direct effect on the standard of living and enables Britain to remain competitive overseas.

Example D shows the effect of higher productivity when coupled with static wages. Such an achievement in higher productivity would result in lower prices; increased competitiveness overseas through price reductions; expansion of overseas markets; and expansion of home industry without the fear of inflation. Economic stability would become a reality resulting in a rapid growth in the standard of living, thus giving Britain the opportunity to assist more in helping under-developed countries. New markets for export programmes would gradually appear as these developing countries could afford more goods.

Production, Productivity and Prosperity

Although during the whole period 1948 to 1978 industrial production has more than doubled, in recent years it has fallen sharply (see Table IV where 1970 is taken as the base year). The highest increases have occurred in chemicals and allied industries, coal and petroleum products, and in engineering. Instrument and electrical engineering show the most rapid growth within the engineering group. Table V indicates the course of production and employment in the years 1968–77. The main reasons for the increase in production are improved management; more intensive competitition and sales promotion; advances in products, processes, machines, and working methods; and the rate of fixed capital formation.

The amount of investment in industry tends to determine the introduction of new techniques and equipment, and new machines and instruments—all tending to decrease the demand for human skilland supervision but at the same time requiring higher skills from fewer people. This trend will naturally result eventually in new patterns of industry, internal organisation, and employment requirements, thus leading to high increases in production and efficiency, and greater prosperity.

Table IV—*Index of Industrial Production 1948–77* (1970=100)

Industry Group	1948	1970	1974	1975	1976	1977	1948–7 change %
All industries	50.5	100	106.3	100.6	101.3	102.5	+ 103
Mining/quarrying	129.1	100	79.2	85.9	88.7	103.6	− 20
Total manufacturing	47.8	100	108.9	102.2	103.2	103.8	+ 117
Food/drink/tobacco	58.4	100	109.9	108.8	110.9	112.3	+ 92
Coal/petroleum products	21.4	100	106.0	92.0	96.5	93.2	+ 336
Chemical industries	25.5	100	126.9	116.0	127.8	132.2	+ 418
Metal manufactures	61.8	100	91.7	78.6	85.3	80.6	+ 30
Engineering industries	34.7	100	113.1	108.7	103.6	103.3	+ 198
Shipbuilding	110.3	100	92.4	97.7	92.0	86.8	− 21
Vehicles (inc. aircraft)	39.0	100	103.0	95.3	91.9	93.3	+ 139
Other metal goods	64.1	100	103.6	95.0	93.8	98.4	+ 54
Textiles/clothing	73.4	100	103.1	99.7	101.9	101.3	+ 38
Bricks, pottery, etc.	54.4	100	117.1	107.9	111.2	108.9	+ 100
Timber, furniture, etc.	45.4	100	112.1	110.2	112.6	105.4	+ 132
Paper/printing/ publishing	42.7	100	108.9	95.6	98.1	114.7	+ 268
Other manufacturing	30.5	100	114.5	105.5	114.7	120.1	+ 294
Construction	56.3	100	93.8	86.1	84.5	83.2	+ 4
Gas/electricity/water	31.4	100	118.5	120.3	123.1	128.1	+ 30

Source: *Economic Trends; Monthly Digest of Statistics*
Reprinted from Britain 1979: An Official Handbook, *by permission of the Controller of Her Majesty's Stationery Office.*

Table V—*Output per Head 1968–77* (1970=100)

	Employed labour force	All production industries			Manufacturing industries		
		Output	Employ-ment	Output per head	Output	Employ-ment	Output per head
1968	100.4	97.2	101.4	95.9	96.0	99.0	97.0
1969	100.4	99.8	101.5	98.3	99.6	100.3	99.3
1970	100.0	100.0	100.0	100.0	100.0	100.0	100.0
1971	98.3	100.1	96.9	103.3	99.4	96.7	102.8
1972	99.0	102.3	94.7	108.0	102.0	93.6	109.0
1973	101.0	110.0	95.8	114.8	110.5	94.1	117.4
1974	101.3	106.3	95.5	111.3	108.9	94.3	115.5
1975	100.7	100.6	91.5	109.9	102.2	90.1	113.4
1976	100.2	101.4	89.3	113.5	103.2	87.3	118.2
1977	100.5	102.4	89.5	114.4	103.7	88.1	117.7

Source: *Monthly Digest of Statistics*
Reprinted from Britain 1979: An Official Handbook, *by permission of the Controller of Her Majesty's Stationery Office.*

The quantity and efficiency of capital assets which employees have at their disposal mainly determine the level of productivity. Investment in industry seems to correlate with the level of demand in the economy. As output increases in response to higher demand the need for increased investment becomes more urgent and eventually investment plans are introduced.

In these circumstances a cyclical pattern of investment should be expected. Since 1961 three discernible cycles appear. First, investment dropped from a peak in 1961 to the start of 1963, then rose to a new peak in 1966. Second, investment dropped in 1967 and rose to a peak at the end of 1970. Third, it fell in 1971 and 1972 and rose to a new peak in 1974.

The more traditional type of investment is still common, however, and much depends upon individual concerns as to how far-reaching their investment programmes arc. Productivity is not the sole responsibility of management; all employees, trade unions, the Government, and educational and research establishments have a responsibility to the community to ensure that the utmost is done to promote increased efficiency in industry. Unfortunately some groups do not see it this way, or they simply pay lip-service to the public and adopt a different policy internally.

Both the employers' and employees' associations actively assist in increasing productivity; the former by providing technical assistance, conducting market surveys, and supporting vocational education and training schemes, and the latter by organising special training schemes and courses to promote a better understanding of modern management techniques. Many specialist concerns also offer assistance in various aspects of productivity.

Most people know that improving productivity results in an improvement in real earnings. The evidence to support this link is overwhelming when Britain is compared with successful industrial economies in Europe and the Far East. Their high rate of productivity growth has been accompanied by a significant and sustained increase in real earnings, whereas in Britain productivity growth has lagged behind but money wages growth has been relatively high.

Increases in money wages which are not related to productivity improvements result in increased industrial costs which eventually mean a higher rate of inflation, thus eliminating the advantages of an increase in money wages. Failure to improve productivity also restricts economic expansion which is essential to provide additional employment.

Between 1955 and 1973 output per head in manufacturing industry grew at an average annual rate of 3.2 per cent in Britain and about 5 per cent in West Germany, France, Belgium, Italy and the Netherlands. These figures indicate that output per operative increased by three-quarters in Britain and about one and a half times in the other countries for the eighteen-year-period.

The cumulative effect over this period is substantial. Real earnings grew at an average rate of 2.2 per cent in Britain, 8.1 per cent in Japan, 6.2 per cent in Italy, 4.5 per cent in West Germany and 4.3 per cent in France.

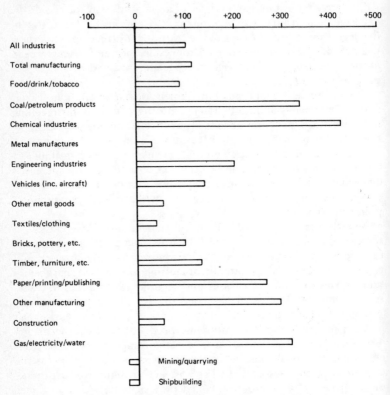

Fig. 14.—*Percentage Change in Production between 1948 and 1977. Source: Economic Trends; Monthly Digest of Statistics.*

A complete analysis would need to include many other factors such as output trends, investment, profitability, and exchange rates movement. Nevertheless the trend is undeniably clear.

Figure 14 indicates the percentage changes in production which occurred between 1948 and 1977. Up to 1978 the census of production reports, based upon output per head, indicate that expansion has been particularly marked in industries using advanced technologies such as electronics, the newer sectors of mechanical engineering, instrument engineering, most of the chemical industry, and man-made fibres.

In other long-established industries such as shipbuilding, marine engineering and electrical engineering, expansion has been slower as it has become essential to meet changing economic conditions by extensive reorganisation, re-equipping, and modernising plant. The various needs of offshore oil and gas industries have provided a major stimulus.

AUTOMATION

One development which can have far-reaching effects on output and productivity is automation. The concept of an automatic factory has become a serious topic for discussion among all the leaders of various groups connected with industry. Automation is sometimes referred to as an addition to mechanisation, which is a totally inadequate description considering the potentialities and unpredictable nature of the subject.

The field of automation extends already to automatic production lines; automatic control of processes; information processing by electronic digital computers; automatic reporting of data; and integrating all the factory systems by a computer which also controls the many variables associated with production.

The trend is clearly indicated in new developments which may be summarised as mechanical handling, automatic control of machines, transfer-machines, microprocessors, and clerical operations by computers. A few "nearly" automatic factories are claimed to be in operation. Some of the larger concerns are adopting various forms of automatic machinery and installing computers for clerical operations.

Although the potential for growth is high, it is difficult to estimate how quickly automation will grow and to what extent it will develop. There are many applications for the small concern as well as the large establishment. Many problems may emerge, however, such as raising capital, shortage of trained employees to cope with increased technical difficulties, integration of plant, higher rate of output level to achieve economy, resistance by employees, and the essential need for managers of high calibre.

If properly organised, automation should reduce costs and increase the effectiveness of industry considerably. Output will rise and prices should be sufficiently competitive to cope with overseas markets. Training in all fields is probably the biggest problem. Provided the training of managers is included, the problem of overcoming resistance from employees and trade unions will be easily met. The introduction of schemes will be balanced by absorption of redundant employees into expanding and new industries which will naturally appear. This account of a topic having far-reaching effects on the country's standard of living and on international prosperity, is of necessity brief and simplified for this book.

QUESTIONS

1. Why do some industries rise and others decline?
2. Give some of the factors which determine the types of industry that develop in a country.
3. Discuss the connection between industrial growth and the standard of living.
4. To what extent has government influence affected industry since World War II?
5. Describe the international influence on British industry.
6. Why are Britain's exports a continual topic for discussion in the press and on television?
7. What is meant by the term "balance of payments"?
8. Discuss some of the barriers to international trade.
9. Give a brief outline of the types of business in the United Kingdom.
10. List the factors that must be considered in the selection of a factory site.
11. Explain the term localisation of industry and its importance in Britain.
12. Why is the effective use of manpower so important to Britain?
13. What can be done to increase the effectiveness of manpower in Britain?
14. Why do prices of products rise?
15. What is the effect of increasing wages in those companies that export goods?
16. Explain the connection between productivity and prosperity.
17. Discuss the introduction of automation and its possible effects on the community.
18. How would you attempt to explain the folly of an employee's attitude who thinks that he should do as little as possible for as much money as possible?
19. Discuss the barriers to international trade and mention the possible results of Britain's entry into the European Economic Community in the long term.
20. Consider the importance of effective manpower planning.
21. What are the main reasons for the doubling of production since 1943?
22. Discuss the effect of labour displacement on the growth rate of productivity in Britain.

CHAPTER VI

THE ROLE OF MANAGEMENT

Introduction

THE role of a supervisor is generally referred to in terms of the relationship between supervisor and operatives, where guiding people is carried out by close contact. Controlling groups by close contact, however, permeates right through the organisation up to the managing director. He also supervises a group of senior executives by very close contact; furthermore, he uses the same techniques and principles recommended to the lowest level of supervision. Obviously this activity forms only part of his job; nevertheless, the supervision of groups commences here and spreads throughout the organisation in a similar pattern. In this sense, a supervisory team exists and the behaviour of each member will be mainly regulated by example set at the top. Generally, supervisors treat their subordinates in a similar fashion to the way their superiors in turn treat them.

All managers who control a group of subordinates directly, may be considered as supervisors who, in addition, undertake the heavier responsibilities of thinking far ahead and formulating policy at a higher range of levels, to meet set objectives. They control many groups remotely by strength of leadership, communication, and the use of management principles. The levels of management are distinguished, therefore, by the amount of policy planning, the total size of the groups underneath, and the amount of problem-solving and decision-making necessary to carry out policy effectively. From this point of view, the management team starts at the top and ends at a point above the highest level of supervision where the emphasis is on problem-solving and decision-making, with a correspondingly smaller proportion of planning and policy-making.

The management team relies extensively on supervision to provide information and make recommendations. Without the aid of supervisors, planning and policy-making become a farce. This reason alone justifies the claim by most managers that supervisors are a part of management. Unfortunately, the recognised supervisory jobs often are considered to be the ladder of promotion for operatives but with no further opportunities of entering management. Furthermore, the highest supervisory post is not thought of as the lowest management level.

The fine line between management and supervision—if there is a line at all in practice—is apparent where a foreman is, in fact, *managing* his department according to definition. He may be indirectly controlling more than twenty-five groups, and forecasting and planning well ahead, although his policy-making activity may be restricted, dependent upon the business.

To summarise, all management positions contain a supervisory element which decreases as the top is approached; all supervisory positions contain a managerial element which decreases as the bottom is approached. Confused thinking and vague terminology in relation to this situation cause many arguments. The line drawn between management and supervision is purely arbitrary, varying from firm to firm. A manager in one concern could easily be a supervisor—with no job variation—in another concern.

Achievement of results rests with all members of a company and their ability to work together as a business team, which includes operatives, supervisors, and managers. A diagram illustrating the teams and flexible borderlines is given in Figure 15.

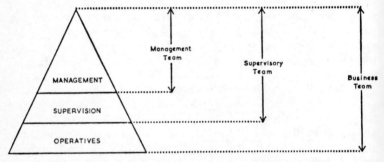

Fig. 15.—*Management, Supervisory and Business Teams.*
The diagram illustrates how the management, supervisors, and operatives should work together, forming a single united business team.

DEFINITION OF A MANAGER

A manager achieves objectives at minimum cost by guiding people and effectively using capital. This brief definition could equally apply to a supervisor. A manager must concern himself with the strategic aspect. He must visualise the over-all scene now and in the future, up to five, ten, fifteen, and twenty years hence. A supervisor, in turn, concentrates on the tactical aspect of solving mainly immediate problems and keeping activities moving towards objectives in line with over-all strategy.

THE SUPERVISOR'S POSITION

The unique position of the supervisor is the subject of constant argument over whether or not he is part of management. Clearly there are three groups involved, namely management, supervision, and operatives; but there are four viewpoints. The fourth viewpoint is that of the disinterested outside observer. General statements are necessary to argue the case.

The management viewpoint claims that supervisors are part of management, but this claim is not upheld in practice. The usual reasons for this attitude are snobbery, social background, and confused thinking. The latter is inexcusable, considering that the same managers who persist in divorcing supervisors from their group would think it ludicrous if a blind man insisted upon having his fingers cut off.

From the operatives' viewpoint, the supervisor represents the management and the concern as a whole. They expect him to represent them to management; but unless the supervisor shows a proper sense of balance (i.e. no particular bias towards management or operators), he will fail in this role.

To the outside observer, the supervisor seems to be in an impossible situation, buffeted from both sides, not receiving sufficient support from management and often operating with insufficient information. Management is inclined to ask for information from the specialist departments, so the supervisor then feels that his authority and responsibility are reduced and that higher authority does not appreciate his problems.

It seems that operatives recognise the supervisor as part of management. Most supervisory training programmes stress this point and attempt to place the supervisor as a representative of management in all respects. Managers should also recognise this fact and treat supervisors accordingly, that is, providing them with sufficient information and authority to manage their groups effectively.

Managerial Activities

The basic managerial activities are: forecasting and planning; organising and commanding; controlling and co-ordinating; and motivating (*see* Chapter VII, p. 94). They can form only a part of the six main business activities: technical, commercial, financial, security, accounting and managerial (*see* pp. 91–2).

Before these activities are described it is necessary to mention the purpose of management, the ownership and control structure of business, and general policy.

PURPOSE OF MANAGEMENT

Management's function is to protect the owner's interests by steering the firm through channels which lead towards sound goals, and which will enhance and ensure the company's future existence.

To survive in the long run, management must build a reputation for the company of supplying goods or services of good quality at reasonable prices. Profitability in these conditions means that management's purpose includes increasing productivity to a high standard of effectiveness, so that owners, consumers, the community and the country benefit, but not at the expense of one particular group.

OWNERSHIP AND CONTROL STRUCTURE

To provide cohesion at the top, a pattern similar to the one in Figure 16 is set up in the joint stock companies which form the major part of British industry. (These and other concerns were discussed under "Business Structure" in Chapter V.)

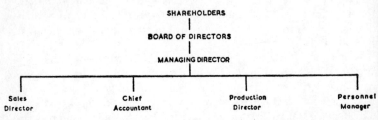

Fig. 16.—*Ownership and Control Structures—Joint Stock Companies.*

Shareholders

Ownership of a joint stock company is in the hands of the shareholders who may be members of the public (either directly or indirectly through the various institutions), directors, or employees of the concern. Under the Finance Act 1978, schemes for extending the ownership of a company's shares to its employees have been encouraged through tax advantages after the schemes have been run for a specified time.

Shareholders are often spread through the country and abroad. Although ownership is vested in the shareholders, control is delegated to the board of directors who are obliged to comply with a large amount of legislation which is designed to protect shareholders' interests.

Future legislation is likely to provide for further protection of the interests of employees and shareholders in addition to implementing E.E.C. legislation on company law and making insider dealing in company securities unlawful.

A great deal of information of both a financial and non-financial nature has to be disclosed in the annual report and accounts to comply with the provisions of the Companies Acts, 1948/1976.

Public quoted companies are obliged to comply with Stock Exchange requirements which are often more onerous than those contained in the statutes. One example concerns the system of voting at meetings; the Stock Exchange insists on the provision of a two-way form of proxy by way of which shareholders can intimate their acceptance or otherwise of the resolutions proposed. Unquoted companies and private companies, however, are not obliged to circulate proxy forms at all.

Some public companies are controlled by a small group of shareholders. By issuing non-voting shares, a small group will continue to control an expanding concern with no change in the balance of power. More is written about shareholders in Chapter XXVII.

Board of Directors

Over-all control of the company is vested in the board of directors, who formulate and approve policy and provide for legal requirements. The size of the board varies considerably. It may consist of full-time directors, working directors and part-time directors who sit on more than one board. Members are generally chosen for their ability; often they hold shares in the concern, and, under the Companies Acts, their holdings have to be disclosed in the company's annual report.

The Managing Director

He is elected by the board of directors and normally holds the position of chairman on the board. He conveys company policy to the senior executives and puts forward policy proposals to the board for formal approval.

Policy

DEFINITION

Company policy is a guide or principle for the use of management and supervision, in order that they may reach objectives by following a set broad pattern of behaviour.

Policies are, by intention, widely defined to allow for individual interpretation in situations which require judgment and initiative. A rigid interpretation destroys policy and turns it into a narrow rule which dispenses with the human approach. A rule has its own place at a lower level in the organisation, where policy is interpreted into detailed principles; followed by even more detailed rules for operational purposes. It is essential for policy to be positive and lasting. Detailed principles and rules, in turn, must be more flexible to adapt to rapidly changing situations.

To summarise, a rule is intended to be interpreted in the same way all the time, whereas a policy allows for discretion in application.

POLICY-MAKING

This multi-stage process may commence with suggestions well down in the organisation structure. Someone has an idea and discusses it with others, who then pass on proposals or information to their superiors, and so on, until definite suggestions reach the managing director. He, in turn, receives many suggestions from other sources which eventually are moulded into concrete proposals that are placed before the board of directors. The board after due discussion may formally approve or disapprove the proposed policy.

On the other hand, the process may be two-stage only; a proposal from the managing director and approval by the board.

ESSENTIAL REQUIREMENTS OF A POLICY

1. Acceptability

The increasing importance of policy being acceptable to everyone is marked by the persistence of employees who want to know why the policy is made or changed. Adequate reasons must be forthcoming, and management ought to provide supervisors with sufficient information to satisfy queries.

The effect of withholding information which leads to gossip and speculation, can be disastrous, causing increased friction between management and operatives, upsetting relationships through general suspicion and lowering morale.

2. Communicated to everyone

There should be no exceptions in communicating policy to employees. In the large concern a group can easily be overlooked, therefore a number of channels should be used.

Convincing people that they were not overlooked intentionally is not an easy task, unless relationships are very good.

3. Genuine application

It is not unusual for management to declare policy for prestige reasons, such as publicity, and then fail to put the policy into practice. Management's policy, in these circumstances, is to ignore the declared policies. Such complete lack of wisdom is hard to appreciate; not one employee is deceived and the word gradually spreads to all interested outsiders

Some managers use "policy" in a negative way, making it an excuse for *not* carrying out some course of action. In these cases policy does not appear in writing and is often made at the time to suit the circumstances. Another practice is wording policy in such a vague way that it can be distorted to fit in with any course of action at the time.

4. Balanced interpretation

The supervisor who rigidly conforms to principles—without due regard for the human situation—would be correctly interpreting policy in his own mind. Something more than correctness is needed in a human society; all the factors, when weighed carefully, might well provide a more balanced interpretation which would not match up with the narrow correct one. Therein lies the art of supervision, which is in no way an abuse of policy.

5. Alignment with the objective

All policies must follow parallel courses on a broad front towards the objective. If they cross or oppose, collective effect is lost and confusion develops. Misunderstandings are often the cause of the problem rather than faults in the stated policy. This danger highlights the need for careful checking that ambiguity or lack of understanding is not occurring at lower levels.

FIELDS OF POLICY

1. Top policy

Broad policy which indicates the general course the company takes is in most cases the one which people have in mind as "top policy". Policy-making is a collective effort and this concept should be communicated to employees to develop a greater sense of belonging. The scheme applies equally in the following two fields.

2. Functional policy

A breakdown of principles for each function (based upon top policy) forms the next logical step, which is the responsibility of the appropriate senior executive, such as the sales manager, the works manager, or the development engineer.

3. Departmental policy

More detailed principles are formulated at this stage. This ensures that everyone who is much nearer to the actual operations, works within more closely defined limits, with a correspondingly smaller chance of misunderstanding. Some flexibility is necessary so that principles form a guide rather than a hard-and-fast rule. Thus, departmental supervisors are actually policy-makers within their own sphere in this sense; and they are responsible for the effectiveness of such policies.

Business Activities

Certain basic activities are essential to all industrial undertakings. These were recognised and published by Henri Fayol in 1925 and are described below. They represent the abilities required by various individuals to perform their functions in the concern successfully.

. Technical activities

The variety of production activities are closely interdependent with buying, for supply of raw materials; with selling, for distributing the finished product; and with capital, for providing machines and equipment. These technical activities include sub-functions: research, development, design, specifications, production planning, production control, production records, work study, quality control, inspection, plant maintenance, and purchasing.

2. Commercial activities
The activities of the distribution staff to market the product are essential, therefore close co-operation between production and distribution must be achieved. Some sub-functions are: packaging, warehousing, transport, despatch, and shipping, sales promotion, advertising, sales statistics, selling, market research, and public relations.

3. Financial activities
Obtaining capital and using it effectively is a critical activity, demanding close control and continual rethinking for success. Within this activity are: investment, accounting, cost accounting, management accounting, and company secretarial and legal work. Part Three explains this activity in detail.

4. Accounting activities
Ideally this function should provide reasonably accurate information on the economic position to date and intelligent estimates of future trends, i.e. it is an indication of the effective use of capital. Management can now operate with greater accuracy and effectiveness. The form it takes includes records, statistics, and accounting records, which include the balance sheet, and profit and loss account. Chapters XXVII to XXIX on Financial Aspects and Costing Aspects explain these activities.

5. Security activities
Safeguarding all the assets against common dangers comes under security. Any measures which reduce the risk, and protect both property and people, are attributable to this activity.

6. Managerial activities
None of the previous activities include the managerial functions of forecasting and planning, organising and commanding, controlling and co-ordinating, which come under this general heading. These are explained in detail under management principles.

The term *management* is used by Fayol to describe an activity which may be applied at *any* level in the organisation. The intention is not to confuse it with position in the hierarchy. Management is interpreted in many different ways: as a subject, an activity, a body of knowledge, a group of individuals holding recognised positions as managers, and status in the company. To avoid this confusion L. Urwick uses th word *administration*, which is a closer translation of the French term in Fayol's writings.

THE FOUR MAIN FUNCTIONS

From the business activities discussed above, it is possible to define the basic functions encountered in a manufacturing concern. These four main functions—financial, technical, marketing, and management—are sometimes reduced to two: technical and marketing. This is because the financial and management functions in simple terms provide cash and control for these two basic functions. Though this explanation is inadequate in concerns where services in various forms are provided instead of a product, it is sound in manufacturing concerns.

The following chapter deals with the management function. The financial function is discussed in Part Three.

QUESTIONS

1. What are the main differences between a manager and a supervisor?
2. Define the terms: management team; supervisory team; and business team.
3. Discuss the question of whether or not supervision is part of management.
4. Why is the supervisor's position in an organisation the subject of constant argument?
5. What are the main business activities encountered in industry?
6. What is the prime purpose of management?
7. Discuss the term "managerial activities".
8. Discuss the responsibilities of management to shareholders; to the community; and to the employee.
9. Carefully explain the term "company policy" and state the essential requirements of a policy.
10. Describe the various fields of policy encountered in a business.
11. Discuss the four main functions encountered in a manufacturing concern.

CHAPTER VII

THE PRINCIPLES AND PRACTICE OF MANAGEMENT

The Principles of Management

ALL principles of management may be grouped to fit conveniently into seven main aspects of management activity. These are forecasting, planning, organising, co-ordinating, commanding, controlling, and motivating. L. Urwick published a logical arrangement of these principles in 1943, in his book, *Elements of Administration* (*see* Bibliography).

These seven main aspects are detailed below.

FORECASTING AND PLANNING

These activities mean looking ahead, and trying to visualise and plan effectively. Certain principles, now described, should be followed from the beginning to cut down the risks of inaccurate forecasting.

1. Research

Although the value of constant investigation is recognised and attempts are made to carry it out, in practice it becomes too difficult for lack of time. People who are "pressurised" at work, must make decisions, based upon less and less information, with the inevitable consequences. The sight of everyone working at high pitch pleases rather than bothers some managers. If a manager is over-worked it is his own fault for not delegating, but there is a limit if top management restricts staff to smaller numbers than is really adequate. Some managers too, are unable to assess work content accurately, even after research has been conducted and the information is presented to them.

The following minor principles should be intrinsic to any research.

(*a*) *Cause and effect:* a belief that effects can be traced back to particular causes provides faith and perseverance in pursuing investigations back to sources.

(*b*) *Comprehension:* the results must be measurable and in an understandable form for practical use in forecasting.

(*c*) *Intelligent observation:* studying an activity requires a certain degree of awareness and appropriate background knowledge, before intelligent interpretation is possible.

(*d*) *Recognition and analysis:* following from intelligent observation, the recognition of similarities is essential for analysing the information, and knowing how to proceed to the next stage of investigation.

2. Forecasting

Armed with sufficient information, the individual must now find a place where he can think without undue distraction. Having found the most suitable place, there he must marshal his thoughts logically and try to visualise or predict future happenings. Some people call this process intelligent guesswork, luck, or being psychic.

Forecasting is often done with very little information, in difficult circumstances; hence the phrase "muddling through". The unknown factor (the missing information) must be taken into account to maintain balance. Consider the serious punter who attempts to marshal as many facts as possible on the horses in a race. He takes everything into consideration, including factors such as the weather and injuries, which make the results unpredictable with any accuracy, in order to lessen the odds as much as possible.

The principles of good forecasting may be listed as follows.

(a) Use of all sources of information.
(b) Maximum information in the time available.
(c) Surroundings conducive to thought.
(d) The unknown factor.

3. Planning

The next step is to determine the targets or objectives and plan a way of reaching these goals.

All industrial activities must be considered in the light of resources available so that plans will be realistic. The good planner will be thinking along lines of economy, which implies that his designs are simple; standardised, with due allowance for changes; and weighted, dependent upon the importance of the plan. Scientific control is not possible unless a plan is based upon a time scale. Planning on this broad front means deciding *what* shall be done, *where, when, how,* and *by whom.* It involves not only readjustment of objectives as new information flows in, but also revision of policies, programmes, budgets, systems, organisation, and controls.

Top management's task is *strategic* planning of over-all policies, objectives, finance, and control. This is implemented by managers or senior supervisors who are responsible for *tactical* planning of how the objectives are to be reached in the time given.

Supervisors then plan—on a short-term or medium-term basis—the actual achievement of broad plans by using the resources available. This is *process* planning and involves scheduling, progressing, controlling, and motivating employees.

The fourth and final phase must logically end on the shop floor where operatives plan their work (*task* planning) in order to complete the jobs allocated to them within the established time limits.

ORGANISING AND CO-ORDINATING

Organising means arranging for everything to be at the right place, at the right time, so that work may proceed according to the plan. Co-ordinating means ensuring that all the formal activities of the concern are combined to form a balanced effective organisation.

The phases which lead to co-ordination are:

    1. planning, which includes organisation design, or establishing the structure;

    2. staffing, which is completed under the aspect of command;

    3. aligning everyone's efforts, which is the eventual effect of co-ordination.

When employees agree to co-operate, and naturally participate willingly, management will be able to co-ordinate successfully. An underlying condition is the ability to lead and motivate people. It is pointless, therefore, for management to complain that employees will not co-operate, when the solution is within its own hands to create the right conditions which encourage and promote co-operation.

Co-ordination is achieved if all the activities are arranged and adjusted in time and situation to ensure smooth economic running and progress towards objectives. Smooth economic operation is an all-embracing term which includes the absence of selfish interests, the balancing of units, and adherence to plans.

The problem of balance begins with the co-ordination of main activities or functions by the managing director and continues through to the level of the supervisor, who co-ordinates the activities of his section or department with other sections. Balance is made possible by allowing unrestricted input of both information and production assemblies from those who supply the section, and unrestricted output to the receiving sections in turn. If the chain of movement is broken, production is off balance and the co-ordinating effect ceases. In this sense co-ordinating is an intentional, active principle.

COMMANDING

Commanding (or directing) means giving orders and issuing instructions, *and* deciding when and how subordinates should carry out the work.

Maintaining command includes making decisions concerning priority treatment for jobs and ensuring that discipline is kept at a reasonable level consistent with good working arrangements. Effective leadership is essential for commanding and motivating.

Although organisation and co-ordination are discussed as one because all the principles of organisation are used to achieve co-ordination, in practice command must come between the two for the following reasons. When the design and planning stage is completed, the next step is to appoint competent staff to the positions drawn up in the organisation plan. Upon completion of staffing, when the individuals are assigned to their jobs and given appropriate duties, authority and responsibilities, they will immediately start to issue instructions. Command becomes operational at this point, and its effectiveness will depend upon the ability of managers and supervisors to raise morale by fair and just treatment; and to lead in the right direction.

The guiding principles for achieving effective command are as follows.

1. Alignment of interest
All effort must be directed towards the general interest. Self-interest must take second place, otherwise command has failed.

2. Staffing
Appointing managers of the right calibre, consistent with company policy.

3. Morale
The acid test of command is unmistakably the general feeling of all employees, majority and minority groups, towards management and the concern. With so much ill-feeling and friction between the two sides, it takes courage and faith to carry out a long-term programme for morale improvement. A permanent change in management's attitude is essential, otherwise relationships will deteriorate rapidly again.

4. Adequate payments and appropriate penalties
Adequate payments for services and appropriate penalties for mistakes are two essential principles which should be second nature to the competent manager. Fairness and justice are essential to maintain a good reputation. Any attempt to show favour to one person results in antagonising the rest. Where it is humane to deviate from the rule, the reason must be made known, whenever possible, if the circumstances are not already common knowledge.

5. Active participation
People must be allowed to expand their capabilities by using their own initiative, criticising, and suggesting openly with no fear of a rebuff. In these conditions they feel more important, and develop enthusiasm and drive in response to the progressive atmosphere. These five aspects are all discussed at length in Part Two.

CONTROLLING

Checking performance and taking action to remedy deviations from the plan involves a constant vigil on all stages of the work and the costs incurred.

Effective control demands, *firstly*, full knowledge of the plans and instructions to proceed; *secondly*, accurate feedback on operations and results; *thirdly*, a common measure to gauge the amount of deviation from the plan; and *fourthly*, positive action to correct the deviations. This subject is detailed in Part Three.

Scientific control is not a haphazard affair; its operation is very demanding, and cannot be switched on and off at random.

The board of directors is supplied with control information by the managing director to check on broad policy and programmes, generally from the financial viewpoint. Management accountancy techniques and all the financial control systems connected with them provide the machinery for control throughout the concern.

On the production side, information on labour, machines, materials, quality, and output, provides supervisors and specialists with control figures. Similarly, information on sales in cash and quantity, and all the distribution expenses, provides management with control statistics. All the information prepared must "pay its way" by providing figures at an economic cost, for some positive purpose.

MOTIVATION

Each managerial activity is dependent upon all the others, hence the main difficulty of thinking about a particular one in isolation. Managing is a combined operation which demands a wide, balanced, human outlook, tempered with the use of a multitude of principles.

Probably motivation, the inner force which stirs people from lethargic attitudes into dynamic action, is the most neglected aspect of management. Half-hearted attempts to improve matters, which are most often abandoned, irritate and depress employees; they naturally fail to respond to fresh encouragement and the blame is nearly always laid unfairly on their heads.

Successful motivation of employees requires a complete change in the outlook of most managers, who are either unenthusiastic, or too cynical or set in their ways to change. Long-term programmes are needed, even though results are sometimes not seen for a few years, to overcome management's faults and misconceptions.

The strong tie between motivation and co-ordination is apparent when the principles involved are considered. These include: job enrichment programmes; constant communication to everyone of all relevant information concerning the business; encouragement of participation and self-discipline; ambitious education and training schemes; joint consultation; personnel counselling; fair schemes of pay, work, and welfare; and sincerity from management (*see* Chapter X).

The Skills Cycle

Underlying and often permeating the principles described above are certain basic management skills which apply equally to supervisors. By appropriate training it is possible to improve these skills through the repetitive process of practice and adjustment. The development of each skill also depends upon the degree of education in certain disciplines or knowledge areas.

Naturally there is a tendency for the disciplines to overlap into more than one skill and in actual operation the dividing line between some of the skills becomes blurred. For the sake of clarity Figure 17

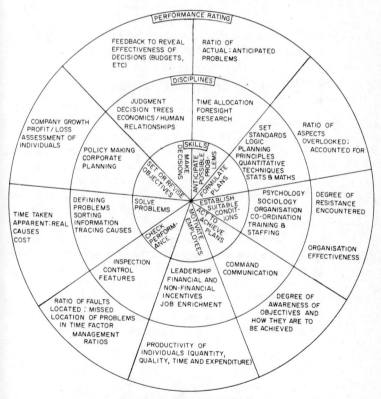

Fig. 17.—*The Skills Cycle.*

Note : This composite diagram is not intended to be complete. It represents certain areas of importance among which are many others not mentioned.

indicates these skills in sector form to show the cycle effect which operates in a clockwise sequence when logical thought is applied to the work process in any situation. The diagram also indicates some ways of checking on the supervisor's performance as he develops. A confusing factor is that during the course of a working day the supervisor will have to cope with many situations and people, which means that a number of these cycles is in operation at any one time.

The diagram can also be used to break down certain principles into component skills; for example, the skills associated with control are to establish suitable standards, to check performance, and to make decisions to correct the deviations that occur. A further use is to locate operating faults; for example, the tendency for some supervisors is to think that so long as an employee has been told what is required of him that is sufficient to provide the essential motivating factor. "I told him what to do but he didn't do it" is a very common saying in industry. Two skills are in fact necessary: firstly, action to achieve the plan which is the communicating skill, followed, secondly, by the motivating skill which will decide whether or not the employee will actually do anything although he may know what is required.

Planning and the Supervisor

Any person who controls a labour force, whether large or small, must plan ahead as far as he can foresee. Employees expect to work to a set plan and schedule, and be controlled in accordance with the plan and changing circumstances. Absence of planning produces chaos on the shop floor. Individuals work from crisis to crisis, frustration develops, and productivity is reduced to a minimum. Clearly the supervisor must allocate time for planning in sufficient detail to satisfy the requirements of his subordinates and production. Time spent on planning is never wasted provided the supervisor is reasonably proficient at the task. The extra thought should result in more accurate and detailed plans, with less risk of overlooking possible difficulties. There is more likelihood, therefore, that the plan will be successful.

PLANNING SUPERVISORY ACTIVITIES

Most supervisory activities lend themselves to planning, which leads to more effective supervision. A cross-section of the main aspects is given below.

1. Production

A large range of separate plans makes up the master plan for production. Machine capacity, labour utilisation, scheduling work loads, supplies of materials, provision for jigs, tools, batch quantities, and all other resources, are planned and combined to form the over-all production plan (*see* Chapter XXV).

Within this plan, the supervisor's section generally forms only a part of the whole production line which means that co-ordination with other sections is of primary importance. He must allow for this factor and be able to accept work in accordance with the over-all production line; supply work in sequence to the next section; and be prepared to help in emergencies.

2. Objectives

Objectives must be intelligently planned to fit into a time scale, within the capabilities of performance. Establishing unrealistic targets is a waste of time. Progress must be controlled and adjustments made as required. The total collapse of efforts to reach specified objectives is bad for morale; therefore, planning with too much optimism should be avoided.

3. Control

Effective control does not happen by chance. A plan of the particular activity must be drawn up on a time, cost, quality, or quantity basis, or some form of standard by which results can be measured. Variances from the plan are now apparent by reference to the data, and control is possible through taking appropriate corrective action (*see* Chapter XX). Planning and control must always be complementary.

4. Organisation

The importance of planning in connection with organisation has been stressed in Chapter III. Haphazard growth, rigidity, and disregard for organisation principles may be avoided with careful planning. Working towards the ideal organisation and making wise changes when the opportunities occur, are made easier by conforming to a plan.

5. Work study

The introduction of work study can be made easier by planning a careful explanation to employees. The programme may include posters, literature, personal letters, films, and introductory talks. Work study can be introduced with a minimum of disruption in this manner.

Planning the actual work to be studied may be based upon those sectors which are (*a*) causing hold-ups, (*b*) expensive to operate, (*c*) trouble-spots, (*d*) relatively high labour turnover areas, or (*e*) where an increase in output is contemplated. Further information is given in Chapter XXI.

6. Communication

Communication may be improved with experience in running the particular section, and a plan of methods, routes, and check systems. Suitable improvements may be planned to eliminate weak spots. A simple plan would begin with an assessment of each communication between supervisor and subordinates, thus revealing its importance, the time factor, the cost and the confidential factor. It should then be possible to select the best means of communication for each kind of message from the methods available. The objective is to ensure that the right person receives the right message, at the right time, and interprets it in the right way. All aspects of communication are discussed in Chapters XI, XII, and XIII.

7. The daily routine

Planning the way each day is to be spent is important. Certain daily tasks cannot be neglected and unless the supervisor plans his day, or week, the risk of some vital activity being overlooked is greater. Simple check-lists are useful reminders of daily and periodic tasks which may be easily forgotten. More elaborate activities which extend over long periods may be charted on the wall by using a time base across the top of a sheet and an activity base down the left-hand side to form a grid. Each square may be either ticked or used to enter details if on a larger scale. Pending jobs may be similarly progressed or listed, a pending tray or file being used for the paperwork.

In conjunction with delegation the supervisor should plan to off-load duties as the opportunities occur and use the freed time for more important tasks which have been rather neglected.

8. Health and safety

Reducing the accident rate and promoting health depend upon detailed planning by management and the supervisor. Planning for safety is an integral part of reducing accidents to a minimum, by making machinery and equipment less hazardous and promoting the right attitudes towards safety. The supervisor's social responsibility cannot be fulfilled unless he plans to prevent accidents rather than wait for them to happen and then reduce the risk. Chapters XVIII and XIX deal with health and safety, and welfare respectively.

9. Maintenance

Planned maintenance is similar in some ways to planned safety. Time and cost may be cut by planning the maintenance of machines to reduce the risk of breakdown. Replacing those components and assemblies whose life is limited before the breakdown occurs ensures smooth output flow. Maintenance is discussed as an aspect of cost reduction in Chapter XXX.

10. Training

Training must be treated seriously as a planned activity to improve productivity by introducing better methods and safer ways of working, with less fatigue and frustration. Planned training includes induction training schemes; training operators for new machines as obsolescent models are superseded; training newcomers at weak points where hold-ups are occurring, or are likely to occur; and making hazardous operations safer by increasing the skill of the operator (*see* Chapter XVI).

11. Motivation

All that was said above regarding management and motivation applies at supervisory level also. All factors which affect motivation closely interact; therefore, the approach must be on a broad front so that employees can develop their capabilities and enthusiasm simultaneously. The plan must be long-term and sustained in application. New techniques of leadership and supervision, group activity, organisation, human relations, and job satisfaction are essentially long-term projects and have a sustained effect; whereas financial incentives are short-term and often short-lived as motivators (*see* Chapter X).

12. Human relations

The supervisor who plans successfully also improves his relationship with subordinates. They have more faith in a leader who defines objectives, plans carefully, and shows command of the situation. Morale will rise as schemes materialise, and operators benefit by effective plans (*see* Chapters VIII and IX).

The above-mentioned topics are only an indication of the many activities which must be planned by the supervisor. Savings in time and nervous energy are possible by planning any activity. Some guides to better planning are now given, together with the characteristics of a sound plan.

GUIDES TO BETTER PLANNING

1. Planning must not be postponed. Planning is hard work but, without plans, work becomes much harder.

2. Planning must not be selfish. The part played by the section within the organisation must be remembered; therefore, co-operative and co-ordinate elements are essential in plans.

3. Always plan within a time scale. Effective control depends upon measurement of work or a project within a period and, furthermore, employees tend to work within periods related to output, which means they work to time targets.

4. Marshal as much information as possible on employees, machines, equipment, materials, and other resources. Use up-to-date information and all resources available.

5. Aim to provide as much detail as possible. There is less chance of overlooking important points and more chance of work proceeding to plan with thorough coverage.

6. Ask for opinions and ideas. Many individuals have something to contribute towards a sound plan, therefore, ask now and avoid adverse criticisms later.

7. Define the problem or objective clearly before planning commences. Look at the whole project, and break it down into its constituent parts to ensure full coverage and to provide a working scheme.

8. A sound, workable, and economic plan is the outcome of something more than logical marshalling of information into a set routine. Certain intangible qualities must be cudgelled into activity within the supervisor's mind. He must be imaginative and creative, exercise judgment and perception in his ideas, and yet retain an objective, critical approach to the problem.

9. Have the courage to stand by the plan.

10. Check and revise the plan as circumstances change.

CHARACTERISTICS OF A SOUND PLAN

1. Economic, within the financial capabilities of the concern.
2. Workable, considering the resources available.
3. Thorough, allowing for most contingencies.
4. Balanced, to blend with other plans.
5. Resilient, to cope with unforeseen changes.
6. Worthwhile, fulfils a desirable purpose.
7. Attractive, creates interest among all who are concerned.
8. Detailed, to establish adequate procedures.
9. Timely, to obtain maximum benefit.
10. Impersonal, avoids personal prejudices.

Problem-Solving and Decision-Making

These important aspects are common to all three basic elements of supervision. Problems and choices are met in all supervisory and managerial activities and must be dealt with, reputations being built or ruined on individual performance. The following discussion puts forward a broad method of approach.

PROBLEM-SOLVING

The supervisor often automatically establishes standards for a vast number of control aspects connected with problem-solving without fully realising the implications to his subordinates. Human behaviour is a typical example, where the supervisor expects a particular code of conduct in many different situations. He is faced with a problem when a standard is violated and if he fails to investigate, find the cause and make a decision, control is lost.

Unfortunately problems do not solve themselves effectively, although some managers will openly admit their belief that if a problem is left for a sufficient length of time it will solve itself. Such managers have not bothered to check on the results of this negative approach, which ultimately brands them as ineffectual. A positive approach to problems is essential.

Operators also apply their own standards to many aspects connected with their job. One operator, for example, may switch off his machine immediately he suspects that a fault has developed, whereas another may wait until a more obvious sign appears. This range of standards among individuals becomes important from the problem-solving aspect. One operator, for instance, may report that a machine failed to start when switched on, whereas another may state that when the machine was switched on, a smell of burning was noticed. Careful definition of the problem in the latter case immediately narrows down the cause of the fault.

The use of standards—in a broad sense—for gathering information should not be ignored. The approach to obtaining the facts, as they appear, should be made on a basis of comparison to find a common factor or an isolating component within that factor. A line of machines for instance, may be powered from the same electricity point; if one machine suddenly ceases to run, the fault may be isolated to a particular section if the basis of comparison is applied, by stating whether or not the other machines continue to run. Investigating a problem in this way helps to isolate areas quickly where the cause is likely to be found.

The use of standard practice or standard "set-ups" is common to many facets of industrial activity. Some examples are the following.

(a) *The use of raw materials in batches.* If faulty work appears it may be isolated to a particular batch which is below standard.

(b) *Planned maintenance programmes.* When a machine develops a fault it may be possible to trace it from the last maintenance job.

(c) *Shift work.* A mistake may be isolated to a particular shift or time coinciding with the changeover from one shift to another.

To summarise, problems must be actively solved; the art of recognising and carefully defining problems must be developed; the causes of faults may be more effectively located by looking for common factors and isolating the unusual aspects within those factors, thus tracking down the trouble by a logical step-by-step approach.

INTUITION

This apparently simple, rapid method is essential to cope with common daily problems. The cause is often immediately apparent, thus simple and complex problems may be solved effectively in this manner by the experienced supervisor. The obvious danger lies in not appreciating the whole problem through lack of experience and knowledge, and jumping to conclusions. Automatic problem solving of this nature can also be dangerous when a recurring problem, normally having a standard cause, suddenly occurs through a new cause not foreseen at the time. Nevertheless, full use of this method is essential considering the time-factor.

GROUP DISCUSSION

This method, also known as "brainstorming", is based upon the idea associated with value analysis (*see* Chapter XXIII). Briefly, ideas (no matter how absurd) are thrown up in committee to provide leaders for discussion and eventual solutions to the problem.

LOGICAL APPROACH

A logical approach to problem solving, already discussed (p. 104), may be established as follows.

1. *Set standards*. Establish standards for as many activities as possible. In other words, set your sights.

2. *Measure activities*. Measure actual results against established standards to highlight deviations.

3. *Assess deviations*. A deviation may be favourable or adverse.

(*a*) Favourable: this is a situation (not a problem), nevertheless, the cause should be traced and identified for revising standards and increasing effectiveness.

(*b*) Adverse: this is a problem which is detrimental to the plan; the cause must be located and decisions made.

4. *Carefully define the problem*. A complete detailed description of the problem is essential.

5. *Investigate*.

(*a*) Judge the time-factor. The supervisor generally has to work within a time scale.

(*b*) Search for information. Haphazard, intermittent fact-finding is unsatisfactory, but often inevitable. Try to build up a system so that information flows in as a continuous process.

(*c*) Learn to distinguish between facts, inferences, and value judgments.

When assessing information, the source and the number of mouths it has passed through are of prime importance. The reliability of the source and the distortion factor—as information passes from one person to the next—cannot be ignored. The well-known game of making up a sentence and passing it round in a group of, say, ten people, often produces bewildering results, bearing no relationship to the original sentence. The only sure way to be certain of a fact is to see it for yourself; unfortunately there is seldom time, and also it is impracticable in many instances.

A further confusing point is the inability of some people to distinguish between facts, inferences, and value judgments. Each one has its usefulness, but the danger lies in mistaking one for another. Here is a typical example of the three: two people decide to walk from A to B along a street which is often very congested with traffic. The lamp-posts are a standard distance apart and as the two people walk at a set pace, one takes the time between two lamp-posts and calculates their speed as, for example, two and a half m.p.h. *This is a fact.* From the calculated speed a further reckoning indicates that they should arrive at *B* five minutes earlier than they intended. *This is an inference*, because any number of situations may arise which will affect their estimated time of arrival, and therefore it is a conclusion or deduction from a given fact. One then says to the other, "It is quicker to walk along this road these days because the traffic is so congested." *This is a value judgment,* because it is an *opinion*, based upon a series of events over a period, but not accurately measured or analysed.

6. *Analyse and establish the cause.* Draw up a detailed analysis from the information available. Look for indications leading to the source, and establish the cause, thus solving the problem. Successful elimination of the cause or avoiding a recurrence depends upon making a correct decision.

DECISION-MAKING

Making decisions involves the consideration of a number of conflicting factors such as the objective, degree of ruthlessness necessary, humane treatment of people, cost, and effectiveness. The supervisor's reputation is directly affected by his ability to weigh these standards sensibly. His choice is tempered also by two conflicting groups, his superiors and his subordinates.

One method of making decisions is to use a logical approach by placing each standard in priority sequence. The natural priority is to establish and reach the objective. Having stated this the next priority may be the cost. Assessment is mainly intelligent guesswork, based upon considering the courses of action and weighing their probable effect on individuals, general effectiveness and the inevitable undesirable results.

Establishing priorities is a personal matter in which good sense is essential. Choice of decision must depend, to some extent, on morale and the prevailing industrial atmosphere. Ruthless decisions which cause a deterioration in relationships indicate the inadequacy of the supervisor to appreciate hidden costs and the intangible effects of causing frustration.

To complete the cycle of events, new standards must be set to check the effectiveness of the decision, so that variances may be seen and any new problems brought to light for further action.

A logical approach to decision-making may therefore be summarised as follows.

1. Aim to reach the objective.
2. Consider various courses of action.

3. Weigh the factors involved, e.g. individuals, cost, undesirable after-effects, morale, etc.
4. Choose a course of action.
5. Set standards to check after-effects.
6. Follow up and revise if necessary.

Management/Supervisor Relations

EXTRA PRESSURES AND DEMANDS ON MANAGERS

The qualities needed in a manager are similar in nature to those needed in a supervisor, but developed to a greater degree because of the manager's more demanding position. Increasing emphasis is placed on creativeness and vision as the top of the hierarchy is approached. The burden of responsibility increases and causes heavier demands on vitality and mental qualities. Personality becomes more important. People expect a higher standard of leadership which means a higher standard of conduct and manners, greater self-confidence and a balanced temperament, together with drive and strength of character.

High ability is needed to assimilate and put into practice all managerial and technical knowledge. Good sense in using that knowledge and hard work are the key factors, in addition to intelligence. The mental and physical strain of working under the pressure of indeterminable problems and risks is wearing on the strongest manager. Being in the limelight is not only rewarding, but also nerve-racking.

A good manager must be ambitious, and possess considerable understanding of people and the world around him. He must create the right image and consistently apply himself to the job. Such devotion cannot be achieved by a façade of qualities. Deep sincerity is essential because employees are not easily deceived. A manager should be judged by results in the short and long term. This highlights the method of achieving results and pin-points the manager of high calibre.

PRESENT STATE OF MANAGEMENT

In the absence of any large-scale surveys, the characteristics of a manager are discussed from the viewpoint of popular belief. Education is very important because of the part it plays in creating a good impression, attaining higher qualifications, and indicating ability. Unfortunately this factor does not take into account leadership, application to work, balanced personality, and experience. Thus, some employees have to suffer under the "raw" graduate from university who is placed in a managerial position by virtue of his degree alone.

Buying the right education helps considerably; a public school background seems to be high on the list of desirable requirements in selection procedures as it ensures that the prospective manager will not be "out of place", but of the "right type". A good social background or good family are considered essential. Furthermore, with some jobs even the prospect's spouse is interviewed to assess whether or not he or she will be able to "mix".

Naturally, the ideal types will emerge from graduates who possess the additional essential qualities. These outstanding people rapidly rise towards the top; nothing holds them back.

There is also the "late starter" group, which includes those who fail to reach university and those who do not even reach grammar school level. The handicap of misfortune or late development is eventually overcome through intense drive and a certain amount of luck.

Another characteristic which is not desirable, but often seen, is the ruthlessness of the person who manages to disregard certain codes of conduct to achieve a position. This unhappy state in a company is not always a one-sided affair; higher management seems to encourage it, possibly unintentionally at times.

A glutton for work is a characteristic which highlights a person immediately. Such people seem to attract work and successfully get through a tremendous amount in a short time. They are not necessarily extra bright, but make up for this by using common sense and working at high speed over long periods.

Finally there is the inescapable characteristic of nepotism which is extended here to include friends as well as relatives. Possibly this tendency is so strong because of the misguided idea that a person's loyalty will be with the one who gives him the opportunity. There may be feelings of insecurity also, which are eased when friends are nearby for support and encouragement.

From this short résumé of qualities and characteristics, it is immediately apparent to those people who are directly connected with industry, that a shortage of suitably qualified managers exists. Demand is increasing for managers possessing higher qualifications in management skills, and more courses for this purpose are becoming available every year.

The present situation is as if someone who cannot read music is conducting an orchestra and expecting the musicians to read music and play well, although he lacks this essential requirement himself. The resulting discord is easily imagined. There are exceptions, however, in business as in the artistic field, where innate ability and experience compensate for lack of training.

MAKING ALLOWANCES FOR MANAGERS

To avoid frustration the supervisor must make allowances for managers. Allowing some latitude for subordinates is easy, mainly because a higher standard is not expected of them, but individuals automatically expect a higher performance from superiors.

In practice it does not always work out that way. Superiors, who are also human beings, have many faults and probably they think that the supervisor acts rather queerly at times too. A sympathetic approach demands cultivation and an understanding of the problems faced by superiors.

Many managers are untrained. A few have a flair for managing, others may be highly intelligent, but something more than ability is required when dealing with people.

When a properly trained supervisor returns to his workplace to continue operating under an untrained manager he will no doubt receive anything but a warm reception. The situation will not return to normal in these circumstances because the supervisor has undergone a change. Instead, frustration will increase. Expanded to national proportions the idea of training supervisors in large numbers, but not managers, is inviting a large pressure group to form with possible disastrous consequences.

The supervisor must not be surprised to receive a negative reaction to a perfectly sound idea. The manager feels rather silly because he did not think of it himself, so he responds in the opposite way by displaying indifference and trying to shrug off the idea as unimportant. Probably a few weeks (or months) later, he will suddenly mention the same idea as if it were his own and expect the supervisor to put it into practice immediately.

Rudeness and offhand treatment by managers must also be expected. Often this form of abuse is due to the manager's complete confusion, lack of ability, or knowledge of how to deal with a particular situation. Resorting to rudeness is the easy way out, in the short run, amply demonstrating inadequacy and lack of human approach. Bearing such indignities gracefully is difficult; nevertheless, a mature person must be tolerant of others and able to accept conditions as they exist, helping to alter them by example.

The ruthless manager invariably is unaware of other more human ways of solving problems. Often this type has temendous drive and when he finally realises that the hidden results of his ruthlessness will offset his achievements, unless he modifies his ways, he becomes an asset to the concern.

The supervisor should not expect managers to know everything; they definitely will not, and it is unfair to expect such a high standard from them. They have limitations, make mistakes and suffer embarrassment which they often attempt to hide unsuccessfully. This applies particularly to young managers who suffer with feelings of nervousness, apprehension, or, in some cases, over-confidence and elation through experiencing a new sense of power. The process of improvement is long without training and, of course, some never change.

Some managers have difficulty in facing reality; to achieve an object they resort to various subtle (or so-called subtle) techniques which, in fact, anyone can see through. Consider, for example, trying to force an individual to leave. The farce may begin with silence from the manager. The general pleasantries such as "good morning" are stopped. The individual's work is by-passed, and some work is passed to other people to create disturbances.

Such practices are not only childish and disrupt the efficiency of the organisation, but are also likely to place the superior in a humiliating position of liability under the unfair dismissal provisions of the Employment Protection (Consolidation) Act 1978. In these circumstances, "constructive dismissal" might arise when all the facts are considered concerning the manager's "nit-picking" attitude towards the employee if the employee "resigns" or walks out for this reason. Whether or not constructive dismissal can be established would be a matter of degree.

QUESTIONS

1. How can a supervisor delegate and still retain effective leadership?
2. Outline the various phases of planning.
3. Why does the supervisor have to make allowances for management?
4. Discuss fully any two principles of management.
5. Describe the activities of forecasting and planning.
6. What supervisory activities lend themselves to planning?
7. Advise a new supervisor how to plan effectively.
8. What are the characteristics of a sound plan?
9. Outline the main principles of a command.
10. If you had the opportunity to participate in the selection of a manager what qualities would you make sure he possessed?
11. Why is decision-making so important in supervision?
12. Outline briefly the practical steps which are essential in decision-making.
13. Describe the principles you would bear in mind when conducting research.
14. Discuss the phases which lead to successful co-ordination.
15. What are the essential requirements for effective control?
16. Outline a logical approach to problem-solving.
17. What are the main basic management skills?
18. Discuss the skills cycle and how it operates in practice.

PART I: SUGGESTED PROJECTS

1. Assess the position and effectiveness of six supervisors in your concern, using such headings as: qualities; estimated effectiveness of each supervisor; any deficiencies in their work and possible reasons; any training schemes for supervision; and management's attitude towards supervisors. Draw up a report of your findings and recommendations.

2. Attempt to assess the productivity level in your establishment by surveying the main aspects which affect this topic.

Draw up a list and write an account of the prevailing conditions under each aspect.

Make recommendations for improving the situation.

3. Conduct a survey on the organisation of the Production Department in your concern and suggest suitable improvements. A diagram is required of the

existing organisation and the proposed organisation. Tabulate the principles which you consider are misapplied; the proposed changes; and the human problems which are likely to occur during the changeover.

4. Conduct a detailed survey on the authority, responsibilities, and duties of two managers and two supervisors in your concern.

Attempt to assess the main differences between management and supervision by conducting your investigation within a framework suitable for this purpose.

Draw up a suitable documentation of your findings and give a careful, detailed opinion of the main differences between the managers' and supervisors' jobs under investigation.

5. Conduct a survey on how supervisors or managers make decisions. The co-operation and assistance of individual superiors will be necessary in preparing a detailed report on the procedure they adopt, in varying circumstances, to arrive at decisions.

Attempt to tabulate your findings in logical sequence and grouped under various methods. Give an account of your conclusions and recommendations.

6. Trace the price alterations of products in your concern and attempt to find out why the changes were introduced.

Tabulate the price changes and dates and list the possible causes for each change, together with any explanations and your findings.

Attempt to draw conclusions from your investigation.

7. Study the organisation of the stores, including the layout, stores control system and the efficiency of the service. Attempt to plan improvements considering the economic factors involved.

8. Study and plan the reorganisation of the Despatch Department.

9. Trace the growth of your company over the past thirty years and attempt to discover the main causes of the pattern produced.

10. Examine the labour displacement aspect in your factory and consider its effects and ways of overcoming the problem.

11. Attempt an assessment of the management skills used by two supervisors and consider ways of improving their performance.

PART TWO

CREATING AN EFFECTIVE WORKING FORCE

CHAPTER VIII

TRYING TO UNDERSTAND PEOPLE

Human Relations and the Individual

THE importance of the individual in a company is becoming more recognised, not only from the financial viewpoint, but also from the productivity aspect. Before a person can be induced to behave in certain desirable ways, i.e. to work better and more happily, a fundamental knowledge of his mind and personality is essential. Being able to understand a person and why he reacts in certain ways, sensing his feelings, and knowing his likes and dislikes, is an extremely difficult task, but the conscientious supervisor must face this challenge.

A vast amount of information on human behaviour is available for study and, when combined with practical application, much can be done to improve bad situations in industry where people's feelings have been largely ignored.

Complete coverage of the field of psychology is not possible in a book of this nature, but the supervisor should supplement the material in Chapters IX and X by selective reading on this subject. The time will be well spent as a knowledge of psychology is very useful in all walks of life.

This survey of human relations first discusses the importance of recognising the individual and creating good relations in industry, also listing some of the main causes of poor human relationships. This provides a suitable background for the study of human behaviour in general. The second part of the chapter outlines the basic needs of individuals and the various outlets of satisfaction. Underlying these topics is the question of levels of mental awareness and temperament, and these are discussed in conclusion.

RECOGNITION OF THE INDIVIDUAL

One glance at a person is usually sufficient to register the fact that he is slightly different from other people. But what is far more important than this visual difference is that each person thinks and reacts slightly differently from others in similar situations. He has inherited and developed certain mental qualities and feelings which make him an individual and he therefore requires individual treatment if the right relationship is to be built up between himself and the supervisor.

True recognition of an individual firstly involves knowing many facets of his nature which are difficult to perceive at the work-place.

Only one side of the person is seen, whereas in fact he has many additional outside interests which affect his outlook. Family ties, religion, politics, hobbies, and sports, all influence his general attitude. There is also an unlimited range of traits in people, such as greed, dishonesty, kindness, carelessness, perseverance, and patience. Everyone is subjected to many pressures which often confuse and trouble. This may lead to distorted thinking and a tendency to keep other people at a distance. This effect is similar to speaking into a microphone with the switch turned off.

Sympathetic observation and treatment help to reduce the mental barriers, although not many people will allow someone to get too close; hence the so-called "mask" is always worn which conceals an individual's true feelings in his daily contact with others.

True recognition of the individual secondly means treating him with respect.

Unless the supervisor believes in people and has a genuine regard for their feelings, their points of view and their potential, he will fail to convey this sense of respect. Fair treatment given in a friendly manner does not amount to grovelling or fawning over subordinates. Diplomacy costs nothing, but it has a tremendous impression on employees. Everyone is sensitive to injustice, bullying, and offhand treatment. The reaction, whether it be active or passive, is inevitable, and both parties are the losers in the long run.

IMPORTANCE OF HUMAN RELATIONS

Unless good relationships exist, most schemes to increase productivity and to motivate people in a particular direction will fall short of their objectives and have no lasting effects. If employees are unhappy, suspicious and generally disgruntled, there will be higher labour turnover, absenteeism and lateness, more risk of waste and accidents, poor workmanship, general slackness, and lack of discipline.

A management policy to improve human relationships must be long-term, as changes do not come about overnight. Deep-rooted distrust and traditional suspicion take time to erase and often the mere act of attempting to improve the situation is treated with doubt. The change must be sustained and genuine.

Employees gradually begin to change their attitude towards work when they see opportunities to use their initiative and abilities to a greater advantage. Feelings of pride and importance in actually contributing something more than the usual day's work, when coupled with the respect received from management and sympathetic understanding from supervision, raise operators well beyond their accepted standards of ability.

SOME CAUSES OF POOR RELATIONSHIPS
1. Traditional treatment of employees

If management in a concern has not moved with the times and continues to treat employees in an autocratic fashion with complete lack of understanding, general resentment grows and possibly leads to increasing friction and strikes.

2. Lack of understanding by management

Although management may have good intentions, if the true situations on the shop floor are not known and instructions are ineffective, its efforts will be wasted. Management must show an appreciation of the situation and relate its instructions to the facts, thus making it obvious to employees why certain courses of action are necessary.

3. Lack of understanding by employees

Assuming that management's intentions are sincere and the right action is taken, nevertheless employee outlook has to be changed before improvements will be noticed. Management has not altered overnight and it is most unlikely and unsound to reason that employees will change more quickly. The inherited feelings towards management are tenacious and unfortunately often correct. For example, the argument that management would quickly revert to its old ways if given the opportunity is a difficult one to answer. Any management presenting a new outlook must understand that one false move will convince employees that management is two-faced.

4. Lack of communication

Unless constant efforts are made to ensure that information reaches all points in a concern, invariably many employees will be neglected. If people are to feel part of an organisation they must be treated as an *essential* part. They want to know what is going on, why changes are made, who the newcomers are. If the formal channels of communication are not used, the "grape-vine" takes over, creating misunderstandings with unconnected, incomplete items of information which leave much to conjecture. The employee feels that management has no faith in him and that he is of little importance to the company.

5. Lack of incentive

Without motivation to work well, in the form of financial and non-financial incentives, severe frustration will appear. (The importance of this factor in human behaviour is discussed further in later sections.) Both forms of incentive are needed, and people must be given the opportunity to participate, set themselves objectives and feel they are doing a worthwhile job.

6. Conflicting viewpoints

The views of management and employees are often opposed on questions of wages, output, working conditions, and terms of employment. One group is thinking in terms of profitability, of cost and output, whereas the other group is thinking of sharing the profit by receiving more wages and benefiting from stability of employment. A better understanding of the other party's position, in both cases, would certainly ease the mutual distrust which defeats many schemes to improve relationships.

A further aggravation is the confusion in employees' minds as to where their loyalty lies. Consideration for the trade union, management, the supervisor, and work-mates, poses a bewildering problem to most employees.

7. Inadequate organisation

The incorrect use of specialists, who appear to come between employees and supervisors, upsets the desired friendly atmosphere. Similarly, unsound application or disregard of the principles of organisation leads to confusion and agitation when conflicts occur. Working harmony is lost until a sound organisation structure is established and understood by everyone.

The Study of Human Behaviour

Observation of human behaviour indicates that each person is different in some respects. These differences play an important part in the productive capabilities of people, for when people act in their own best interests they work much better. There are also basic needs or similarities in everyone, which are called instincts. In addition, people are flexible and able to change their ideas, outlook, and general behaviour.

THE DISTRIBUTION OF HUMAN DIFFERENCES

If any one physical characteristic of people is measured and plotted on a graph, provided the sample is sufficient, a symmetrical, bell-shaped curve will be drawn, as in Figure 18. (Frequency distributions are discussed more fully in Chapter XXIV.)

A similar distribution also exists in the hidden and more basic characteristics of people, such as desires, ability, and disposition. These are exceptionally difficult to measure and considerable training and experience is needed before reasonable assessment is possible. Most people have realised their mistakes later when they have formed strong first impressions of a stranger. Keeping an open mind and continually observing the person is very necessary to achieve a true evaluation. As opportunities occur for people to demonstrate their particular skills and natural abilities their individual characteristics gradually appear. The supervisor should make sure that such opportunities do occur.

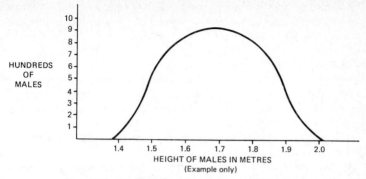

Fig. 18.—*Distribution of Human Differences.*
Distribution curves are normally bell-shaped, since most of the data fall around the average. This is particularly so with natural statistics, e.g. more people are of approximately average intelligence (or height, etc.) than are very far above or far below average.

BASIC NEEDS

What happens to an infant in the very early stages of life governs to some extent attitudes, traits, character, and general outlook. At birth the fundamental need of a baby is probably to be loved and cared for so that the child's basic needs—to eat, drink and move around— are satisfied. A general opinion is that there is a complete absence of the instincts which are noticeable in lower forms of animal life.

Fixed behaviour patterns or instincts apparently severely restrict an animal's learning capacity and socialisation, whereas people are able to use language as well as possessing animal needs, impulses, and some innate capacities. If people are not given the opportunity to mix or socialise, however, ability does not develop. The assumption is that biological drives account for the baby's basic needs, not instincts. Thus the transmission of culture and the establishment of most individuals in an organised society is made possible.

A complication arises, however, when psychological needs—self-assertion, belongingness, self-esteem, aggressiveness and creativeness—are considered. Whether these are inborn (instinctive) or acquired (learned) is a subject for debate and theorising.

BEHAVIOURAL THEORIES

The two main theories associated with an understanding of basic needs, motivation and job satisfaction are the process theory and the content theory. Research findings in these fields so far have been found to be inconclusive.

The process or *mechanical* theories attempt to explain the processes involved which lead to choices among alternative courses of action, the amount of effort expenditure, and persistence over time.

Content or *substantive* theories try to specify the substantive identity of the variables that influence behaviour, such as rewards, basic needs, and incentives.

Process theory

Various theories under the general heading of process theory attempt to postulate a formal explanation for the direction, amplitude and persistence of behaviour. The main ideas, in sequence, leading up to these theories are as follows.

1. In earlier centuries, it was thought that rationality and free-will decided behaviour.

2. Early twentieth-century concepts retained rationality for people but animal behaviour was thought to be a mechanical response set in motion by instincts. Darwin's evolutional model introduced biological explanations which led to the idea that instincts explained behaviour. McDougall (1908) gave the term *instinct* respectability but its use was stimulated beyond acceptable limits. A proliferation of instincts emerged and became difficult to manage experimentally, resulting in Woodworth (1918) creating a new concept: drive. He defined drive as a unitary concept which represented an over-all activity level.

3. Mid-twentieth-century ideas assumed that man makes choices among behavioural alternatives on the basis of his knowledge. Thus people consciously calculate the relative pleasures and pains of various outcomes provided by alternative actions and seek to maximise their total pleasure.

Within this concept there are three major determinants of action: reinforcement, drive (a need) and incentives. Either singly or in combination they formed the major motivational models which were developed up to 1960. Simplified, reinforcement means the effect on the individual of learning habit-forming activities. Thus habit strength is dependent upon the situations that the individual has been subjected to in terms of magnitude and frequency. The energiser or motivational component, drive, indicates the general level of pressure for activity. Incentive represents the pulling effect of rewards.

Within the process theory concept lies the expectancy theory which attempts to explain the reactions of individual behaviour by arguing that they depend upon the discrepancy between what the environment offers and what the person expects, or has adapted to, at the time. In other words, a person will be expecting a particular outcome when he performs a particular act. If expectancy fails there may be a pleasant or unpleasant surprise, possibly with emotional reactions.

Content theory

Theories under this heading attempt to suggest the specific identity of variables discussed in general terms by the process models. The history of content theory is located in the theories of instincts which fell into disrepute at the beginning of the century as a result of the propensity to postulate a specific need for almost any human act. They achieved respectability again, however, when they were changed in concept to one of needs being acquired through the learning process.

Content theories are more concerned with specific rewards, the basic needs that may be identified, and the strengths of incentives on offer. For example, considering job performance a theory may attempt to classify the strength of achievement possibilities, recognition, responsibility, promotion prospects, and salary increases. Another theory may propose a different list.

Typical content theorists are Freud, McDougall, Murray, McClelland and Maslow. Examples of the latter two theorists' ideas are given in Chapter X, Motivation.

BASIC DRIVES

Research has revealed five inclinations or drives which are of particular significance in business life. They are significant because suddenly they may appear in the conscious mind and, it is claimed, pressurise the individual into taking a certain line of action which he might not have taken if given sufficient time to think. If the drive is suppressed, however, it is likely that frustration could result, causing loss of energy unless an adjustment is made.

The five drives referred to are self-assertion, acquisitiveness, aggressiveness, gregariousness, and constructiveness. Each of these drives and its importance to the supervisor is now discussed.

1. Self-assertion

The strong desire to be important closely associates itself with constructiveness. A person likes to consider what he makes as belonging to himself, but this concept becomes difficult to reconcile with the facts when work is divided into many processes, each one being performed by a different individual. The operative finds compensation instead in the group spirit.

Lack of security, poor wages, unsatisfactory working conditions and bad relationships between management, supervision, and operatives can also destroy pride of ownership in the work. On the other hand, efforts by management to improve human relations generate the group spirit and give the operator confidence in his individual ability and importance. This can be achieved to a great extent by consistently fair treatment, careful selection procedures and training schemes, and attention to individual problems. Opportunity for advancement also provides an outlet for people who feel that progress is an essential element in their lives. Although some people may only desire security and appear to be content in "dead-end" jobs, they still like to know that the opportunities are available for advancement and more money.

Making a person feel important means something more than paying him high wages. It is for management and the supervisor to show him their respect and appreciation in positive action.

2. Acquisitiveness

The feelings connected with this drive are protection and possession. The desire to possess extends to include people, property, and ideas. This drive may appear as the strong urge to control and have power over people. It can frequently appear as a need for security, which may be satisfied by material and abstract possessions. Security as a form of protection is also found in employment, superannuation and insurance benefits, as a protection against accidents and old age.

If management does not provide secure working conditions for its employees, they will lack confidence in the management and be generally disgruntled and suspicious. The value placed on secure employment is probably considered of less importance when there is full employment, but threat of unemployment is, consciously or unconsciously, very real to people and they instinctively react against lack of job security.

3. Aggressiveness

The desire to be powerful is stronger than the urge for prominence, which comes under self-assertion. This drive for power finds expression in aggression, as a generally hostile, quarrelsome attitude or even physical violence. The reason for its importance is its close connection with the drive to escape, often felt in difficult situations.

Many employees have felt the urge to strike a superior under unjust treatment and to run away from the job. When an employee is unhappy at work, the drive to escape is often frustrated by circumstances, and conflict appears. Outside commitments force him to continue with his job, causing him mental suffering and nervous tension, or he may day-dream as a means of escape. The desire to escape may subside to give the aggressive urge the opportunity of emerging, through the voicing of a multitude of complaints and grievances which are often imaginary.

Further developments may create a trouble-maker; his own work deteriorates along with his associates' work as he gathers support. The whole chain of events can be avoided by good supervision.

4. Gregariousness

The desire to belong to social groups and to be accepted as part of the group is fundamental. The urge to unite with others is related to man's mating and parental drives. Being "sent to Coventry" or excluded from the group is a severe punishment; the supervisor should avoid participation in any such activity and attempt to solve the problem quickly. The supervisor also should continually encourage his group's efforts by appropriate praise and reference to their achievements, as opportunities occur.

5. Constructiveness

The urge to create is often satisfied by giving people the opportunity to express themselves in various ways, such as suggesting improvements, putting forward ideas and opinions, and allowing some flexibility in how they do their jobs. The chance to have a say is an essential element of communication which produces feelings of influence and participation.

The employee should also receive open credit for his proposals if they are adopted; where the ideas are not feasible the reason—which must always be valid and acceptable—should be given with adequate explanation.

OUTLETS

When any drive grows strong enough to prompt action, it can be expressed in the natural way, or repressed where there is no natural outlet available, or it can be controlled and redirected.

These three outlets are important to the supervisor because, with practice, he can recognise symptoms and redirect his subordinates' energies towards more appropriate fields.

1. Expression

The natural outlet for a drive is through expression, which means freely satisfying the desire in appropriate action, thus relieving the feeling. Such free expression is not possible in many instances and when restriction occurs, the choice lies between repression or control.

2. Repression

Restraining a natural impulse creates nervous tension. This may be eased by repressing the urge, or "forgetting about it" and transferring it from one's conscious thoughts into the unconscious, or the "back of the mind". Employees have to restrain themselves, for example, when they feel they might retaliate against unjustified action by a superior. Suppressing this desire may be permanent or only of a temporary nature, hence the sudden retaliation by a subordinate at a later time will take the supervisor completely by surprise. The real reason for the outburst remains unknown to him. Repression is the cause of many troubles, including obstinacy, apathy, lack of interest in the job, maladjustment, poor concentration, and distorted outlook.

3. Control and redirection

Being able to recognise the nature of a drive, and attempting to control it by aiming at some goal, is the gift of a well-developed personality. Redirection of the drive into other lines of satisfaction is an excellent way of relieving the conflict which would occur if it were repressed. The experienced supervisor will recognise these drives as they come to the surface in individuals and direct them to advantage, not only on the shop floor, but in social, athletic, and other pursuits within the company. This form of personnel counselling is most important, and also includes dealing with emotional problems, which are discussed shortly.

MENTAL LEVELS

There are three mental levels: the conscious, the subconscious, and the unconscious. Some of these have already been mentioned. The supervisor should have some knowledge of the working of these levels, so that he may show a sympathetic understanding towards subordinates in certain situations, such as the examples given below.

1. The conscious level

Consciousness may be described as knowing what is happening around us and being aware of our actions. Being able to concentrate on a particular task means that a person can successfully block out all those counter-attractions which are happening around him at the time. If his thoughts are disturbed by a van passing by, a whistle blowing, or any unusual noise, concentration is lost and an error may occur.

Some people find concentration more difficult than others; the slightest noise which they cannot identify upsets them, or even a familiar sound may disrupt their train of thought. Their workmanship capacity may be excellent, but unless local conditions are satisfactory, results will be poor.

2. The subconscious level

All instructions and information flow into the subconscious mind which retains the messages for recall at any time. Recent messages, which include information and experiences, are easily recalled within days, weeks, or months, depending upon the particular individual. Some people find it hard to remember an event after a few weeks, others find it easy. Failing to remember is not a crime; in fact, it is both thoughtless and inefficient to ignore the handicap when it is known, instead of making a due allowance for the unfortunate person. The sensible supervisor will avoid placing people with poor memories in situations which call for a good memory, where they are likely to fail.

3. The unconscious level

The subconscious connects with the unconscious mind, and passes on all information and experiences for permanent storage. Although all past experiences are stored, it seems that automatic recollection at any time is not possible. Recalling an event at will does not seem to work; often there is a time-lag and suddenly, without any apparent effort, it springs into the conscious mind. A difficult problem may be put to one side and then, without warning, the answer presents itself. Similarly, all manner of information will appear without any conscious effort.

Another effect occurs when a person takes an instant dislike to another for no obvious reason. Psychologists say that this is due to an unconscious connection of the person with someone who caused unhappiness in the past. The danger of allowing first impressions to affect one's judgment is plain.

TEMPERAMENT

Individuals cannot be held responsible for their temperament or nature (though they can learn to control or modify it) because it is moulded mainly upon previous environment and inherited nature. Often it is associated with the disposition of a person, but there are other considerations which indicate temperament. Certainly disposition is an important aspect, judged by the sudden changes of mood in an individual for no obvious reason. One minute he may be happy but within a short time he is gloomy and generally antagonistic. In other words, he is unpredictable from one hour to the next.

Stability is associated with disposition. It is difficult to judge how well a person can control his emotions under various circumstances unless the supervisor has known him for a long time and has been in a position to note his reactions under emotional stress. Even so, the supervisor does not know everything, and should not jump to conclusions. In general, people are unpredictable; they react in odd ways which do not follow a set pattern.

QUESTIONS

1. How would you establish desirable superior/subordinate relationships?
2. "Every individual is different." Explain this statement and how it affects supervision.
3. Why has human relations been neglected in industry?
4. "Human relations and higher productivity go together." Give your views on this statement.
5. How would you proceed to improve human relations in a department where poor relations existed between supervisors and employees?
6. Can the viewpoints of managers and employees be reconciled?
7. What is meant by "divided loyalty" in connection with management/employee relationships?
8. Explain the importance of understanding human instincts as a means of improving the *industrial climate*.
9. What advantages can be gained by a supervisor who recognises the fact that each subordinate is a separate individual?
10. Discuss fully the problem of trying to understand people.
11. How would you deal with a situation where an employee complains about his colleague who sits next to him and suffers from B.O.?

12. How would you react if a subordinate "pulls your leg"?

13. What action would you take if a subordinate complains that *your* superior ignores him?

14. If a subordinate offers you a gift of fifty cigarettes which he says were given to him and that he does not smoke, what would you do? Explain your action.

15. How would you cope with a situation where a subordinate is continually critical of your actions but does not make constructive suggestions?

CHAPTER IX

IMPROVING HUMAN RELATIONS

The Practical Aspects

THE previous chapter on human relations gave a short survey of human behaviour which should serve as an introduction to the practical aspects which are discussed now.

Before the supervisor can deal effectively with people, he must be able to appreciate the stresses and strains within individuals which affect their daily working life. These emotional problems are discussed in more detail below, together with sections on the emotional range of normal people, the problems of resistance to change, and the various types of individual encountered on the shop floor. The importance of group activity is then discussed with illustrations of research into this aspect. The chapter concludes by describing the fundamental problems of human relationships, and lists the many methods of improving relationships on the shop floor.

EMOTIONAL PROBLEMS

Emotion is much deeper and more pronounced than simple feelings associated with "drives" since it involves environment, training and temperament, among other factors. Three responses occur with emotion: some *physical or organic change*, accompanied by *an impulse* to do something active about the situation, and *a feeling which* hastens the process of action.

A person's temperament is recognised by the way he controls his emotions, his moods, outbursts, and by his general emotional maturity.

Further detail of this complex topic is outside the range of this book, but the supervisor will already be able to recognise the problem employee who is emotionally unstable, because he will be spending more than the usual amount of time with him. This unhappy employee has problems which cannot be solved in the usual way because of his inability to adjust easily. The signs are antagonism towards management, the group, and certain employees; ill-health and absenteeism; generally miserable mood; frequent and trivial complaints; and in extreme cases, complete breakdown, violence, and excessive drinking.

THE ATTITUDES OF NORMAL PEOPLE

A normal person's attitudes are formed by arriving at personal balanced opinions which are, under suitable conditions, open to adjustment through the acceptance of logical reasoning and provision of sufficient information to justify the change.

Although people may behave in different ways, tending to suit their own particular needs or best interests, they are all acting normally. Each person has his own method of dealing with problems, depending upon his emotions, reasoning, and past environment. Moreover, what seems to be an abnormal or extreme reaction may be caused by further factors unknown to the supervisor.

RESISTANCE TO CHANGE

Any new scheme or change will instinctively be examined from the selfish aspect and, if it pleases, acceptance follows generally. An element of doubt will create the tendency to reject the idea, or to demand more information, or assurance.

To some people security is very important and, if this seems to be threatened in some obscure way, a form of guarantee is necessary before the change visualised becomes acceptable. Any proposed alteration affecting wages, safety, working conditions, and methods, needs clarifying in the employee's mind to remove resistance. Perfectly healthy people will resist change from outside, as already pointed out. Individuals do change, however, as it suits them. The process of living requires continual adjustment to social and industrial environment, although it is often a slow and laborious task. The fortunate ones adjust quickly; to others the problem is insurmountable, and they require special treatment before their minds can accept a change. An example is where a person suffers a bereavement and cannot face up to the drastic change in family life.

The supervisor should accept the fact that people do change their habits, outlook, and attitudes, and have the capacity to improve. He should be able to recognise the ill-adjusted employee by a variety of indications, including nervousness, difficulty in concentrating, ailments, misunderstandings, unusual behaviour, and poor general attitude towards work and people.

The Supervisor and Emotional Problems

This simple classification of people with emotional problems (and their responses under industrial conditions) defines three classes of people—normal, emotionally troubled, and convalescent.

NORMAL PEOPLE

This group adjusts readily to problems, provided that the supervisor treats each person with proper understanding and sympathy when emotional stress is evident. The industrial climate must be right, with a friendly atmosphere throughout the organisation, a feeling of belonging, and support from superiors.

EMOTIONALLY TROUBLED PEOPLE

There are many different types of people who feel unhappy and suffer generally. Their working efficiency is impaired and relationships with others are often unsatisfactory. They are misunderstood and their problems are aggravated further through general ignorance of their complaint. Trying to understand these people, who are fortunately in the minority, is wearing for the supervisor. They take up a lot of his time; often they cannot express themselves adequately; they do not make sense of situations; and are generally looked upon as a nuisance. Making the effort to understand them is worth while for the supervisor; it saves time in the long run and greatly assists them. Some of the types are given below.

1. The insecure person

Insecurity is apparent when the need for praise is exaggerated to a point where any sign of apparent neglect, although unjustified, will cause the person either to react strongly against the supervisor, or to resort to sulking for long periods. When approached he will possibly state that there is nothing the matter, or he may pick on little faults and grossly exaggerate their importance. He is commonly known as difficult, or touchy, and he needs regular strong assurance of his usefulness and his capabilities.

2. Over-dedication to the job

The person who places too much importance on his job, at the expense of outside interests, will find job satisfaction increasingly difficult to achieve unless he is able to advance in step with his aims.

Because of his unbalanced outlook, it is most unlikely that he will possess the right characteristics for promotion. Frustration generally appears as his demands are thwarted. Possibly the supervisor may be able to persuade him to take up other interests in the social activities of the company.

3. The temperamental person

This "time-consuming" type is continually pestering the supervisor with a whole range of problems, registering dissatisfaction, making excuses, and generally being a nuisance. He appears to be suffering from a number of emotional problems, openly expressed through continual upsets with his colleagues and authority.

The supervisor should try to restrain himself from direct reproach, and attempt to help the subordinate by seeking the cause of the trouble. This method is easily written about, but hard to practise, as the supervisor also has feelings and emotions which can stand so much provocation and no more.

Within this group are the types who are often absent and have accidents fairly regularly. Developing the group spirit so that these individuals feel a stronger obligation towards their colleagues may help considerably.

THE CONVALESCENT
Due allowance should be made for the person who has suffered a long illness or a breakdown and now wishes to lead a normal life again. The supervisor should treat the matter straightforwardly, informing his subordinates of the person's return and making it plain that the convalescent will be expected to be treated as an ordinary employee, with no special concessions. This should provide the right atmosphere, which might otherwise cause embarrassment if too much fuss were made on his return. Most people are naturally sympathetic and understand the person's feelings on these occasions.

Group Activity

Many supervisors have been puzzled by the sudden change in an individual they have known before, when he joins a group under their control. The reasons are that a person in isolation possesses more individuality, possibly has more responsibility, but may feel less powerful, and may be restricted in his outlook, thoughts, and actions, through fear of the consequences.

When a person joins a group a drastic change occurs; he loses some of his individuality and the group tends to mould his feelings, thoughts, and actions. He senses a *new* feeling of power, having the strength of numbers, and his attitude and general behaviour are affected accordingly. His feeling of responsibility is now spread into the group's responsibility and, as a result, he now acts in different ways. The pressure of mass suggestion also tends to make him think along similar lines to those of the group. The amount of change in the individual will depend naturally upon the nature and type of group, and the strength of character of the person involved.

This explanation of the *individual* and the *group individual*—although both the same person—should make clear the need to draw a subordinate to one side and reprimand privately, or to carry out any unpleasant task connected with an individual away from the group. A stronger reaction is guaranteed if any attempt is made to embarrass the subordinate in front of his colleagues.

TYPES OF SOCIAL GROUPS
There are many types of social group which all tend to merge into each other. Three main types can be distinguished: (*a*) the gathering or crowd; (*b*) the club; (*c*) the community.

Firstly, the gathering of people at a football match, theatre, or public meeting occurs when they have something in common. They are guided by events and are inclined to act impulsively and emotionally with no real objectives in mind, as a body.

Secondly, the club type of group is formed through active participation in sports and social activities, welfare, and religious work. Club members have definite objectives and generally possess strong sentiments which create the desirable group spirit.

Thirdly, the community type of group is a powerful, complex, stable organisation of individuals with strong common interests and high motivative potential. It is formed by force of circumstances and members play an important part in its organisation, daily operations, and objectives. Each member has particular responsibility and exercises self-discipline; his group loyalty provides a spirit often known as *esprit de corps* and this stabilises the group. The individual identifies himself directly with the group which allows him to assert himself through the group structure and satisfy his basic needs.

Although something near to the community type of group is very desirable in industry, it is not frequently seen; the crowd type is more familiar. Some of the essential requirements for building up community groups in a concern are: (a) forming the right organisation within each group of individuals and relating each correctly to other groups, on soundly based principles; (b) creating stability, i.e. a low level of movement of group members; conditions must be such that labour turnover is minimised; (c) reaching that stage of development in the industrial climate where each employee feels part of the concern, and has a pride in belonging to his particular group which is recognised by management.

RESEARCH IN HUMAN RELATIONS

The early pioneers of scientific management, such as F. W. Taylor and F. B. Gilbreth, had concentrated on improving productivity by studying the operator, the job, tools and equipment, and working conditions. Although outstanding improvements were achieved by the introduction of financial incentives, new methods, time and motion study, rest pauses for workers, new types of tools, improved layout and specialisation, these innovations did not always achieve the visualised targets.

In 1924 the Western Electric Company, near Chicago, decided to call in Elton Mayo, a professor of Harvard University, to study human behaviour. The company had already installed the systems of Taylor and Gilbreth, but the results were not up to expectations. Apparently productivity depended upon other factors that remained unknown.

The basis of the investigation was to test the effect of various factors on productivity by altering working conditions. Two equal groups (A and B) of female operatives were formed and studied by Elton Mayo and his colleagues over a number of years. Lighting intensity was increased with A group and, as expected, output increased in sympathy. For no apparent reason B group also increased its output, although the lighting was unchanged. The lighting was returned to its original intensity in A group and output increased further instead of falling back in sympathy.

In view of this unusual result a whole series of experiments was conducted over a period of five and a half years. Two voluntary female groups were formed and observed by the research workers who worked closely with the operators. All changes—which were made regularly every few weeks—were communicated to the operatives, who had the opportunity of commenting, asking for additional information, seeking advice, and airing any grievances.

This particular series of investigations was carried out in the Relay Assembly Test Room at the Hawthorne plant. Communication was ideal as information was allowed to flow freely in both directions. The supervisor had frequent conferences with the girls, their views were requested and in some cases they were allowed to veto a proposal. The girls had complete freedom to voice their thoughts and to decide their own working conditions.

A happy working group developed. The girls worked freely and confidently, with very little anxiety. A supervisory relationship was established which allowed them to feel a new sense of responsibility for their work. On the social side, they seemed glad to be together in outside activities and enjoyed themselves through a sense of group solidarity which reflected itself in both the social and work environment.

A summary of the experiments and their effect on output is given below.

Stage	Change	Hours (5½ day week)	Output in units per week
1.	Commencement of experiment (5 weeks' duration).	48	2400
2.	Group piece work introduced instead of fixed weekly wage (8 weeks' duration).	48	Increasing.
3.	Two rest periods introduced; five minutes in the morning and in the afternoon (5 weeks' duration).	47 hr. 5 min.	No change.
4.	Rest periods increased to two 10 minute pauses daily (4 weeks' duration).	46 hr. 10 min.	Substantial increase.
5.	Rest periods revised to six 5 minute pauses daily (4 weeks' duration).	45 hr. 15 min.	Slight drop, complaints that frequent interruptions upset work flow.
6.	Further revision of rest periods (15 minutes in the morning, 10 minutes in the afternoon) and a free lunch (11 weeks' duration).	45 hr. 40 min.	Increased output to Stage 4 level.

7. Working day terminated at 4.30 p.m. instead of 5.00 p.m. (7 weeks' duration)	43 hr. 10 min.	Further increase.
8. Working day terminated at 4.00 p.m. (4 weeks' duration).	40 hr. 40 min.	No change.
9. All changes withdrawn. Return to Stage 2 (12 weeks' duration).	48	Reached record level of 3,000.
10. Return to Stage 6 except for free lunch (31 weeks' duration).	45 hr. 40 min.	Increase to new high record above Stage 9.

GROUP SPIRIT

This series of experiments, and many others, became known as the Hawthorne Investigations. They provided sufficient evidence to prove that other factors beside wages and working conditions have a significant effect on output.

When employees are in the limelight they feel important, they begin to feel part of the organisation—and a vital part when their opinions are requested—and the climate is improved to a point where group spirit can freely express itself.

Self-discipline is established because a new feeling of responsibility emerges in a group which has freedom to develop its potential, make decisions, and take pride in its achievements.

Some Fundamental Problems of Human Relationships

1. Selecting and training operatives

Every operator must be able to do his job sufficiently well to achieve satisfaction and develop a feeling of pride. The responsibility of management for ensuring that this is possible is twofold: it rests with those who must select the suitable personnel for each job, and with those who are responsible for training personnel to perform their tasks properly. Encouragement, patience and tact are needed by the supervisor to see the operator through the training period.

2. Selecting and training supervisors

Management must appreciate the importance of providing each group with a carefully selected supervisor, who is trained in the art of dealing with people. A plan which includes continual search for supervisory ability within the company is essential, coupled with effective education and training schemes. Such a plan demands expenditure, and often a change in management attitude towards supervision and its importance in industry.

3. The position of management

The type of outlook required by management to establish good working arrangements with employees has been stressed already. This fundamental change of attitude is hard for senior and long-established managers to accept and, in some cases, it is totally unacceptable. Similarly, breaking down the traditional outlook of employees towards management is exceptionally difficult.

4. Company loyalty

Employees should be able to connect the company, its products or service and its aims, with themselves in such a way that they feel the job is worth while. They should feel proud of the concern, otherwise the correct attitude towards work will not follow.

5. Trade unions

Harsh supervision is often said to be the cause of the rise of trade unions. The modern supervisor recognises that collective bargaining is an essential part of developing human relations, and that training in the art of consultation is needed. True recognition of the union, and its influence, does not exist until consultation becomes a regular, acceptable form of communication. When the union, management, and employees work together as a team, the problem of loyalties falls into the background. Many managers recognise the practical use of the union for negotiating with employees, where the majority are members. All three groups have a similar interest in the company's prosperity and amicable co-operation solves problems and speeds progress.

The essential requirements are sincerity and continual demonstration of management's intentions to seek agreement by peaceful means. Provision of actual figures accompanied by plans showing the effects of changes contemplated by both management and the union, help to reduce unnecessary tension between the two.

6. Divided loyalties

To many employees the industrial situation is confusing and irritating, especially to those who are conscientious and strongly desire satisfaction from work. Loyalties seem to lie in opposing directions; to colleagues, the group, the supervisor, management, and the union. Other pressures complicate the problem, and it is not surprising to see some people reach a state where they are prepared to submit to anyone's schemes, thus abandoning their own principles, to secure some peace of mind. Others withdraw from industry and seek employment elsewhere.

7. Understanding each other

Being able to understand each other is probably the biggest problem. Simple conversations are misunderstood, people's words are easily distorted; in fact, very few individuals manage to be really in tune with each other all the time. Some people try very hard to get on with others without much success, while the fortunate few find it an easy task, but everybody finds that a large degree of tolerance and self-restraint is necessary.

8. Working conditions

Good working conditions are an essential background to good relationships. The atmosphere created by poorly decorated premises which are not cleaned regularly is depressing and degrading to operatives. Such poor conditions hardly match any attempts to show personal regard for employees. The contrast of bright and airy offices for other grades of employees in the same company aggravates the situation.

Good and ample amenities, cleanliness, and regularly decorated premises help to lift a person into a more congenial frame of mind.

Ways of Improving Human Relationships

1. The supervisor must show a genuine interest in other people, and display this interest openly, but he should not try too hard to impress in an attempt to win subordinates' interest.

2. He should ensure that the conversation is directed towards the subordinates' interests, as these are most important to him. The company's interests can be more fruitfully discussed when good relationships are established.

3. Remember the futility of arguing. The other person thinks he is right regardless of the supervisor's viewpoint, otherwise he would not argue. Although the supervisor may win the argument, the cost of upsetting the bond which existed between him and the other person far outweighs his own satisfaction; hence the saying, "You cannot win an argument."

An argument should not be confused with constructive discussion. Where people put forward their opinions—which must be respected— and intelligent discussion follows, obviously only good can result.

4. Try to imagine the other person's viewpoint, his feelings and divided loyalties which tend to distort and confuse his reaction to a situation. The supervisor will not be so ready to criticise or blame a subordinate if he does so; in fact, if he gives the subordinate a good name to live up to, this objective may help the subordinate to clarify his thoughts and realign his aims.

5. Do not make promises that cannot be kept. Straightforward talk is much safer and avoids misunderstandings. Always clarify instructions with subordinates and check that they have clearly understood the meaning of statements. People tend to put their own interpretation on what is said and unless care is taken to explain carefully, with illustrations where necessary, the wrong impression is given.

6. Find time to have a good talk with each man periodically.

However, the supervisor should avoid giving the impression that he is delving into private affairs. Attempting to give advice on private matters may be dangerous as the supervisor will possess only that information which the subordinate cares to divulge.

7. A supervisor should not attempt to bluff his way out of situations where he is at fault. There is nothing clever in concealing mistakes, which may cause more trouble and expense to correct at a later stage of development. Admit an error or inadequacy and most people will immediately feel sympathetic. Any admission of mistakes should be followed by prompt action to correct the fault.

8. Avoid direct criticism wherever possible. A better way is to make a constructive comment and so avoid an argument with someone who is probably already agitated by the situation. The supervisor will not necessarily appear too easy-going as one may expect; instead the individual will appreciate his sense of understanding and tact, and working harmony will be kept.

9. Always give a subordinate the opportunity to speak; it does not matter if he complains so long as he can air his thoughts. His criticisms will become more constructive eventually, with a little prompting, as he realises that the supervisor is consulting instead of insulting him by ignoring his ability. Where changes are necessary, less friction will occur when the subordinate has taken an active part in suggesting ways of altering the system.

Subordinates should be encouraged to talk about themselves and their problems. The supervisor must be careful to give them his undivided attention, or his advice and sympathy will not be sought again.

10. The supervisor should be pleasant and try to develop a friendly atmosphere. Resentment and misunderstandings are caused by abruptness and putting on a tough front. Use common courtesies always, such as "good morning", and "good night". Avoid addressing employees by their surnames only; remember there is a handle to the name—always *Mr.* Jones. Try to have a few words with each man every day.

11. If a man is doing well, then he should be told. Do not allow praise to go unspoken; always show appreciation actively. Supervisors are often quick to complain, but slow to praise extra effort.

Continually impress upon employees that their jobs are important. The desire to feel important, and be appreciated, spurs people on when they see recognition of their efforts, but not in financial terms alone.

12. Try to allocate the right jobs to the right people. The supervisor should always make sure that he knows what is involved in a particular job before assigning it, otherwise he may place an unnecessary burden on someone. Make sure that the subordinate also understands clearly the instructions.

13. The reason for policy and rules of organisation should be carefully explained and discussed. If employees are not satisfied,

endeavour to find more information, or obtain explanations from management.

14. Try to be a patient listener to grievances. The supervisor will have even less time available later if he allows problems and complaints to remain unsaid and repressed. Gain confidence by showing sincere interest and taking positive action where necessary.

15. Supervisors must be particularly careful in their dealings with employees of the opposite sex. Avoid being familiar, and bear in mind the emotional relationships which may exist in groups consisting of men and women. Words should be chosen carefully, the correct approach being essential. Someone nearby will always be ready to misinterpret a supervisor's intention, and pass on the incident and conversation to everybody, suitably distorted, of course.

16. Be just and fair in all dealings with subordinates. The danger of being easy-going should be borne in mind, as this will retard the supervisor's efforts to treat everyone in the same way. The supervisor must have his facts right, so he should be continually on the look-out and not trust to chance. His action should be timed well, and alertness to situations will ensure that the slackers do not escape his reprimands.

Fair treatment is essential at all times, and standard ways of dealing with subordinates in similar situations will show objectiveness or lack of personal bias. Avoid having favourites; these are guaranteed to upset all efforts to improve relationships.

17. Stress the permanence and security offered by management to employees. Any feelings of insecurity, such as rumours of redundancy, will immediately affect morale and output. Of course it is management's responsibility to provide the right climate before security can be impressed upon employees.

18. A good rule is to question every action involving operatives, to ensure that their self-respect is not affected in any way.

19. Promotion should be open to everyone. Opportunities for advancement should be well publicised and, when appointments are made, the reasons should be stated clearly to those who are unsuccessful; thus resentment is minimised.

20. Make sure that the members of the group are not in conflict. Although people of different temperaments will work together happily, some will be antagonised through conflicting beliefs, e.g. racial, political, or religious ideals. Where a clash occurs it is cruel to force such people to work together; they must be separated, otherwise the group will suffer unduly.

QUESTIONS

1. Discuss the various types of emotional problems that an employee may have to face at work.

2. How would you recognise the emotionally troubled employee and what would you do to help him?

3. What is meant by the term "a normal person"?

4. "People don't change." Discuss this statement.

5. What is meant by "resistance to change"?

6. How would you deal with the insecure individual?

7. How would you explain the change in an individual when he joins a working group?

8. Discuss the various types of social groups, illustrating your answer with suitable examples.

9. Write an essay on the Hawthorne experiments and include your personal opinion on the unusual effects that were discovered.

10. What is meant by "group spirit"?

11. Why are selection and training important factors in the problem of establishing good relationships with subordinates?

12. "Traditional outlooks tend to thwart attempts to improve management/employee relationships." Explain this statement.

13. Discuss the various ways of improving human relationships.

14. On your first day as supervisor, an employee makes a rude remark as you go by. On the second day a similar remark is passed by the same employee. What would you do?

15. If your best subordinate receives permission to attend a relative's funeral and on your journey home you see him leaving the local football ground, what would you do?

16. How would you cope with a situation where an employee complains that his colleagues refuse to speak to him?

17. An employee suddenly becomes very quiet and cuts himself off from his colleagues. Outline the action you would take.

18. How would you deal with the following types of employee: sensitive; casual; aggressive; and constantly grumbling.

CHAPTER X

MOTIVATION

Introduction

In Chapter VIII certain characteristics of people were discussed which are of direct relevance to motivation. The distribution of human differences, basic needs, drives, outlets, mental levels, and temperament were all considered. An in-depth study of people is a lifetime's work: everyone is different to some extent yet predictable in certain ways. In other ways people are absolutely unpredictable: they do not respond in a set way every time; they have likes and dislikes, individual fears, and various ideas; and some even think differently.

The only means an individual has of assessing his effect on another person is to note the other's behaviour at the time. A detailed analysis is often impossible; therefore this very limited assessment through noting behaviour may be totally inaccurate in terms of cause and effect. Many factors govern behaviour, each factor varying in strength dependent upon the person. If it were possible to put anyone through the same set of circumstances twice, varying one factor slightly the second time, the difference in behaviour could be noted.

The chance of coming to the right conclusion the first time as to the cause of anyone's behaviour is slim. For example, an employee suffering with exhaustion through sleepless nights with a newly-born child could be labelled as lazy if he did not disclose the problem. Similarly a wrong word from the supervisor may unintentionally upset the employee and cause erratic output, or a change in working position on the shop floor may cause the employee to feel unsettled and affect the quality of his work.

Consideration should be given to the vast number of aspects likely to affect behaviour at any one time. It is not unusual, however, for superiors to say, "The reason for his behaviour is his attitude." This statement assumes that attitude tends to lead to behaviour, whereas it may be more correct to assume that behaviour tends to lead to attitude when all the psychological motivation factors are considered.

Before examining this theory the background and factors affecting motivation are first considered, because although it may be true that factors other than motivators govern behaviour it is stressed again that this is the only means of seeing the effects of people's efforts.

The Background to Motivation

A central point in motivation research was reached in 1924 when Elton

Mayo was invited to study a productivity problem at the Western Electric Company (*see* Research in Human Relations in the previous chapter). Spending money on such factors as financial incentives and methods, and varying rest pauses for workers, were not producing the desired results. Mayo's attempts to solve this problem became the starting point for a continual programme in human behaviour undertaken by a number of behavioural scientists in the U.S.A.

Behavioural science includes psychology, sociology, anthropology, and other complex disciplines. Costly research undertaken over many years has covered firstly types of management behaviour which seem to encourage higher productivity and more profitable structures, and secondly the investigation into whether or not the findings associated with successful managers can be applied in other situations.

The simple question "How are people motivated?" can lead into the most bewildering, complex answers. To maintain some form of logical approach to motivation it is essential, therefore, to consider carefully the physical and mental make-up of people, the psychological aspects of motivation, the industrial environment, society, previous attempts to motivate, modern theories, and current attempts. These will shortly be discussed.

In many companies at present managers are being forced to resort to financial incentives in an attempt to increase productivity because they claim that other forms of motivation are unsuccessful. Employees, in turn, are accused of being lazy and wanting more and more money for less and less work, but they claim to be thoroughly discontented. The behavioural scientists claim that people are forced to behave badly through the way they are treated at work and that they will continue to behave in this manner until they are given challenging, mentally rewarding, and more meaningful jobs. One observation is certain: the various methods of motivating people in industry have failed miserably over the past fifty or so years.

Factors affecting Motivation

The main factors which affect motivation of people are the job itself, the company environment, external pressures on people, internal human pressures, individual capacity, and over-ride features. There are many aspects within each main factor (*see* Fig. 19). Furthermore, there is no way of accurately assessing each factor, or aspect within that factor; therefore the idea of calculating which mix is suitable for motivation is strongly suspect at present. In other words, it seems that the priorities and correct mixtures of factors vary with each individual

There are many different ways of grouping all the aspects to form main factors; this particular approach in Figure 19 takes into account the various current theories, but at the same time adds other factors which are often not mentioned when a certain concept is considered.

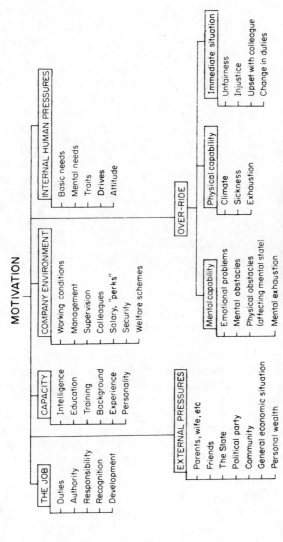

MOTIVATION

- **THE JOB**
  - Duties
  - Authority
  - Responsibility
  - Recognition
  - Development

- **CAPACITY**
  - Intelligence
  - Education
  - Training
  - Background
  - Experience
  - Personality

- **COMPANY ENVIRONMENT**
  - Working conditions
  - Management
  - Supervision
  - Colleagues
  - Salary, "perks"
  - Security
  - Welfare schemes

- **INTERNAL HUMAN PRESSURES**
  - Basic needs
  - Mental needs
  - Traits
  - Drives
  - Attitude

- **EXTERNAL PRESSURES**
  - Parents, wife, etc
  - Friends
  - The State
  - Political party
  - Community
  - General economic situation
  - Personal wealth

- **OVER-RIDE**
  - **Mental capability**
    - Emotional problems
    - Mental obstacles
    - Physical obstacles (affecting mental state)
    - Mental exhaustion
  - **Physical capability**
    - Climate
    - Sickness
    - Exhaustion
  - **Immediate situation**
    - Unfairness
    - Injustice
    - Upset with colleague
    - Change in duties

Fig. 19.—The Main Factors Affecting Motivation.

Each factor is now discussed before continuing with the various concepts.

THE JOB

The breadth of the job undertaken by an individual seems to have undergone a cyclical effect. Craftsmen possessed a very wide job breadth a few hundred years ago. Gradually the breadth has diminished: in fact a policy of job narrowment has been adopted over the past seventy years up to a point where an operator will simply turn a spanner, for example, many hundred times daily.

Now the vogue is job enrichment, which means not only continuing the cycle by increasing the job breadth, but also ensuring that the individual actually gains genuine achievement in the tasks, gains recognition for this achievement, has a definite interest and responsibility for the job, and is allowed to develop himself so that he may advance to even more complex jobs.

Management, it may be assumed, has not thought much of this factor as a motivator during the twentieth century. Possibly the job width cycle is due to a natural process of production development alongside technological advancement. This trend may give the employee of a few generations into the future the opportunity to develop in a narrow but complex technological field after passing through an interim stage of suffering very narrow jobs.

THE COMPANY ENVIRONMENT

This factor includes all the features associated with a concern except the job itself. Naturally there is a large variety of features such as the organisation structure; managers, supervisors, and colleagues at all levels; company policies, rules, and regulations; working conditions; all the welfare schemes—pension, social facilities, clubs, "perks", and other benefits; salary, wages, and bonus schemes; status; and security arrangements.

Many managers have used these features in an attempt to achieve motivation, but they have often fallen far short of projected targets. This does not mean, of course, that employees do not think these features are important. The question is whether or not they motivate employees.

EXTERNAL PRESSURES

A person is subjected to a whole host of external pressures which presumably affect his behaviour to some extent. The strong desire to mix with other people often results in an individual seeking advice, listening to opinions, being subjected to political views, and generally being indoctrinated. The main sources and features are his parents, wife, friends, relatives, the State, political parties, the community, colleagues, superiors, the economic situation, various advertising media, and the amount of capital in his possession.

The effect that some people have on others is frightening: sheer strength of personality is sometimes sufficient to make an impressionable person go against logical reasoning and behave in very odd ways. The element of confusion caused by many external pressures also should be taken into consideration. If this factor plays an important part in motivation it then becomes the responsibility of everyone in a country to ensure that his influential powers are used to encourage motivation. The well-known chain effect now applies because someone, in turn, needs to take the responsibility for ensuring that each individual is capable of exercising this responsibility.

It should not be forgotten that an external pressure, such as an ambitious wife, can motivate, if she can use subtle powers of persuasion which appear to her husband as an intense inner desire on his part.

INTERNAL HUMAN PRESSURES

These pressures come from within the individual in the form of basic needs, mental needs, traits, drives, and attitudes. Some of these features are an inherent part of a person—he is born with them—while others depend partly upon many external features encountered during growth.

Whether or not it is the responsibility of each individual to know himself and make certain adjustments which will favourably affect his behaviour is debatable. Again the chain effect may apply where, for example, it could be the responsibility of the Department of Education and Science to ensure that people receive sufficient education in particular disciplines which would allow them to benefit by self-adjustment.

So often people enter business with very little knowledge of what it is all about: a completely new environment is encountered with no real understanding of the importance of co-operation, co-ordination, self-discipline, and self-control. The "do this, do that" type of environment soon moulds people into attitudes involving suspicion and antagonism towards management. Frustration soon sets in as management's emphasis on certain features becomes obvious and the opportunities to satisfy higher needs become more and more remote. Such a situation tends to force a person into behaving irresponsibly, not necessarily because his attitude is at fault, but rather through a healthy reaction to an unhealthy situation. Resorting to highly absorbing hobbies and arriving at work absolutely exhausted could easily be a symptom of low satisfaction from the employment situation.

CAPACITY

Capacity is closely coupled with the previous factor. The main features are education, training, background, experience, and intelligence. The extent to which capacity affects behaviour depends upon matching the individual with the job not only from the "square peg, round hole" aspect but also from the individual's ability to develop within that field.

Although it is healthy to stretch a person's mind, over-reaching the limit of his capability will cause frustration. Conversely under-utilisation is just as dangerous. The need in these circumstances for rapid detailed feedback on performance and careful adjustment of the job based upon results is vital.

OVER-RIDE

For want of a better name the so-called over-ride factor upsets the effect of all the previous factors regardless often of their combined strength to motivate. Over-ride comes into play on the spot: it has an immediate, powerful, and dominating effect on motivation by altering behaviour through some mental incapability, physical incapability, or sudden change in the situation surrounding the individual.

From the mental aspect an emotional problem, a mental obstacle, or a physical obstacle can suddenly appear which may completely throw the employee off balance and produce erratic behaviour. Similarly, from the physical aspect, feeling off-colour, sustaining an injury, or suffering with a physical disability may produce unpredictable behaviour. A sudden change in a stable situation such as unfair treatment, an injustice, or a change in the environment without due consultation will again induce a similar effect.

All these features associated with over-ride tend to destroy a great deal of effort to motivate in other factor areas. Indeed, their effect frustrates many managers who abandon perfectly healthy schemes for the wrong reasons. In these cases employees are often branded as being lazy, which really means either that they are suffering with some mental or physical incapability or that they are reacting strongly against some unfairness or injustice. The use of the word "lazy" should be avoided as it immediately highlights the superior's complete inability to diagnose the individual's problem, as will be seen from the next section.

The Psychology of Motivation

The remaining aspects for analysis are those associated with internal and external motives, and the various obstacles that prompt particular forms of behaviour.

The motives that dominate behaviour may be subdivided in various ways such as grouping them into basic needs and mental needs. Another method of subdivision is to group them into internal motives such as the wish to satisfy hunger or thirst and external motives such as taking shelter if a gale is blowing, or lighting a fire if it is cold.

Motives may also be divided into known and unknown. The actions of eating and sheltering are obvious and would group conveniently into known motives, but other actions such as suddenly punching someone on the nose could be due to an unknown motive, unknown often both to the aggressor and to the victim, the real reason being obscured by an apparent reason. Motivation in this sense is essentially a force that comes from within a person, or, put another way, an internal cause produces motivation. Understanding this aspect is most important.

These known and unknown needs vary in strength along similar lines to the main factors and features of motivation outlined in the previous section. Some needs are easily satisfied while others, unfortunately, are subjected to barriers or obstacles. If these are not overcome the individual suffers some disappointment and frustration. The barriers are divided into two groups: external and internal obstacles.

EXTERNAL OBSTACLES

Barriers are raised by the society in which the person is a member, by the people who are associated with him, and through various objective factors.

The type of society exerts considerable influence by expecting certain forms of conduct from its members. If the rules and norms associated with this behaviour are broken by an individual he is subjected to certain sanctions such as disapproval, punishment, or even banishment. People learn through normal upbringing and education what is expected of them in their particular society; some, however, find the rules unacceptable and conflicts occur which may result in either the rules being altered, or the erection of insurmountable barriers for the individual, or eventual individual adjustment.

People associated with the individual may also disrupt or completely block his aims either intentionally or unintentionally. Interdependence is unavoidable in a complex industrial society; therefore restraint, tolerance, and understanding, and a generally sympathetic outlook on life become very important if everyone's needs are considered. Each person's actions impinge on many other people who are often powerless to react effectively, thereby resulting in inner conflicts and emotional upheavals which, if solved, require the utmost effort to adjust continually to rapidly changing situations. Unfortunately many people become bitter and it seems that maladjustment is inevitable.

Closely connected with people's actions are the resultant objective factors such as the economic situation, international conflicts, and taxes; also there are the completely objective factors such as weather conditions and earthquakes which can upset plans.

INTERNAL OBSTACLES

In addition to the external obstacles, a person possesses a highly complex and delicately balanced brain. He suffers with physical and mental limitations which tend to cause inner conflicts when associated with his traits, and create problems which he sometimes finds impossible to solve.

These problems appear through his inability to make a correct assessment of his capability in physical or mental terms. They cause conflicting interests which confuse and irritate him, resulting often in tiredness and apathy. His aims are sometimes set too high if self-assessment is inaccurate.

Behaviour and Obstacles

There are many different ways and combinations of ways of reacting to obstacles which are recognised through behaviour. These behavioural patterns are often called frustration symptoms; they are generally divided into characteristics such as aggression, regression, rationalisation, compensation, rejection, day-dreaming, and flight. Within some of these groups are further divisions; each one is now discussed.

DIRECT AGGRESSION

If needs are blocked through a weakness there is a tendency to become depressed, sour, sullen, and generally displeased with life. This tendency can suddenly result in a direct physical attack on the obstacle, examples of this primitive reaction are often seen in children and animals. Refined forms are shouts, derision, oaths, and sarcasm.

This tendency should be avoided if possible because calmness and sensible judgment are affected and there is always the risk that aggression may be answered by aggression; in other words, the person may hit back.

TRANSFERRED AGGRESSION

This form occurs either when the obstacle is unknown or when the obstacle is known but when it is unwise to show direct aggression. The aggression is transferred to a false barrier upon which irritation can be directed; it is controlled when compared with direct aggression and recognised by symptoms of pedantry, peevishness, complaints, criticism, and a negative approach.

A typical example is seen when a disgruntled employee continually picks on a weak colleague who is, in fact, not interfering with him at all. The weak colleague may eventually react through direct aggression.

INTROVERTED AGGRESSION

This type of aggression is indicated by depression, lack of initiative, self-accusation, and low energy. The individual either has suffered some failure or has a sense of failure which results in self-punishment, and anger is directed inwards.

Such self-denial may appear, for example, if an employee refuses a reasonable promotion because he was unsuccessful in gaining a more senior post. In extreme cases this form of frustration leads to suicide.

REGRESSION

A person who retires into earlier primitive habits and at the same time seems to have forgotten later-acquired, more adaptive habits is suffering from regression.

This regressive way of reacting to an obstacle is recognised when behaviour becomes less practical than normal. An employee, for example, may insist that he cannot do a task when it is quite obvious that he possesses the capability. Any form of inability to use knowledge or skill could apply along with typical tendencies towards vague thinking, careless dress, and a quick temper. A person's normal work becomes more difficult for him in these circumstances through loss of interest and inability to concentrate.

RATIONALISATION

This emotional reaction occurs when self-respect is hurt. Failure in an examination, for example, may cause a person to comment that it was not worth passing or that he did not care whether he passed or not. This unconscious twisting of motives occurs to justify silly actions or a humiliating personal situation.

When an individual does not act sensibly or he fails for some reason, he rationalises to justify his behaviour. Naturally the true reasons are ignored, and thus it becomes more difficult for him to solve problems logically.

DIRECT COMPENSATION

All efforts are directed to conquer the obstacle which is generally of an inner kind such as a weakness or lack of something. If the efforts are successful and socially acceptable it is good adjustment, but over-compensation may occur such as assuming an arrogant and exaggerated self-confident manner to cover shyness and a feeling of inferiority.

The symptoms are exaggeration and stiffness in behaviour; also a person may continually return to the same lines of thought although they have already proved worthless. This form also is called *fixation* because all the person's energy seems to be concentrated along certain tracks resulting in narrow thought patterns, stubbornness, unresponsiveness to argument, and poor reasoning. Underlying this behaviour is a feeling of uncertainty which forces the individual into desperate attempts to protect his self-esteem.

INDIRECT COMPENSATION

Failure to reach a goal may result in indirect compensation if a substitute goal takes its place and all the individual's efforts are directed towards it.

This obsession sometimes results in extraordinary performances or extreme actions such as wearing odd clothing and expressing way-out opinions. Examples of such failure are a family upset resulting in an obsession at work, or failure in an occupation and resorting to self-employment.

REJECTION

Rejection or repression means casting aside previous unsuccessful efforts and trying to forget the problem. Self-respect and self-esteem force unpleasant memories into the back of a person's mind so that his conscience is clear. Similarly his needs or desires which do not conform to a certain code are rejected and he pretends he has not been tempted. These unpleasant occurrences, including failure to reach a goal, are mentally pushed aside into the subconscious where they affect outward behaviour and dreams.

Symptoms of rejection are projection and lack of courage or energy. Projection is obvious when someone is known to have a fault and yet continually refuses to admit it or sees this fault in others and openly advertises it. Thus his own needs, wishes, and failures are projected into other people's behaviour; he feels better if his weaknesses can be seen in others. Lack of drive can also be attributed to financial worries, unhappiness at home, or unfair treatment which have resulted in rejection.

DAY-DREAMING

Resorting to fantasy is a way of seeking release from petty annoyances, difficulties, and apparently insurmountable problems.

The day-dream overcomes all obstacles as the goal is close and it can be useful if it provides a release and allows the person to regain his stability and drive. The danger lies in allowing the success in dreaming to be preferred to real life, for this results in maladjustment. The maladjusted day-dreamer is sometimes seen as the operator who often makes mistakes, seems unable to improve his performance, and continually lapses into blank expressions.

FLIGHT

An external obstacle allows a person to take flight or retreat from it, such as leaving a job to avoid the superior's moans. Such action could be good adjustment if a better job were located or bad adjustment if it ended in a worse employment situation.

Internal obstacles naturally cannot be subjected to flight, but a form of flight may result in drug-taking or resorting to alcohol to remove the obstacle temporarily. Lateness and absenteeism of a persistent nature are a sign of partial flight.

RESIGNATION

Closely associated with flight is resignation, where people openly admit that they have "given up" for various reasons associated with the job and colleagues. The usual comments from these hopeless and apathetic employees are: "It's no use trying to do anything round this place"; or "I've put up with it this long and I can wait until I retire"; or "I've learned to put up with the place"; or "It's always been like this and always will be." These unfortunate people, often through no fault of their own, quickly affect their colleagues and the atmosphere surrounding them is unmistakable.

CONCLUSIONS

So far the motives which govern behaviour are seen to be extremely varied and capable of complex classification. The barriers which tend to destroy motivation force people into reacting in a variety of ways which are known as forms of frustration. Knowing the terms associated with frustration does not help unless the supervisor has the time to think and to analyse his employees. The supervisor can assist in promoting emotional stability with the aid of further information and with the idea of trying to help employees adjust to situations often outside their control.

A vast amount of information on motivation is available; in the following section some of the main authors and their work are discussed by way of an introduction only. An essential requirement for understanding the work of behavioural scientists is to read their books and papers.

The Behavioural Scientists

A cross-section of the best-known behavioural scientists includes Abraham Maslow, Frederick Herzberg, Douglas McGregor, Chris Argyris, David McClelland, Saul Gellerman, and Rensis Likert. The main features of their research findings are given below, followed by a short conclusion before proceeding with further general observations.

ABRAHAM MASLOW

In 1943 Maslow wrote a paper on motivation ("A Theory of Human Motivation") which put forward what has become the most widely accepted theory on the subject. He maintained that the process of satisfying human needs is continuous; as soon as one need is satisfied another one takes its place. This implies that needs form a hierarchy of importance and that when one need is satisfied it no longer acts as a sustained effective motivator. Maslow subdivided needs into the following groups: physiological needs—hunger, thirst; safety needs—security, order; belongingness and love needs—affection, identification; esteem needs—success, self-respect; and self-actualisation needs—desire for self-fulfilment. These groups are in ascending order of importance commencing at the lowest level.

The hierarchy breaks down when all the needs are developed; the needs remain, but energy is spent differently on a continually changing basis as an attempt is made to satisfy all or any one of them. Furthermore, if a lower need is at risk a higher need will be given up as the

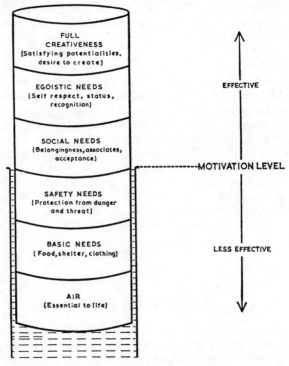

Fig. 20.—*Motivation Levels.*

Imagine the tube contains the needs of an individual arranged in a series of levels. The tube is situated inside the container of liquid. As each need is satisfied in ascending order, the one above becomes the need most urgently requiring fulfilment. The previous need, being satisfied, submerges the tube below the motivating point. Only those needs above the liquid level are effective motivators, unless a lower one is at risk.

hierarchy reasserts itself. All the needs stay with a person regardless of whether he is at work, at home, or at play.

A slightly adjusted arrangement of these motivation levels in Figure 20 illustrates that, when lower needs are satisfied, increasing those factors such as wage rates, working conditions, and fringe benefits will have only a slight effect on motivation. If a person is suddenly deprived of air, however, the immediate effect is to motivate the individual to satisfy this vital need, thus over-riding the higher levels temporarily. This reverting effect applies in varying degrees of strength at other levels dependent upon changing circumstances.

Higher standards of living and increasing social legislation affect the motivation level up to a point where social and egoistic needs become more important. If these are neglected, individuals will tend to be indolent and unwilling to accept responsibility and to behave in an unreasonable manner.

Concentrating on one motivating factor alone has, at the most, only a temporary effect if it is already sufficiently satisfied. All factors connected with motivation closely interact with each other, and management's approach to motivation must cover all areas if the knowledge, intelligence, and enthusiasm of employees are to be released into channels conducive to higher productivity.

Maslow's theory was first published in the *Psychological Review*, Volume 50, 1943. He also wrote many other papers, including "A Preface to Motivation Theory" in *Psychosomatic Medicine*, Vol. 5, 1943, and various books, among which was one in conjunction with B. Mittleman, *Principles of Abnormal Psychology*, published in 1941.

FREDERICK HERZBERG

How the needs described by Maslow actually operate has been studied by Herzberg, who has drawn certain conclusions which have received much publicity and achieved popularity in Britain. He has analysed the main factors which result in either satisfying or dissatisfying experiences at work and has arrived at the conclusion that satisfaction and dissatisfaction are not attached to the same factors.

Satisfaction, Herzberg says, is induced through the job itself by the adjustment of achievement, recognition, the work, responsibility, and professional growth; these are the motivators. Dissatisfaction is induced through the environment by adjusting company policies and administration, supervision, working conditions, interpersonal relations, money, status, and security. This environmental aspect Herzberg refers to as "hygiene" and he considers that, although the hygiene factors are important and that dissatisfaction should be kept to a minimum, only a fair day's work is possible if management concentrates on the environmental approach. Approach through the job itself, however, seems to have a larger and more lasting effect. Concentrating on job design or job enrichment provides more satisfaction to the employee and in turn increases his productivity.

For a full appreciation of this motivation–hygiene theory there are two books written by Herzberg that should be read. They are *The Motivation to Work* and *Work and the Nature of Man*. Herzberg is Chairman of the Department of Industrial Mental Health, Case Western Reserve University.

DOUGLAS McGREGOR

McGregor's work was based on his idea that effective leadership depended upon a manager's assumptions of the nature of management and about people in general. This idea was the keystone to his best-known contribution—Theory X and Theory Y.

Although the reasoning behind these two theories is in fact very subtle, it does have the appearance of being simple. This misconception has resulted in a tendency to oversimplify McGregor's thoughts; to be sure of the correct concept it is essential to read his books *The Human Side of Enterprise* and *The Professional Manager*.

McGregor stated there were two sets of assumptions about people; since then these assumptions have been interpreted in many different ways. Briefly Theory X and Theory Y—the terms given for these two assumptions—attempt to account for the way a manager can deliberately influence the behaviour of an employee. This influence is exerted through an underlying philosophy which is communicated by the use of all the techniques associated with contact between two people, such as speech, written notes, gestures, tone of voice, atmosphere, expressions, and so on.

Theory X is a philosophy where a manager sees employees as inherently disliking work; being unimprovable; needing to be coerced, controlled, directed, and punished; avoiding responsibility whenever possible; and generally being unambitious.

Theory Y involves coaxing people through reward, praise, permissiveness and attention; it assumes that people will work naturally, will exercise self-discipline and self-control in certain circumstances, and will have potential for further development.

Both theories assume that productive work is an unnatural form of behaviour and that some form of pressure is essential to achieve it. The strategy behind Theory Y not only involves coaxing but also demands the structuring of work so that opportunities for further achievement and personal growth are possible.

Some people incorrectly interpret Theory Y as completely abandoning the limits or boundaries associated with discipline and control. In other words, people are allowed to do as they wish with no pressure to conform. This interpretation really amounts to anarchy, and unfortunately when such an approach is tried employees tend to take full advantage of the situation.

McGregor's work clearly anticipated the present vogue of job enrichment; he thought that trust should be established by a collaborative effort where mutual support encouraged high motivation. He was Professor of Industrial Management at Massachusetts Institute of Technology. He died in 1964.

CHRIS ARGYRIS

According to Argyris apathy and lack of effort are due to healthy reactions by normal employees to an unhealthy industrial situation which has been created by management policies. He feels that most people are naturally motivated to act responsibly and to be self-reliant and independent. Most jobs are structured, however, to create a child-like role and as a result lead to frustration which is demonstrated as a defensive manœuvre, indifference, and contempt, so that the individual preserves his self-respect.

Argyris feels that people must have a sense of pride and accomplishment at work, but management still concentrates on financial reward, job security, and fringe benefits. Thus employees find little stimulation or dignity in work and employment becomes a necessary evil partially compensated by applying for more wage increases as a penalty payment to offset lack of job satisfaction.

He also points out the difference between happiness and motivation. Making a person happy does not necessarily motivate him. Conversely a motivated employee is not necessarily happy.

A further aspect examined by Argyris was that of interpersonal relationships, which are the characteristic way of perceiving and dealing with each other. Apparently there is a tendency for managers and supervisors inadvertently to filter information and to have difficulty in giving their real views. This lack of interpersonal competence can be improved, he says, by sensitivity training or T-group training.

The method involves placing people in a unique situation which encourages openness and risk-taking but discourages defensiveness and mistrust. Thus their behaviour should give them the opportunity to improve their communication effectiveness, to reduce the barriers affecting relationships with other people, and to remove the filters that tend to distort information flow.

This unique atmosphere is created by operating very informal sessions without a chairman or an agenda. When the session commences, the participants soon realise that a framework is needed where each individual plays a predetermined role if anything is to be achieved. The learning occurs as the group copes with this problem, each person seeing the effect of his tactics on the others, observing the personal bias effect and noting the distortion of information flow between them.

Argyris emphasis that T-group training does not solve management problems and that he would not recommend its use in certain cases.

Evidence shows that this training helps to make a person a better listener, and that he becomes more receptive to information from other people.

Argyris has written many articles and books; the best known books are *Organisation and Innovation, Interpersonal Competence and Organisational Effectiveness*, and *Integrating the Individual and the Organisation*. These should be read to appreciate his work, including his analysis of executive behaviour patterns. He is Beach Professor of Administrative Science at Yale University.

DAVID C. McCLELLAND

According to McClelland, most people feel they have an achievement motive. Research, however, shows that in the U.S.A. only about 10 per cent are strongly motivated for achievement.

McClelland's definition of an achievement motive is "the tendency when you are not required to think about anything in particular to think about ways to accomplish something difficult and significant". Apparently a person with a strong achievement motive is likely to surpass the accomplishments of an equally able but less strongly motivated man, especially if he is employed in such occupations as sales and marketing, or management, or is an independent businessman. People with a strong achievement motive possess three major characteristics: first they set their own goals; secondly they prefer moderate goals; and thirdly they prefer immediate feedback on their progress. They have a high opinion of their value in the form of wages, but it is questionable whether high reward makes any difference to their output as they normally work at peak efficiency. It would seem to follow, therefore, that monetary incentives have more effect on weak achievement drives. McClelland stresses that achievement motive is not the only source of high achievement; other drives can also play a part in different occupations.

There are reserves of achievement motive which can be utilised by introducing into jobs more achievement characteristics such as personal responsibility, individual participation in selecting production targets, moderate goals, and rapid feedback of results. Thus many standard supervisory practices are not appropriate and may even hinder employees' performance.

McClelland's best-known books are *The Achieving Society* and *The Roots of Consciousness*. He is Professor in the Department of Social Relations at Harvard University.

SAUL D. GELLERMAN

According to Gellerman it is possible to make some generalisations on motivation from research findings. These are that many motivational problems stem from the method of managing an organisation rather than the reluctance of employees to work hard; that managers have a tendency to overmanage by narrowing employees' jobs and by making too many decisions at too high a level; and that studying the employees' environment indicates reasons for their behaviour.

Gellerman's principle of psychological advantage explains that employees are motivated by their own desire to get by in the best possible way in the kind of world they think they live in. Thus employees are less susceptible to the influence of other people and more susceptible to their own drives, which presumably are partially governed by the standard of education, degree of independence, and the demand for what they have to offer. Managers can play a part, therefore, by ensuring that these desires can be satisfied by offering a change in the role an employee can play rather than concentrating on financial reward alone, although it is important.

Gellerman recommends three approaches which have a positive motivational effect. These are to "stretch" the employee by giving him more difficult duties above the level normally considered suitable for him; to apply the principles of management by objectives; and to encourage participation by asking the employee for his opinions before making decisions affecting his work. These and many other concepts are given in Gellerman's books entitled *Management by Motivation*, *Management of Human Relations*, *Motivation and Productivity*, and *People, Problems and Profits*. He is President of the Gellerman Kay Corporation.

RENSIS LIKERT

The research undertaken by Likert is particularly interesting to supervisors. His findings indicate the importance of quality of leadership and that certain basic patterns of supervision give the best results. According to the data, supervision and leadership style usually influence productivity far more than attitudes towards the company and job interest.

Likert states that supervision is always a relative process; a supervisor must adapt his behaviour to allow for the expectations, values, and interpersonal skills of his subordinates, colleagues, and superiors. He maintains that there are no specific rules of supervision which work well in all situations, but broad principles do apply to the supervisory processes and provide useful indicators to behaviour. These principles should always be used bearing in mind the situation and the employees involved.

A fuller understanding of leadership styles and Likert's research work and empirical tests is very useful and these can be studied in his book *New Patterns of Management*, published in 1961. He is Director of the Institute of Social Research, University of Michigan.

CONCLUSIONS

Even a brief study of motivation theory as propounded by the above authors is sufficient to indicate the complexity of the science. There is a tendency for managers and supervisors to hear about a theory or a technique, try it, and abandon the idea for the wrong reasons. This is mainly due to misinterpretation of the theory, or arriving at apparent causes of failure instead of the real causes, or failing to appreciate other factors that over-ride the behaviour of people in certain situations.

The social organisation it concerns is another important aspect affecting productivity. Society is rapidly changing and it is not easy to maintain close touch with reality. People are reacting more strongly against undue pressure and general unfair treatment by management; and the trend towards satisfying the more sophisticated needs is increasing along with more opportunities to develop to a higher educational standard. The strong demand for management to adapt to these changes is obvious and cannot be ignored if attempts to motivate are to succeed and people are to be relieved of the multitude of senseless obstacles that frustrate them in many companies.

To complete this survey of the motivation scene the remainder of the chapter deals with some topics which although they have already been mentioned require a closer examination. These are discussed under the headings Financial Incentives; Management; Leadership and the Supervisor; The Group; The Individual and Human Relations; and The Job. Each of these topics is interrelated and interconnected. If one is not adequately considered by management, efforts in other fields tend to be wasted; enthusiasm and morale are lowered immediately. These topics are now dealt with in random order.

Financial Incentives

The desire to work is strongly coupled with the desire for financial reward through the very nature of society and the need to satisfy basic urges or drives. The degree of influence financial incentives have on output, however, depends upon many factors such as the wealth of the individual, the standard of pay already being received, the relative influence of social factors, the strength of the greed trait, general character, and intelligence. If wages are high, the effect of a further increase may be negligible—perhaps a short burst of effort followed by a rapid fall to the original output level.

Two strongly opposing views are often heard in connection with financial incentives. One view is that a fair system is one where people are paid for what they produce; in this way the slackers are not supported by the energetic workers. Another view is that this system upsets human dignity when people have to jump for the so-called "jelly-beans". The emerging questions are: why do some people want to slack, and how are scrupulously fair schemes arranged and operated?

Successful motivation in non-financial terms eventually overcomes the first problem; the second question, however, does conform to a number of conditions that must be satisfied before non-financial forms of motivation can be applied. The main aspects are that management must be completely open with its intentions, and be fair when operating the scheme; employees' acceptance is essential and they should have confidence in its operation by possessing a complete understanding of the system; substantial incentives, promptness of payment, just penalties for poor work, and prompt attention to queries are all necessary.

METHODS OF REMUNERATION
The main types of wages schemes are day work, measured day work, graded day work, graded level day work, piece work or premium bonus schemes, the points system, and bonus schemes.

Day work
Day work is a simple, easily understood scheme where the operator is paid a standard rate or flat hourly or daily rate. This method is also called "time work" and is suitable where standardisation of work is not possible and quality is important. The method may include a lieu bonus where operators are working near others who receive incentive bonus.

The method is also used when it is not considered economic to introduce an incentive scheme or when output is not governed by the operator. Strong leadership is needed to make up for the lack of incentive.

Measured day work
A flat rate is provided, as in day work, but performance is also measured and used to assess the payment of annual increments. This method thus provides a form of competitive incentive.

Graded day work
Another variation is to base payment upon a graded structure according to ability. The pay level is reviewed regularly and is partly subjective in nature through the application of merit rating if increase in skill is the yardstick. Alternatively length of service may determine the increases or output levels may be determined over the period under review and used for appropriate increases.

Graded level day work
This is a more sophisticated scheme utilising work measurement. Payment is based upon a graded structure of proved performance levels. Advancement depends upon the operator demonstrating his ability to perform at the next higher level for a probationary period. The scheme is operated on a basis of mutual trust: the operator

undertakes to work at a determined level, while management guarantees his wage level regardless of any change in circumstances.

Piece work

Where operators need rewarding for exceptional ability straight piece work is suitable. A fixed amount is paid for each unit of work produced of a set quality, payment being directly proportional to output. The sum is calculated by timing the unit of work at a reasonable speed of operation and relating it to the wage rate, plus an allowance to give the operator the opportunity to earn a bonus.

Setting rates may pose problems: the rate must be fair and should be fixed with great care as any change contemplated because of an error in the original rate-fixing may disrupt good relationships. Some agreements are made not to pay less than the basic rate. Close inspection for quality is essential, but close supervision is not so necessary as the scheme provides a strong incentive.

Signs of overstrain should be borne in mind and the scheme must be run fairly. Clocking-off the job may be necessary if delays occur and certain rules are needed to clarify situations where additional tasks are involved which are outside the rate set. Normally allowances for fatigue and incidental tasks are built into the rate.

Other forms of piece work are simply variations such as differential piece work which provides steps in the earnings to accommodate increased or decreased rates at certain levels. Many geared schemes may be used to make payment regressive or progressive at appropriate levels where, for example, quality falls off rapidly or more enthusiasm is needed to reach a level where higher bonus becomes operative.

Premium bonus schemes

The basis of all premium bonus schemes is to share the savings, provided by working faster than the set standard time to do the work, between operatives and the company. The three main schemes are the Halsey, Weir, and Rowan systems, although there are many schemes in operation, which are the offshoots of these three.

One-third of the saving is given to the operator under the Weir system, whereas half the saving is given under the Halsey system. The proportion of saving is variable under the Rowan system. An example of each scheme is given in the table of premium bonus schemes in Figure 21 and a graph illustrating bonus schemes based upon the table is shown in Figure 22.

The Rowan system allows a bigger bonus for small savings compared with the other two. When half the time is saved, however, the Halsey and Rowan systems give the same bonus. The Rowan system also limits the increased earnings to nothing more than double.

A prerequisite of any system is the careful use of work study to determine the best way of doing the job and to set a reasonable time for its performance (*see* Chapters XX and XXI).

System	Hours			Formula	Hourly Rate (R) £ p	Bonus £ p	Total £ p	Average Hourly Rate £ p
	Standard Time (S)	Actual Time (A)	Saving					
Weir	6	4	2	$\frac{1}{3}(S-A) \times R$	1.35	.90	6.30	1.57
Halsey	6	4	2	$\frac{1}{2}(S-A) \times R$	1.35	1.35	6.75	1.69
Rowan	6	4	2	$\frac{A}{S}(S-A) \times R$	1.35	1.80	7.20	1.80

Fig. 21.—*Premium Bonus Systems.*
The three main bonus schemes are shown comparatively. Figure 22 shows these data graphically.

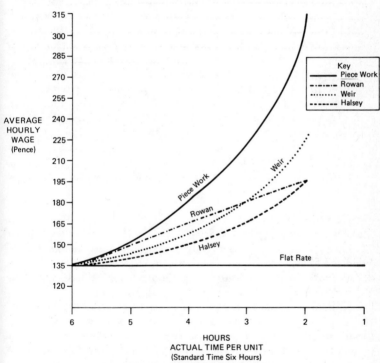

Fig. 22.—*Graph of Bonus Schemes.*
The graph is based on the data given in Figure 21.

Points system

The job is carefully evaluated on a points basis to provide a set number of minutes in which an operative working at a reasonable speed could complete the process. A point usually represents one minute, as in the Bedaux system, and an average operative is assumed to work normally at a speed of sixty points an hour.

A basic rate is guaranteed and the bonus is calculated on about 75 per cent of the time saved.

BONUS SCHEMES

The remaining schemes involve either a group of operators who work as a team and are paid a bonus on group output or various ways of distributing a proportion of company profits to all employees.

Group bonus

Financial reward is based upon the combined output of the group. The effect is to bring each operative's work under the scrutiny of the rest of the group. Operatives become dependent upon each other's work and, where they can help each other within the group, the group spirit grows and output should improve.

Precautions are needed to ensure that the group does not suffer unduly when a member is absent. Group size becomes critical and the bonus schemes should be so arranged that *all* groups have *equal opportunities* to earn more at the same differential of payment.

A degree of flexibility or allowance is essential so that those employees who naturally work quickly are not restricted. Group incentives also seem to induce a better standard of quality compared with individual bonus schemes. Close supervision is not so necessary as the group attends to the lazier members automatically. The system is essential where individual effort is difficult to measure, as in the case of track-laying teams.

Profit sharing

There is a variety of profit-sharing schemes which are extensions of the group bonus system. Generally all employees are included, provided they have completed about two years with the concern. The object is to build up a collective effort, though some individuals cannot correlate their own work with the over-all concern.

The bonus fluctuates because of other factors besides employee effort, which some people consider unfair. Ideally profit-sharing should at least join the interests of employees with those of the company, and provided the scheme is operated fairly with full disclosure of figures, there should be more confidence in management.

Management

RELATIONSHIP WITH EMPLOYEES

The employees' reliance upon management is fundamental. Management ought to appreciate the employees' desire to be proud of their managers; they should be right and look right in employees' eyes. To reach such an exalted position, managers must possess and display a number of qualities. Sufficient knowledge of management principles, organisation, motivation, and human relations, is essential; managers should know what life and work are all about. They must be vital and dynamic, to a point where their enthusiasm becomes infectious. Managers' achievements are measured in growth and financial success, but they must conduct internal affairs in a human way and not by ruthless methods.

The organisation should be treated as a community, where a network of human relationships seethes with activity, controllable only by sensitive understanding and a high degree of skill.

Supervisors should be allowed to develop their operators' capabilities so that ambition and self-improvement are considered normal, and a sense of opportunity is felt by everyone. Appointments should be conducted on sound scientific lines for the most efficient deployment of labour, and with impartiality and fairness to maintain good working relationships.

Finally, objectives and information on performance are just as important to employees as they are to management, and these should be communicated fully and promptly to every member of a concern.

MANAGEMENT BY OBJECTIVES

One method of motivating both managers and supervisors is by using a technique called management by objectives. The title is misleading, considering that everyone normally works towards given targets. Management by *acceptance* of objectives is more accurate.

Briefly the technique of persuading a subordinate to accept objectives is achieved by:

(*a*) allowing him to clarify his job by establishing his own ideas of its content and purpose;

(*b*) coming to a mutual agreement with him on his responsibilities;

(*c*) allowing him to decide what his targets for a given period should be and agreeing them with his superior;

(*d*) letting him work on his own as much as possible during the target period, asking his superior for professional advice (rather than direction) whenever he feels the need;

(*e*) conducting an appraisal of personal performance at the end of the period with a view to improving his effectiveness by further training and general assistance as required.

Successful application of the scheme depends upon using the appropriate strategy; this is based upon modern methods of influence and control which allow people to feel unrestricted and free to develop and improve their performance according to their own ideas.

Naturally there is a degree of restriction according to company objectives and economic factors.

Leadership and the Supervisor

Employees' motivation can be considerably improved by good leadership. Suitable supervisory leadership depends mainly upon circumstances in the particular concern, the lead given by management, and management's attitude towards supervision. Discovering supervisory ability, training supervisors and motivating effective supervision play an important part in the process. (The qualities of a good supervisor were discussed in Chapter II.) The good leader weighs up a situation and acts accordingly. An assessment of one situation may indicate that powerful leadership is needed where subordinates feel they need firm direction, encouragement, and support; whereas in another situation a more subtle support role is needed with emphasis on assisting, consulting, and co-ordinating.

Assessment of the situation should include all the factors connected with the organisation, the industrial climate, state of the business, and general morale and attitudes.

In general, the supervisor will successfully motivate operators by taking a personal interest in them. Being friendly and sociable is insufficient. A true understanding is desirable, which means studying them, finding out their problems and feelings, and working out solutions together. In other words, the desirable form of leadership is creating confidence, interest, and enthusiasm, by indicating courses of action, discussing the choices, and then making a decision. Overcoming the problems caused by mistakes should receive more emphasis than blaming people for the errors.

Knowing how closely to supervise is another problem. Subordinates are inclined to resent very close supervision which may produce less job satisfaction and less feeling of responsibility for the work performed. Given more freedom the opposite effect applies; the supervisor has the opportunity to delegate and to use the techniques for improving human relations and motivation.

Probably the most difficult task faced by the supervisor which affects operatives' motivation is the negative job of disciplining operators. The test of a good supervisor is being able to deal with good and bad operators without upsetting relationships. Although he is friendly and co-operative, there are occasions when he must assert his authority by reprimanding or disciplining those operators who do not respond to the treatment already described. Good operators will expect him to act justly when dealing with those who do not conform to normal working arrangements. If he shirks this responsibility he will lose respect and operatives will be less willing to work well for him.

The key to motivation through leadership is in allowing operators to influence the supervisor by actually taking part in daily activities, having a say, and seeing the efforts of participation rewarded in improved working conditions and output. The operator is given the chance to see and understand the facts of the situation or problem, which becomes an objective exercise to solve. The *personal* aspect, where the supervisor demands action from the operator, becomes insignificant and the operator's thoughts and energies are directed towards dealing with the situation.

Leadership is an essential part of supervision. Without adequate direction there will be uncertainty and lack of co-ordination. Without sufficient drive there will be less motivation, and without representation group adhesion will suffer as imbalance is created in the organisation structure.

The Group

Successful handling of a group depends upon supervisory skill and adequate knowledge of group activity. This was discussed earlier in Chapter IX and a brief summary here is sufficient.

GROUP BEHAVIOUR

Within the group every individual invariably supports its activities, finding security in it and working to a common goal. The peculiarities of group behaviour are, firstly, that the group is very sensitive towards the treatment of its members. Secondly, the group is stronger than the sum of its members, more emotional and open to ideas; but it takes longer to change and therefore seems to be more set in its ways. Thirdly, when aroused to achieve an objective, its driving force can be tremendously strong and sustained. There is a definite connection between productivity and group activity.

The supervisor's job is to satisfy the group's natural desire for solidarity, which gives individuals a sense of security and importance.

SOCIAL ACTIVITIES

Adequate accommodation and financial support for social activities encourages the development of group spirit. Although some managers have been bitterly disappointed at the lack of enthusiasm or wavering interest in such schemes, no doubt they should look elsewhere for the cause rather than blaming employees entirely.

If employees suggest the facilities required and organise the activities themselves, there should be more personal identification and hence more satisfaction. Managers should actively support, but possibly not take any part in controlling the proposed programmes.

The supervisor should also be active and enthusiastic. He can often recommend certain employees whom he knows have a flair for sport and other interests. The sphere of recreation allows him to gain a better understanding of his subordinates outside the working environment.

There are many opportunities open to social clubs to represent their firm in the outside community, e.g. joining local sports leagues, assisting in charitable work, taking part in parades, holding joint dances with other companies; all are ways of encouraging pride in the group and the organisation, and enabling employees to appreciate their role in the community as a whole.

The Individual and Human Relations

Although the importance of the group should be recognised, and techniques used to develop this motivation factor, similar emphasis on the individual is necessary to provide employees with a balanced outlook.

As mentioned previously, people are too complex even for expert psychologists to understand completely. The supervisor can with perseverance, however, use certain techniques effectively. Being more objective in his approach towards people and finding out as much as possible about them, will produce the desired results.

Any supervisor who attempts to apply principles in isolation, without considering the human factor, will inevitably receive a poor reaction from a subordinate. The chances of choosing an effective course of action, based upon principles alone, are remote. Human factors can easily over-ride the most elaborate plans. An obvious method of increasing employee motivation may produce a negative reaction because an equally obvious human factor has been ignored. Negative reactions must be accepted as a failure to weigh up the true interpersonal relationship. Reasons for failure must be thought out and new approaches tried, with more emphasis on human relations. Understanding people, therefore, is a vital part of successful motivation.

The Job

The job itself plays a part in providing the operator with sufficient scope for motivation. A thorough knowledge of job content (i.e. duties, status, and line of command as laid down in the organisation plan) is essential otherwise the difficult task of matching a suitable operator to the job becomes impossible.

The job should be kept sufficiently broad to give the operator some flexibility and initiative. A very limited job may rapidly produce boredom, and frustration, as the opportunity to contribute is reduced.

Committees, conferences, suggestion schemes, competition, and personnel counselling provide further outlets for active participation, once the familiar barriers of lack of time and reluctance to accept responsibility are broken down. Some of these activities are discussed in more detail below (*see also* Chapters XII and XIII).

MEETINGS

The right atmosphere at committees and conferences is created by the chairman, who should be well versed in the art of persuading all the members to make some contribution to the discussion. Often operators are reluctant to speak in front of their supervisors, especially if they disagree with their views.

The purpose of a committee is defeated if one side dominates and all the parties concerned do not contribute and share information, opinions, and ideas.

SUGGESTION SCHEMES

Many employees are already aware of better ways of doing their jobs. Others are capable of thinking about the problems and coming up with ideas which would save the concern a great deal of money. A well-organised suggestion scheme, combined with good relationships, provides encouragement for employees to put forward their ideas.

Everyone gains under a fair suggestion scheme; relationships are improved, an excellent outlet for participation is provided, and employees are able to identify themselves more closely with the concern. Even generally inactive employees are known to have submitted excellent proposals as the impetus to take part catches on. The element of competition and the chance to be recognised incite people into action.

Launching the suggestion scheme

(*a*) *Publicity*. A full-scale campaign is essential to diffuse information through every part of the concern. Posters should be prominently displayed and supported by letters in pay packets; supervisors should be carefully briefed to give any additional information that may be required.

(*b*) *Boxes*. Suggestion boxes should be placed in well-chosen positions and accompanied with a supply of forms. The conditions of the scheme should be clearly stated on the form and brought to the attention of the employee, where the signature is required.

(*c*) *The supervisor's position*. The attitude of the supervisor is most important in generating a successful scheme. He should understand that suggestions are not personal reflections on himself, and it is his responsibility to encourage and stimulate interest in contributing ideas.

Operation of the scheme

A manager should be given the responsibility for operating the scheme.

Finer details of the system will depend upon circumstances, but the essential points are that collections should be made regularly, recorded, and acknowledgments sent promptly. If privacy is requested, notification through the outside mail to the employee's home address could be used.

A recording system is necessary to avoid errors; each form should be numbered and a file raised to accommodate the correspondence and findings. A sorting scheme is essential to cover all the areas of likely suggestions, each area being represented by an executive who can study and investigate fully each proposal, before recommending a course of action. Possibly a committee should finally approve or reject the suggestions, and award appropriate sums.

A rejection requires a carefully prepared, adequate explanation. On occasions a similar idea may already be in hand; in these circumstances proof is needed to show the employee that he was not the first to think of the proposal (one very important reason for keeping careful records).

The amount of award varies considerably from about 10 to 50 per cent of the savings for a year. Suitable publicity of awards should be given, and additional benefits, such as a free summer holiday, attending special functions or theatre visits, could be given periodically to all award winners.

The main reasons why the scheme may fail are: long delays in administering the system; poor rewards; inadequate reasons for rejecting proposals; poor supervisory support; or that suitable relationships were not established before commencement.

A successful scheme demands time, expense, and additional managerial effort. The gains are mainly twofold—financial economies and higher motivation of employees.

Periodic comparisons of the number of submissions and acceptances give an indication of the trend, and for this purpose the following formulae may be used:

(a) $\dfrac{\text{Total suggestions submitted}}{\text{Average number of employees}} \times 100 = \begin{array}{l}\text{Submission rate per 100}\\ \text{employees}\end{array}$

(b) $\dfrac{\text{Total accepted suggestions}}{\text{Average number of employees}} \times 100 = \begin{array}{l}\text{Acceptance rate per 100}\\ \text{employees}\end{array}$

COMPETITION

Fostering a competitive spirit between individuals and groups provides them with an additional interest in the job. The easiest way to stimulate rivalry is to give everyone all the information on production, including operator and group performances on output, quality, economy, and productivity.

The information should be presented with some highlighting effect to arouse interest and, after a while, followed up with targets which should not be unreasonable. A production drive for one month, to achieve a delivery date for a particular order, is a typical example. The output targets should not be over-demanding; the drive needs staging properly with, say, an opening ceremony and well-publicised daily progress.

The scheme may be extended into the fields of quality, waste prevention, absenteeism, and accidents. Suitable rewards for efforts could include extra privileges, besides financial gain.

QUESTIONS

1. How would you recognise high motivation and what are the essential factors which are needed to achieve it?
2. Discuss fully financial incentives and give your personal opinion of their effectiveness.
3. What part should management play in promoting high motivation?
4. What type of supervisory leadership is needed to motivate subordinates?
5. How can a knowledge of group behaviour help the supervisor to achieve higher motivation?
6. Discuss the methods open to the supervisor for developing group spirit.
7. In your opinion how important is the human factor in connection with motivation?
8. How would you organise a suggestion scheme?
9. Do you think a suggestion scheme is worth while? Explain your viewpoint thoroughly.
10. If an employee is continually leaving his workplace and spending a considerable amount of time in the cloakroom and he has been warned once, what action would you take?
11. If an operator accuses you of always giving him the difficult jobs, and it is not true, what conclusions would you draw and what action would you take?
12. What fundamental requirements are needed before a suggestion scheme will be successful?
13. How would you explain the fact that operators may receive wage increases but no difference in their attitude towards work is seen?
14. What would you do about a situation where your group starts openly to "carry" an operator for no apparent reason?
15. "Behavioural Science is based upon the assumption that behaviour tends to lead to attitude." Discuss this statement.
16. List the main factors which affect the motivation of people.
17. Outline the external and internal barriers which may stop an individual from satisfying his needs.
18. List the ways that people may react to obstacles which thwart their needs.
19. Write brief notes on the work of Abraham Maslow.
20. Discuss job enrichment.

CHAPTER XI

INTRODUCTION TO COMMUNICATION

Importance of Communication

SUCCESSFUL communication of information to operators, fellow supervisors and management is an essential part of the supervisor's job. Surveys in recent years have indicated that over one-third of clerical workers' time is spent on moving information from place to place. It is said that in a highly-civilised society about four-fifths of the working day is spent on communicating.

SOME DIFFICULTIES

Poor communication accounts for about one-third of the strikes in Britain and causes a considerable amount of misunderstanding between employees and management. As companies grow, the problem of achieving good communication and overcoming feelings of remoteness between the different parts becomes more difficult.

Communication forms the link between every individual in the concern and all instructions, information, concepts, opinions, and attitudes must flow through individuals. It is essentially a two-way process of imparting information to others and attempting to receive information, both with as little distortion as possible.

A high degree of skill and care is needed in communicating with people. Misunderstandings are so common that a determined attempt is needed to cut down the possibilities of mistake.

The various aspects of communication to be considered to this end are the channels of communication, methods of transmission, the language and tone of the message, and the attitudes of the sender and receiver.

EFFECTS OF POOR COMMUNICATION

Poor communication will have a drastic effect on production and individual relationships. Continual misunderstandings lead to confusion, mistakes, wastage and accidents. Employees become frustrated and morale drops, resulting in lack of motivation and low productivity. When changes occur and reasons are not communicated, unrest and, possibly, strikes follow. Very little information flows upward to managers who are unaware of the situation as the complaints, grievances and trouble spots reach the lower levels of supervision, and stop there. The general feeling of dissatisfaction spreads and poor co-operation is general throughout the concern. Employees leave, and labour turnover increases until the situation is recognised by management and attempts are made to improve communication. Many of the symptoms mentioned are measurable, so trends should be watched and appropriate steps taken.

Channels of Communication

TYPES OF CHANNELS

The channels are divided into formal and informal groups, as listed below.

1. Formal channels

The Scalar Chain or line of command.
Joint consultative committees.
Discussion groups.
Personnel interviews and counselling.
Liaison with trade unions.
Company magazines, posters, and literature.
Policy publications.

Direct Letter
Notice boards
Conferences
Conventions
Suggestion schemes

2. Informal channels

The "grape-vine" (*see* p. 170).
Discussions with trade union officials.
Informal consultation.
Outside services (newspapers, television, radio, magazines, and contacts with friends or relatives).
Airing grievances and complaints.

USING FORMAL AND INFORMAL CHANNELS EFFECTIVELY

Formal channels of communication operate through the lines of command throughout the organisation. The effectiveness of these channels is probably measurable by assessing the time factor, the accuracy of the message, responsiveness of employees, and the cost per unit of manufacture. The time taken to achieve a good response from employees is the important factor. The quickest way of passing information and making decisions is a one-way communication process from supervisor to subordinate. The amount of response, however, depends upon the supervisor's influence and powers of persuasion and the amount of consultation and participation in making decisions, involving two-way communication which slows down the process.

Other factors must also be taken into account when dealing with communication problems and the correct balance must be achieved between speed of transmission, accuracy and effectiveness, depending upon the particular circumstances.

Employees should be given as much information as possible. Information flows in from a number of sources. Some of these are very unreliable and unless the sound, official sources of information operate effectively, people are given wrong impressions that cause considerable harm to relationships. The easiest and quickest way to squash rumours is to publish the facts and demonstrate by positive action the truth of the issued statements. This method cannot work in circumstances where poor communication blocks the upward passage of information in the organisation. The supervisor should bear in mind that executives cannot make statements explaining away rumours until they are aware of the situation.

Some supervisors have the mistaken idea that withholding information demonstrates power to subordinates. The reverse is the case, as employees will find out through other sources and, if it is obvious that the supervisor was aware of the information, he will be despised and distrusted.

A similar situation will occur when the supervisor withholds any information from his superior. Regardless of whether the superior will be pleased or annoyed at receiving the information, it is better for it to come from the supervisor rather than from another source.

No manager or supervisor likes to be in the position of being taken by surprise. He would much rather learn about problems and mistakes from a subordinate than first hear of them in the form of complaints or reprimands from his superiors, since early information will give him the opportunity to investigate and correct the trouble, and prepare an adequate explanation.

THE GRAPE-VINE

This informal channel of communication operates through all members of the organisation. They pass on gossip, scandal, and rumour to each other during their daily contacts at the workplace, in the canteen, and during social activities.

When used properly the "grape-vine" is a quick way of assisting the formal channels and it provides a guide to the effectiveness and accuracy of other channels.

Dangers of the grape-vine

Management is usually to blame if the grape-vine plays a dangerous part in the communication system by betraying confidential information and spreading rumours based upon odd scraps of information and conjecture. Invariably the leaks may be traced back to managers' lack of circumspection; e.g. careless remarks over the telephone, leaving confidential papers lying around, imparting information to close associates without authority to do so. Few people are able to keep confidences *completely* "under their hats".

Subordinates expect their supervisors to know the facts about any rumours which are circulating. If the supervisor does have confidential information he is then placed in a difficult position where he must either deceive his operators, antagonise them by withholding the information or betray management's confidence. Management should prevent such situations by issuing statements in advance or ensuring that no leakage is possible.

When any instructions are issued without acceptable reasons, or when breakdowns in formal channels occur, the grape-vine promptly takes over and creates the information which is lacking. If the facts are not available from official or unofficial sources, someone always gives an opinion which is accepted as fact until proved false.

Employees want to know about the concern, any current news which may affect them, proposed changes and development of existing programmes. If information is withheld, the inevitable rumours will quickly destroy good relationships. Rumours cannot be stemmed unless management understands the situation and provides sufficient information for supervisors to pass on.

Uses of the grape-vine

1. As a control check to ensure that information reaches everyone in an undistorted form.

2. As an informal means of supplementing formal channels of communication. Certain subordinates have a reputation for always being "in the know". Many are informal leaders of groups and are usually good workers with a genuine interest in their job. The supervisor should make sure that these people are supplied with the right information to pass on. Often this method of passing information is more effective if used properly because individuals pay more attention to those employees "in the know".

3. As a means of keeping up to date on events so that further information may be obtained from management and passed on quickly to subordinates before rumours can develop.

4. To counteract rumours. Management should supply the facts and demonstrate the truth whenever possible by definite action.

5. As a means of locating the malicious gossiper. There are generally one or two employees in a concern who try to ruin personal reputations and lower morale by continually running down managers and supervisors. The slanders can be discredited quickly if the true facts are fed into the grape-vine. An interview with the person responsible is essential to find out why he acts in this manner, and disciplinary action may be necessary to protect others against his spiteful activities.

Methods of Transmission

There are many means of communication between individuals in a concern. Each has its advantages and disadvantages and particular uses. The main methods of transmission discussed are: speech, writing, signs, actions, silence, and general behaviour and attitudes.

1. Speech

Although oral communication is direct and more personal than written instructions, great care is needed in choice of words and expressions. The message should be given a little thought before it is prematurely announced to someone, otherwise the risk of misunderstanding is increased. Wherever possible use simple words and state the message slowly and distinctly.

After all precautions have been taken, the risk of misunderstanding is still high, therefore always check to be sure that the employee understands clearly. Remember that absolute concentration is difficult in noisy conditions, with other subjects on the mind at the same time.

2. Written communication

From the sender's viewpoint, writing is more difficult as he must make up for the lack of face-to-face contact which affects the tone of the message. Facial expressions and gestures are missing, which means that much of the impact is removed from the communication.

Being able to express a message clearly in writing demands practice. The danger of writing too much or too little is always present. The receiver is inclined to jump to conclusions—nearly always the wrong ones—without checking first because of the remoteness factor.

3. Signs

Signs and indicators form a particular class of visual communication where the loss of impact is a special problem. Notices such as "No Smoking", "Danger", "Handle With Care", "This Way up", "Press Here", "Keep within the white lines", are examples which are often ignored. The usual excuse is that the sign was not noticed. Similarly the use of flags, coloured lights and mechanical devices also has limitations because concentration is necessary. People need constantly reminding, otherwise they tend to forget or overlook the most glaring signs.

4. Actions

Positive demonstration by actually doing something is the best means of communication, it is immediately recognisable by everyone and is the least likely to confuse. The effectiveness of an individual's various senses is not the same. The sense of sight is about 87 per cent effective; hearing 7 per cent and smell, touch, and taste, about 6 per cent. A well-worn saying, "Actions speak louder than words", makes good sense in communication.

5. Silence

The use of silence is probably the most subtle form of communication, but when misused is the stupidest form. As a means of showing displeasure because a particular code of conduct has been ignored it is very effective and harsh. Sending someone "to Coventry" causes the offender feelings of uneasiness and frustration, followed eventually by near panic in some cases.

Another example occurs when an operator is given a thirty-minute job, five minutes before time, by a supervisor who does not bother to enquire if the operator wishes to stay late. The operator's silence may be accompanied by a facial expression which is more than sufficient to indicate his feelings.

Silence can be interpreted in many ways. If the object is to confuse, silence will succeed because the chances of the receiver choosing the correct interpretation of the situation are very remote. Consider for a moment the married man who arrives home and is greeted by silence from his wife. As he runs through all the likely causes, he becomes more and more confused, hence the continued use of this situation in films and television. Although treated as a comedy situation in fiction, this practice has very serious consequences in industry.

Some of the effects of silence on people are: annoyance, indifference, disgust, hurt feelings, fear, suspicion, distrust, amusement, and antagonism. They form an excellent list of feelings which must not be generated in employees. The danger of allowing false impressions to develop generally outweighs the effectiveness of silence and this approach should be used with great caution.

Superiors should also realise the dangers of remaining silent from sheer lack of thought. Imagine the case where a superior leaves and his deputy takes over automatically as people come to him for instructions. Management is silent on the subject, no official communication is issued and the weeks go by. After a while people begin to assume that the deputy has taken over permanently with the approval of authority; he is doing the job well and no word from management indicates otherwise. Suddenly the new superior arrives one morning, quite possibly with no previous word of warning from management. Subordinates, deputy, and new superior are all placed in an uncomfortable position and organisation is disrupted.

6. General behaviour and attitude

Gestures and facial expressions can substitute or reinforce other forms of communication. Another method which should be taken into account is the creation of "atmosphere".

Compared with continental countries people in Britain have very few generally-recognised gestures. These signs are very helpful because everyone knows exactly what is meant when they are used. The "V" sign is a typical example.

Closely associated with atmosphere are the effects of facial expressions. The "sour" face depresses and the bright, cheery face enlightens. Changes in expressions indicate changes in feelings, although some people manage to hide their feelings successfully while others use expressions to gain particular ends. Appropriate expressions are an essential part of conveying a message and help to give it impact and make it more easily understood.

Every person has the ability to create atmosphere, which should not be confused with silence. One person within a group can destroy a friendly atmosphere; this may result in either a tolerable or an intolerable situation. It is highly catching, which probably accounts for the saying about the "bad apple in the barrel".

Causes of Misunderstanding

PROBLEMS OF EXPRESSION

1. Educational level and experience

Allowance for a person's level of education and his amount of experience is essential, otherwise a message can be so worded that it goes completely over his head. Embarrassment may prevent the individual from querying the message in these circumstances. The situation is not revealed until later, when a problem arises because no action was taken by the operator. This problem requires careful treatment when it seems that a subordinate has deliberately ignored an instruction. It is always wise to ask first if the message was clear.

2. Interpretation of words

Words that have definite meanings such as those describing buildings, furniture, tools, machines, and work benches are easy to understand. Confusion occurs, however, when the word describes an object of which there is more than one. Additional words of description are essential in cases where misinterpretation is possible.

Words that have vague meanings should be avoided whenever possible when describing the degree, condition or manner of things. Otherwise they must be explained or their meaning demonstrated.

Some examples of vague words are given in the sentences below.

The job will be finished *soon*.
Give the end of the tool a *light* tap.
Hold the wire in the cutters *gently*.
Slowly withdraw the assembly from the furnace.
This job is *urgent*.
Fix the bolt *securely*.
Make sure the nut is *tight*.
When the liquid is *hot* dip the assembly in and out *quickly*.
Press the valve in a *little bit*.
Mix well before replacing the cap *firmly*.

A moment's thought will show how these instructions could be made more clear and precise.

3. Abstract terms

Words which describe qualities or intangible things should not be used carelessly, as their meaning varies from person to person. Abstract words are often used when people wish to avoid being precise or have not thought about exactly what they mean. The tendency to be vague is because a person feels more secure when he does not commit himself and it requires less mental effort. The effect on subordinates is frustrating because they do not know where they stand.

These are some carelessly-used abstractions: Democracy, Virtue, Peace, Morality, Responsibility, Conformity, Truth, Liberty, Honour, Religion, Power, Poverty, Standard, Progress.

4. Technical jargon

Although the use of technical terms has its place this practice should be avoided in communications intended for those who are not acquainted with the terms. The full meaning is seldom conveyed and often completely misunderstood. Using jargon becomes a habit and some people even think its use makes them appear superior.

5. Gobbledygook

This American word describes the style of speaking or writing which confuses through its complexity. Too often a number of words are used where one would do, or long and uncommon words are used instead of short, simple ones. Here is an example of "gobbledygook":

"The general arrangement in the drilling section has now been made untenable from the risk of fire point of view. The positions of the benches and drill stands have been altered considerably from the previous working layout which allowed the fitters, drillers, and female assemblers free access from the gangways to the emergency exit which was installed three years ago in case of fire."

A suggested revision is:

"The rearrangement of benches in the drilling section has blocked the emergency fire exit."

PROBLEMS OF RECEPTION
1. Company size

As a concern grows, the problems of communication and misunderstanding increase in proportion. More specialists are introduced, each with their own problems of communication. When dealing with others who are unfamiliar with their function, specialists are often misunderstood and so misused. In the growing concern information passes through many more hands and remoteness becomes a danger as keeping in touch with everyone gradually becomes more burdensome. People are less familiar with the whole situation, thus it is easier to misunderstand information.

2. Poor organisation

If each person is not sure of his own authority, responsibilities, and duties in the concern, and also those of his colleagues, inevitably there is considerable uncertainty concerning instructions, official backing, and the importance of a message. Surveys show that poor organisation is common and that many misunderstandings stem from this which could be improved rapidly by clearly defining everyone's function.

3. Previous environment

Memories of past treatment at home and in industry, shape the attitudes of employees. If they have suffered injustices or harshness before, they will be on the defensive. They are often suspicious and prejudiced against their superior's intentions, although the communication may be clear. This inherent tendency to distort the message to suit the individual's attitude towards the sender should be recognised.

4. Class consciousness

Some people seem to thrive on continually emphasising how much better they are by standards of bank balance, blood line, residence, previous schools, culture, or accent. Such people are bores, and some are unaware of the gulf they create with colleagues and subordinates by their immature attempts to assert themselves. This form of assertion is short-sighted, since other people's reaction is more likely to be dislike, jealousy or contempt than admiration. Such feelings will distort messages received and misunderstandings are inevitable.

5. False reasoning

Reasoning must follow a set logical pattern, otherwise it is easy to fall into the trap of associating a statement of fact with some item of knowledge or another factual statement, assuming a connection and jumping to the wrong conclusion. An example of reasoning by deduction, using logic, is given below, followed by a statement of ridiculously obvious false reasoning.

> All dogs have four legs;
> An alsatian is a dog;
> Therefore, an alsatian has four legs.

> All dogs have four legs;
> A cat has four legs;
> Therefore, a cat is a dog.

Although the second example is obviously false, people are inclined to reason along similar lines, confusing facts with possibilities. A cat *may* be a dog on this basis, but without further information one cannot be sure. Always be particularly careful to check the sense of a statement when it is based on the relationship of two connected statements or facts in this way.

6. The wrong context

When conversations are overheard, a misunderstanding may occur because the opening remarks which clarify the subject and throw light on the meaning are missed. An example of how the wrong impression can be caused is given below:

> "He was inhaling oxygen, when suddenly the supply was cut off and he was dead a minute later."

The correct context was an incident in an operating theatre, but it could have been in an aircraft flying at forty thousand feet or in a space capsule on the moon.

7. Thinking in terms of extremes

Some people develop a habit of judging or thinking in terms of extremes at each end of the scale and not appreciating that problems and situations are multi-sided affairs. Not many events are so clear-cut and simple that they fit conveniently into a set pattern. There is a whole range of sides to a problem, each requiring separate consideration. For example, if a machine breaks down because a fuse has blown, the fuse could be replaced immediately. An engineer however, might reason why the fuse burned out, make several checks on the machine before replacing the fuse, and so save the concern money and wasted time on future delays.

DIFFICULTIES OF THE SENDER

The sender must be able to assess the outlook, problems of understanding, and particular interests of the receiver. The right approach produces a more positive reaction and a better response to the message. Every person needs individual treatment which means that judgment plays an important part in successful communication. A friendly approach and giving information form only part of a far more complex programme discussed under human relations and motivation.

The idea that communication is simply passing information from one person to another is quite common, and some companies spend large sums of money with this thought alone in mind. Negligible results are achieved because the full process of communication must include motivating employees by modern leadership. This concept encourages self-discipline through persuasion and consultation, and aims at convincing the employee that management and society want him to develop fully his capabilities.

QUESTIONS

1. Explain the term *communication* and its importance in connection with production and human relations.

2. Discuss the main channels of communication and how the supervisor should use them.

3. Discuss the existence of the grape-vine as an essential channel of communication.

4. Consider some of the common causes of misunderstandings and how they can be overcome by the supervisor.

5. How would you assess the effectiveness of communication in a concern?

6. Why is communication so important in industry?

7. Outline the means of communication and the possible dangers involved, if any, with each one.

8. How can a supervisor use the grape-vine effectively?

9. State the advantages and disadvantages of one-way communication and two-way communication.

10. Why is it essential for formal channels of information to be supplemented by informal channels?

11. "Withholding information unnecessarily can be dangerous." Explain this statement.

12. Discuss the effects of silence as a means of communication.

13. What advice would you give to a supervisor who cannot understand why employees ignore signs, such as "This way up", that he arranges for display at various points?

14. Why do operators and supervisors easily misunderstand information?

CHAPTER XII

COMMUNICATION: PRACTICAL APPLICATIONS

Introduction

IN the previous chapter the importance of communication was outlined, and the various channels and means of communication were discussed. The last section described some of the obstacles to effective communication.

This chapter and the next concentrate on those practical aspects of communication with which the supervisor is mainly concerned.

This chapter discusses the art of listening; how to communicate effectively; order-giving; discipline; grievances; and group discussion. Chapter XIII deals with interviewing; the new employee; committees; report writing; and external aspects of communication.

The Art of Listening

The ability to listen with genuine interest and concentration is an essential part of supervisory skill in communication.

As thought is faster than speech it is easy to be inattentive and let one's mind wander ahead. Much of what is said is missed and the real message is not absorbed. If the speaker senses inattention, then the desire to communicate is lost and communication breaks down in the early stages.

The use of rules for better listening can improve performance considerably if they are followed with persistence.

Rules for better listening

(a) *Maintain undivided attention.* Use the spare time caused by higher thought speed to sift what is said into important and irrelevant points, examine them for validity, try to classify them and decide what is missing. Try to imagine what is coming next and link it with the change of mood or actions of the speaker. This flexible technique will fill the spare thought time and ensure that the mind does not have the opportunity to wander.

(b) *When practicable, find a place with a minimum of distractions and interruptions.* Noise and disturbances will ruin the continuity of a message for both parties, and lead to mutual irritation.

(c) *Show a positive interest.* Some supervisors deliberately pretend not to be interested, but this should only be done when some diplomatic action is called for, e.g. to discourage a request which will cause

resentment to refuse. Intelligent questions and comments in appropriate places help to convince the speaker that he is being heard with
interest and understanding. The atmosphere should improve, and the
sender is more likely to gain confidence and expand on his thoughts.
In other words, listening should be dynamic and magnetic.

(d) *Make due allowance for distortion.* This applies both to supervisor and subordinate. The supervisor must recognise that he is
capable of distorting information as he receives it and of discarding
those parts that do not fit into his own outlook. He should try to
treat the message objectively and ignore any personal feelings towards
the speaker which might influence his reaction to the message. (This
does not mean that the personal approach of being friendly should
be discarded.)

(e) *Be co-operative: allow the speaker to hold the floor and say
everything on his mind.* Anything left unsaid grows and nags soon
after. The supervisor should bear in mind that he does not learn anything while he is talking.

(f) *Do not rely on memory in a long conversation.* Recognise that
memory lets a person down later when a number of points have been
raised which demand some action.

Make a written note and give the reason for doing it. This also
reassures the speaker.

(g) *Improve the art of listening by practising.* There are many
opportunities for experimenting away from the workplace, such as
trying to decipher a relative's conversation at home, using the radio
and television, and listening to conversations on buses and trains.
Attempt to determine the main topic by sorting the major points from
the side-issues and padding. Look for particular techniques in emphasising the subject matter and note the words which arouse particular
feelings and emotions. If there is time, write a summary and check
on the facts for correctness and ambiguity. Look for ideas from facts
and reason out why there is an objection to certain words or phrases.

How to Communicate Effectively

Any plan for communicating effectively should conform to a scientific
or logical method. A general approach is suggested below, which may
be applied to most types of communication, including orders, reprimands, grievances, policy, rules, induction, interviewing, and information passing.

The twelve main steps which the supervisor should practise are as
follows.

1. Clarify the purpose of communication.
2. Classify the type of communication.
3. Obtain the relevant information.

  4. Assess the individual (the recipient).
  5. Determine the best means of communication.
  6. Decide on the channel or channels to use.
  7. Assess yourself (the sender).
  8. Make any necessary arrangements.
  9. Transmit the message.
  10. Check that the message is clearly understood.
  11. Listen carefully.
  12. Follow up.

1. Clarify the purpose

The question to be asked is: what should be the result of the communication? Care is needed to avoid stopping short of the real objective by shallow thinking. For example, if a reprimand is necessary the true purpose of the communication is not to reprimand the individual, but to point out his error. Assist him by trying to help him readjust, if necessary, and by showing fair play to other subordinates. The purpose cannot be achieved unless it is correctly identified at the beginning.

2. Classify the type

The means of achieving the purpose may now be decided and the type of communication chosen, e.g. an order, a reprimand, a discussion, a report or an interview. The communication will often consist of more than one type and the particular points which apply should be studied before proceeding further.

3. Obtain the relevant information

Although the time factor is nearly always against the supervisor, he must make an attempt to gather as much information as possible on the topic. Information is often more easily obtained informally, by talking to the people who are close to the trouble-spot or situation, and their information will contain less distorted material. After the information is found it should be examined and classified. Unnecessary information should be discarded and the remainder translated into simple, straightforward language for easy transmission.

The receiver's viewpoint must be borne in mind; if any vital piece of information is missing, the "grape-vine" will fill the gap. The supervisor ought to check that the message is complete, otherwise he is deliberately or unintentionally creating a distorted picture in the receiver's mind.

4. Assess the individual

Make sure that all aspects have been considered when assessing the person who is to receive the message. The individual's job, background, education, experience, and present social and domestic life all mould his outlook and account for his present mood. His past history should be taken into account and any possible past injustices and problems noted. Many factors will affect his reaction to the message and knowledge of the individual helps in the choice of the best method of communication.

5. Determine the best means

Choosing the best means of communication depends upon such factors as speed, security, accuracy, impression on the recipient, need for a permanent record, and the complexity of the message. When the information is complicated, the answer is to combine different means by using speech, diagrams, notes, and visual aids such as files and charts. Further considerations are the type of impression it is desirable to make and the cost involved. In a large company, information may be announced through a public address system, or in a small company, the general manager may call the employees together and speak directly to them as a group. Naturally, some personal contact is lost but in some circumstances, such as a threatened strike, it may be justified to speak to employees as a group instead of individually. The best means to use will vary as each situation varies.

6. Decide on the channel

The choice depends upon a variety of factors, such as the number of people involved, the importance of the information, status of the individual or individuals concerned, and the time available.

If one person is involved and the message is important, a face-to-face discussion through the formal line of command may be needed. Unimportant information can be passed verbally through a third party, or a note may suffice. A number of channels could be used simultaneously if many people are involved, and they should all receive the information at about the same time. This may be essential to maintain good relationships when union officials and fellow supervisors are concerned with the information. When in doubt it is wiser to use many channels, to avoid the repercussions if someone is overlooked, and the dangerous effects when individuals resort to the grape-vine.

7. Assess yourself

Being honest with yourself is not easy. Self-analysis means recognising your own faults and personal prejudices and your good points. You are influenced by your own background and experience in exactly the same way as other individuals. Consider your objectives and what you will gain or lose by your intended actions. These factors will determine your tendency to understate or overstate your case.

All these points add up to you as a person. Unless you are familiar with your own bias you will be unable to counteract the tendency to twist information you receive and transmit. A common fault is to allow your particular specialisation to distort your outlook which means that you fail to see other specialists' points of view.

8. Make the arrangements

The timing depends mainly on the type of communication. With reprimands or the discussion of grievances, promptness is essential, but there is often more latitude with other types of communication. There may be unavoidable delays if arrangements have to be made for another person to be present, such as a union official or a superior, in which case the delay must be explained to the individual as soon as possible.

If the message is important and requires emphasis, timing again must be given some thought. A message given two minutes before lunch break will obviously get a half-hearted reception, with little or no response from the receiver. Notification of appointments for important communications, e.g. interviews, new policy announcements, reprimands, are communication problems in themselves and similar principles apply.

A further aspect is the question of privacy, and lack of interruptions and distractions. Although very important and essential with some types of communication, these requirements are often out of the question in some establishments owing to pressure of work and poor working conditions. Tact is vital in such situations.

9. Transmit the message

To minimise distortion there should be a friendly atmosphere, clear simple language should be used, and a genuine sense of security created, so that the receiver responds without fear or suspicion.

A careful note of instructions or promises is essential so that future communications on the subject agree with the original statement. Although a mistake made later may be unintentional, the supervisor will have difficulty in convincing subordinates.

10. Check that the message is understood

Do not assume that the message is understood. It is only too easy for people to take it for granted that they have understood. Some nod their heads, indicating that they understand, although they have only partially heard the message; others do not understand but cannot be bothered to query it.

Effective communication implies that checking is an integral part of the process. Failure to check is like setting the hands of a clock correctly and forgetting to wind the spring. A further advantage with the check is that in the process of repeating it, the message is impressed more deeply on the receiver's mind.

11. Listen carefully

Although the point was stressed as the beginning of effective communication, it is listed again here as an essential step in checking that the message is received and acted upon as desired.

The advantages to be gained by listening far outweigh the satisfaction received when transmitting information. People respect those who are prepared to listen attentively. The person who listens is nearly always up to date because individuals will go out of their way to speak if they are sure of a sympathetic hearing.

12. Follow up

Any promises made by the supervisor should be put into action quickly, just as the supervisor expects, and should check, that subordinates take note of his communication without delay. The immediate effect on the individual and his colleagues should be noted. A careful check on the long-term effects is essential until it is apparent that no trouble-spot is developing.

Try to visualise the possible problems which may arise, be ready to spot danger signs and attend to them quickly.

The aspects of communication for the supervisor which are discussed in the rest of this chapter are: order-giving; discipline; grievances; and group discussion.

Order-Giving

The main purposes of giving orders are as follows.

1. To stir people into action to achieve an objective—by giving them information on a situation which demands attention.

2. To indicate that a particular person is held responsible for performing a task—by approaching him, discussing the situation, and arousing in him a strong desire to deal personally with the particular situation.

3. To give the superior the opportunity of contacting the subordinate and issuing instructions—in a way which will be most acceptable.

4. To give the subordinate the maximum opportunity of consulting and participating in the situation—so that he may develop his capabilities fully and display his potential qualities for promotion.

To achieve these purposes the supervisor must treat order-giving as a continuous process of passing information, checking and controlling. True assessment of each individual's capabilities is not possible otherwise.

TYPES OF ORDERS

Although it is possible to classify orders into six types according to method, there are many combinations possible, based upon the words used, the tone of voice, facial expressions, and gestures.

Four other factors also must be borne in mind.

(a) The job to be carried out. The order must be modified to suit the circumstances; these may involve dirty work, difficult tasks perhaps with risks, disagreeable work, actions which may have a detrimental effect on future relationships, or work of high importance.
(b) Personalities involved whom the subordinate may find difficult to approach or deal with.
(c) The type of subordinate who is receiving the order.
(d) The relationships which exist between supervisors and employees, and the general industrial climate.

The six common methods of giving orders are discussed below.

1. The command

A direct or autocratic order is essentially one-way and will get a job done quickly provided it receives an acceptable response. Simple or straightforward tasks, carried out by normal people under favourable conditions, are especially suited for this type of order where there is little to discuss. Such phrases as "Leave that and do this", "Help him now", "Do this", "Get that", are typical examples.

The sensitive operator will often be antagonised by a direct order, whereas the lazy worker may be jolted into action. The order is emphatic and useful when more diplomatic methods fail. The unreliable or troublesome operator may respond to this treatment and, of course, in emergencies immediate response from direct orders is essential.

2. The request

The request is more personal and tactful, arousing a friendly atmosphere of co-operation. The emotionally unstable operator is less likely to take offence as the request softens and displays understanding and sympathy. Examples of opening phrases are "Could you look into this one?" "I wonder if you could arrange for ...?" "Would you mind having a look at...?" "How about having a go at...?" "Do you think you could find out...?"

The request is particularly useful for dealing with subordinates who have made mistakes. Generally they are aware of the error and even when they do not know, it is soon obvious after the request. Some ways of opening the request are "Would you mind correcting it?" "Perhaps you could have another look at this?" "Maybe you could go over this one again?" "Possibly you could improve on this?"

3. The suggestion

This is the mildest form of a request. Mentioning the subject is sufficient to the reliable experienced person, who immediately sees the implication and acts accordingly. There is no demonstrated weight behind the order, which is really thinking aloud, e.g. "Lateness seems to be on the increase", "The floor is rather dirty", "There are more rejects this week", "I have not seen the new assembly yet." This technique allows the receiver to develop his capabilities, but the sender should remember the importance of follow-up in case the remark was not fully understood. A further danger is obvious if this method were used on a new inexperienced employee.

4. The open order

This type gives the receiver the maximum opportunity to experiment and develop his capabilities. The supervisor gives information on what is required, but leaves an adequate allowance for the operator to work out how to perform the tasks. The degree of allowance depends upon the subordinate's experience, his ability to perform the tasks within a time schedule, and to deal effectively with any problem that may arise. The open order provides guiding principles, together with additional essential information, such as deadline dates. This type of order is particularly useful for developing potential leaders.

5. Mutual effort

This advanced type of order is only practicable under conditions of high morale and active participation in a concern where everyone is pulling in the same direction—towards the company's objectives.

The order takes the form of discussing the situation with operatives and the union, when they have a common objective in view; it takes longer to arrive at a solution but the results are more effective and permanent. This form of "combined operations" uses everyone's knowledge and experience and the actual order is unnecessary. All concerned already know what has to be done and they go ahead and solve the problem without any persuasion. The basis of this technique is called the *law of the situation*, which is discussed shortly.

6. Volunteers

Asking for volunteers is useful when it is obvious that choosing a subordinate will upset relationships, and when the task is particularly unsavoury or detestable. The call may arouse in someone the desire to be important, though the same person would probably refuse if approached directly. The danger of receiving no volunteers should not be overlooked when morale is low.

CAUSES OF LOW RESPONSE TO ORDERS
1. Poor approach

If the supervisor adopts the old approach of being the boss and completely ignoring modern methods of leadership he will receive negative reactions. Today's employee is more independent, more aware of his rights, possesses increased power, and will not tolerate harsh, illogical methods of supervision.

Mary Parker Follett wrote an interesting paper on giving orders. One of her ideas was to depersonalise order-giving by supervisors and operatives exchanging information and studying the situation together. This approach reduced any personality problems and indicated that the *law of the situation* itself demanded action, which was far more acceptable to individuals than a superior's instruction. The collected papers written by Miss Follett are published under the title *Dynamic Administration*.

2. Lack of information

If insufficient information is provided by management, or passed on by the supervisor, the chances are that the receiver will not fully understand the order. Errors may occur, and subordinates are less likely to react properly to a situation.

3. Poor assessment of the individual

Unless the true attitude of the receiver is known and his experience is used through genuine consultation, the supervisor will not be able to communicate with him or gauge his response accurately. Poor assessment stifles the individual and wastes his knowledge and capabilities, to the detriment of other employees and of the company.

4. Low morale

A good response to orders is not possible when morale is low. Human relations need improving as well as communication, before any results will be noticeable.

Apart from sensing morale by atmosphere, variations can be measured through productivity, the amount of information flowing to the top, the number of mistakes, complaints, grievances, and strikes, wastage, labour turnover, and the degree of co-operation.

Although morale is difficult to define accurately most people know what is meant by the term. State of mind, outlook, enthusiasm, collective attitude, sensitivity, and co-operation, all add up to morale. Building up morale takes a long time, but knocking it down is easy and rapid.

Causes of low morale have all been mentioned before. They are:

(*a*) poor leadership;
(*b*) very little fairness and justice in all aspects of industrial life, which includes wages, promotion and working conditions;
(*c*) no chance to display initiative;
(*d*) no satisfaction from the job;
(*e*) no feeling of importance.

Discipline

People tend to think of discipline as a system of rules and appropriate punishments when they are disobeyed. This system is quite common. Other forms of more sophisticated discipline demand high morale and enlightened management which, of course, go together. The problem employee, who is instinctively hostile towards authority, calls for reprimands based upon a fair standard of rules and punishments; therefore, such a system is essential and cannot be removed entirely.

A higher form of discipline emerges automatically if employees are well-trained and are allowed to take more part in their work than the simple performance of tasks.

SELF-DISCIPLINE

When employees are given the opportunity to develop their capabilities, the group spirit and general working arrangements with supervisors foster a personal driving force within each individual. This drive is often called *positive discipline*, which urges employees to conform to rules and unwritten codes without restricting their enthusiasm.

The application of negative forms of discipline, such as penalties or fear of dismissal, fall into the background as people find new outlets for their energies through creativeness, sense of belonging, and greater freedom to develop their abilities. The supervisor must be sensitive to the degree of change as individuals begin to practise self-discipline and the organisation structure fosters it. The application of consultation and participation is a long process which means that both types of discipline have to be varied in proportion to suit the situation as it progresses. This process does not give the supervisor the opportunity to shirk his responsibilities for the group he controls. He must continue to use his authority to make unpleasant decisions which someone will probably disagree with at times. A policy of fairness and justice includes imposing penalties, not only to correct the offender, but also in fairness to those who are conforming to regulations. (These matters were raised when discussing Leadership in Chapter IV.)

REPRIMANDING

Negative or imposed discipline uses the system of punishments, which may be rebukes or penalties. The reprimand can easily destroy good relationships unless it is acceptable to the individual and the group to whom he belongs. Although basically acceptance depends on high morale, the way the supervisor handles the actual reprimand will be the main deciding factor in individual cases.

A number of questions must be satisfied before the offender will feel that he has received a square deal. He must understand clearly why he is being rebuked, why the offence demands a reprimand, and, even more important, he must be aware that other offenders have not been allowed to "get away with it". Provided he receives a fair hearing and he is not emotionally unbalanced, the reprimand should be acceptable.

Some basic rules are given below, but the supervisor should remember that *he* is also an individual with good and bad points. He should try to assess and develop his good points so that his technique in dealing with these awkward situations is improved.

Basic rules for reprimanding

1. Be impartial. Treat everyone alike.
2. Make sure the information on the case is correct and complete.
3. Be human. Remember that rules and regulations are guides for the supervisor. He should not interpret them too rigidly. Sympathetic understanding of other people's actions is essential.
4. Always check the information. A good opening is to ask the offender for facts, his views on the case, and his opinion of the rules. This technique gives the employee's "safety valve" a chance to blow a little and may avoid an emotional outburst later. His feelings are made known to the supervisor early in the proceedings which is an advantage.
5. Do not allow your temper to interfere with the discussions at any time. Although the employee may make outrageous remarks about the system and the company, remember that he is under stress and also he is entitled to his views, especially if you have asked for them.
6. Most people have a sense of fairness and are conscientious. If they commit an offence they expect repercussions; therefore, it is pointless to prolong a reprimand by lecturing on the subject. This just encourages feelings of antagonism and disgust to develop in the employee.
7. Be straightforward. Tell the offender what you think has occurred, why you think it must not be overlooked, and the consequences if it occurs again. Make sure that he is aware of all the facts.
8. Try to help the employee. Find out why the offence happened; perhaps something may be bothering him and unless you can win his confidence the true cause will not be found. Avoid arguments and listen carefully to all his comments.
9. When all the information is known, try to be constructive by doing something positive whenever possible. Avoid any form of threat as this will immediately arouse aggressiveness and fear.
10. Another good opening is to praise the employee. Generally there is something you can praise him for, such as good timekeeping, consistently high output, or low absenteeism.
11. Never be sarcastic. Some people do not realise they are being sarcastic until someone points out the fault. The habit easily develops

because it inflates feelings of self-importance. Unfortunately, the receiver is sadly deflated and intense dislike, lack of confidence, and insecurity soon follow.

12. Although timing is important do not hold up reprimands without good reason. Allowing reprimands to accumulate amounts to shirking responsibility and when a supervisor eventually loses his patience, the offender will be astounded and puzzled. He will have the excuse that nothing was said on previous occasions.

Some sense of proportion is essential, however, otherwise the supervisor may be continually rebuking, which is pointless.

13. Always think in terms of the offender's feelings, not your own. Avoid lowering his prestige in front of the group and placing him in a position where he is forced to retaliate to save face. In brief, make sure that any unpleasantness or difficulties are discussed privately, out of sight and hearing.

14. Do not be offhand after the reprimand. You have carried out your responsibility and your relationship should continue to be firm and friendly. Only immature supervisors hold grudges after they have reprimanded and subordinates quickly recognise the fact.

Procedure for reprimanding

A suggested logical approach to reprimanding which uses the basic rules above would be on the following lines.

1. Get your facts right. Check with the employee.
2. Listen carefully to his views and any special circumstances.
3. Explain the rule, why it is necessary, the reprimand for breaking it, and penalties for further violation.
4. Weigh and decide in the light of evidence, previous cases, and the human aspect.
5. Make the reprimand in a straightforward manner and in private.
6. Ask the employee if he has anything further to say; allow the "safety valve" to blow a little.
7. Give any help he may require. If you feel that you have not really got through, and there is something bothering him, follow up until you are satisfied.

Types of reprimand

1. Probably the mildest form of reprimand is a disapproving look, or a few short words to remind the employee of the code of conduct expected from him.

2. The straightforward reprimand would follow the procedure outlined above when an offence is committed. Dependent upon the nature of the offence, the reprimand may be given and forgotten officially, or a note may be given to the next level of authority, or perhaps a written account will be made on the employee's record card.

An indication of a routine would be as follows.

First offence—Verbal reprimand.
Second offence—Written reprimand.

Third offence—Written reprimand, mentioning that the works manager
has been informed and a note has been entered on the employee's
record card.
Fourth offence—Written reprimand and three days' suspension.

Such routines vary considerably depending upon existing agreements and company policy.

3. Some offences may warrant a reprimand and an immediate three
days' suspension. Care must be taken to conform strictly to any
management procedure or trade union agreements in this connection.

4. After a number of reprimands for a similar offence, the question
of terminating employment must again conform to official procedure
and to statutory requirements (*see* Chapter XV).

Serious offences

Although the supervisor may be sympathetic towards an employee
who has committed a serious offence, he must not shirk his social
responsibility in these circumstances. Such cases as gross carelessness
which endangers life, malicious damage to property, indecency, steal-
ing, violence, or insulting behaviour, must be severely dealt with in
fairness to other employees. Invariably this form of offence leads to
instant dismissal.

Grievances

A grievance is any situation or act which is unfair in the eyes of the
complainer. The cause may be the act of a manager, a supervisor, or
an operator, or a situation which is allowed to continue and develop.
The grievance may be held by an individual, a group, a section, or
even a department, and the complainer may be personally involved
or he may act as a representative for others. At this stage, whether
the grievance is right or wrong is unimportant. The employee thinks
he has a legitimate complaint which is very important to him; other
factors are by the way.

The supervisor's role is essentially active, seeking out employees
with grievances and solving the problems quickly in the most effective
way. Knowingly allowing employees to seethe for weeks is inviting
disaster when the upheaval occurs.

BASIC CAUSES OF GRIEVANCES

Some knowledge of the reasons why employees complain, and the
causes of their complaints will help in minimising grievances. Early
action ensures that the grounds for complaint are prevented from
appearing. Sufficient information should be passed to satisfy any
suspicion concerning a particular action to avoid a complaint in a few
days' time.

Employees complain for two main reasons: either because they are emotionally unstable or because they feel there is some unfairness or injustice.

1. The problem employee

The problem employee is easily recognised by his continual waves of complaints, mostly settled by carefully explaining the truth that is distorted in his mind. Unfortunately, some of these employees are beyond the stage where the supervisor can help. When readjustment is not possible, replacements may be necessary and every effort should be made to persuade the individual to seek medical advice.

The inexperienced supervisor may easily confuse the problem employee with one who has a deep legitimate grievance which is hidden by a steady stream of petty complaints. These minor grievances are a symptom of a more basic grievance, which does not emerge until the operator has full confidence in the supervisor, who should listen carefully with sympathy and understanding.

2. Lack of understanding

The second basic cause of grievances covers all those activities of management and supervision which, for many reasons, are unacceptable to employees. This could be summed up as lack of training and understanding of people by managers. In more detail, the problem includes poor communication when breakdowns occur in both directions; poor organisation which is aggravated by violation of principles; unsound policies and rules; general lack of fairness and justice; poor working conditions; overloaded supervisors who do not have sufficient time to assess subordinates and ensure smooth running of the section; inability of supervisors to assess subordinates; favouritism, which may be intentional or unintentional; poor training schemes for managers, supervisors, and operators; jealousy between individuals and sections; and rumours and gossip. There are many more causes, but the above cross-section indicates the depth of the problem which faces the supervisor.

RECOGNISING GRIEVANCES

A grievance is recognisable in two stages. Firstly, when the event occurs which causes the grievance to materialise in the person's mind and secondly, when the person voices the grievance to someone in authority. The second stage does not require any effort from the supervisor except to listen initially, but by this time the complainer has been turning over the grievance in his mind for some time, with obvious effects.

The real problem of recognition occurs at the first stage. Such recognition is very demanding on the supervisor who must be continually on the alert, watching for the danger signs to appear. He should be looking for: changes in attitude in seasoned employees; antagonism; suspicion; indifference; carelessness; day-dreaming; rudeness; slacking; absenteeism; frequent cloakroom visits; gossiping and general carelessness.

Successful discovery of a grievance in its early stages is time consuming; the supervisor must be continually in close contact with subordinates to assess the situation. He must know each individual sufficiently well to notice changes and be able to identify the likely causes. When the supervisor has gained the employee's confidence, the employee feels that he can ask the supervisor immediately for more information, for reasons, or for fairer action and the natural tendency to hold back complaints and suffer unnecessarily is lessened.

In the long run, time spent on observation and settling of complaints in their early stages is economical, compared with the adverse effects and long sessions spent later in sorting out and trying to solve grievances that have reached a complex stage of development.

SOLVING THE GRIEVANCE

Each supervisor should gradually develop his own technique of solving grievances as he becomes more experienced in understanding individuals. How to assess their problems, and their reactions to suggestions and advice must also be considered. Some basic steps are useful as a guide and they indicate the main stages in any investigation of employees' complaints.

1. Knowing the individual

The supervisor should attempt to know as much as possible about the individual. This essential requirement includes studying the employee at work and on the social side, knowing his sentiments and his background, and his attitudes and outlook generally. Accurate assessment is a long, painstaking process. A proportion of the supervisor's time must be allocated for this purpose to avoid an increasing amount of time being spent later on grievances.

2. Watch for change

Being constantly on the look out for changes in individuals is habit forming and becomes a sixth sense after some practice. A change may be due to any number of reasons outside the working environment such as a domestic upset, and is often indistinguishable from a work problem. The change is difficult to correlate with a particular type of problem unless the individual is well known and responds in the same way each time. For example, a close colleague could sense when his mate has had a row with his wife, if he has them fairly regularly.

The supervisor may find it useful to connect events with individuals. Instructions, change in workload, or any alterations in conditions might cause complaint. If the alteration coincides with some change in a subordinate's behaviour, the cause is probably self-evident and the supervisor is provided with some form of opening topic to discuss with him.

3. Analyse change and any information

Attempt to assess the change and what it means in connection with other close associates. Perhaps one subordinate looks distinctly unhappy, while another looks very happy, both being unusual for the two people concerned. The whole group may be antagonistic and this may not be apparent until several people within the group are contacted. A study of the information available and some attempt to couple events with people could give a clue to the problem. A word with other supervisors might help if the situation is puzzling.

4. Consult with employee

(a) *Do not delay in approaching the employee.* Take the initiative and try to persuade him to talk about the grievance. Ask him appropriate questions and lead him on to those topics which may be the cause of the change in attitude. Remember to listen with sympathy and openly show that you understand. If you do not understand, ask more questions until you are sure that everything is clear.

(b) *Presentation of grievance by employee.* If the employee takes the initiative before the supervisor has the opportunity, or because the situation was not known, remember that the person is already emotionally aroused. Allow him to give full vent to his feelings and keep your temper in check. If there is an outburst, let it subside before proceeding along the lines stated above.

People often have difficulty in explaining their thoughts clearly and they may be embarrassed or nervous because of this problem. They may not be sure of the real cause of the grievance themselves until the whole question is talked over carefully and calmly. A combination of events at work and at home may eventually arouse the person into action. People are complex and easily upset. They need help, friendly advice, and often seek it from a supervisor who creates the right atmosphere. A small irritation often becomes a large grievance in the employee's mind and it must be treated as it appears to him.

5. Treatment

Some grievances can be solved by patient listening and showing a complete understanding of the complainer's feelings. If the employee's position is sincerely appreciated and consolation is given, although no action is possible, it relieves the tension and emotional disturbance. The employee may then feel his position is understood and the grievance is solved. Similarly, genuine praise for good work and an assurance that all the conditions under which he works are known and understood, relieve the complaint.

Other grievances demand some positive action—not reassurances or promises that cannot be kept. Shallow promises are fatal and highlight the weak supervisor. If he cannot deal with the situation because it is outside his authority, the facts must be reported *objectively* to his superior. The risk of distorting the story to cover any error on the supervisor's part is not worth while. If the superior interviews the employee and if his story does not agree with the supervisor's report the supervisor's position is not an enviable one.

Often a grievance is solved simply by providing the employee with information, in which case, where the supervisor has not himself withheld the information, he should check on the breakdown in communication.

Finally, some grievances are beyond the solving point. Sometimes there is no way out and unfortunately the problem ends in termination, or perhaps a transfer. Possibly the cause can be traced back to poor interviewing for the job or a drastic change in the individual's outlook through no fault of the concern.

6. Follow-up

No sound grievance-solving procedure is complete until some form of follow-up and checking is made, at intervals, after treatment. If the treatment has been unsuccessful, another discussion is necessary, and so it goes on until a more acceptable solution is found. Patience, understanding and courage to take action are the essential requirements.

Group Discussion

The supervisor may decide to hold a group discussion to talk over a grievance, a problem, or a situation. He assumes the role of discussion leader and preparation for the discussion is normally his responsibility. He should define the objects of the meeting and outline the main topics in some form of order for discussion.

A careful selection of members is essential and should be restricted to those who will be able to contribute their knowledge, experience and ideas on the particular subject. Choosing the right number is generally based upon the inclusion of those who have a direct interest in the problem. About five or six is a good number for ensuring that each member has the opportunity to participate.

Any information which may be needed to supplement the discussion should be provided. Without essential information, valuable time is often wasted arguing over opinions, instead of being spent in intelligent discussion based upon factual information.

CONDUCTING THE DISCUSSION
1. Introduction

(*a*) Establish a friendly relaxed atmosphere and remind members of the purpose of the meeting. Generally, notice of the purpose and main points for discussion should be distributed well in advance to give members sufficient time to think over the problem and make a few notes.

(*b*) Continue with the background information and hand out any further details. Do not expect members to hold figures or complex information in their heads.

2. Stating the case

When the members have settled down a lead should be given by mentioning the controversial or important aspects and asking for opinions or ideas. Perhaps a question could be put forward to stimulate the group or, if this fails, the group leader's opinion may be stated to bring out any reaction.

3. Controlling the discussion

When the discussion is under way the leader must control carefully, keeping to the point, but not stopping any member from having a say. The reluctant member should be encouraged to give his opinion, because the best ideas do not always come from those who have most to say.

When the discussion warms up, control becomes more difficult, as personalities become involved and feelings run high. The tension may be removed by summarising at appropriate points and clarifying a person's remarks to make sure that he is not being misunderstood.

4. Conclusion

When everyone has had the opportunity to speak and fully discuss the problem, the leader may reach a conclusion and recommend certain actions. He should note any further comments and thank the members for attending.

The work of committees is dealt with in the next chapter, with other aspects of communication.

QUESTIONS

1. State how the supervisor can improve his performance in the art of listening.
2. What are the main purposes of giving orders?
3. What factors should be borne in mind when giving orders?
4. Discuss the main ways of giving orders and suggest suitable situations for their use in each case.
5. In what circumstances would a supervisor resort to a direct command and when should he avoid its use?
6. "Many supervisors blame their subordinates when they receive a low response to their orders." Comment on this statement.
7. How would you encourage self-discipline among your subordinates?
8. When should a supervisor use negative forms of discipline?
9. What precautions should be taken before reprimanding a subordinate?

10. What advice on reprimanding would you give to a newly promoted supervisor?

11. Suggest a logical procedure for dealing with a reprimand.

12. What action would you take, as a supervisor, if you saw an employee who was not in your department deliberately damaging a machine?

13. How can a supervisor use subordinates' complaints constructively?

14. Discuss the basic causes of employees' complaints and the role of the supervisor when dealing with this problem.

15. How would a supervisor recognise the symptoms of a complaint before it is aired by the employee?

16. Outline the basic steps in solving a grievance.

17. How would you conduct a group discussion?

CHAPTER XIII

COMMUNICATION: FURTHER ASPECTS

Interviewing

WHENEVER the supervisor is conversing with another person and information is being exchanged, he is interviewing or being interviewed. The broad concept of an interview goes well beyond the general impression that interviews are solely connected with employment. A wide range of interviews takes place every day on topics such as induction, training, grievances, suggestions, wages and merit rating, discipline, policy, regulations, operating problems, and personnel counselling. *Interviewing*, in this sense, becomes an active two-way process of exchanging information, ideas, and opinions between people, while the term *communication* forms the passive link between people throughout the concern. The exception which illustrates the difference is a *direct order* which is one way, not an interview, but nevertheless a communication.

Although experience is invaluable in the art of interviewing, the supervisor should also take full advantage of books written by specialists on the subject (*see* Bibliography). Reading soon dispels any common misconceptions that interviewing is easy and that individuals can be assessed accurately at first sight, or in thirty minutes.

The inherent problems of interviewing are: making people feel at ease; knowing the right questions to ask; recognising faults and elaborations; being able to size up people, and not allowing personal prejudices to interfere.

Interviewees tend to create impressions of what they think they are or would like to be, which of course is natural, but misleading to the interviewer. Similarly, when individuals pass on information, the tendency to give favourable impressions of themselves causes them to slant the information to conform with this pattern.

TYPES OF INTERVIEW

There are five types of interview used in various situations, including the application for employment:

1. Closed. 2. Open. 3. Self-controlled.
4. Group discussion. 5. Board or Committee.

1. Closed interviews

This type follows a set pattern of asking questions which are

planned to cover all the requirements of a particular job. Considerable skill is required to overcome the stereotyped approach. Learning the questions and being able to vary their order helps to break
up a rigid or formal effect.

An advantage is that all the essential information is gathered
together, and the interviewee is also given sufficient information to
make a decision. Careful planning is needed to cover all the aspects
of the job and, whenever particular skills must be demonstrated,
the interviewee is passed to a specialist who checks the requirements
personally.

The closed interview can be very impersonal unless the right
atmosphere is established by the interviewer.

2. Open interviews

This type offers more scope for the skilled interviewer to make a
better assessment of the individual. Although a job specification and
information on the concern is used, the object is to put the interviewee at ease, draw him out on the subjects under discussion, and
steer him carefully on to new topics.

The open interview is closely coupled with the closed type as both
have a certain object in mind, that is, to obtain and give particular
information.

3. Self-controlled interviews

When suggestions, complaints, or grievances are presented, the self-
controlled interview allows the interviewee to express himself fully
without worrying about time limits. The interviewer plays a "near
passive" role by listening sympathetically and agreeing periodically
with the interviewee.

If the interview starts "drying up", the interviewer must be sufficiently skilled to encourage the interviewee to gain confidence and
air his thoughts openly.

4. Group discussions

A well-conducted group discussion is an excellent way of exchanging
information and fostering new ideas. The right atmosphere of co-
operation and enthusiasm must be induced.

The discussion may be conducted with a specific subject in mind,
or as an open discussion to see what may develop. The group
approach was discussed more fully in the previous chapter.

5. Board or committee

This technique subjects the individual to a number of interviewers
who are known as a board or committee. The interviewee will
probably feel very nervous when confronted by, say, six people who
in turn ask questions based upon their own particular experiences.

Facing up to such an ordeal is part of the technique, but there are variations; for example, where the individual is interviewed privately by each member of the board. The opinions of each member are then examined and analysed by the board and if agreement is unanimous, the choice is made.

EMPLOYMENT INTERVIEW

The interviewer must have a sound knowledge of the job, including the degree of authority and responsibility and the duties involved, to form a clear picture of the personal qualities required. A questionnaire should be designed which includes all the information needed from the applicant. In addition, the applicant will be interested in the company, its policies and regulations, the products, working conditions, social activities and pension schemes. All this information should be available and accurate.

Various plans have been designed to assist the interviewer in his assessment of the candidate and his suitability for a particular job. The Seven-Point Plan of the National Institute of Industrial Psychology is one example. This plan was devised by Professor Alec Rodger and used in vocational guidance work by the Institute. There are seven headings and each one contains a number of questions, as detailed below.

The Seven-Point Plan

1. *Physical make-up.* Has he any defects of health or physique that may be of occupational importance? How agreeable are his appearance, his bearing and his speech?

2. *Attainments.* What type of education has he had? How well has he done educationally? What occupational training and experience has he had already? How well has he done occupationally?

3. *General intelligence.* How much general intelligence can he display? How much general intelligence does he ordinarily display?

4. *Special aptitudes.* Has he any marked mechanical aptitude? manual dexterity? facility in the use of words? or figures? talent for drawing? or music?

5. *Interests.* To what extent are his interests intellectual? practical-constructional? physically-active? social? artistic?

6. *Disposition.* How acceptable does he make himself to other people? Does he influence others? Is he steady and dependable? Is he self-reliant?

7. *Circumstances.* What are his domestic circumstances? What do the other members of the family do for a living? Are there any special openings available for him?

A development of the Seven-Point Plan was introduced in 1950 by John Munro Fraser in his well-known book *Employment Interviewing*. This plan is called a five-fold framework and Table VI illustrates the main features. An assessment for each grade is based upon the distribution of human differences which was mentioned in Chapter VIII.

The final arrangements which should be made before the interview are to ensure that:

1. all the questions to be asked are clear;
2. sufficient time is allowed to complete the interview thoroughly;
3. the applicant is notified of the arrangements.

The introduction

Reception arrangements and appropriate accommodation are an important aspect for establishing the confidence of the applicant. Every attempt should be made to put the individual at ease. Naturally he is nervous, and time should be allowed for him to settle down. Any quick assessment should be avoided and the interviewer must be extremely careful not to give the wrong impression because the applicant will be judging him as well during these critical early stages.

A short chat on any topic which is familiar to both parties helps to relieve the tension and establish a friendly relationship.

Exchange of information

As the interview develops, information will flow in both directions. The interviewer should be seeking attitudes as well as facts, which can only be found by listening carefully to assess pauses, evasiveness, embarrassment, over-elaboration or sketchiness.

The interviewer is not there to impress, nor to show his personal feelings. True assessment demands concentration and, if there is a doubt, the topic should be clarified by asking further questions until the position is clear.

The interview must be controlled smoothly and scientifically.

The conclusion

The interview will gradually draw to a close quite naturally, and sufficient time should be allowed for this to happen. Both sides will run out of questions, but the interviewer should allow the applicant a little time to think of any further points which are often forgotten under stress of the interview.

The applicant should be thanked courteously for attending and the conclusion given to him, if possible. No doubt should be in the applicant's mind about the job or the company. He will then feel that he has had a fair interview with the fullest opportunity to state his case.

THE NEW EMPLOYEE

The importance of communication to the new employee is often neglected because most existing employees take their surroundings for granted and fail to see the strange picture presented to the new-

Table VI—The Five-fold Framework

		Grade E (bottom 10%)	Grade D (lower 20%)	Grade C (middle 40%)	Grade B (upper 20%)	Grade A (top 10%)
Impact on others		Dirty clothes and sullen expression. Difficult to understand, with manner causing others to avoid him whenever possible.	Rather scruffy in appearance, with local accent and limited vocabulary. Manner rather off-putting through lack of self-confidence.	Undistinguished in appearance, while his speech and manner attract little attention. Difficult to call to mind after we have met him.	Well turned out. Expresses himself with enough confidence to meet most situations.	Very pleasant to talk to; shows interest in what one says. Has considerable attraction in other ways.
Qualifications and Experience	General education	Incapable of normal education; school for educationally subnormal	No recognised qualifications in examination passes. Lower-streamed classes.	Some passes in C.S.E. at lower or middle grades.	G.C.E., "O" Level to "A" Level.	University degree from pass to Honours level.
	Vocational training	Left to pick up the work by himself.	Unsystematic on-the-job training, limited to work to be done.	Systematic training at work with part-time classes, but no publicly-recognised qualifications.	Higher National Certificate or Diploma or similar standard at local college.	Equivalent to a university degree at polytechnic or similar institution.
	Work experience	Unskilled work on simple tasks that call for a minimum understanding.	Semi-skilled work on jobs that have been pre-planned and are carried out to set standards.	Work calling for varying levels of skills and knowledge. Mainly routine involving little planning or decision-making.	Middle or supervisory management posts, responsible for day-to-day operations.	Higher management, mainly concerned with long-term planning.

Innate abilities	Mentally subnormal.	Slow in understanding and tending to reach over-simplified interpretations.	Capable of taking in everyday affairs but has difficulty in understanding new or complex ideas.	Above-average intelligence, but lacks the extra spark that would push the pendulum into grade A.	Quick and active mind capable of taking in all sorts of information, interpreting it effectively and thinking up new ideas.
Motivation	Incapable of supporting himself and completely dependent on other people.	Lacks initiative to find means of applying his effort satisfactorily. Tends to rely on others to organise his work and spare time.	Motivation adequate for routine work, provided someone is available to deal with unexpected problems.	Hard-working, with enough initiative to overcome day-to-day difficulties.	Very high level of drive and enthusiasm; always succeeds in finding outlets that provide self-realisation.
Emotional adjustment	Incapable of adapting to normal social roles and frequently requires special treatment.	Has difficulty in meeting the demands of normal roles and tends to be found "awkward" by colleagues.	Fits into normal roles acceptably, but may become emotional when anything unforeseen crops up.	Tends to be accepted in central roles as others find they can depend on him in difficulties.	Capable of social roles that involve continuous stress; remains calm and rational in the most difficult situations.

comer. First impressions tend to mould attitudes towards individuals, the concern, and the job. These attitudes remain fixed and are very difficult to change, hence the increasing interest in induction schemes which help the newcomer to adjust rapidly to his surroundings and which create more favourable impressions.

The main points to remember are as follows.

1. First impressions are important.
2. Be friendly.
3. Try to put the new employee at ease.
4. Show him all the amenities.
5. Have patience when teaching him the job.
6. Praise him when he does a good job.
7. Check for any problems periodically.

The question of induction is discussed in Chapter XV on Employment and Remuneration.

Meetings and Committees

The object of committee work is to provide opportunity for people representing the functions or sectors which come under the committee's sphere of activity to meet and act as a group. Under the guidance of a chairman, information and ideas from each sector can be pooled and discussed in order to reach more accurate and balanced decisions. Provided the meeting is conducted properly, closer co-ordination between sectors should automatically follow.

A good chairman is essential. He must conduct the meeting firmly, using the correct procedure, and planning carefully throughout the life of the committee.

Each member must be conscientious to a point where his own and his group's interests are subordinated to the common interest, that is, the objective set for the committee. The chairman can control this factor when it is obvious, but unfortunately self-interest can be shielded when specialists are drawn together. Besides problem-solving, the meetings help people to appreciate other points of view, and so broaden their outlook. As the body of knowledge grows, people have to specialise on narrowing fronts, which increases the problem of trying to understand the over-all picture and the problems of other specialists.

The type of authority given to a committee affects its status and procedure.

The first type is *direct*, where members vote and are responsible as a committee for the decisions implemented.

The second type is *advisory*, assisting the manager, who is chairman of the meeting. He gathers the knowledge and experience of members, and proposals are discussed; then he makes the decision and is responsible for it.

The third type makes *recommendations* to the manager, who is not the chairman. He considers the proposals later, and either accepts or provides the committee with an adequate reason for rejection.

Committees also are held for other purposes, such as *consultation*; for example, where representatives of management and employees are brought together to give their views, and "communication by committee" ensures that information is received by all interested parties.

To summarise, ideally committee work is an excellent means of supplementing the organisation framework providing a meeting-ground for individuals from different parts of the concern, who normally would not have much direct communication. Purposeful control and suppression of self-interest are difficult to achieve, and as a result, some committees have a poor reputation and become known as "time-wasters". However, much invaluable work is done at meetings to co-ordinate activities and to improve the effectiveness of organisation.

ATTENDING MEETINGS

The main points to consider when attending meetings are as follows.

1. Study the constitution of the meeting which gives the rules for conducting proceedings.

2. Enquire from the secretary for suitable dress.

3. Study the previous minutes of the meeting, the agenda and any information forwarded in advance.

4. Prepare any facts or figures which you will need to state your views.

5. Send a written apology or telephone the secretary if you are unable to attend, as soon as you are aware of the fact.

6. Plan to arrive five minutes before the meeting commences.

7. During the meeting, always address your words to the chairman unless directed otherwise.

8. Think carefully before you speak as you will be judged by your words and ideas.

9. Make your speeches clearly, slowly, and with brevity.

10. Do not take offence at criticisms of your views. They are probably made with as much sincerity as your suggestions. Remember the object of group discussion is to discuss the best solutions to problems by team effort, which means constructive criticism, putting forward ideas, and arriving at several conclusions.

11. Listen attentively and use the spare time to think over proposals.

12. Criticise constructively and tactfully.

13. Ask questions if you are uncertain about any point or if you do not understand clearly the decisions reached.

14. Avoid any comments and suggestions after the meeting. The time to speak is at the meeting and failure to comment until later indicates that you are uncertain of yourself.

NOTE: The main technical terms used at meetings are given in Appendix I.

THE MEETING AS A MEANS OF PERSUASION

On some occasions the supervisor may have difficulty in persuading management to take an obvious and essential course of action. When these circumstances are known to everyone and management remains indifferent, it is possible to ask for a meeting to be arranged to discuss the question.

In many cases this will be agreed and, by the time the meeting is held, the chances are that management has already acted to avoid embarrassment.

Report Writing

An efficient communication system has to rely, to some extent, upon the conscientious provision of written reports. Neglecting to render worthwhile reports has resulted in disastrous blunders, poor decisions, and wasted time.

A report is a written account of an event or situation, together with relevant facts, figures and recommendations where required. The purpose is to provide information to those who are concerned with or responsible for taking some action on the matter.

Every supervisor who is responsible for a number of subordinate supervisors soon realises the importance of the reports he receives from them; but he, in turn, must attach a similar importance to the report he conveys to his superiors. He will expect the reports received to be clear, accurate, concise, logically arranged, and on time; and he must conform to similar standards in making his own reports.

READABILITY

The report must be easy to read and understand otherwise the reader will be distracted by the wording. One method of calculating readability is called the Fog Index, which increases in value as the writing becomes "foggier".

The index is calculated in the following way.

1. Work out the average number of words in each sentence in a passage of about 100 words by dividing the total number of words with the number of sentences. The final sentence in the passage should be included or excluded depending upon which word count is nearest to the 100 word total.

2. Count the words containing three or more syllables in the passage, but excluding proper nouns and easy compound words, i.e. words beginning with a capital letter and words such as "extend" or "repress' when they appear as "extend*ed*" or "repress*es*" should not be included.

3. The results of one and two are added and multiplied by 0.4 to give the Fog Index.

A passage with an index of six is very easy to read, while an index of seventeen is extremely difficult. Any figure above twelve is considered to be difficult to read. The Fog Index may be improved by restricting a sentence to about two ideas and eighteen to twenty-two words; keeping sentences short, but varying their length and structure; linking and relating sentences to each other; and using short-syllable words wherever possible.

Other points to note are: use adequate conjunctions (and, but, with, that, etc.); avoid lengthy prepositional phrases (for the reason that = because); wherever possible use short-syllable familiar words; and avoid passive verbs ("The rollers' position is changed to ..." becomes "The rollers move to ...").

TYPES OF REPORTS

One method of classifying reports is to split them into their main types:

1. personal accounts;
2. routine reports;
3. special reports.

The first two are fairly straightforward accounts of incidents or events, including facts and figures. Personal accounts include presenting information, as witnessed at the time, on events such as accidents, social disturbances, and disciplinary action. Routine reports include all information passed to control points on topics such as production progress, machine breakdowns and idle time, which are everyday occurrences.

The third type is for unusual events which are generally far more involved. The report includes investigations, analysis of information, illustrating the significance of findings and often recommending courses of action. Careful planning and a logical approach are needed, otherwise the reader will spend considerable time wading through the material in an attempt to sort out the sequence of events and the points to be noted.

PROCEDURE

A recommended approach is detailed below.

1. The object of the report.
2. Preparation—method of investigation, area, etc.
3. Collecting information.

4. Collating the report.
5. Revision.

1. The Object

Make sure that the aim of the report is perfectly clear. Any ambiguity or uncertainty in the terms of reference should be clarified before proceeding further. The terms of reference must give sufficient detail to establish accurately:

(a) the topic of investigation;
(b) the limitations, if any, of the enquiry;
(c) the purpose of the report.

2. Preparation

Before enquiries and the collection of information commence, it is essential to prepare a framework of investigation. Work can then proceed to a flexible plan which may be revised as necessary when fresh information becomes available. The plan should be based upon such factors as assessment of the likely difficulties, the time factor, amount of co-operation from employees, degree of secrecy, amount of detail required, known availability of facts, possible repercussions from certain individuals, and any special requirements for the report.

The reader must be considered when drawing up the plan. An assessment through personal knowledge, previous experience, or by discreet enquiries, will enable the writer to decide how much detail is needed, depending on what information is already known to the reader, whether technical jargon or plain language should be used, and the reader's likely reaction to the significance of the findings as they may affect him.

3. Collecting Information

Collection of information and ideas should proceed according to the plan. The sources of information are found by personal knowledge, or by using the "chain method" of asking one person, who suggests another, and so on. Careful observation, reading and experiment form part of the technique.

Notes should be made immediately whenever possible, and in sufficient detail, for very brief notes are often difficult to decipher later. The use of rough sketches assists the writer in refreshing his memory. An important precaution is always to identify the source of information.

4. Collating the Report

The first draft of the report should be written within a suitable framework, usually made up of headings, such as the ones given below.

(a) The subject.

(*b*) Introduction.
(*c*) Findings.
(*d*) Conclusions.
(*e*) Recommendations.
(*f*) References.
(*g*) Summary.

The report must also be dated and signed.

(*a*) *The subject.* Terms of reference should be stated in full. In some instances the source and date of directive should be given, especially if copies are to be sent to various departments.

(*b*) *Introduction.* The method of conducting the investigation should be given, together with any major difficulties which were encountered. Any major gaps in the report must be mentioned and an assessment of their importance given. If background information is considered to be of use, it may be mentioned at this stage. Any relevant information which does not fit conveniently into the rest of the framework of the report may be included in this section. Examples are: the general attitude of employees towards the subject; degrees of secrecy; explanations of courses of action, or necessary technical jargon.

(*c*) *Findings.* This section forms the main body of the report which includes all the facts presented in logical sequence and in an unbiased manner. Whenever possible, it is a good plan to tabulate the facts; this has the advantages of clarity to the reader and easier preparation for the writer.

(*d*) *Conclusions.* An analysis of the facts, and all the inferences and value judgments should be included in this section. Adequate explanations of conclusions drawn from the facts are essential, otherwise the reader will be unable to assess their value. Logical conclusions based upon a number of facts are generally straightforward and immediately acceptable, but if experience and judgment are included in the basis, this should be stated.

(*e*) *Recommendations.* Recommendations are based upon the findings and conclusions. If there are a number of choices available, they should be weighted with arguments for and against each one. Some of the important factors may be: the cost, time, disruption of production, human problems, availability of supplies, and space.

(*f*) *References.* References to any documents or books should be listed in this section. Sufficient information should be given for easy location. Naturally this section may be omitted if there are no references mentioned.

(*g*) *Summary.* A brief outline of the report is essential for some people who have insufficient time to read the full story. Care is needed to ensure that the correct meaning of each section is conveyed. Figure 23 gives an example of the layout of a summary page.

```
┌─────────────────────────────────────────────────────────────┐
│                  TITLE                    Page 1              │
│                                                              │
│  Terms of Reference..........................                │
│                                                              │
│  Introduction. . . . . . . . . . . . . . . . . . . . . Date............│
│                                                              │
│  Summary of Findings                                         │
│                                                              │
│  1 :                                                         │
│                                                              │
│  2 :                                                         │
│                                                              │
│  3 :                                                         │
│                                                              │
│  4 :                                                         │
│                                                              │
│  5 :                                                         │
│                                                              │
│  Conclusions.................................................│
│                                                              │
│  Recommendations............................................ │
│                                                              │
│                                              Signature       │
└─────────────────────────────────────────────────────────────┘
```

Fig. 23.—*Summary page of Report.*

A single-page summary of a report is necessary for those who will not have sufficient time to read the full report, and is also convenient for those who have. Clear, logical layout is important, and the figure shows a sample layout and the points to be included.

5. Revise

Whenever possible, wait at least a few hours before attempting to revise the first draft. A slight change of mood provides sufficient variance of insight which helps considerably in rendering a more balanced report. The document should be read critically and objectively. Try to be scathing and remove all unnecessary words.

If a person can be found who will give an honest constructive view of the report, the second draft should be submitted to him for comment.

ESSENTIAL REQUIREMENTS OF A REPORT

1. On time.
2. Accurate, concise, and clear.
3. Tactful and unbiased.
4. Logically arranged and complete.
5. Depth of investigation consistent with importance of subject.
6. Conclusions and recommendations aligned with the facts.
7. Illustrations used where words are inadequate.
8. Stimulates interest, otherwise no one will read it.

External Aspects of Communication

All employees are subjected to many external forms of communication which affect their attitudes and opinions regarding the company, the management, supervisors and the work.

MASS MEDIA

The information comes either from individuals, or from the many forms of mass media: the press, radio, television, hoardings, illuminated signs, and publicity handouts. Although advertising, news, and entertainment predominate in these external forms of communication, there are many occasions when commercial and industrial activities are featured. Such activities often form the basis for reports, broadcasts, films, exhibitions, conferences, educational talks, and group discussions.

A few examples illustrate the point. Results of research and development programmes, a new machine, new products, new buildings, anniversaries, take-over bids, moves to new areas, and many other topics of interest are frequently featured as news items in various media.

Some large concerns employ specialists who develop suitable news stories and ensure that the firm's noteworthy activities are properly publicised. Their work is discussed further in the next section.

Writers with controversial viewpoints and persons of experience or in prominent public positions, including personalities from industry and commerce, are often quoted and invited to publish articles, or to appear on radio and television. This democratic freedom of speech provides an important source of information and opinion for the public which, of course, includes employees.

IMPACT OF EXTERNAL COMMUNICATION

The impression on the public is difficult to assess when such problems as strikes, wages, productivity, economic survival, management, ownership of industry, industrial disputes, and union activities are discussed and reported through the different media. The effect on the community depends on factors such as the individual's ability to reason for himself, educational background, the degree of experience in connection with a particular topic, open-mindedness, and the amount of attention paid to the communication. People tend to pay less attention to matters which do not affect them, to unpleasant news, and to announcements from people or organisations they dislike. On the other hand, repetition of information tends to break down resistance, especially when several channels of communication are used, and people are inclined to follow the crowd.

In many ways the community is becoming more enlightened and

sophisticated as a result of the large increase in these external forms of communication. The spread of information and constructive discussion on the shop floor break down those rigid, traditional outlooks which are no longer realistic, and which constantly hinder Britain's efforts to compete economically with countries like Japan, France, West Germany, and the U.S.A.

SOURCES OF INFORMATION

If the supervisor can keep himself well informed of current developments and opinions he will be better able to guide and advise his subordinates, influencing their outlook for the mutual benefit of employees, the organisation, and the nation's economy. Besides the external forms of communication already mentioned, there exists a vast range of reference and textbooks available from libraries. Books are continually appearing on the market dealing with the latest techniques and ideas, but only a limited number of people read them; the majority of those who should be vitally concerned with these matters (including managers) often remain blissfully ignorant of their very existence. Cost should present no problem as any library will obtain a book on request. Some reference books which are of general interest and useful sources of information are listed separately in the bibliography.

PUBLIC RELATIONS

In recent years many companies have begun to appreciate the importance of establishing good relationships with the community. Less advanced concerns, which concentrate on advertising their products alone, have failed to realise how far changed social conditions and technical progress have given greater weight to public opinion, often with far-reaching effects.

A company cannot afford to ignore the community, for a number of reasons. The community provides: the market for the product; present and future employees; suppliers of materials and services; and the cash to finance the business. A company's prosperity depends to a large extent on whether the public feels that the concern is worth supporting, i.e. on its public image. Poor quality products, bad service, unsatisfactory treatment of employees, general inefficiency and also lack of publicity will detract from a firm's image. People tend to be influenced by the opinions and experiences of friends and relatives, and satisfied customers will attract others.

The aim of public relations

Public relations seeks to expand the field of company promotion well beyond the normal channel of advertising its products. Explanations of policy, news of improvements and any factors enhancing the prestige of the company are part of a publicity programme which is designed to appeal to an individual's community spirit, national pride, general curiosity and self-interest. Some companies publish their annual accounts, which include the balance sheet and parts of the profit and loss account. Statements on progress are made to the press and a report on the company appears as an advertisement in national newspapers. This sort of publicity helps to build the company image, as well as attracting investors. A further practice is to circulate half-yearly and yearly reports to employees. These reports explain the financial accounts and indicate future objectives, helping to foster pride and personal interest in the firm's progress.

Company policy is also influenced directly and indirectly by Government measures and policies in the various fields of industrial activity. Public relations departments must be careful not to provoke political controversy and Government disapproval inadvertently.

The breadth of external communication may pose serious problems in public relations. For example, an independent report in the press or on television may present facts (or just other points of view) which completely undermine a carefully-planned publicity campaign and reveal errors and failures in company direction.

The role of the public relations officer

The Public Relations Officer (P.R.O.) must be able to convey the most favourable image of the concern to the community. He achieves this aim by choosing the appropriate media for the different groups of people whom the message will affect, e.g. a particular trade journal for purchasers of one product. The various groups interested must be analysed and their importance for the purpose of the campaign assessed.

The need for the right type of psychological approach makes public relations an art. Creating favourable impressions involves assessing the possible reactions to the information to be conveyed and then circulating the message in the most suitable ways.

A common example illustrates this psychological approach. Electricity Boards often make no attempt to hide the fact that they are digging up the road and causing traffic congestion, although to many people it would be difficult, at a glance, to know which public service was at work. A large sign is displayed stating that the Electricity Board apologises for the inconvenience caused to the public and explaining the reason for the work, such as a new main to feed a housing estate.

On a national level, P.R.O.s can contribute towards convincing the community of the urgent need for higher productivity. Raising the prestige of companies helps to create better relationships between the community and industry, eventually, it is hoped, increasing the public's desire to co-operate towards this vital objective. The ignorance and suspicions which led employees to violent action in the early years of the Industrial Revolution today take more subtle forms—machine smashing has been replaced by "go-slows", apathy and dissension—but a similar problem of communication remains. Public opinion as a whole must be changed, through the psychology of public relations, before any permanent effect will be felt within industry itself.

QUESTIONS

1. Discuss the importance of developing a good interviewing technique in connection with supervision.
2. Describe how you would conduct an employment interview.
3. "The importance of reports is often overlooked." Discuss this statement.
4. Outline a logical approach in preparing a written report.
5. Discuss the essential requirements of a report.
6. What advice would you give to a colleague who is going to attend his first meeting as a member of a committee?
7. Put yourself in the place of a new employee and describe your feelings and what information you would hope to receive from your supervisor.
8. Outline a logical method of communicating effectively.
9. Discuss the importance of external aspects of communication in connection with the supervisor's role as a leader.
10. Why is public relations considered so important today?
11. Outline the various types of interview.
12. Discuss the Five-fold Framework illustrating the main features of the plan.

CHAPTER XIV

THE PERSONNEL FUNCTION

Introduction

THE purpose of the personnel function is to provide a specialist who is capable of creating and administering a suitable working environment in a concern which will attract and keep an effective complement of employees.

The personnel specialist must be highly skilled and experienced in such topics as employment negotiations, wages structures, industrial relations, education and training, health and safety, and general welfare services. He must be a good communicator, really understand human beings, and possess a deep understanding of his function in a concern. If any of these qualities are missing he will quickly gain a poor reputation.

A supervisor cannot be expected to possess the knowledge of a personnel manager and yet all the above essentials of personnel administration are needed to maintain an effective working force. In medium- and large-size concerns such a specialist can be afforded and full use of his capabilities must be made by all line supervisors. In the small concern the function cannot be ignored, but by necessity it has to be carried out by supervisors and managers alone. Regardless of company size the functions of personnel work should be clearly understood and practised by all supervisors.

Maintaining a stable force of employees is an economic necessity. The cost of finding suitable employees is continually growing in an age of rapid technological change, housing shortage, and rising wage rates. Training an individual is often unavoidable and expensive. He must fit the job otherwise he will be frustrated and probably leave or be dismissed. Careful selection and reasonable working facilities are essential. Good relations between management, trade unions, and employees must be created and maintained, otherwise industrial unrest will ruin any attempts to improve productivity. All these factors are part of the personnel function.

The success of the personnel specialist can be seen by improvements in labour turnover, the degree of satisfaction in performing jobs, higher productivity, and the advancement of individuals through improved capabilities. The spirit of an organisation should show considerable improvement in the long run.

A closer examination (in the next section) of the activities of a personnel department soon reveals that a personnel manager cannot work successfully in isolation. He needs full support from management and supervisors in all aspects of his duties. Similarly, those supervisors who cannot see the necessity for using an expert in personnel work will be unsuccessful.

Management of people is recognised today by many concerns as being of equal importance to managing finance, machines, equipment, and materials. The strong need for centralising and co-ordinating personnel functions throughout an organisation has resulted in the employment of personnel managers in many establishments, but employing a specialist alone does not solve the problem. Top management must be prepared to use him effectively which often means that high ranking managers must change and come into line with the personnel policy prepared by the specialist.

Some managers give the impression that they employ specialists to be in the fashion, not because they sincerely believe in the function they perform. Frustrated personnel managers are not uncommon. Management policies and personnel policy must be reconcilable, and both ought to be actively pursued.

Naturally there are good and bad specialists in any profession and personnel management is no exception. To some extent it depends upon what management is prepared to pay. The supervisor should try to assess the specialist, noting carefully the effectiveness of his advice.

Many personnel departments have been very successful where management has co-operated and the importance of the personnel function will continue to grow at a time when more emphasis is being placed on selection, training schemes, and co-operation with unions.

Activities of a Personnel Department

The activities which are generally recognised as coming under the province of a personnel manager are given below.

1. Employment
In order to fulfil this activity successfully, it is necessary to begin with consideration of the job itself. Surveys of existing and proposed jobs are needed in order to plan ahead and to draw up accurate descriptions of requirements.

Further activities cover these aspects: liaison with the sources of prospective employees; knowledge of terms and conditions of employment; understanding of existing and proposed legislation affecting personnel; interviews connected with engagement, transfer, termination, and dismissal; procedure for any employee movement; maintenance of personnel records; preparation of personnel statistics; committee work associated with personnel; and induction procedure for new employees.

2. Remuneration

The personnel department is responsible for providing accurate information on wages and salaries for the wages section of the accounts department. The wage and salary structure should be administered fairly by careful application of scales of pay, merit rating schemes, and bonus systems. Any changes in remuneration must be properly authorised.

Assessment of pay in similar industries and consultation with unions and work study engineers concerning pay rates also form an important part of personnel work.

3. Education and training

Procedures for training new employees and schemes to improve employees' capabilities form an important part of personnel work, with the aims of increasing productivity, increasing employees' pay by improved performance and promoting from within wherever possible. Such training would include schemes for management, supervisors, instructors, apprentices, transferees and newcomers. Encouragement of further education generally would include the use of internal training schemes, Government skillcentres, technical colleges, and evening institutes. This activity also covers the maintenance of records showing attainments and the publication of information on training opportunities; circulation of educational publications and company magazines, and the organising of any special lectures; training in safety; operating suggestion schemes, and conforming to the Industrial Training Act 1964.

4. Industrial relations

The roles of mediating, negotiating, and conciliating between employees' trade unions and management form an exacting part of a personnel manager's work. He must have a thorough knowledge of collective agreements, conciliation and arbitration procedure, company policy and rules, and appropriate legislation.

He must also work to maintain and improve joint consultation, fostering good relationships and making full use of joint committees.

Liaison with unions should include ensuring that personnel policy is clearly understood and that all procedures within the policy are fairly conducted. These procedures include wage negotiations, complaints, and grievances, apprenticeship schemes, application of rules and regulations, dismissals and transfers, redundancy, social activities, and general conditions of employment.

5. Health and safety

The promotion and maintenance of good physical health is achieved by attending to working conditions, including accident prevention. Statutory requirements under the Health and Safety at Work etc. Act

1974 and related legislation must be complied with. Government health and safety inspectors, who enforce the legislation, normally work through the personnel manager.

The large concern may employ a full-time nurse and provide certain medical facilities for the well-being of employees. Some companies use the services of doctors and dentists on a part-time basis. This medical service normally comes under the control of the personnel manager, who keeps health records, attends to problems connected with hazardous work, arranges for visits to the sick and provides for convalescence and rehabilitation.

Further activities connected with safety may include attending accident prevention meetings, inspecting workshops, minimising fire risks, investigating accidents and providing management with accident statistics.

6. Welfare

Welfare services and facilities vary considerably from firm to firm. Some of these, including social facilities, are as follows.

> Various pension schemes.
> Savings schemes, benevolent funds and sick clubs.
> Co-partnership and profit-sharing schemes.
> Financial assistance for house purchase.
> Advice and assistance with transport and domestic problems.
> Information services such as a library, advice, and legal aid.
> A dining room.
> Rest rooms and rooms for various types of clubs.
> Sports pavilion and grounds.
> Dance hall and bar.
> A theatre.

If a concern does not employ a personnel manager, many of the activities mentioned above are undertaken by other executives as a sideline. For example, the sales manager may look after the canteen, while the accountant may attend to any savings and pension schemes.

Personnel Policy

Ideally there should be a clear, written personnel policy which is fully supported by management. The personnel manager is responsible for maintaining and interpreting the policy.

An example of a typical personnel policy is outlined below.

1. Fairness and justice should be accorded to all employees irrespective of status, position, sex or race.
2. A fair system of adequate wages and salaries.
3. A merit-rating scheme to compensate those employees who achieve increased effectiveness.

4. Every employee should be allowed to develop his capabilities fully.

5. Suitable education and training facilities, thus enabling employees to progress and have equal opportunity in applying for vacancies within the company.

6. Reasonable working conditions consistent with good health and safety (*see* Chapter XVIII for legal requirements).

7. Personnel selection based upon placing each individual in the work situation most suitable for his requirements.

8. Help employees whenever possible with domestic and industrial problems.

9. Conduct all activities between management and employees in a friendly and co-operative spirit.

10. Provide and encourage social activities.

Organisation of a Personnel Department

In the small concern there may be a personnel officer who is often known as the labour manager. In addition there may also be a secretary, and perhaps a younger clerk who acts as a receptionist and deals with general enquiries. As the firm grows an assistant may be introduced.

Continued growth will call for additional specialists such as a welfare officer, safety officer, training officer, and industrial relations officer. The personnel office will expand to include clerks and typists who deal with records, statistics, time cards, and other related jobs. A typical example of the organisation of a personnel department is given in Figure 24.

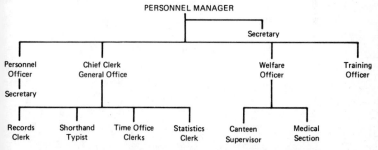

Fig. 24.—*Organisation Chart of a Personnel Department.*

As a firm grows in size, the importance of the personnel function increases. This organisation chart shows a typical breakdown of a personnel department into specialist functions.

QUESTIONS

1. What is the purpose of the personnel function?

2. Discuss the main activities of a personnel department and how they affect the supervisor.

3. In what ways can the supervisor assist the personnel manager in connection with employment?

4. Outline a typical personnel policy and discuss two of the items you consider to be high on the list in order of importance.

5. Comment on the advantages and disadvantages of establishing a personnel department in a concern.

6. Discuss the importance of providing welfare services and facilities in the large concern.

7. Consider the various ways in which a personnel manager can help the supervisor.

CHAPTER XV

EMPLOYMENT

CERTAIN topics under the general heading of employment are of particular interest to the supervisor, who will be concerned with them either directly or indirectly.

These topics are job evaluation; engagement, the employment contract, equal opportunities, induction, transfers and promotion, terminations, redundancy; lateness and absenteeism; and remuneration.

Job Evaluation

Job evaluation is a systematic approach to the problem of determining the value of a job in relation to others, so that a fair wage scale may be applied. A scientific basis of assessment of *all* the factors involved in a job is essential. Although personal bias or opinion cannot be eliminated completely, new techniques are being developed which will eventually place job evaluation on a more scientific basis.

Judging the relative values of jobs is difficult even within the same department and becomes exceptionally difficult when applied to different industries. With sufficient experience the superior should be able to make a reasonable assessment. Opinions vary among supervisors, however, and a determined attempt to be as objective as possible is recommended.

Successful introduction of job evaluation depends to some extent on the ability of supervisors to make sound assessments and on the careful compilation of the wages structure. A good scheme should result in a reduction in labour turnover and an increase in morale and output. Correct placement of employees in suitable jobs is made easier and publication of the job classifications clearly indicates the duties, authority, and responsibilities of each employee.

PROCEDURE

The scheme is generally based upon particular standards which provide a fair comparison between various jobs. The main factors under consideration are as follows.

Physical and mental effort.
Education and training.
Experience.
Degree of authority and responsibility.
Particular skills and aptitudes.
Working conditions.

A detailed examination of the job is essential. A suitably designed form should be completed for every job, and the findings then carefully assessed on a comparative basis. When all the jobs are assessed they are arranged in sequence of value and related to the wages structure by using the most logical method possible.

METHODS OF EVALUATION

The two main methods of evaluating jobs are called points rating and ranking. The *points rating* system attempts to rate each factor of the job by allocating an appropriate weighting of points. Each factor may be assessed within a range of 0 to 10 points, or 0 to 20 points if a wider choice is desired. An example of a form using the points rating system is given in Figure 25. The total number of points is calculated and matched against a wages table which is designed on a points/wage-rate basis.

JOB EVALUATION		
Job Title.		
Name. . . . .**Clock No.**.		
Department..		
Responsible to..		
Job Summary		
Job Requirements	**Assessment**	**Points (1–10)**
Education Experience Learning Period Responsibility Physical Conditions Hazards		
Job Grade..	**Signature.**.	
Total Points.	**Title.**.	
	Date..	

Fig. 25.—*Job Evaluation Form.*

This shows the layout of a typical job evaluation form, using the points rating system.

A variation of this method is known as *factor comparison*. The main difference between the two schemes is that only five factors are used for factor comparison. These are: Mental; Physical; Skill; Responsibility; Working Conditions.

Key jobs are chosen to represent various wage levels and the wage for each job is proportioned among the five factors. From this information a value can be placed on each point and an appropriate rate may be calculated for those jobs which come between the key posts.

Ranking is the other main method, which involves judging each job as a whole and attempting to assess its relative value by ranking a whole job against another whole job. This simple system includes preparing a job description and grading the levels for allocation of wages. The system does not indicate the degree of difference between jobs, which is a disadvantage for the large company where a wide variety of jobs usually exists. In the small business this method is likely to be more suitable because of its simplicity and the reduced range of jobs are probably easier to define.

FUNCTIONAL ANALYSIS

In connection with job evaluation, the supervisor may feel that a complete or partial revision of the activities within each job is required. This situation often arises when a company is growing rapidly or has developed on a "stop-gap" basis. The analysis may be conducted in two stages.

Stage 1. Functional analysis

A complete survey of all the activities conducted within a department is recorded. The two main details noted are the particular activity and the operator who is responsible for it. In many situations a number

ACTIVITY	A	B	C	D	E	F	G	H	I	J	K	L	M	N
1 Assemble packing carton	▨	▨	▨	▨	▨	▨								
2 Pack carton	▨	▨	▨	▨	▨	▨								
3 Check contents	▨	▨	▨	▨	▨	▨								
4 Seal carton							▨	▨	▨					
5 Label carton							▨	▨	▨					
6 Weigh carton							▨	▨	▨					
7 Load on pallet							▨	▨	▨					
8														
9														
10														
11														

Fig. 26.—*Functional Analysis of all Activities (Stage 1)*.

This form is used to record all the activities conducted in a department, as the first stage of functional analysis. Each activity and the operator responsible is noted.

of operators will be performing similar activities. A typical example of a form which may be used for analysis is given in Figure 26.

Stage 2. Job analysis

The activities can now be rearranged to form a more logical pattern among the operators. The knowledge and experience of operators will be taken into consideration, along with any other relevant factors which will affect the allocation. Figure 27 illustrates the type of form which can be used for this purpose with a simple example. This information provides valuable data for the preparation of job evaluation forms.

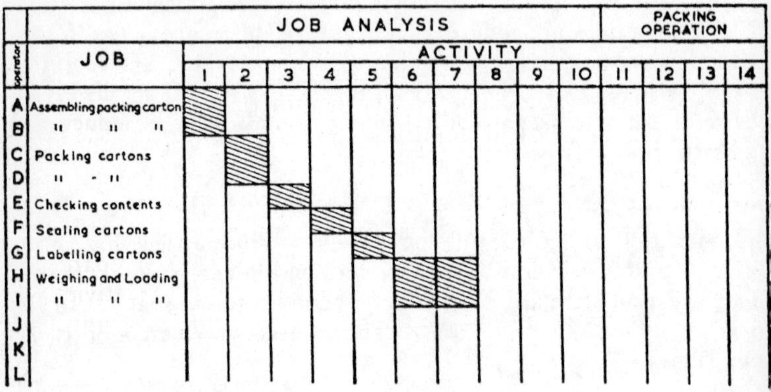

Fig. 27.—*Job Analysis Form (Stage 2)*.

This analysis forms part of a procedure for assessing and improving the organisation described in Chapter IV on the Growth of Organisation.

Engagement

The supervisor is often asked to interview a prospective employee to assess his suitability from the technical aspect. Generally the personnel manager conducts an initial interview to check details and assess personal qualities. The newcomer is then passed to a specialist or supervisor who assesses the individual for a particular function. Usually the supervisor also makes a general assessment, which is compared with the personnel manager's opinion, and a mutual agreement is reached.

Interviewing techniques were discussed in Chapter XIII as an aspect of communication.

Where no personnel department exists, either the departmental manager or the foreman engages employees. Such an arrangement is wasteful—unless a check is kept on all vacancies—as suitable employees may be available in other parts of the concern. Moreover, planning for future vacancies is virtually non-existent.

The employment contract

The Employment Protection (Consolidation) Act 1978 requires that an employee be given written particulars of his terms of employment within thirteen weeks from the date of commencement.

The written statement must include the following.

1. The names of the parties to the contract of employment.
2. The date of commencement. If the contract is for a fixed term, the date of expiration should be stated.
3. The scale or rate of pay, or the method of calculating remuneration.
4. The intervals of payment, i.e. weekly, monthly, etc.
5. Hours of work, including any terms or conditions associated with this aspect.
6. The terms and conditions relating to holiday periods and holiday pay. These should include calculations for accrued holiday pay and rights to pay during sickness and injury.
7. Length of notice the employee should give and which he is entitled to receive.
8. The name of an individual to whom the employee may consult and apply for redress of a grievance. The procedure to follow and any relevant details.
9. A statement of any works rules and a statement of the title of the job.
10. Details of pension rights if any.
11. Whether a contracting-out certificate in respect of the State Pension Scheme is in force.

Any changes made after commencement of employment must be given in writing to the employee within a month. If the employer fails to provide any of the above information the employee may apply to an industrial tribunal to establish the missing details. These particulars will then be recorded and deemed to have been given by the employer.

Equal opportunities

Discrimination in employment on the grounds of sex or marriage is prohibited under the Sex Discrimination Act 1975. This applies to interviews and other selection procedures, benefits such as opportunities for training and promotion, and any action which may be detrimental to employees such as short-time working or dismissal. The Act goes further by stating that discrimination is unlawful in relation to membership of, and benefits and facilities provided by, trade unions and any other organisations (such as professional bodies) which substantially influence the possibility of an individual carrying on an occupation. Any pressure exerted on another individual to discriminate unlawfully and the publishing of discriminatory advertisements are also prohibited.

The Equal Opportunities Commission (E.O.C.) was established to promote the objectives of this Act and the Equal Pay Act 1970 (see p. 312). It can carry out formal investigations into discriminatory practices, and issue "non-discrimination notices". Breach of such a notice may be enforced by injunctions in civil courts. The Commission carries out research, advises the Government on ways in which the legislation may need to be improved, and may assist and represent individual complainants.

An individual feeling discriminated against in employment on the grounds of sex can make a complaint to an industrial tribunal. A conciliation officer of the Advisory, Conciliation and Arbitration Service (ACAS, see pp. 236, 267) will attempt to settle the problem. If this fails the complaint will be considered by the tribunal which has the power to declare the complainant's rights and/or award compensation against the employer, and recommend action which, if not complied with, could lead to increased compensation.

The tribunal may also declare a case of general discrimination which can then be made the subject of a formal investigation by the E.O.C.

The Act provides for exceptions in certain posts where a person's sex is a genuine occupational qualification. The criteria are as follows.

1. For reasons of physiology or authenticity.
2. In social and personnel work where teams of both sexes are essential.
3. In a predominantly single-sex institution where members of one sex are legitimately important to the character of the institution.
4. On grounds of propriety and privacy which would be affected if the appropriate opposite sex were employed.

Induction

The importance of introducing the new employee correctly has already been discussed in Chapter XIII. First impressions form a permanent mark in the newcomer's mind and, if they are unfavourable, it takes a long time to change the individual's outlook towards the firm.

The personnel department has the opportunity to create a good impression from the beginning, if given a free hand. In view of the high cost of labour turnover and the importance of first impressions, it is surprising to see some personnel departments housed either in huts tucked away in the most unattractive part of the concern or at the end of long, bleak corridors.

THE PERSONNEL DEPARTMENT'S PART

A list of information which the personnel department normally provides for a new employee is given below.

1. Organisation charts and an explanation of where his particular job fits into the over-all plan of production.

2. A booklet on terms and conditions of employment; the personnel officer should explain any items which are not clear and mention those which are likely to be altered in the near future.

3. A clear statement of the authority, responsibility and duties of the job, and the job title.

4. An outline of possible channels of promotion.

5. Details of the concern's education and training schemes and the name of the training officer.

6. A plan of the workshop showing all the usual facilities, which should include cloakroom, washrooms, medical services, and the canteen.

7. The names of his immediate superior and the superior in charge of the department.

8. Full details of his commencing wages rate, the scale of pay increases and any financial incentives which are in operation. Personnel should make sure that the new employee understands the pay scheme properly.

9. An outline of the social activities and the name of the welfare officer or the individual who arranges such activities.

10. The hours of work, including tea break times, lunch times, starting and finishing times. Any allowances for clocking and times for washing should be explained.

11. The general amenities such as bicycle sheds and car parking arrangements.

12. Information on the trade unions and where to locate the union representatives.

13. Advice on safety and a copy of the company's written safety policy.

14. Background information on the company, its achievements, products and objectives.

As well as providing all this necessary information, the personnel officer should carefully point out that the new job will no doubt mean some amount of adjustment to new surroundings, new colleagues, and work methods. He must emphasise that the personnel department is there to assist and offer advice whenever anything is bothering the new employee.

Further it helps to create a good impression if employees' legal rights are made known. For example, legislation on health and safety (*see* Chapter XVIII) and industrial relations (*see* Chapter XVII).

After a formal introduction to his supervisor, the personnel department officially hands over the newcomer.

THE SUPERVISOR'S PART

The next step of induction begins at this point and preparation by the supervisor for this time is just as important as planning for induction in the personnel department.

He should make sure that the following arrangements are made.

1. Preparation

(*a*) *The individual.* Know all essential information such as the employee's name, clock number, his job, background, education, experience, and assessment.

(*b*) *The section.* Pass on the necessary information about the newcomer to his colleagues and other individuals who may contact him.

(*c*) *The workplace.* Make sure the place where the newcomer will be located is tidy and clean and that all tools and equipment which can be obtained beforehand are available and in good condition.

(*d*) *Procedure.* Make all the arrangements beforehand which may be needed for special passes, forms for social activities, tea tickets, and any hand-outs which are not covered by the personnel department.

2. Arrival

Give the newcomer a warm welcome. Show that you are pleased to see him; you probably are, so why hide the fact? Introduce him to all his colleagues and mention in passing any special interests. This will give him an opening when he sees them again.

Try to put him at ease by conversing on general topics, but without giving the impression of being personal or over-inquisitive about his affairs. If you feel he is reacting against your approach take the initiative and proffer some information about yourself and your own interests.

Provide him with as much information as you feel he can assimilate. Do not expect him to remember everything; he definitely will not. Be prepared to repeat information several times on different occasions. This technique may seem tedious, but remember that strangeness is caused by lack of information on people, the job, and surroundings.

Make sure that his job is clear to him as regards his authority, the person to whom he is responsible, what he is responsible for, and his duties. Explain the job in greater detail and question him to see if he clearly understands. The learning and teaching period is covered as a separate topic in the next chapter.

Supplement earlier stages of induction by discussing the terms of employment and regulations in more detail. This procedure is essential as there may be small but important variances due to local conditions which the personnel department could easily overlook. The employee is also given a further opportunity to clarify any queries which may have arisen since his interview with the personnel officer. Matters such as transport problems, holidays, insurance schemes, social activities, pay problems, and working arrangements often require additional on-the-spot advice.

Naturally there is a vast number of small points to be covered under the general topic of working arrangements and it is only too easy for the supervisor to overlook a few. Keeping a complete check-list of all the points to tell the new employee can save embarrassment later. The list would include the following points.

Danger areas.
Special regulations concerning smoking.
Departmental and sectional boundaries.
Allowances for washing.
Locker and cloakroom facilities.
Maintenance rules.
Fire hazards and procedure.
Special routines concerning tools, oils, and equipment.
Use and issuing of safety devices.
First aid.
Emergency arrangements.

3. Work assignment

Check that the employee already understands the assignment. If the job involves manning a particular machine or control point, make sure that the employee realises the importance of being at the point and knows the procedure to follow if he leaves the workplace for some reason. The procedure for tool and materials requisitions should be clearly outlined.

The chargehand, leading hand or a responsible operator should act as guide during the initial period, helping as much as possible to develop the right attitudes in the newcomer. The importance of the work and its place in the general pattern of production should be stressed.

4. Follow-up

The object of induction is to make the newcomer feel part of the organisation, which enables him to contribute his capabilities to the full. This sense of belonging is not achieved in a few days; it takes weeks and often months before a new employee really settles in.

Induction must be treated as a lengthy process of indoctrination and the supervisor should check periodically to note progress, see if he can assist and help out with any problems. There will be at least one problem which is bothering the newcomer, and the supervisor should try to gain the individual's confidence by asking him how he is progressing and noting his general reactions.

The supervisor should not expect good results immediately. People learn at different speeds and improvements often depend upon the patience and understanding of superiors.

When progress is made, appropriate praise is essential and any pay increase should be awarded in accordance with the scheme. The employee should be told how he is progressing and if there is a problem, more attention should be given to help him over the snag.

Transfers and Promotion

The personnel department acts as a centre for dealing with transfers and promotions. By keeping records and checking on all employee movements, it can ensure that the most suitable members are given the opportunity for promotion.

The problem of balancing the labour force in time of expansion or contraction becomes easier when controlled from a central point. The supervisor, however, has considerable responsibility in deciding upon transfers which he cannot offset as the personnel department's responsibility. He must be very careful not to make mistakes on transfers, promotions, and terminations, as the responsibility for such action rests squarely on him and mistakes may be disastrous.

The supervisor should be constantly on the look-out for changes which occur in individuals and in jobs, which are the main reason for transfers. The employee may be unsuitable for the particular job because his capabilities are not up to standard or his health may be suffering because of the strain involved. The job may have gradually or drastically changed, but the operator may not be able to adjust or he may have new interests.

Reorganisation within the company often provides a surplus in some sections and a shortage in others, which can be solved by a careful selection of transfers.

As an employee develops his capabilities through experience in the job and through education and training schemes, the possibilities of a suitable transfer or promotion should always be considered, otherwise he may become frustrated and possibly leave. Schemes for improving employees' performance and capabilities must be related to a policy of up-grading employees.

INTERDEPARTMENTAL TRANSFERS

The usefulness of the personnel department is well illustrated when the problem of transferring employees between departments is considered. Successful placing of individuals in the departments depends upon adequate information on vacancies or likely transfers and on assessments of employees. The personnel department can co-ordinate this activity smoothly with the help and co-operation of supervisors.

The responsibility for such transfers lies naturally with the personnel department, and all supervisors should realise how they can assist and also avoid any friction with fellow supervisors. A supervisor should never try to entice an employee away from another department. Providing sufficient information and referring all cases of transfers to the personnel department usually ensures a smooth running scheme.

PROMOTION

The importance of finding the right person for the right job is recognised by most employers. The principle applies at all levels. Employees, however, become more critical of appointments as the levels of supervision are ascended. The responsibility involved in making a promotion, therefore, is always highlighted. Any mistakes made by the personnel department, or by supervisors who make recommendations, receive considerable attention from most members of the concern. Promotion generally includes a pay increase, additional privileges, a rise in status, and more authority and responsibility.

The main points for consideration are whether the scheme of promotion is fair and whether the concern as a whole will benefit. For the concern and all employees to benefit, it is essential that the best man is found for the particular job. A fair scheme with this view in mind is to assess all possible internal applicants and if a suitable man is found he should be appointed, provided a more suitable person is not available outside the company. Such a policy of promotion from within whenever possible is sound and is seen to be fair by existing employees. Fair operation of the scheme depends upon the supervisor, who must continually assess his subordinates and recommend on a strictly objective basis those he considers are suitable for promotion.

Some of the problems which arise concern those who have given long, loyal service, but are unsuitable material for promotion; and those who may be excellent workers, but lack other essential qualities. Favourites or friends of the supervisor also pose a problem as possibly they may be suitable, but the opinions of colleagues are often against such people and ill-feeling may develop.

Terminations

If an employee wishes to terminate his employment with the company the personnel officer should conduct a termination interview to find out the true reason for leaving. This form of personnel counselling may prevent a good man from leaving the concern because a particular grievance has not been aired. Of course, the supervisor will have interviewed the employee earlier, but the truth might not have appeared at that stage.

The reasons for leaving are important, as personnel policy—and the success of management and supervision—is difficult to assess unless actual accounts of employees' opinions are sought and classified.

The trend of labour turnover indicates the level of morale and the effectiveness of selection, induction, and training among new employees. Comparison may be based upon the following formula:

$$\frac{\text{Number of terminations a month}}{\text{Average number of employees}} \times 12 \times 100 = \begin{array}{l}\text{Monthly labour turnover} \\ \text{expressed as an annual} \\ \text{percentage}\end{array}$$

The reasons for leaving may be categorised as follows.

1. Dismissal—poor performance, violation of rules, or poor code of conduct.
2. Redundancy—market depression, seasonal business, or organisational change.
3. Resignation—promotional gain, better company located, domestic problems, dissatisfied, or personal circumstances.
4. Retirement—reaching retiring age, physical ill-health, mental ill-health, or company succession plans.

DISMISSALS

The authority to dismiss an employee is a serious and very responsible duty which demands the application of absolute fairness. Where a personnel manager is not employed, the right to dismiss may rest with the supervisor at departmental level generally. Higher management would normally sanction such an action first.

The introduction of a personnel manager normally changes the system and final responsibility for dismissal is taken by him. The supervisor recommends the action to the personnel manager; he is in the position of being able to consider the case objectively, without bias. In the eyes of the employee, an appeal to an individual outside the immediate jurisdiction of his superior is much fairer.

The supervisor in these circumstances often feels that his status is lowered, some power is lost, or his authority is reduced. If the supervisor is relying upon such forms of authority and power he is obviously out of date, and he does not appreciate the value and effect of modern democratic supervision, which allows appeal to an outside authority.

REASONS FOR DISMISSALS

The real blame for the dismissal may lie with management when employees are placed in unsuitable jobs, or when no attempt is made to help the employee to adjust to new surroundings, changes, or incapacity.

The dismissal should be avoided if possible, especially where the fault is two-sided. Much can be done to help employees to adjust and on grounds of economy and morale alone, the effort is worth while.

Disregarding the problem employee, some of the reasons leading up to a dismissal involve personality clashes which make adjustment to the job very difficult. Lack of co-operation, absenteeism, lateness, laziness, rudeness, dishonesty, and carelessness all seem to point to a supervisory problem. Help at the time when the employee becomes disgruntled may prevent an untenable situation developing.

Further reasons concern the individual and his ability to carry out the tasks allocated to him. In the case of the trainee, if he is unable to do the job after training, the reasons are either that he is lacking in the necessary ability or that he has not been taught properly. Basically this means that selection procedures are faulty or that the training scheme needs revising. The employee is not to blame in either case.

Another reason connected with work is where the person actually loses his ability and finds that he can no longer cope with the job. This state may be due to the development of mental trouble, or physical incapacity. Some large companies provide rehabilitation centres to assist the employee with a physical or mental handicap. New jobs are located which often mean a demotion, but provided the approach is made in such a way that the employee feels it is worth while and is not down-graded in front of his colleagues, the demotion is generally acceptable.

EMPLOYEES' LEGAL RIGHTS
Under the Employment Protection (Consolidation) Act 1978, an employee (subject to certain exceptions) has the right not to be dismissed unfairly and may seek a remedy by complaining to an industrial tribunal.

Some brief details are now given but in view of its comprehensiveness, the Act itself should be consulted before taking any action.

Meaning of dismissal
Dismissal may be defined as employment termination by the employer, with or without notice; employee's resignation, with or without notice, where the employer implies that he is not to be bound by the contract of employment; the expiry of a fixed-term contract without renewal; or the employer's refusal to allow an employee to exercise her legal right to return to employment after the birth of her baby.

Restrictions
Independent contractors, freelance agents, and other non-employees

are outside the Act. Similarly employees who have not completed twenty-six weeks' continuous employment cannot complain of unfair dismissal. This period is reduced to four weeks for certain dismissals following intervals of statutory medical suspension. No qualifying period is necessary for employees who have been dismissed on account of their trade union membership or activities.

Other exclusions include the following.

1. Part-time employees who normally work less than sixteen hours a week, unless they have been employed by the same employer for eight or more hours a week for five years. Whatever the hours of work of employees, however, they may complain to an industrial tribunal of dismissal on account of trade union membership or activities.

2. Employees who, before their effective date of termination, had reached the normal retiring age for their employment or, if there is no normal retiring age, had reached the age of 65 for men or 60 for women. Whatever the age of employees they may complain to an industrial tribunal of dismissal on account of trade union membership or activities.

3. Employees with fixed-term contracts for two years or more where the dismissal consists only of the expiry of the contract without renewal and the employee has previously agreed in writing to forego his or her right of complaint in such circumstances.

4. Employees with fixed-term contracts for two years or more where the dismissal consists only of the expiry of the contract without renewal and the contract was entered into before 28th February 1972 (or, in the case of dismissal on grounds of pregnancy, 1st June 1976).

5. Employees who are married to their employer.

6. Employees who, under their contract of employment, ordinarily work outside Great Britain. Most merchant seamen on British-registered ships and most employees working on off-shore oil, gas and other similar installations in British areas of the Continental Shelf *can* complain of unfair dismissal.

7. The police and armed forces.

8. Registered dock workers engaged on dock work.

9. Those engaged in share fishing who are paid solely by a share in the profits or gross earnings of a fishing vessel.

10. Staff of the House of Lords.

Fair dismissal

Dismissal can only be fair if the employer can show that the reason for it was one of those listed below and that he acted reasonably in the circumstances in treating that reason as sufficient to justify dismissing the employee.

The reasons are as follows.

1. A reason related to the employee's capability or qualifications for the job.
2. A reason related to the employee's conduct.
3. Redundancy.
4. A legal duty or restriction on either the employer or the employee which prevents the employment being continued.
5. Some other substantial reason which could justify the dismissal.

Unfair selection for redundancy

Dismissal on grounds of redundancy will be unfair if:

1. the employee was selected for dismissal on account of trade union membership or activities;
2. the employer unreasonably disregarded the customary arrangements or the agreed procedure relating to selection of employees for redundancy;
3. the selection was unfair for some other reason. For example, the employer failed to give adequate warning of redundancy or failed to consider alternative employment for the employee.

Dismissal relating to trade union membership and activities

If the main reason for the dismissal was any of those below, then the dismissal will be held to be unfair.

1. If the employee was or proposed to become a member of an independent trade union; or took part or proposed to take part in the activities of an independent trade union, unless the activities were within working hours and there was no arrangement with the employer permitting the employee to take part in such activities during working hours.
2. If the employee refused to belong to a non-independent trade union.
3. If there was a trade union membership agreement (closed shop) covering the employee, and the employee objected, on grounds of religious belief, to membership of *any* trade union.

These are called inadmissible reasons. Employees who consider they may have been dismissed for the first one mentioned above can apply to an industrial tribunal for interim relief pending a full hearing of their complaint of unfair dismissal. If the tribunal considers it likely that the full hearing will uphold the complaint the tribunal will either order reinstatement or re-engagement or will make an order for the temporary continuation of the contract of employment.

Dismissal on grounds of pregnancy

It is unfair to dismiss an employee because she is pregnant or for any other reason connected with her pregnancy unless at the effective date of termination she will, because of her pregnancy, be incapable of doing her work adequately or her continued employment would be against the law. For dismissal to be fair the employer must have no suitable alternative vacancy. If there is a suitable alternative with not less favourable terms and conditions of employment then the employer must offer the employee a new contract.

Dismissal during a dispute

Where, at the date of dismissal, there is a lock-out by the employer or a strike or other industrial action by the employees, an industrial tribunal will not determine whether the employee was fairly or unfairly dismissed unless it is shown that not all the relevant employees have been treated equally.

Special cases

For those employees who consider they may have been dismissed for a special reason, for example, trade union membership, or in special circumstances such as arise from a woman's right to return to work after pregnancy, the Department of Employment guide, *Dismissal—Employees' Rights*, will be of particular use.

APPLICATION TO AN INDUSTRIAL TRIBUNAL

An application to an industrial tribunal claiming unfair dismissal may be made as soon as the employer has given notice of dismissal and it must normally be received within the period of three months beginning with the employee's effective date of termination. If the application is received any later than that date the tribunal will consider the complaint only if they believe it was not reasonably practicable for the employee to have made the complaint earlier.

Remedies

The remedies for unfair dismissal are:

1. reinstatement (the employee is to be treated in all respects as though the dismissal had not occurred);
2. re-engagement (the employee is to be re-employed but not necessarily in the same job or on the same terms and conditions of employment);
3. compensation.

Conciliation

ACAS receives a copy of the employee's application to the tribunal and a conciliation officer will contact one or both of the parties involved. The officer then considers whether or not the parties can be helped to reach a settlement without the need for a tribunal hearing. Conciliation can take place at the request of both parties (or their representatives), or, if there is no such request, if the officer thinks there is a reasonable chance of success. If a settlement seems possible the parties may apply for a postponement of the tribunal hearing, but the time-limit for applying to an industrial tribunal is not extended because of any such discussions.

Where a complaint of unfair dismissal could be made to an industrial tribunal but this has not yet been done, conciliation may take place at the request of either or both of the parties or their representatives.

Conciliation officers encourage employees to use any procedures that exist within their employer's organisation for appeal against their dismissal. While these procedures are running their course the employee should ask both the conciliation officer and the tribunal not to take any further action on the complaint to the tribunal.

Tribunal hearing

If a settlement is not reached beforehand, the employee's application will be heard before an industrial tribunal. Each tribunal consists of a legally qualified chairman and two lay members. The hearing is conducted in a simple and straightforward manner in such a way that applicants may put their own cases. Applicants can ask a friend, trade union official or lawyer to represent them if they wish. Applicants may also be eligible for a limited amount of legal advice and assistance.

If the dismissal is disputed, the tribunal must first be satisfied by the employee that there was a dismissal. It is for the employer to show that the dismissal was for one of the reasons specified under the Act. The employer must also show that he acted reasonably, in all the circumstances of the case, in treating that reason as sufficient for the dismissal. If it is claimed that the employer's conduct entitled the employee to resign, the onus is on the employee to prove this and also to prove any claim made about sex or race discrimination which is being considered at the same time as the unfair dismissal claim.

Reinstatement and re-engagement

When a tribunal finds that an employee has been unfairly dismissed it explains what orders it can make for the employee to be reinstated or re-engaged and asks the employee whether such an order is wanted.

In deciding whether or not to make an order for reinstatement or re-engagement, the tribunal will take into account the employee's wishes; the practicability of the employee returning to work for the employer; and in cases where the employee was partly to blame for the dismissal, whether or not it would be just to make such an order.

Where a tribunal orders re-engagement it will be on terms which are, wherever possible, as favourable as if the employee had been re-instated, unless the employee was partly to blame for the dismissal.

Awards of compensation

Where the tribunal finds that an employee has been unfairly dismissed and makes no order for reinstatement or re-engagement, it provides the alternative remedy of an award of compensation. Such an award will usually consist of a basic award and a compensatory award. The basic award is based on the employee's age, length of service and weekly pay and is calculated in the same way as a redundancy payment. The compensatory award is an amount which the tribunal considers just and equitable for the loss which the employee has suffered because of the dismissal.

SUPPLEMENTARY PROVISIONS

Supplementary provisions include interim relief, recoupment of un-employment and supplementary benefit, provisions relating to the death of employer or employee, and the right of employees to receive on request a written statement of the reasons why they have been dismissed. These are dealt with in more detail below.

Interim relief provisions

These provisions apply to any employee who is complaining of unfair dismissal on the grounds that he was dismissed because he was, or proposed to become, a member of an independent trade union or because he took part, or proposed to take part, at any appropriate time, in the activities of an independent trade union. An employee whose complaint of unfair dismissal is based on any of these grounds also has a right to apply to the tribunal for an order for him to be temporarily reinstated or re-engaged or for his contract of employment to be continued until his complaint of unfair dismissal has been finally settled by agreement or decided at a tribunal hearing.

A tribunal cannot consider an application unless it reaches the tribunal within seven days of the employee's effective date of termination, *and* during the same period the tribunal receives a certificate, signed by an authorised official of the employee's union (or the union which he had proposed to join). The certificate must confirm that the employee was a member of that union (or proposed to join it) at the date of his dismissal and that there are reasonable grounds for supposing that the reason, or main reason, for his dismissal was the reason connected with his trade union membership or activity which he has alleged in his complaint.

The main aim of the provisions is to prevent an industrial dispute developing at the time of the dismissal by suspending the effects of the dismissal until the complaint of unfair dismissal has been fully dealt with.

Death of employer or employee

Provision has been made for the case where the employer or the employee dies after the employer has given the employee notice of dismissal.

If the employee dies before he has been able to make a complaint of unfair dismissal, a personal representative of the deceased employee may make the complaint or, if a complaint had been made before the employee's death, may continue the industrial tribunal proceedings concerned with the complaint. If there is no personal representative of the deceased employee, proceedings may be instituted on behalf of the estate of the deceased by a person appointed to do so by the tribunal. He may be either someone who was authorised to act on his behalf by the deceased employee before his death or the widower, widow, child, father, mother, brother or sister of the deceased employee.

Recoupment of unemployment and supplementary benefit

When a tribunal is assessing arrears of pay under an order for reinstatement or re-engagement or compensation for loss of wages as part of a compensatory award, it will ask the employee whether he has received unemployment or supplementary benefit between his effective date of termination and the date of the tribunal hearing and, if so, for what period. Unless the tribunal is satisfied that he has not received unemployment or supplementary benefit, it must follow a special procedure in making the award.

A written statement

The Act gives employees whose employment is terminated with or without notice, or whose fixed-term contracts expire without being renewed, the right to receive from their employers, on request, a written statement of the reasons for dismissal or the non-renewal of their fixed-term contract. An employee who has been dismissed has no right to receive such a written statement unless he asks for one. His request can be made orally or in writing.

Employers are required to comply with an employee's request within fourteen days. The written statement can be used in evidence in any subsequent proceedings.

Should an employer refuse or fail to provide a written statement of the reasons for dismissal and the employee considers that his refusal or failure is unreasonable, the employee may complain to an industrial tribunal. He may also complain if he considers that a statement he has been given is inadequate or untrue.

If an employee makes a complaint, an ACAS conciliation officer will be available to help the employee and his employer try to reach a settlement without the need for a tribunal hearing. If no settlement is reached and the tribunal, on hearing the complaint, decides that it is well-founded it will require the employer to pay the employee compensation equivalent to two weeks' pay. It may also make a declaration of what it finds to be the employer's reasons for dismissing the employee.

Redundancy

An unhappy fact of industrial life is that often companies are forced into declaring some of their employees redundant through such circumstances as a market depression, a seasonal variation in business, or essential organisational changes. To remain competitive at home and abroad a company may need to increase mechanisation or automation programmes which also could result in redundancies.

The social responsibilities of management in these situations are complex. For example, a decision not to automate may throw the *whole* labour force into unemployment if the company becomes insolvent.

In addition to the company's social problems there are a number of legal requirements under Part IV of the Employment Protection Act 1975 (now incorporated in the Employment Protection (Consolidation) Act 1978). Where redundancies are planned, independent trade unions and employees are given certain rights. The Act and any special orders should be studied before taking any action.

RIGHTS OF TRADE UNIONS

An employer has a duty to consult with appropriate trade unions about proposed redundancies to see whether there are ways of reducing the numbers involved or of mitigating the effects of redundancy. This consultation must be conducted before redundancies are announced.

An employer who wishes to dismiss an employee as redundant and who recognises an independent trade union to which the employee belongs, must consult the T.U. representative about the dismissal before it occurs. If the employee is not a member the employer must still consult the trade union.

Minimum periods for consultation are given in the Act dependent upon the number of employees involved. An employer must provide reasonably full information in writing and include the reasons, the numbers and descriptions of employees involved, the total number of employees of any such description, the proposed method of selecting the employees, and the proposed method of conducting the dismissals, taking into account any agreed procedure including the period over which the dismissals will occur.

If the trade union replies, the employer must consider the points raised and reply to them giving reasons if he rejects any of them. If the trade union does not reply the employer need take no further action.

The trade union may complain to an industrial tribunal if it feels that an employer has not met the consultative requirements. Before the hearing, an ACAS conciliation officer must have the opportunity to consider whether he is able to help the parties settle the dispute. He may be asked for help by either party or he may proceed independently.

The tribunal, after hearing the complaint, may make a declaration if the union's complaint is justified. This declaration may tell the employer to postpone dismissal notices if there was failure to consult so that consultation may proceed.

The tribunal may also make a protective award which safeguards the employees' remuneration. It requires the employer to pay a normal week's wages for a specified period, regardless of whether or not the employees are still employed.

RIGHTS OF EMPLOYER

In certain circumstances it may not be reasonably practicable for an employer to meet fully the requirements for minimum consultation periods, disclosure of information, or the manner of dealing with the union's representations.

In these special circumstances the employer must do all that he can reasonably be expected to do to meet the requirements. In defence, an employer must show that he *did* fully comply, or state the special circumstances, or show that he took all possible steps to comply as far as he could.

RIGHTS OF EMPLOYEES

If an employee is covered by a protective award he has a right to be paid his normal week's pay for the protected period whether he is still working for the employer or not. However, there are certain conditions for claiming these rights.

An employee who is still employed will be paid under a protective award only when he is entitled to payment under his contract of employment or under his statutory rights during a period of notice. For this purpose the whole remaining part of his employment is treated as if it were a statutory period of notice. Thus an employee who goes on strike, or is absent from work without leave and without good reason, or is granted leave at his own request, or has time off from work under certain other provisions of the Employment Protection (Consolidation) Act, will not be entitled to payment.

An employee who is absent under contractual holiday arrangements, or who is ill, or during any period where the employer has no work available for him, will be paid.

An employee who is fairly dismissed for a reason other than

redundancy, or who gives up his job during the protected period without good reason will, however, lose his right to payment for the rest of the protected period.

Offer of renewed or new employment

An employer may offer to re-engage an employee in his old job, or in a different but apparently suitable job, before the end of the protected period. If the employee refuses the offer without good reason he loses his right to payment for the rest of the protected period.

Right to a trial period

An employee who accepts an offer of a different type of job is allowed a trial period to see if the job is suitable. For calculating continuity of employment this trial period will be regarded as starting from when the employee's old job ends even where there is in fact a gap between the two jobs. The trial period will normally continue for four weeks after the employee starts work in his new job but may, however, be extended by agreement between employer and employee in order to retrain the employee for the new job.

An employee who leaves the job for any adequate reason or who is dismissed for a reason connected with the new job during the trial period, keeps his right to payment under the protective award. If, however, he gives up the job or the training without adequate reason or the employer dismisses him fairly for reasons not connected with the changed terms of employment, he will lose his right to payment for the rest of the protected period.

Extension of trial period

The trial period may be extended to retrain the employee for the new job, by agreement between the employer and the employee. The agreement must be made before the employee starts work in the new job; must be in writing; and must specify the date that the trial period ends and the terms and conditions of employment which will apply after the trial period ends.

The period allowed for trying out the new job is the same length as under the redundancy payments provisions. However, the employee has a right to a trial period if he starts a different job with his employer at any time during the protected period. Nor does it matter whether the employer offers him the job before the end of the old job or after.

Complaints

If an employer does not pay the money under a protective award the employee has a right to complain to an industrial tribunal. Where a number of employees is concerned in a single protective award a test case could be arranged by agreement between the parties, including the union concerned.

A complaint can be made within three months from the last day for which there has been failure to pay but if tribunals consider that it was not reasonably practicable for the employee to make his complaint in time they can allow longer. Application forms can be obtained from local offices of the Department of Employment and the Employment Service Division. A copy of the completed form will be sent to a conciliation officer of ACAS who will at the request of the parties, or on his own initiative in appropriate cases, consider whether he can help settle the complaint without the need for a tribunal hearing.

A conciliation officer will also act at the request of the employee or the employer who can get in touch with a conciliation officer through his nearest ACAS regional office.

Where conciliation is not possible, or fails, the tribunal will hear the complaint. If justified it will order the employer to pay the employee or employees concerned the money due to them under the award.

THE DEPARTMENT OF EMPLOYMENT

An employer must also notify the Secretary of State for Employment if there is a proposal to make ten or more employees redundant at one establishment within a relatively short period. This action allows the Manpower Services Commission to take any necessary measures to redeploy or retrain redundant employees, and Government departments and agencies to consider any further steps to avoid or minimise the redundancies.

Similar enforcements apply in terms of disclosure of information. Moreover, the employer's defence of "reasonable practicability" also applies. There are penalties for non-compliance.

Lateness and Absenteeism

The adverse effects of lateness and absenteeism on output and morale are well known. Poor supervision is commonly revealed as the underlying cause although there are some genuine direct causes for bad timekeeping.

The importance of the problem is demonstrated when the effects are shown to permeate the whole concern. The burden of covering for latecomers and absentees often falls on the rest of the employees who must apply extra effort and suffer the additional strain of trying to do more than one operation at once. Such unnecessary strain on supervision and employees is unfair. Continually trying to rearrange operations and machine loading inevitably causes some hold-ups and idle time, which is reflected in lower output and possibly poor work quality.

The personnel department, through personnel counselling,

attempts to improve those employees who are constantly causing this trouble. The true causes should be sought and the supervisor should note such cases for reference when up-gradings and pay increases are considered.

Some of the reasons put forward for lateness are domestic problems, transport difficulties, ill-health, fatigue and over-sleeping. In cases of continued employee negligence, the supervisor ought to investigate and pass the case to personnel if the situation does not improve.

Similar treatment is needed for absentees. Some of the reasons are domestic difficulties, sickness, accidents, fatigue and the weather. Some employees fail to give reasonable excuses after a while and develop into chronic cases who need firm treatment to protect the conscientious employees.

The drag on operational effectiveness results in higher costs and increasing discontent if bonus schemes are affected. Those employees who have avoidable reasons for lateness or absenteeism should be interviewed and given a clear understanding of the effects of such irresponsible actions. Some companies apply pressures by cutting pay, stopping bonuses, suspension, discharge after a number of warnings, loss of seniority and loss of holiday rights.

Although there are many external influences which cause employees to act in certain ways, the supervisor who practises good human relations and takes a genuine interest in each employee will have less difficulty with lateness and absenteeism.

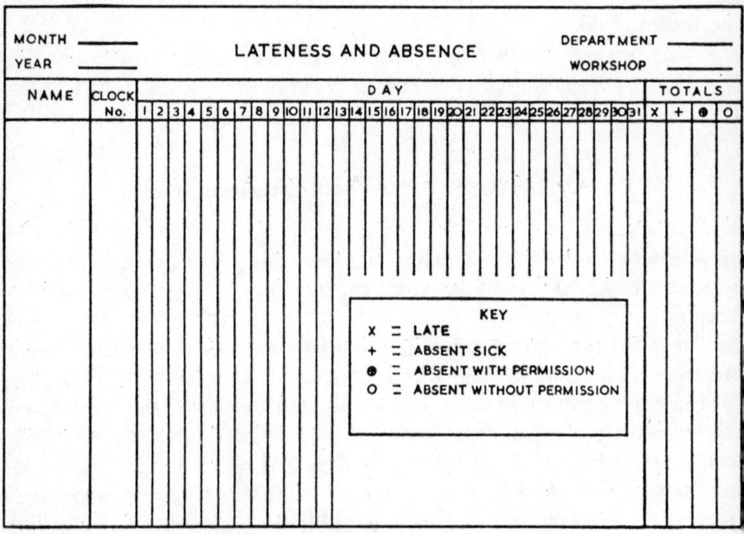
MONTH ______ YEAR ______

LATENESS AND ABSENCE

DEPARTMENT ______ WORKSHOP ______

NAME	CLOCK No.	DAY 1	2	3	4	5	6	7	8	9	10	11	12	13	14	15	16	17	18	19	20	21	22	23	24	25	26	27	28	29	30	31	TOTALS X	+	●	O

KEY
X = LATE
+ = ABSENT SICK
● = ABSENT WITH PERMISSION
O = ABSENT WITHOUT PERMISSION

Fig. 28.—*Lateness and Absence Chart.*

This is a typical control chart for a department, recording any lateness and absence among the operators for each day of the month.

A typical control chart for lateness and absence is given in Figure 28. Comparisons may be made for each period such as a month or a year by using the following formulae:

1. $\dfrac{\text{Total number of days lost through absence}}{\text{Average number of employees for period}} =$ Average number of days lost per employee for period

2. $\dfrac{\text{Total number of days lost}}{\text{Total planned days}} \times 100 =$ Days lost expressed as a percentage of planned working time

This second formula may be applied on a basis of hours, shifts or days. Although the particular age distribution will affect the percentage, a guide may be taken from the national average, which is 3 per cent for men and 5 per cent for women.

Remuneration

The question of financial incentives has been covered in Chapter X, Motivation. The other major aspect of remuneration is achieving a fair system.

Responsibility for recommending wages policy and negotiating wage rates comes under the personnel department which operates the wages scheme as fairly as possible. Within such a scheme the maintenance of correct differentials—through the operation of a merit rating scheme—is of particular importance to the supervisor. His recommendations provide the personnel department with appropriate information for establishing new rates, potential up-gradings, and promotions.

MERIT RATING

Rating each employee's performance is a demanding part of the supervisor's duties. Accurate assessment is a continuous task of checking and noting the capabilities of individuals and their responsiveness in particular situations.

Some standard of comparison is necessary for each quality to be measured against. The standard may be a simple arrangement such as "well below average"; "below average"; "average"; "above average"; and "well above average". A possible alternative is to use a points system from one to ten, using five as the average position. An indication of the measurable qualities would be to assess work output, work quality, self-discipline, interpretation of instructions, ability to take effective action, conscientiousness, supervisory qualities, ability to train, ability to learn, general outlook and attitudes, and loyalty.

The scheme should be carefully explained to employees and the individuals should be notified of their ratings. Incentives to improve could include a higher rate of pay, extra benefits such as higher bonuses and increased holidays, and other appropriate privileges.

Unfortunately, such schemes tend to lose their effectiveness as employees are often influenced by trade unions to regard merit rating as an expected annual increase, whereas the true purpose is to recognise good operator performance.

QUESTIONS

1. Outline a method of conducting a job grading scheme and illustrate your answer with suitable diagrams.
2. How would you assess a candidate's suitability from the technical aspect?
3. Discuss the question of induction.
4. Outline a list of information that you think a new employee should receive before he commences employment.
5. What arrangements should be made to receive the new employee on his first morning at work?
6. Discuss the problem of transfers and promotion in connection with fairness and justice.
7. How would you conduct a termination interview?
8. What action would you take if labour turnover began to increase in your department?
9. Explain the implication of the statement "Employees are often discharged through no fault of their own."
10. How would you deal with an employee who is continually late? Include in your answer the reasons for your actions.
11. As a new supervisor, outline a plan to improve lateness and absenteeism which is particularly bad in your section.
12. State how you would conduct a fair programme of assessment for each subordinate under your control.
13. What advantages are likely to accrue from the establishment of an efficient selection procedure in a company?
14. Discuss the problem of labour turnover and the importance of keeping records on this factor.
15. If the company were forced to contract, discuss the various ways of deciding which operator's employment should be terminated. Give your personal choice of the method to be used and explain the reason for your choice.
16. List the records you would expect to find in a personnel department and explain their uses.

CHAPTER XVI

TRAINING

Importance of Training

ANY country possessing a highly-trained industrial labour force has a distinct advantage over others that may have neglected this vital factor in economic development and increasing productivity. In Britain there has been a shortage of skilled labour since World War II and many companies have shirked their responsibilities for training employees. This situation has contributed towards the slow rate of economic expansion.

Every supervisor has a responsibility to improve the level of skill of his staff so that there is more readiness to cope with changes in work and organisation. The personnel officer also has a responsibility for assessing education and training requirements of the company as well as advising on the methods and suitability of training courses.

MANPOWER DEVELOPMENT

The Government's attempt to deal with the problem of skill shortages was to introduce the Industrial Training Act in 1964 to supplement the good work of the Industrial Training Federation which had been established in 1958 by the Trades Union Congress, the British Employers Confederation (now the C.B.I.) and the nationalised industries.

The Act gave the Secretary of State for Employment the power to establish training boards for each industry. Twenty-five Boards are now in operation covering about 15 million employees. As a result of the Employment and Training Act 1974 these boards are controlled by the Training Services Division of the Manpower Services Commission, established by the same Act.

The imposing of levies by the Boards and the reimbursement of grants to companies who send employees on approved courses have encouraged managers to become more training conscious.

The M.S.C. is separate from the Government but accountable to the Secretary of State for Employment. The Commission advises the Government on manpower policy issues and its aims are to enable the country's manpower resources to be developed and contribute fully to economic well-being, and to ensure that there are available to each worker the opportunities and services needed in order to lead a satisfying working life. Most of its activities are financed from public funds, expenditure for 1977–8 amounting to £432 million.

The main public employment services are operated by the M.S.C.'s

Employment Service Division which provides a comprehensive service for employers requiring staff and for people seeking jobs.

The M.S.C.'s Training Services Division is responsible for improving the supply of trained manpower needed by the economy, for providing opportunities for people to acquire new skills, and for generally improving the efficiency and effectiveness of training.

A number of other direct training services are also offered by the M.S.C. These include the Training Within Industry (T.W.I.) scheme to develop the skills of supervisors, refresher and up-grading training at skillcentres, and a mobile instructor service. Other services offered include Occupational Guidance, Professional and Executive Recruitment (P.E.R.), and services to the disabled.

THE SCOPE OF TRAINING

Training is a natural part of the sequence of selection and induction of employees. If this important stage does not receive sufficient attention from supervisors or managers, the possibility of using each individual's full capabilities becomes very remote. In this sense training becomes a continuous programme of employee development, achieved by formal education and training schemes, run or arranged by the personnel department, and by localised training, which is mostly given by immediate superiors.

Certain fundamentals of good supervision cannot operate effectively unless training is recognised as an integral part of supervisory policy. For example, increased proficiency, delegation of responsibility, and safety, all depend upon proper training.

Increased proficiency

Newly-trained employees and raw recruits naturally need special attention until they are fully proficient and capable of working entirely on their own. Even new employees who are already skilled expect and should receive training in the particular job, which invariably differs in some respects from similar jobs they may have done previously.

An essential part of issuing instructions on work, rules and regulations, and procedures is to provide training on any aspects which are new or unusual. New methods are introduced periodically, on the recommendation of work study engineers or as a result of the supervisor's study of existing methods, and such changes obviously make additional training necessary.

Where employees are below standard and lack the essential knowledge or dexterity to improve quality and output, additional training will help to improve performance.

Delegation of responsibility

Successful delegation depends upon the recognition of employees' potential and their effective training for the tasks to be delegated.

Further training of employees to expand their abilities and prepare them for promotion is essential, both for morale and improved efficiency. Often the supervisor must rely on his subordinates to assist and take over part of his planning and organising activities as well as more straightforward tasks. His responsibility then is to ensure that his subordinates are adequately trained to cope with these tasks. The supervisor has frequent opportunities during the daily routine to demonstrate his methods and the reasons for his actions to his deputies, thus giving them an invaluable insight into the job.

Safety

Proper training, as well as sufficient close supervision, is needed if the accident rate is to be kept down. An assessment of accidents over a period will indicate particular areas where more training is required to cut down dangerous practices. Extra instruction will help to convince employees of the full danger of various bad habits, such as: not using protective clothing or goggles; operating machines without using appropriate guards and safety devices; abusing machines by working above specified speed limits; standing in dangerous positions near equipment; ignoring precautions for conveyors and transport systems; interfering with other employees and distracting their attention from their work.

The legal requirements for safety which affect both employer and employee are discussed fully in Chapter XVIII. The supervisor should remind his staff of their duties under ss. 7 and 8 of the Health and Safety at Work Act, and of the powers of inspectors under s. 20.

Training Methods

TRIAL AND ERROR

The employee is either placed on his own and learns the job by performing operations, making mistakes and correcting them or he watches another employee, asks questions, and copies the operations. Such unsound methods are still very common.

In this way the trainee picks up bad habits which are very difficult to break, so that he is unlikely to become a first-class operator. If an operator is asked to help a trainee he has no incentive to assist, as invariably time is wasted which affects his wages in the case of piece work and bonus schemes. These forms of training are slow, disrupt organisation, are relatively expensive and generally ineffective.

PLANNED PROGRAMME

This scheme is based upon scientific principles of learning and psychology. A set pattern of procedure is followed on a step-by-step basis, which allows the trainee to develop rapidly towards using the most effective and economic methods of performing the job.

One of the main problems in training schemes is how to overcome the *learning plateau* which generally appears when the trainee is about half-way towards the speed of a proficient operator.

Figure 29 illustrates the learning plateau which generally occurs when the traditional method of training is used. The analytical method of training shows considerable saving by dispensing with the plateau. While conducting the basic exercises at the beginning a short time lag occurs before production commences. Both methods are described below.

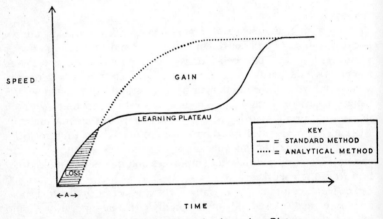

Fig. 29.—*Overcoming the Learning Plateau.*
This diagram shows how the analytical method of training overcomes the "learning plateau" normally met with the standard training method. The analytical method employs initial exercises with no productive work involved, therefore a time lag occurs (A) before production begins.

The psychological effect on the trainee under the standard method may be severe as frustration sets in through lack of further advancement at the plateau stage.

Many reasons have been suggested to explain the cause of the learning plateau. One reason is that the skills which are acquired in the early stages of training are not capable of development to the advanced stages of full speed operation without being modified. This suggests a strong case for learning each small part of the job separately, using the advanced skills from the beginning, until full speed is attained. The trainee can then concentrate on increasing speed by intensive repetition without concerning himself with the over-all job until he is proficient at all the required skills.

On assembly-line type jobs where the operator controls the speed of work, the feasibility of the scheme (the analytical method), should be carefully examined. There may be snags such as increased training time, breaking down the job into skills, and the problem of slowing down advanced skills to speeds that can be readily assimilated, but these should be weighed against the savings through dispensing with the learning plateau.

A summary of the two schemes is given below.

Traditional method of training

1. Explain the whole job.
2. Demonstrate the operations.
3. Practise the operations slowly and carefully.
4. Increase speed until the learning plateau is reached.
5. Place trainee on the job under some form of supervision.
6. Eventually increase speed to that of a proficient operator.

Analytical method of training

1. Conduct basic exercises.
2. Break down job into individual skills.
3. Demonstrate each skill separately.
4. Practise each skill until full speed is reached.
5. Gradually combine the skills and parts of the job, maintaining full speed, until the whole job is performed.
6. Place trainee on the job and allocate periods of practice at full speed under supervision.
7. Gradually increase the practice periods until the whole day is spent at full speed.

The Training Environment

Training may be carried out at the workplace or at a separate training centre. The correct attitude and approach to learning is also a factor to be considered.

LEARNING AT THE WORKPLACE

The supervisor is generally responsible for training at the workplace, acting as instructor. This is an additional burden, nevertheless, it is an important aspect of his job. Allocation of his time becomes more difficult as less time will be spent on actually supervising; the success of this scheme depends upon his ability to instruct and to spend sufficient time with the trainee.

LEARNING AT A TRAINING CENTRE

There are certain advantages if a training centre is utilised. Less distraction provides the trainee with suitable conditions for concentrating and learning although reality is probably missing. The use of a specialist instructor is an obvious advantage, provided suitable discipline makes up for loss of workshop atmosphere. The trainee receives more attention and guidance on his weaknesses and, therefore, he should progress more rapidly.

THE BACKGROUND TO LEARNING

A number of useful guides have been discovered through research into the learning process.

1. Planning

Although it is essential to draw up a careful plan of training such aspects as current alterations, difficulty with a particular topic and coping with particularly slow learners must be allowed for in the schedule. A degree of flexibility is required, otherwise adherence to a rigid programme becomes the objective, whereas the aim must be to produce trained employees.

2. Trainee ability

The instructor should assume that effective selection of trainees has provided individuals who are capable of learning and have sufficient ability to perform the tasks involved. Lack of confidence in the trainees is immediately apparent to them and has an adverse effect on the learning process. Displaying confidence in trainees builds up enthusiasm and spurs individuals on to greater efforts.

3. Motivation

Creating the desire to learn, i.e. being able to motivate trainees, is part of the instructor's job. The reasons and advantages of learning a job should be given to make the trainee feel he is doing something of importance with definite objectives in mind such as financial gain, regrading, or increased status.

4. The learning rate

Although people learn at different rates there is a certain amount of uniformity in learning progress: it starts from a low position, rises rapidly and levels out to a plateau, already mentioned under Training Schemes. The position of the plateau varies with individuals and the type of job.

Generally the quick learner progresses more rapidly in the long run as against the slow learner, but invariably any individual learns some processes quickly and others more slowly. The main factors are intelligence and a flair for the particular task. Further factors affecting learning speed are lack of interest, physical weaknesses, resistance to change, established working habits, lack of incentive, and sometimes deeper psychological reluctance. Age itself is of less importance as a single factor, except that it has some bearing on strength and experience. Very old operatives, however, are frequently incapable of being retrained as their mental and physical powers are failing.

5. Correct sequence of learning

Whenever possible the operation should be taught in correct sequence; that is, in a logical pattern from the beginning to the end of each operation. Although this procedure may not be economic in some circumstances through excessive waste, the fact remains that skill is acquired by performing movements in correct sequence. Skill is largely developed through muscle sense which feels the movement of a lever for example, and automatically decides by the degree of sensation the next movement to be carried out. Familiar examples of this effect are handling the steering wheel in a car, and changing gear.

6. Depth of understanding

Creating a deeper understanding of the job and the process is better than imparting a superficial knowledge of the job. The success of this more sophisticated training scheme largely rests with the intelligence of the trainees and their keenness to possess a deeper understanding of principles and their wider application.

Those with considerable insight into their work as well as ability are more versatile and become valuable assets to a concern.

7. Instruction

The process of instruction, i.e. passing on information, may be carried out in a variety of ways, including explanation by direct speech or written notes, and practical demonstration and examples, illustrated by a range of visual aids such as the blackboard, models, diagrams, and sketches.

The process of passing knowledge must, however, be distinguished from the process of learning. Learning is an active process where the trainee must be physically and mentally involved.

8. Simplification

Some instructors fall into the trap of making things more difficult for trainees in order to stress their own importance because they know the answers. Such feelings must be replaced by aims to make training schemes as simple and easy as possible to assimilate. It is psychologically bad to impress trainees with continual propaganda on the difficulties and complexities of the job. The instructor must make the operations look easy, show that he can perform them easily and not allow trainees to form the impression that even the expert finds the job difficult.

Encouragement and confidence are important to the trainee, therefore, it helps considerably to arrange the programme so that teaching the easy tasks comes first followed by the more difficult ones later.

9. Ability to discriminate effectively

Many jobs involve processes or operations which demand a particular type of response to certain situations. The response may be to push a button, pull a lever, stop a machine, or to process a piece of material in many different ways dependent upon requirements. The situation which demands attention may be made evident by lights, sound, touch, visual appearance and measurement.

The training process should develop the correct response to situations; associations should be built up so that the trainee learns to use the most suitable sense organs to provide an adequate response to the situation as it arises. A simple example would be to check the smoothness of a surface by touch rather than by sight.

Another example would be the operation of a transfer machine where the operator is expected to press a button when twenty-four red lights are all glowing. The response to a number of lights may be much slower to learn than reaction to more familiar signs, like a bell or a buzzer sounding. The operator must learn to judge when the critical moment is coming.

10. Practice

Continued practice or participation forms an essential part of the learning process. The trainee must be given the opportunity to ask questions, examine the machine or tools or the work in hand, try out the process, show the results of his efforts, discuss the queries or problems and so become absorbed in the process of learning. A genuine interest in the job should develop as the trainee notices his improvements and is appropriately encouraged when he performs the operations correctly.

The instructor should point out any errors, or bad practices, and demonstrate the differences to show the advantage of performing the process correctly.

11. Use of analogies

When a trainee is confronted with strange or complex assemblies or operations it can be helpful to explain the assembly, for example, by showing a similar device which is more familiar to him and then pointing out its likenesses to the unfamiliar assembly.

12. The importance of repetition

As already stated, the trainee develops skills through continual practice. The instructor should apply the same principle: learning is easier and lasting impressions are achieved by repeating the information or demonstrating the technique many times.

Most individuals' powers of absorption are limited, so repetition is essential. If difficulty is experienced, repetition should also be supplemented by varying the approach, giving different forms of examples.

13. Spaced repetitions for learning skills

Skills are acquired more easily in a carefully planned number of regular learning periods over a length of time, than in the same number of lessons grouped closely together over a short period. Although this scheme is often difficult to arrange in many industrial conditions, wherever possible the principle should be used.

14. Continuity

Through the nature of change in processes, design and machines, training is essentially a continuous activity. Newcomers, transferees, and existing employees, all require training as changes occur. Follow-up becomes very important also, to ensure that the correct methods of performing operations are being practised.

15. Progress reports

Each trainee should have immediate and regular reports on his progress so that he can correct and practise to a scientific programme.

Unless criticism or praise is given quickly, valuable time is wasted by all concerned. Emphasis during the early stages of training should be placed on the correct method. The incorrect ways will continually appear, but they should not be highlighted by drawing attention to them unduly. Repetition of the correct method at these times is more positive and directs the efforts of the trainee in the right direction.

Asking questions regularly helps to keep trainees alert and fosters the feeling of actively taking part in the learning process. The question should be phrased so that an explanation is required, which will immediately show whether there is a true understanding of the subject, rather than a simple yes or no which tells the instructor nothing. If any particular difficulty is highlighted the instructor should deal with the problem immediately. Regular reviews of progress also provide an excellent opportunity to summarise the important aspects.

The Training Programme

A planned programme of training is discussed in three stages.

Stage I.   Available facilities.
Stage II.   Choice of methods.
Stage III. The plan.

Under Stage I an investigation of available facilities will provide sufficient information to prepare the plan. Information on accommodation, visual aids and learning material will also assist in the choice of methods discussed in Stage II. Methods include lecturing, hand-outs, discussion, practical demonstration, examples, practice, and improvisation.

Finally, Stage III outlines the important aspects of the plan, such as objectives, the budget, organisation, the programme, allocation of trainees, methods of instruction, training environment, progress reports, and follow-up.

STAGE I: AVAILABLE FACILITIES
Accommodation
The supervisor has to cope with the accommodation which management is prepared to offer. Often this is inadequate and simply amounts to a rearrangement of existing space at the workplace. In some establishments, however, a separate training centre is available to supplement training at the workplace and allowances are made to accommodate trainees on the shop floor so that they can practise, listen to lectures and watch demonstrations all in the most suitable surroundings.

Visual aids
The object of using visual aids is to assist the instructor, supplementing verbal explanation. Many very useful aids are cheap and require a small amount of preparation. Such items as blackboards and white chart pads allow the instructor to develop his ideas visually stage by stage. Diagrams and models can also be made up cheaply and are most effective in demonstrating practical work. There are many more expensive aids such as overhead projectors, slide and cine projectors and television, but it should be borne in mind that they are aids and not ends in themselves.

Only one aid should be used at a time and without any fuss, otherwise the trainees give more attention to the aid than to the subject matter. To avoid any delays the aid should be checked beforehand so that the operation runs smoothly.

Learning occurs when the trainee becomes mentally involved in the process by seeking out knowledge, asking questions and visualising the operation. Actual practice is the natural complementary process, so that the trainee learns from relating physical experience and visualisation of the operation.

Lecturing material: the job breakdown
Adequate preparation of lecturing material is an essential part of the instructor's job. Besides the obvious advantage of presentation of the procedure to be learnt in correct sequence without hesitancy, it provides an excellent opportunity to check the method currently used. The critical points in the operation should be given particular emphasis, with additional explanation and practice to overcome the crucial stages.

A job breakdown should contain an up-to-date, step-by-step account of the operation. The usual method is to watch the operation, build up the steps by asking questions and ensuring that the steps are in the correct sequence. If a work study department exists then probably records may be obtained from there.

Make sure that the most effective method or standard method is being used by the operator. If there is time, another opinion is a good way of assessing the job breakdown.

The following is an example of a job breakdown scheme for using a public telephone.

Step	Points to note
1. Consult dialling instructions.	1. Check that S.T.D. code is available.
2. Lift the receiver.	2. Listen for dialling tone.
3. Dial the number.	3. Make sure the dial fully returns every time before dialling the next digit.
4. Listen to number given.	4. Check number and dial again if incorrect.
5. Insert coin.	5. If coin passes through machine and out, retrieve and reinsert.
6. Insert further coins if additional time to converse is required.	6. Have further coins ready.
7. Replace receiver.	7. Essential before attempting to dial again.

Preparation of a job breakdown similar to the one above demands an intimate knowledge and great care in scheduling the sequences correctly. The amount of work involved is worth while; the instructor will be fully prepared and the actual teaching will be in correct sequence.

Any questions should be answered with confidence and understanding of the difficulties which trainees are likely to experience.

STAGE II: CHOICE OF METHODS

The various methods of instructing are detailed below. Instructors use all these methods as part of a full training programme where courses are included for acquiring both knowledge and skill.

1. Lecturing

In its narrowest sense the lecturing method is used to give information to trainees; their approach to the topic is strictly limited to playing a passive role of listening.

As their knowledge of the topic increases the one-way process of lecturing is gradually replaced by a two-way process of participation with the questioning technique, i.e. teaching rather than lecturing. The instructor continually checks by asking questions to see whether the knowledge has been absorbed accurately and trainees are encouraged to ask questions to supplement the lecture.

Lecturing is a fundamental method of imparting information, concepts and explanations, but although the theory and a guide to the practice of a skill can be imparted, the reality of performance is still something remote.

2. Hand-outs

A useful supplement to lecturing is to distribute duplicated copies of notes on the subject matter and any additional information. The dictation of notes is avoided which saves considerable time and energy. Suitable reading matter such as textbooks and periodicals may be recommended for further reading.

Part of a training programme may be conducted by basing the training periods upon previous preparation by the student. The particular topics to be dealt with are outlined in a programme so that the student can read in advance of the lecture. The scheme encourages discussion and permits questions to be asked by the instructor to assess the degree of absorption. He may then supplement the trainees' reading by elaborating on particular topics.

3. Discussion

The essential requirements for successful discussion are a group of individuals who possess similar basic knowledge of the topic for discussion, but preferably with varying backgrounds and experience to provide a balance of opinions. The size of the group will also affect the discussion. Such stringent requirements may limit the use of this method for operator training.

The discussion technique is becoming increasingly popular as a method of airing problems in order to stimulate individuals into thinking up new ideas. The use of discussion groups in supervisory and management training schemes is commonplace.

Such schemes include seminars, case studies, role playing, and business games. Seminars are conducted either by asking a member to give a lecture on a given topic or by holding a discussion on a topic to stimulate an exchange of ideas under the chairmanship of a group member. The use of case studies is another method where information on a problem is given and the group attempts to find a satisfactory answer by discussing and analysing the case. Role playing involves members in actually taking part in controlled situations by assuming the identity of a supervisor, for example, and dealing with a complaint. The business game is similar to role playing, but more involved. A number of members may participate on similar lines and, when properly conducted, they soon tend to "live the part".

Gathering a group of operators from the workplace often causes a certain amount of disruption to which management may object. The gains may be considerable, however, not only from the training viewpoint, but also because of the excellent suggestions that can emerge from such discussions.

4. Examples

Some topics are difficult to explain adequately by speech alone. This predicament can often be solved easily by using suitable examples to illustrate the situation or point. Some of these aids are sketches, diagrams, models, pictures, and analogies.

5. Practical demonstration

Skills are mainly acquired by imitation and practice. Naturally the only way a trainee can imitate an operation is to watch a practical demonstration and be provided with facilities to copy and practise what he has seen.

The demonstration must be clear, in strict logical sequence and according to the standards given in any hand-outs. The complete operation should be demonstrated and any particular problem pointed out and accompanied by illustrations of special techniques and critical points.

6. Practice

As already stressed, the vital stage of acquiring skill is reached when practice begins. Continual practice is essential, together with assistance from the instructor who should regularly check and correct when necessary. He must encourage the trainee if progress is poor as it is easy to be disheartened at this time. Criticism should be positive in nature by showing the correct method and techniques. Quick learners must be watched to see that speed is not leading them into bad habits. Slow learners need plenty of encouragement and sympathy.

7. Improvisation

All instructors should practise the art of improvisation because the moment straight lecturing ceases and the opportunity is given for trainees to ask questions it will be necessary to some degree.

If a topic is difficult to understand, invariably the instructor will have to think up examples and illustrations on the spur of the moment which are in tune with the atmosphere at the time and meaningful to that particular group.

Successful improvisation demands a broad and deep knowledge of the subject matter, plus the ability to expand a point and to construct suitable teaching material at a moment's notice.

8. Programmed learning

This method uses a technique of learning by breaking down the subject into simple stages which are presented to the trainee in sequence; he learns, tests himself, moves to the next stage, and so on. The sequence should be designed to motivate the trainee to learn quickly.

STAGE III: THE PLAN

The main aspects of the training plan to be considered are given below.

1. Objectives
A good plan is based upon clear objectives which should be stated and understood by everyone who is concerned with the training scheme. Some of the aims of training are to improve quality of work, increase output and to increase productivity by reducing errors, reducing the accident rate and creating positive attitudes.

2. The budget
Management must agree a budget to cover all possible expenditure such as for equipment, teaching materials, training centre and instructors.

3. Organisation
The appointment of individuals who are responsible for training generally and for particular training schemes is essential. They must have sufficient authority to act within the over-all framework of training programmes so that arrangements may be put into practice and controlled effectively.

4. The programme
An assessment should be made of all the training schemes which can be accommodated. Each scheme should be titled and timetabled with sufficient detail and suitable progress points to form a logical sequence of training at different levels. An over-all schedule may now be drawn up to accommodate the schemes, e.g. on a half-yearly or yearly basis.

The programme should be as simple and flexible as possible to cope with probable alterations later on.

5. Allocation of trainees
Allocation should be made on a fair and logical basis in accordance with personnel policy. Selection of suitable trainees and choice of training are additional factors which will depend upon circumstances. To avoid any misapprehension the method and results of allocations should be publicised.

6. Methods of instruction
Deciding upon the methods of instruction will depend upon a number of factors including training environment, the budget, the standard of trainees and existing facilities. The initial decision on methods depends upon whether the aim is to acquire knowledge on a particular subject or to acquire a skill.

7. Training environment
Where a choice of facilities is available, full use should be made of the advantages of each training environment. As a general guide the quiet atmosphere of a classroom is ideal for lecturing and discussions; the training centre may accommodate lectures, demonstrations, and

practice, while the workplace provides the atmosphere of reality and is, therefore, useful for advanced practice.

8. Progress reports

Adequate control depends upon conscientious recording of progress and results. Measuring performance and improvements at appropriate stages in training ensures that corrective measures will be taken such as additional tuition or, in extreme cases, removal of a trainee from the course.

The reports are normally recorded on personnel records and statistics are prepared for management appraisal. The trainee should also see the reports as part of the normal practice of informing the individual of his progress.

9. Follow-up

A good training scheme is essentially a continuous process. Genuine interest in the progress of trainees after the course is essential for successful follow-up. Further training or retraining may be necessary in some cases whereas in others rapid progress may result in promotion. Recording such information is vital for statistical purposes when coupled with progress reports. Assessment of long-term results may indicate changes in the training programme. Individuals might develop particularly bad habits after certain periods on machines and these may be corrected in subsequent training schemes by additional emphasis at the appropriate stage of the operation. Long-term effective control of training relies upon conscientious follow-up.

Sequence of Instruction

The main steps in an instruction plan are as follows.

1. Prepare the trainee.
2. Explain the job.
3. Demonstrate the operations.
4. Practise.
5. Check performance.
6. Follow-up.

The plan follows a logical sequence of training which is fundamental to all schemes for acquiring skill.

The basis of most of the schemes is taken from the work of Charles R. Allen whose writings were published in 1919 in a book called *The Instructor, The Man and The Job.*

The main points connected with each step are given below.

1. Prepare the trainee

Reduce nervousness and concern by attempting to establish friendly relationships with the trainee. Take his mind off the subject of training for a while.

Useful information can be gained by getting him to chat about his previous jobs and this provides a lead to give general information on the product, the processes involved, where this particular job fits in, and its importance.

His interest should be further aroused by giving more details of the objectives of the company and his particular part in achieving them.

2. Explain the job

The job should be explained in outline, but with sufficient detail for the trainee to appreciate its significance. At this stage explanations should be given on special tools, standard layouts, measuring devices, specifications, drawings, job language, and materials. The trainee should also be told the value of the equipment, tools, materials, and assemblies, and be instructed on safety precautions, cost of waste and the importance of quality standards, to encourage conscientiousness.

3. Demonstrate the operation

Each important step should be adequately explained, shown and illustrated. Each key point must be stressed. The trainee should be as near as possible to the operation position. The instructor should be certain that all stages are clearly understood, which means that he must be painstaking and check the effectiveness of his teaching by constantly asking questions.

A run-through at normal operating speed is followed by a sloweddown version to a point where each movement may be clearly seen and connected with preceding and subsequent movements.

4. Practise the operation

When the trainee feels sufficiently confident to attempt the operation, he should be allowed to have a trial run under close supervision. A complete run of the whole operation at normal speed is recommended, but, as mentioned previously, it is not always possible owing to economic considerations such as high cost of scrap.

Mistakes should be corrected immediately by showing the correct way with more detailed explanations. Often the cause of error is forgetfulness and a quick reminder is sufficient. If the trainee explains the tasks as he performs them it helps to bring the key points into his mind and hastens the learning process. Practice continues until the instructor is satisfied with the performance.

5. Check performance

At this stage the trainee is placed on his own and put to work. A nearby colleague or supervisor should take over to offer immediate assistance when needed, while the instructor should check frequently for any deviation from the correct method.

Continued personal contact is required to boost the trainee's spirits at this time. Questions should be asked on any work problems. Extra coaching should be gradually diminished as performance improves.

6. Follow-up

The final stage of follow-up ought to be considered as a process which continues indefinitely. If good relationships have been established the instructor will be able to encourage and make employees feel more important by taking an interest in their progress on a long-term basis. Any bad working habits that may appear later must be checked and any advice which is desirable should be given freely.

This broad interpretation of follow-up should be encouraged as such a scheme provides a close-knit system of communication for promotion and other purposes. Sufficient information should flow between the Personnel Department, the supervisor, the instructor and post-trainees, to provide more reliable indications of the true working situation.

Training Existing Employees

A supervisor is often faced with the difficult tasks of persuading existing employees to change their present jobs, stimulating them to learn new jobs and actually training them.

The main reasons for job changes are as follows.

1. Incapacity

The employee's physical or mental health may deteriorate and so prevent him from performing the job successfully. He may have suffered an illness, had an accident, or be under emotional stress.

This condition may be difficult to deal with. Sometimes the employee persuades himself that the blame for his shortcomings lies with the supervisor, who continually gives him the "hard jobs" to perform.

2. Production method

Most employees will appreciate the economic necessity of keeping up to date with production processes in the face of competition. Obsolescent machines must be replaced, new and more suitable materials must replace the old and the introduction of better methods is essential. Unfortunately, these changes often cause human upheavals which include retraining and regrouping employees. Adequate explanations are essential otherwise there is less chance of achieving co-operation.

3. Fluctuations in output

Seasonal lines and changes in demand through competition cause output fluctuations which often result in temporary redundancy. The introduction of patterned seasonal lines (such as ice-cream in summer and hot dogs in winter) solves the problem of output, but probably demands a more versatile labour force, with many employees capable of performing more than one job.

It is essential to encourage and persuade existing employees so that they want to learn new jobs. Important factors such as losing face in front of colleagues, breaking up working groups, separation from a particular colleague, and resistance to changing a long-established routine, should all be considered. Reasonable solutions to such problems must be established before interviewing the employee.

Adequate information on the background to these changes helps considerably. If the employee can see and accept the reasons for any changes, the possibility of agreement and co-operation is much greater.

The Results

The aim of a training programme is to produce a highly trained versatile labour force.

Some top managers strongly contest the installation of a training programme on the grounds that it is costly and time-consuming. They claim that many other pressing jobs should receive priority and that training is uneconomic because the trained employees leave and other firms receive the benefit.

More enlightened managers refuse to shirk their social and industrial responsibilities and gain the following advantages.

1. Higher productivity.
2. Increased output.
3. Improved quality.
4. Less waste.
5. Less machine maintenance.
6. Fewer accidents.
7. Shorter learning periods.
8. Less labour turnover.
9. Higher morale.
10. More confidence in management.

Training is an essential part of the supervisor's job. If this activity is neglected the time spent on other aspects of supervision increases sharply. The vital point is that neglect of this aspect to spend more time on other matters is false economy. Other matters demand far more time, cost, and effort than training, without showing such effective results.

QUESTIONS

1. Why is training considered to be so important today?
2. Discuss the supervisor's fundamental task of training.
3. Discuss the question of training schemes, mentioning their effectiveness and any limitations.
4. What is meant by the "learning plateau" and how can it be overcome?
5. Discuss the analytical method of training, mentioning the advantages.
6. Suggest some useful guides to training which would assist the supervisor in improving his capability as an instructor.
7. Discuss the problem of acquiring a skill.
8. Outline a planned programme of training.
9. Draw up an instruction plan for acquiring a skill.
10. What difficulties should a supervisor be prepared to overcome when retraining existing employees?
11. What are the aims and advantages of an organised training programme in a company?
12. Discuss the Industrial Training Act 1964.

CHAPTER XVII

INDUSTRIAL RELATIONS

Introduction

THE current trend is to employ the term "industrial relations" to cover all the complicated bargaining and discussions between management and trade unions, and management and employees. Such consultation may be formal or informal, may involve certain legal machinery and use accepted negotiation procedures.

Both managers and supervisors require a thorough knowledge of these procedures and the background of previous negotiations and agreements in their particular industry. Many trouble-spots are allowed to grow through lack of understanding of the consultative bodies and their functions. Working together is essential and demanding; both sides must be prepared to give and take to maintain co-operation and mutual understanding.

The main areas of industrial relations are now considered by examining collective bargaining over the past ten years and the consultative bodies involved. The main aspects of disputes and consultative machinery are then discussed along with the individual rights of employees and the role of the supervisor.

Collective bargaining

In 1968 when the Donovan Report was published, about 500 negotiating arrangements for manual workers were known to exist between employers (or employers' associations) and trade unions, and about two-thirds of the working population had their terms and conditions of employment regulated by collective bargaining.

In 1971 the Industrial Relations Act was passed in an attempt to create a legislative framework acceptable to all parties. The enactment caused considerable controversy mainly on the grounds that legislation is not the proper vehicle to carry the many facets of relationship between employer and employee.

A change of Government occurred in 1974. The new Government prepared a threefold labour legislative plan:

    1. to repeal the 1971 Industrial Relations Act;
    2. to legislate afresh on collective and individual employment rights;
    3. to launch "industrial democracy". (Research for this part of the plan was conducted by the Bullock Committee.)

Many of the issues were studied in depth in the U.K. and in overseas countries. Each phase of the threefold plan is now discussed.

1. REPEAL OF THE INDUSTRIAL RELATIONS ACT 1971

The statutory replacement of the Industrial Relations Act was the Trade Union and Labour Relations Act passed in 1974. TULRA, as it is often called, repealed the 1971 Act but re-enacted with some changes the provisions of the older Act regarding unfair dismissal, along with certain supplementary provisions.

The 1974 Act provided a new and fuller portrait of the trade union, its immunities and the legal position of the collective agreement. Schedule I of the Act received much publicity; this covered the basic rules regarding unfair dismissal as well as the jurisdiction and procedure of industrial tribunals. In 1976, for example, over 31,000 applications were received by the industrial tribunals on unfair dismissals alone, thus illustrating the importance of this single region of employment law. (It should be noted that these provisions are now contained in the Employment Protection (Consolidation) Act 1978.)

2. THE EMPLOYMENT PROTECTION ACT 1975

This comprehensive statute, containing 129 sections and 18 schedules, made many inroads into labour law. Many quarters have heavily criticised the Act but the general aim was to establish statutory minimum requirements of employment for those who did not happen to work for "enlightened" companies.

Undoubtedly the Act forcibly squashed the old "hire and fire" philosophy. Moreover, it has been generally recognised that Britain compares unfavourably with its E.E.C. partners in the area of indirect labour costs, which is money expended on the general well-being of a company's labour force. The E.P.A. went some way towards bringing Britain in line with its Common Market partners in this field of "benefits".

The implications of the Act were so large that it was phased into the U.K. working situation by degrees, mainly during 1976 and 1977. Thus on 1st January 1976 the Advisory, Conciliation and Arbitration Service (ACAS) was placed on a statutory basis, while 6th April 1977 saw the commencement of "maternity pay".

Two areas of major significance were Part I, which dealt with the machinery for promoting the improvement of industrial relations, and Part II, which covered the individual rights of employees. Basic coverage was also given to such items as the procedure for handling redundancies and the law dealing with terms and conditions of employment. (The provisions of the Act relating to individual employee rights are now contained in the Employment Protection (Consolidation) Act 1978.)

Apart from establishing the well-known ACAS, the Act also set up the Employment Appeal Tribunal to hear appeals from industrial tribunals and the office of the Certification Officer who is appointed by

the Secretary of State after consultation with ACAS. He is responsible
for functions which were formerly performed by the Chief Registrar
of Friendly Societies and for certifying that a trade union is "independent", which means that it is free of such control by employers which
may inhibit the union from acting in its own best, independent
interests.

3. INDUSTRIAL DEMOCRACY

There has been wide debate for many years on the role of industrial
democracy or employee participation. Since the publication in 1977
of the Report of the Committee of Inquiry on Industrial Democracy
(the Bullock Report), immense controversy has developed but as yet,
no legislation is in force.

Probably the British business interests' hostile comments could be
summarised as implying that the Bullock proposals, regardless of
whether they were right or wrong, were too radical for employers.
Indeed, this 120,000 word report was not without its own division
of opinion. A minority report of employers' representatives, published
by three of the Committee's members, broadly alleged that industry
in Britain was not yet ready for such fundamental changes as were
envisaged in the majority report.

In the body of the report the Committee envisaged its creed as follows: "We believe that there must be a joint approach to decision-
making in companies, based on equal representation of employees and
shareholders on the board. In our view it is no longer acceptable for
companies to be run on the basis that in the last resort the shareholders' view must by right always prevail."

The Committee envisaged that a basic legal framework—"of
necessity, complex"—should be laid down but that, within this sphere
great freedom should be allowed for each individual company to create its own board of directors. This device clearly indicates that the
success or failure of industrial democracy depends on co-operation
between management and trade unions.

Also, an independent Industrial Democracy Commission was advo-
cated to provide "advice, conciliation, and ultimate decision for those
within a company whose task it is to devise an agreed system of
employee representation on boards."

The German model of a two-tier board was considered unsuitable,
although the minority group favoured it. The unitary board was
favoured with an "ultimate responsibility for decisions".

The philosophy of industrial democracy

The disastrous consequences of poor relationships between employers
and employees in Britain are well known. Equally obvious is the need
for Britain's managers and trade unionists to revise their ideas on
industrial democracy, individually and collectively.

Many reasons are often given for lack of industrial harmony. Some of the glaring examples are: failure by employers to recognise the growing strength of trade unions; the continual use of outdated methods of treating employees; reliance on obsolescent managers who are out of touch with reality; failure in appreciating the educational level of employees who understand far more about industrial and commercial operations than is generally imagined; and, finally, completely underestimating the ingenuity and capability of employees.

Employees must also take some of the blame. Often there is a tendency to take advantage of management and the company if the opportunity arises, such as improving on their share of "perks", slacking whenever possible, bargaining for excessive wage claims if they think they can hold the company or an industry to ransom, and in general not co-operating. This selfish approach often at the expense of fellow workers in other industries is indicative of one of the basic problems that prevails in industry and commerce.

Finally the trade unions also must take their share of the blame for lack of industrial harmony. Some trade union leaders openly declare their political beliefs and even go so far as to admit that their aim is to overthrow the Government in office at the time. Others develop a minority interest through improving earnings and conditions for a particular group of trade union members, despite the discontent created in other groups. Certain unions have held the public to ransom at times and also issued grave warnings such as anticipating industrial chaos under particular conditions. Excessive militancy by some shop stewards, outdated policies, and general misuse of trade union power have also been levelled against trade unions in recent years.

Government intervention to stem the increasing chaos in order to protect the community does not seem to work. The adoption of a philosophy by all parties concerned—to avoid economic disaster— would need to be based upon an overriding objective of company survival and growth so that everyone's interests would be seen to be at stake in the long term. Thus all parties need to be consulted and take part in decisions which directly and indirectly affect them. Wherever they have sufficient expertise to contribute this capability must be used, otherwise frustration is inevitable. Moreover, this concept implies the subordination of individual and collective self-interests to the common good.

Problem areas

Such a philosophy outlined above raises many fundamental issues. Some examples are given below but there are many others.

1. Does a particular formal approach to industrial democracy seen operating well in a foreign country mean that a similar approach would be successful in Britain?

2. How can a trade union equate nominating some of its members to a board of directors with its freedom of action?
3. How would collective bargaining be affected considering (2) above?
4. Would employee nominees to a board of directors have sufficient expertise to contribute at this level in the organisation?
5. How can enthusiasm be generated among employees to participate effectively in management decision-making?
6. If one of the declared objectives of a trade union is to develop a minority interest through improving earnings and conditions for its members, despite the discontent of other groups, how does it reconcile this aim with the national interest?

The Whitley Committee

Up to World War I negotiations concerning terms and conditions of employment were conducted mainly at area or district level with very few on a national basis. During that war the power of the unions increased considerably because of labour shortages and closer co-operation of employment areas with the State. The need for improving industrial relations and conditions was recognised by the State and in 1917 a committee was established under the chairmansip of J. H. Whitley to investigate and make proposals.

The reports were based upon full recognition of trade unions, the idea of self-government in industry and no legal compulsion. The proposals included setting up Joint Industrial Councils to fill the need for negotiating machinery at a national level. There are now about 200 joint committees at national and district levels, and over half are Joint Industrial Councils. Procedure and structure of these bodies are not standardised; they are generally composed of equal numbers of employers' and employees' representatives. The majority of national agreements on wages and conditions of employment have been negotiated through these councils.

The chairman is generally an independent person with no voting rights as the purpose of the committee is to help both sides to reach a mutual agreement. If the parties fail to agree then the case is taken to arbitration or left to some form of conciliation.

In the Civil Service and local government service, these permanent bodies are also known as Whitley Councils. They are also found in some minor industries but not in the basic industries.

The consultative bodies

The main consultative bodies are the employers' associations and the trade unions. At this level negotiations for wages are usually handled directly without referring for active assistance to the two central federations, the Confederation of British Industry and the Trades Union Congress.

The federations advise, provide information and statistics to their members, and give their views to the Government, the national press and international organisations. Their officials sit on a number of councils and committees which advise the Government and statutory bodies.

Employers' associations

Employers have grouped together generally within the particular industry, but not to any set pattern. Their associations vary in size from small local groups, to sections of an industry, to a whole industry on a national level. Some of these associations were formed to cope with industrial relations problems while others were organised to deal with trading problems in addition. In some cases an association deals only with trading questions.

The role played by employers' associations varies, dependent upon over-all policy. Some have an enlightened policy and actively promote good relations between employers and employees, offering such facilities as practical advice and information on wages standards and conditions of employment, training programmes and specialised services. Others are rather negative in their approach. They will examine proposals and advise revisions, based upon the protection of members' interests, but seldom initiate action themselves.

A typical organisation consists of a small number of full-time staff, controlled by a director who is responsible for the daily activities of the association, plus representatives from member firms and officials who form a central committee. This committee meets about four times a year to formulate policy and to elect such committees as are considered necessary. The chairmen of these committees usually meet regularly with the association's officials to co-ordinate activities.

There are approximately 1400 employers' organisations and most of these are federated to about eighty-five national organisations. Most of the national organisations are members of the Confederation of British Industry and they negotiate with trade unions to reach national collective agreements.

THE CONFEDERATION OF BRITISH INDUSTRY

This confederation represents the employers' associations at national level and internationally. The nationalised industries and many individual companies are affiliated to the C.B.I., which puts forward the views of all these groups to the Government. C.B.I. representatives are members of a number of Government advisory committees and voluntary bodies who deal with labour problems.

Table VII—Trade unions [1]

At end of year:	1966	1967	1968	1969	1970	1971	1972	1973	1974	1975 [2]	1976 [2]
Number of trade unions	622	604	583	562	540	522	504	515	501	492	462
Analysis by number of members:											
Under 100 members	126	126	114	111	108	100	83	84	79	77	68
100 and under 500	147	135	136	133	133	128	135	135	135	134	135
500 and under 1,000	68	70	63	66	57	60	45	52	52	54	47
1,000 and under 2,500	89	85	88	74	66	64	67	74	69	66	60
2,500 and under 5,000	65	63	59	57	54	53	55	50	51	44	44
5,000 and under 10,000	30	31	32	32	33	33	32	35	30	29	29
10,000 and under 15,000	22	21	18	12	14	11	13	11	11	11	8
15,000 and under 25,000	18	18	19	24	22	19	18	18	18	17	15
25,000 and under 50,000	19	18	15	14	13	16	18	18	17	20	17
50,000 and under 100,000	20	18	20	17	17	15	13	18	14	15	17
100,000 and under 250,000	9	10	10	13	14	12	14	13	14	14	14
250,000 and over	9	9	9	9	9	11	11	11	11	11	11
Membership (Thousands)											
Total	10,259	10,188	10,191	10,470	11,178	11,126	11,351	11,447	11,755	12,184	12,376
Males [3]	8,003	7,903	7,829	7,965	8,437	8,374	8,445	8,443	8,579	8,721	8,816
Females [3]	2,256	2,286	2,362	2,505	2,741	2,752	2,905	3,005	3,174	3,462	3,560
Analysis by size of unions:											
Under 100 members	6	6	5	5	5	5	4	4	4	4	3
100 and under 500	37	34	34	33	33	31	35	34	35	34	35
500 and under 1,000	48	49	43	46	40	41	31	37	37	39	34
1,000 and under 2,500	146	141	142	121	111	106	101	114	107	105	99
2,500 and under 5,000	227	218	202	200	186	176	179	168	170	144	151
5,000 and under 10,000	206	214	216	218	221	227	216	232	196	195	196
10,000 and under 15,000	274	265	226	145	166	130	150	129	135	129	100
15,000 and under 25,000	332	333	343	447	419	342	333	335	343	327	296
25,000 and under 50,000	666	647	512	492	452	540	609	624	609	664	621
50,000 and under 100,000	1,379	1,274	1,434	1,205	1,202	1,101	912	997	948	1,045	997
100,000 and under 250,000	1,477	1,539	1,539	1,875	2,188	1,718	1,879	1,810	1,958	1,995	2,053
250,000 and over	5,461	5,469	5,495	5,684	6,155	6,709	6,901	6,963	7,213	7,503	7,790

...more than once in the figures, but the effect on the aggregates is relatively insignificant. [2] The 1976 figures are confined to organisations which appear to satisfy the statutory definition of trade union in section 28 of the Trade Union and Labour Relations Act 1974. This has had the effect of excluding from the statistics 31 organisations, with a combined membership of about 167,000, which were previously regarded by the department as trade unions. More than half the membership was accounted for by organisations representing members of the police service, which are specifically excluded from the statutory definition by section 30 of the 1974 Act. Calculated on this new basis the number of trade unions at the end of 1975 was 461 and the membership was: Total membership 12,017; Males 8,592; Females 3,425. [3] The subdivision of the total membership into males and females is partly estimated, as some trade unions are unable to state precisely the numbers of males and females in their total membership.
Source: Department of Employment.

Figures are taken from the Central Statistical Office, Annual Abstract of Statistics 1979, by permission of the Controller of Her Majesty's Stationery Office.

Table VIII—Registered trade unions in Great Britain [1]

	1961	1962	1963	1964	1965	1966	1967	1968	1969	1970	1972
Number of unions on register	393	388	372	369	356	351	345	337	328	326	229
Number of members (thousands)	8,545	8,532	8,524	8,620	8,683	8,584	8,472	8,529	8,753	9,277	891
Income (£ thousand)											
From members	27,004	29,226	30,424	31,969	33,301	35,951	36,561	37,081	38,280	43,785	4,808
From other sources	3,906	4,357	4,329	4,884	5,768	5,912	6,821	7,241	7,502	8,441	2,496
Expenditure (£ thousand)											
Working expenses	15,870	16,981	17,988	19,199	20,619	22,486	23,768	25,412	27,384	30,222	3,710
Unemployment, etc. benefit	178	309	464	209	216	251	521	478	427	533	149
Dispute benefit	539	697	462	489	649	919	730	1,162	1,619	3,583	13
Provident benefits [2]	6,810	7,184	7,528	7,528	8,171	9,663	10,278	10,454	10,393	10,804	716
From political fund	605	606	1,063	975	658	1,155	700	712	718	1,566	23
Other outgoings	2,078	2,109	1,881	2,798	2,539	2,989	2,462	3,424	2,696	3,694	598
Funds at end of year (£ thousand)	95,134	100,839	106,179	111,324	117,572	121,882	127,249	129,762	132,746	134,599	14,216

[1] The figures for 1961 to 1970 given in this table relate to trade unions of employees in Great Britain which had registered voluntarily under the Trade Union Acts of 1871 and 1913. The legal definition of a Trade Union was changed by the Industrial Relations Act 1971 and provisional figures for 1972 relate to 170 of the 229 organisations registered voluntarily under the new Act. No information is available for 1971. Number of members, income from members and expenditure (other outgoings) have been adjusted to eliminate duplication in respect of registered unions that are affiliated to a registered federation or are branches of another registered union. [2] Expenditure on sickness and accident benefit, superannuation and other benefits. Figures are not available after 1972.
Sources: Registry of Friendly Societies; Registry of Trade Unions and Employers' Associations.

Figures are taken from the Central Statistical Office, Annual Abstract of Statistics 1976, by permission of the Controller of Her Majesty's Stationery Office.

TRADE UNIONS

Employees have organised themselves into trade unions in most industries today. The process has been long, involved and often haphazard in growth, resulting in a complex structure of many different types of union. Gradually the movement is becoming more organised and uniform, as amalgamations and mergers of the smaller unions into larger ones continue.

Table VII gives the number of trade unions and membership between 1966 and 1976, and Table VIII provides the last available information on registered trade unions, membership, expenditure, and funds in hand. The total membership of trade unions in the United Kingdom in 1969 was 10.3 million, which represented about 40 per cent of all employees.

Objects

The main object of a trade union is to protect and help its members. So far this object has been partially achieved by negotiating for higher wages and better conditions of employment. The trend now is towards more joint consultation, to be distinguished from joint negotiation which is limited to questions of wages and conditions of employment.

Forms of organisation

In general there are four main forms of organisation: the professional workers' union for clerical, administrative or executive workers; the craft-type union for skilled trades; the industrial union for all workers in an industry such as mining; and the general labour union for workers below the skilled level. The first-mentioned is expanding rapidly, while the others tend to be static now.

The structure

The varied forms of growth in the union movement have inevitably resulted in many different types of internal organisation. The general structure of trade unions is described below, taking each level of control in turn.

First level: shop steward. In many unions the first level above members is an official who is known as a shop steward, delegate or collector. His job ranges from collecting dues to handling complaints and grievances and he operates from the shop floor.

Second level: branch secretary. Most trade union organisations are divided into branches and every member belongs to a particular one in his area, which may vary in size from a few members to thousands. In some industries branches are based within each company and are known as chapels (in the printing industry) or groups. Officers are elected and matters within the area of the branch which are local in nature are dealt with by the secretary. The secretary of a branch controls a very important link in the chain of command.

Third level: district controller. Branches are grouped into districts, under the district or regional controller, who is generally salaried and full-time. The regional level usually operates committees which are powerful within the district controlled. In large unions the methods of linking up regional levels with the central organisation become very complex through the use of coupling committees.

Fourth level: general secretary. Generally the fourth level forms the central organisation, headed by a general secretary. He is responsible to a national executive committee, which may vary considerably in nature and size. The general secretary is usually salaried, full-time and elected in various ways. Unions also have a president. Full-time staff are employed at head office for administration purposes.

Similar problems of organisation and communication are found in any large concern and trade unions are no exception.

THE TRADES UNION CONGRESS

The trade union movement is represented as a whole by the T.U.C., to which most large unions belong. About 180 unions are affiliated, which represent over 8 million members. The remaining unaffiliated unions account for about a million members, who are mainly Government servants and teachers.

Objects

The objects of the T.U.C. are "to promote the interests of all its affiliated organisations and generally to improve the social and economic conditions of the workers." In practice, the objects are extended to include consideration of the broad issues of national policy where they affect trade unions.

Delegates to Congress

A trade union must be affiliated to the T.U.C. before it has the right to provide a delegate. One delegate is allowed for every 5000 members and one vote for every 1000 members.

The T.U.C. meets annually to discuss the report of its General Council and the work of the committees. Each paragraph of the report is discussed and motions from affiliated trade unions' delegates are considered. The resolutions passed by Congress are based upon majority votes by delegates who voice an opinion, show hands, or vote by card, dependent upon the importance of the issue. These resolutions provide the framework of policy which the T.U.C. General Council uses throughout the year in its negotiations and general activities. They do not commit the unions to any particular course of action.

The unions remain completely independent, therefore, the T.U.C. has very limited executive control and acts in the capacity of a deliberative body whose resolutions are mere recommendations. This situation has been the subject of strong comment by specialists in this field.

In emergencies and when a unified decision is required by the T.U.C. for policy purposes at a national level, a special conference is convened. All the trade unions' executives attend and pass resolutions on a majority vote. These decisions carry the full support of all the affiliated trade unions when represented by the T.U.C.

The T.U.C. General Council

The thirty-two members of this council are elected annually by Congress. The functions of the General Council are to represent the trade unions, to co-ordinate any action by a particular union and to promote the trade union movement generally.

To achieve these aims a large range of activities is carried out. Among other involvements, the General Council consults with other associations and with the Government, takes note of and, if necessary, initiates labour legislation, sits on advisory councils and committees, adjusts disputes, promotes common action among unions, undertakes educational propaganda and research projects, and prepares an annual report for Congress.

The General Council's executive powers are strictly limited and in the main it recommends courses of action with no power to enforce them.

REGISTRATION

Any organisation of workers (such as staff associations) or employers may apply for registration to the Certification Officer who is appointed by the Secretary of State after consultation with ACAS. Certain provisions are necessary, including having the power to alter its own rules, being independent, and controlling the application of its own property and funds.

The advantages of being registered and granted a certificate of independence are many and real and include the right to demand information from an employer for collective bargaining purposes; the right of employees who are members of an independent trade union to have time off work—with pay—to engage in union duties, the right to refer a "recognition" issue to ACAS and the right to tax exemptions in respect of investment income and in capital gains devoted to the payment of provident benefits.

Disputes

Failure to settle a dispute by collective bargaining generally leads to a stoppage of work through either a strike or a lock-out. The number of deadlocks of this nature has reached alarming proportions in recent years. Such cessations of work not only affect the interests of the parties concerned but also have serious repercussions on the national economy. An examination of Table IX which shows the number of stoppages and working days lost indicates clearly the disastrous trend.

For many years successive Governments have attempted to introduce effective machinery to promote settlements. This machinery has taken the form of advice, conciliation and arbitration. Conciliation means introducing a third party who attempts to help the parties in dispute by suggesting possible solutions which may be acceptable to both. There is no question of compulsion.

Similarly, arbitration is a voluntary process where both parties agree to submit the dispute to a person (or persons) who will give a valued opinion. The parties also agree to accept this opinion or award beforehand.

Figure 30 gives a simplified indication of the negotiating machinery which is available in the settlement of disputes.

THE ADVISORY, CONCILIATION AND ARBITRATION SERVICE

The aim of ACAS is to promote the improvement of industrial relations by strengthening collective bargaining and by assisting in various ways when a dispute arises. It is independent of Government control—this is its distinguishing feature.

Employers are offered advice on a wide range of industrial relations and employment matters. They may ask for assistance from its officers in helping to settle disputes and arbitration can also be arranged. In addition, employers may, in most cases, seek the assistance of an ACAS conciliation officer when a trade union or employee complains to an industrial tribunal. The officer will try to settle the dispute by agreement between the parties rather than resorting to a tribunal hearing. Indeed, a copy of the complaint submitted to an industrial tribunal is sent, as a matter of course, to a conciliation officer.

ACAS may conduct inquiries into industrial matters and publish its findings. A Code of Practice has been produced called *Disciplinary Practice and Procedures in Employment* which provides guidance on how to draw up disciplinary rules and procedures and how to operate them effectively. This is discussed in detail below.

ACAS may refer disputes to the Central Arbitration Committee (C.A.C.) for arbitration provided the parties concerned agree. The C.A.C. has powers in connection with trade union recognition and disclosure of information, and it took over the functions of the Industrial Arbitration Board which included cases involving fair wages.

The Employment Protection Act 1975 established a new Employment Appeal Tribunal which hears appeals from the decisions of industrial tribunals on points of law and appeals from the decisions of the Certification Officer on points of law and fact when the dispute concerns either an entry on the list of trade unions or applications for certificates of independence.

Table IX—Industrial stoppages [1]

Number of stoppages and workers involved

	1967	1968	1969	1970	1971	1972	1973	1974	1975	1976	1977
Numbers of stoppages beginning in each year											
Analysis by industry [2]:											
All industries and services [3]	2,116	2,378	3,116	3,906	2,228	2,497	2,873	2,922	2,282	2,016	2,703
Mining and quarrying	399	227	193	?65	138	229	305	196	217	283	272
Metals, engineering, shipbuilding and vehicles	910	1,103	1,430	1,521	1,107	1,249	1,342	1,326	1,045	800	1,121
Textiles	41	54	72	96	70	66	92	94	72	49	77
Clothing and footwear	19	15	24	27	27	31	31	31	45	31	38
Construction	256	276	285	337	234	243	217	203	208	244	248
Transport and communication	208	342	540	584	269	236	298	305	189	193	245
All other industries and services	293	387	576	777	383	443	591	774	517	418	702
Workers directly and indirectly involved in these stoppages: Total (thousands)	732	2,256	1,656	1,753	1,175	1,726	1,513	1,622	789	670	1,155
Analysis by industry [2]:											
Mining and quarrying	42	30	145	113	23	342	47	307	28	39	54
Metals, engineering, shipbuilding and vehicles	459	1,911	750	784	665	680	819	733	465	415	603
Textiles	6	12	18	34	11	18	26	31	39	9	20
Clothing and footwear	3	4	10	30	4	7	14	6	12	6	16
Construction	37	47	44	51	38	210	25	22	26	51	34
Transport and communication	113	145	393	347	306	218	147	135	81	43	56
All other industries and services	73	107	296	429	127	251	435	388	138	107	372
Analysis by duration of stoppage:											
Not more than 6 days	572	2,075	1,093	1,075	702	821	1,025	710	473	449	547
Over 6 but not more than 12 days	82	77	146	162	127	137	191	226	111	107	241
Over 12 but not more than 24 days	28	73	222	268	65	155	152	499	113	78	193
Over 24 but not more than 36 days	34	16	158	199	28	352	96	105	66	16	63
Over 36 but not more than 60 days	13	4	24	58	244	56	35	71	14	14	90
Over 60 days	?	11	14	30	9	206	14	11	13	6	20

Working days lost as a result of stoppages (thousands)

	1967	1968	1969	1970	1971	1972	1973	1974	1975	1976	1977
Working days lost through the stoppages which began in the year [4]	2,783	4,719	6,925	10,908	13,589	23,923	7,145	14,845	5,914	3,509	10,378
Analysis by workers involved:											
Under 100 workers	201	250	318	485	320	406	378	440	374	293	377
100 and under 250 workers	256	352	419	708	389	591	598	668	579	399	662
250 and under 500 workers	278	364	578	752	535	890	648	887	671	570	873
500 and under 1,000 workers	361	559	774	1,171	687	1,151	738	1,071	834	563	1,205
1,000 and under 2,500 workers	595	821	1,226	1,671	1,059	1,897	1,248	1,604	1,092	773	1,473
2,500 and under 5,000 workers	289	507	558	1,123	623	2,155	879	1,054	1,272	426	1,944
5,000 workers and over	802	1,867	3,053	4,998	9,976	16,834	2,654	9,121	1,094	485	3,843
Working days lost each year through all stoppages in progress [5]:											
Analysis by industry [2]:											
All industries and services	2,787	4,690	6,846	10,980	13,551	23,909	7,197	14,750	6,012	3,284	10,142
Mining and quarrying	108	57	1,041	1,092	65	10,800	91	5,628	56	78	97
Metals, engineering, shipbuilding and vehicles	1,422	3,363	3,739	4,540	6,035	6,636	4,800	5,837	3,932	1,977	6,133
Textiles	25	34	120	192	58	236	140	236	257	39	208
Clothing and footwear	6	7	19	192	13	38	53	19	93	26	56
Construction	201	233	278	242	255	4,188	176	252	247	570	297
Transport and communication	823	559	786	1,313	6,539	876	331	705	422	132	301
All other industries and services	202	438	862	3,409	586	1,135	1,608	2,072	1,006	461	3,050

[1] Excluding stoppages involving fewer than 10 workers or lasting less than one day except any in which the aggregate number of working days lost exceeded 100. [2] Figures from 1967 to 1969 are based on the 1958 Standard Industrial Classification and those for 1970 onwards, on the 1968 edition. [3] Some stoppages involved workers in more than one industry group but have each been counted only once in the totals. [4] The figures for working days lost include days lost in subsequent years where the stoppages extended into the following calendar year. [5] This analysis shows the total working days lost *within* each year as a result of stoppages in progress in that year whether beginning in that or an earlier year.

Source: Department of Employment
Figures are taken from the Central Statistical Office, Annual Abstract of Statistics, 1979, by permission of the Controller of Her Majesty's Stationery Office.

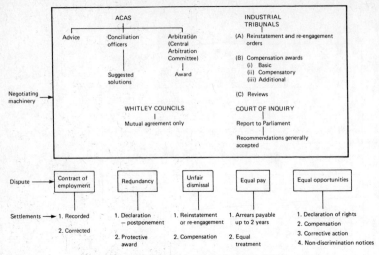

Fig. 30.—*Settlement of Industrial Disputes*.

THE CODE OF PRACTICE ON DISCIPLINARY PROCEDURES

The aim of the Code is to help employers, trade unions and individual employees by providing practical guidance for promoting good industrial relations to encourage improvements in individual conduct. Failure to observe any provision does not render a person liable to proceedings. However, in the event of a dispute being taken to arbitration or being put before the Central Arbitration Committee, the Code shall be admissible in evidence and if any provision in the Code appears to be relevant to the case it will be taken into account.

The essential features of disciplinary procedures are that they should:

1. be in writing;
2. state to whom they apply;
3. provide for matters to be dealt with quickly;
4. indicate the disciplinary action which may be taken;
5. state the levels of management which have the authority to take various forms of disciplinary action, ensuring that immediate superiors do not normally have the power to discuss without reference to senior management;
6. arrange for individuals to be informed of the complaints against them and to be given the opportunity to state their case before decisions are taken;
7. give individuals the right to be accompanied by a trade union representative or by a colleague of their choice;
8. ensure that no employees are dismissed for a first offence except in the case of gross misconduct;

9. ensure that no disciplinary action is taken until the case has been carefully investigated;
10. ensure that individuals are given a proper explanation for any penalty imposed;
11. provide a right for the individual to appeal;
12. specify the procedure to be followed in the event of an appeal.

The supervisor and the Code

The initiative for establishing adequate disciplinary rules and procedures lies with management, but for them to be fully effective they need to be accepted as reasonable by both supervisors and employees. Thus all levels within the organisation should be involved when new or revised rules and procedures are being formulated.

Some degree of interpretation of rules is inevitable and the supervisor should ensure that employees know and understand them. Verbal explanations are needed as well as written copies; these should form part of an induction programme for new employees.

To avoid misunderstandings the supervisor should make known the likely consequence of breaking rules and indicate clearly the type of conduct which could lead to summary dismissal.

The following items could well constitute an acceptable disciplinary procedure.

1. Establish the facts immediately, including statements from witnesses.
2. Consider a brief period of suspension with pay while the case is investigated.
3. Interview the individual before any decision or penalty is imposed. Give him ample opportunity to state his case.
4. Advise the individual of his rights under the procedure, including the right to be accompanied.
5. Decide whether to give a formal oral warning in the case of a minor offence or a written warning if it is more serious. Set out the nature of the offence and the possible consequences of further offences. The individual should be told that the warning, oral or written, constitutes the first formal stage of the procedure. If, however, the supervisor decides to give only an informal oral warning for the purpose of improving conduct, then naturally this does not apply. Remember to satisfy the test of reasonableness of action in all circumstances, not forgetting also the employee's record and any other relevant factors.
6. A further breach of discipline could warrant a final written warning. This should include a statement that any recurrence would lead to suspension or dismissal or some other penalty as the case may be.
7. The final stage could be disciplinary transfer or disciplinary

suspension without pay provided these are allowed for by an express or implied condition of the contract of employment, or dismissal, according to the nature of the misconduct. Disciplinary suspension without pay should not normally be for a prolonged period and it demands special consideration before proceeding with such a course of action.

8. Details of the disciplinary action should be given in writing to the employee or his representative. This does not apply to an oral warning.
9. Notify the employee of any right of appeal and how to conduct such an appeal in terms of procedure and the people involved.

Exceptional cases

Occasionally special consideration must be given in circumstances where the use of the standard disciplinary procedure may be too rigid or difficult to comply with. Three typical examples are the following:

1. If the full disciplinary procedure is not immediately available for some reason then special provisions are essential. Nightshift workers may not be able to consult a trade union representative, there may be no one in authority to take appropriate action, or there could be problems associated with remote working sites.
2. There may be an apparent attack on a union's functions if a union official has committed an offence. This could lead to a serious dispute and, therefore, it may be more diplomatic to give an oral warning until the circumstances of the case have been discussed with a senior union official.
3. A criminal offence outside employment may not be sufficient to dismiss an employee. Consideration should be given as to whether the offence makes the employee unsuitable for his type of employment or whether he would become unacceptable to his colleagues.

INDUSTRIAL TRIBUNALS

Although these tribunals have already been explained in Chapter XV, Employment, they feature generally in disputes. Complaints are heard in the main from individual employees, on a range of jurisdictions given to the tribunals under employment laws passed since 1964.

COURTS OF INQUIRY

Under Part II of the Industrial Courts Act 1919 the Minister may appoint a Court of Inquiry to investigate the causes and circumstances of a trade dispute and submit a report. Such a dispute would naturally be of high importance where an impartial opinion is considered necessary in the public interest and when other methods of negotiation have broken down.

The Court has the power to call witnesses who give evidence under oath, to ask for any relevant documents and to sit in private or public as it so desires. Its findings or recommendations carry no legal weight, but because of its impartiality the decision is invariably either accepted outright or as a firm foundation for further negotiation between the parties, leading to an agreement. Any report (and any minority report) must be laid before both Houses of Parliament, "as soon as may be".

Individual Rights of Employees

Employee rights were established by a number of Acts, including the Redundancy Payments Act 1965, the Contracts of Employment Act 1972, the Trade Union and Labour Relations Act 1974 and the Employment Protection Act 1975. The provisions of these Acts relating to individual rights are now contained in the Employment Protection (Consolidation) Act 1978. The rights are not altered in any way, nor are the corresponding obligations on employers.

A summary of these rights is given below.

1. To take a complaint to an industrial tribunal on a wide range of jurisdictions under the various employment laws passed since 1964.
2. To receive a written statement of the terms and conditions of his contract of employment after thirteen weeks of continuous employment with his employer.
3. To a certain minimum period of notice after four weeks' continuous employment. Duration is dependent upon length of service and the employee will usually be entitled to pay during notice. After four weeks' continuous employment the employee is required to give a minimum of one week's notice.
4. To qualify as a person entitled to a full range of legal protection provided continuity of employment of sixteen hours a week or more can be shown. A person also qualifies if he has worked for the same employer for eight or more hours a week (but less than sixteen) for five years or more.
5. To receive itemised pay statements showing gross pay, take-home pay, and the amounts and reasons for all variable and fixed deductions. As an alternative, fixed deductions may be shown as a total with the amounts and reasons supplied in a separate annual statement which must be amended during the year when the occasion arises.
6. To receive guarantee payments for a limited period during short-time working or lay-offs. The employer must make this payment only if a full day's work is lost. The limit is £6 a day and guaranteed for five days in any calendar quarter. Payment is excluded if there is no work due to action involving other employees of the same or an associated employer.

7. To receive normal pay (up to a maximum of twenty-six weeks) during medical suspension covered by special health and safety regulations following examination by an employment medical adviser or an appointed doctor.

8. To be a member of, or take part at an appropriate time in the activities of, an independent trade union.

9. To refuse to join a non-independent trade union or to object to joining on religious grounds any trade union whatsoever.

10. To be allowed reasonable time off with pay during working hours to carry out trade union duties if the employee is an official of an independent trade union. Furthermore, this applies to receiving training in trade union duties provided it is concerned with industrial relations.

11. To take reasonable time off without pay for the performance of certain public duties such as the holding of offices as Justices of the Peace, members of a local authority, members of any statutory tribunal, and members of certain health, education, water and river authorities.

12. To take reasonable time off with pay while under notice of redundancy, to seek new employment or to make arrangements for retraining. Entitlement is also based upon the employee being continuously employed for at least two years by his present employer.

13. If a woman is expecting a baby she has a right not to be dismissed because of pregnancy, or for a reason connected with her pregnancy. If her condition does not allow her to do her job adequately or her continued employment while pregnant is against the law she must be offered a suitable alternative job if one is available. Furthermore there are other rights involving return to work and receipt of maternity pay.

14. To complain to the Certification Officer or industrial tribunal against any unfair or unreasonable disciplinary action. This aspect is discussed in detail in Chapter XV, Employment, along with rights on redundancy pay.

15. To claim from the Department of Employment any pay outstanding as a result of an employer becoming insolvent.

The Supervisor and the Shop Steward

Although the supervisor needs a sound knowledge of the procedures and regulations controlling industrial relations, his day-to-day contact with these problems will be through the shop steward.

A sound and friendly relationship between supervisor and shop steward is essential to keep industrial friction to a minimum. The problem of establishing and maintaining such a relationship is complex and demanding on a number of individuals, for the superviso and shop steward not only have to consider the other's viewpoint, but are also under pressure from employees and management in various ways. When a difficult situation is aggravated by temperamental employees and outdated management, disputes can scarcely be avoided.

The problem is therefore examined from the viewpoints of the employee, the shop steward, the supervisor and management.

THE EMPLOYEE

Although the employee lives in a period of comparatively full employment and little hardship, he is continually reminded through daily occurrences at work and a steady stream of publicised cases, of injustice and victimisation of various descriptions and intensity. It is difficult for him to resist the influence of this constant external pressure, therefore he feels insecure and sensitive to any suggestion of injustice or harshness.

An employee obviously feels the need to belong to an association which will support him and fight for his rights. Even those who are not members of any employees' association are mindful of the role it plays and would probably join very quickly if their continued non-membership meant disbanding the association.

Whether employees are misguided, have incorrect attitudes or wrong impressions is beside the point. They distrust management, strongly feel the need for protection, and are prepared to stand by the association which will support them.

THE SHOP STEWARD

Most shop stewards are very conscious of their responsibilities to the union and its members. They are voluntary representatives of the union and recognised as officials in negotiating procedure.

Many are untrained in a role which is practically impossible to fulfil adequately without a true understanding of industrial relations and all the other matters connected with it. Both trade unions and educationists are aware of this lack and are actively engaged in improving the situation.

The shop steward's job is time-consuming and such qualities as leadership, patience, and the ability to sift fact from opinion are essential. He has the power to improve the atmosphere within an establishment with due co-operation from supervisors and management or he can destroy relationships, often with disastrous consequences for all concerned, including employees.

Although he is appointed to represent the will of his colleagues and the policy of the union, he also has a social responsibility to act in an impartial and fair manner. In circumstances where he sincerely feels that his colleagues are biased to a point beyond a reasonable limit, he must have sufficient courage to disagree with their demands and stand by his word.

A shop steward's official duties vary, dependent upon the rules of the union to which he belongs. In general they include collecting fees, recruiting new members, checking membership cards, dealing with complaints from members and supervisors, handling infringements of agreements at shop floor level, negotiating piece and and bonus rates, relaying information about the work of the union to his colleagues, and passing any relevant information to the union.

THE SUPERVISOR

Any attempt—whether real or only apparent—by a shop steward to undermine the supervisor's authority will naturally get a hostile reception. Unfortunately, shop stewards often create this impression in performing their duties and the supervisor feels he is losing prestige in the face of criticism and interference.

The soundness of the supervisor's position depends to a large extent on management's policy towards supervision and the degree of active participation in negotiations which is allowed at supervisory levels. If queries, complaints and grievances are to be settled quickly, the closest point to the trouble is on the shop floor, which gives the supervisor a distinct advantage. He is more familiar with the situation than is management and, provided that he is adequately informed of all communications and agreements with the union by management, he should be able to deal effectively with the problem with a minimum of disruption.

MANAGEMENT

Management's attitude and relationships with the shop steward vary with general policy, which is largely governed by procedure agreements and awareness of the need to work together.

Individual managers may find themselves working strictly to set terms that tend to cause unnecessary rigidity and narrowness of outlook; this is not conducive to friendly working relationships with employees.

A progressive management recognises the importance of supporting the supervisor and developing friendly relationships among the parties concerned. The vital need to work together must be recognised, and active steps to encourage co-operation must come from management, otherwise the efforts of supervisors and shop stewards will be wasted.

WORKING TOGETHER

Good relationships between supervisor and shop steward depend on each party appreciating and recognising the other's position and the role he plays. This foundation of understanding and the good sense of both parties will provide the opportunity to improve industrial relations considerably.

The supervisor should appreciate the need to keep the shop steward fully informed of any problems, plans, grievances, complaints and possible changes, so that the steward is not surprised by any action and likely to lose prestige in front of his colleagues. Similarly, the supervisor looks for an adequate return of information from the shop steward; this exchange of information is vital if the improvement of communication and confidence is to be maintained. Furthermore, the information should include adequate explanations of changes and all the known facts, whenever possible. Any reasonable man will respond to this straightforward approach and try to co-operate.

Naturally, there is always the possibility of being faced with an antagonistic shop steward who is suffering with some emotional problem. The importance is stressed of standing firm in these circumstances and being scrupulously fair. Most employees recognise fair play when they see it, but the provision of full information is essential, otherwise the employees are not made aware that the supervisor is acting fairly.

The supervisor reserves the right to discuss any problems that his subordinates put forward, but if they involve a union agreement he should recognise the need for the shop steward to be present. Similarly he should try to settle all problems at this level with the co-operation of the steward, who should ensure that his colleagues abide by the set procedure. Each case should be judged on its merits and sufficient facts—as opposed to mere opinion—are essential in order to reach a solution that satisfies both parties.

Working together in the way described produces mutual respect and a marked improvement in atmosphere on the shop floor.

Joint consultation

During the early part of World War II, proposals were put forward to establish joint committees of employees and employers so that workpeople could have the opportunity of actively helping in production problems. The objects were to raise production and morale. By 1942 a number of establishments had set up Joint Production Committees. Although they suffered some criticism of their real usefulness, they helped to provide common ground for discussion with management, and thus improved relationships. The committees have continued and grown since then, with the support of the Department of Employment.

Similar committees were established at national and regional levels in 1939, linking employers' and employees' associations and the Department of Employment. These committees are still in existence; they advise on a wide range of topics and provide an outlet for the State to divulge any relevant information. At national level the National

Joint Advisory Council meets four times a year and a Joint Consultative Committee acts as an assisting body, which meets as required. They deal with problems of industrial relations while the National Production Advisory Council on Industry concentrates on production problems.

At regional level a number of Regional Boards meet monthly to liaise with the National Production Advisory Council.

QUESTIONS

1. Discuss the function of the Industrial Relations Officer.
2. Why should the supervisor need a reasonable knowledge of industrial relations?
3. What is meant by the term "collective bargaining"?
4. Explain the role played by employers' associations and the Confederation of British Industry.
5. Describe the growth and organisation of trade unions. Comment on the organisation and effectiveness of their activities.
6. Discuss the part played by the Trades Union Congress in industrial relations.
7. What is meant by the terms "conciliation" and "arbitration"?
8. Explain the purpose and effectiveness of arbitration.
9. What is a Court of Inquiry?
10. Give your personal advice to a new supervisor on his dealings with the shop steward.
11. Discuss the functions of shop stewards.
12. What are the main difficulties that the supervisor and shop steward have to face when trying to work together?
13. Outline the use of joint consultation in industry.
14. Discuss the changing role of the shop steward.
15. State the main tasks of the Certification Officer.
16. What is meant by the term "industrial democracy"?
17. Outline the general aims of the Employment Protection Act 1975.
18. Explain the role of a Whitley Council.
19. What are the aims of ACAS?
20. List the essential features of an acceptable disciplinary procedure under the ACAS Code of Practice I.
21. Explain the use of industrial tribunals.
22. Give ten examples of an employee's individual rights.

CHAPTER XVIII

HEALTH AND SAFETY

The Background

THE need for more effective programmes to improve occupational health and safety has been recognised for many years. However, until recent years such schemes have been neglected as can be seen when the number of working days lost annually through accidents is compared with those lost through strikes.

A typical year, 1970, illustrates the case: 23 million days were lost through accidents, 342 million days through certified sickness, and nearly 11 million days through strikes. Included in the 23 million are 1 million days lost through prescribed industrial diseases. In addition, 911 people were killed in industrial accidents and 642 cases were reported of industrial disease.

More recent estimates suggest that on an average working day four workers will die and over 3000 will be seriously injured sufficient to lose three or more days from work.

The nation's total accident costs probably are as high as £1500 million apart from the distress and anxiety of employees and their families. Accidents are a complete waste of human effort.

Sources of Law

In addition to the social obligations of health and safety there are two main sources of law which protect the employee. The first is "common law" which is *unwritten*, established by custom, and is supported by precedents (created by judges) which are referred to as *case law*. The second source is "statute law", i.e. Acts passed by Parliament, and these over-ride "common law" in the event of conflict.

COMMON LAW

Under common law there is a liability for safety of employees. An employer may be sued for damages if he does not provide reasonably safe systems of work. If the employer ignores this obligation to take reasonable care and avoid unnecessary risks, a civil wrong or tort of negligence is committed. The injured person may sue for damages and, in serious cases, the State may consider the offence a crime and prosecute.

Another legal aspect of safety arises when an employee commits a civil wrong or tort during the course of his employment, such as injuring another person. This means that if an employee carries out an improper action which causes injury to a colleague, although he may have been expressly forbidden to do so, his employer is liable for the civil wrong and damages, provided the employee was told what to do and how he was to do it. This is known as *vicarious liability*. If a person is told what to do but has complete freedom as to how the work is done, the relationship changes to one of employer and independent contractor, in which case the employer is not liable.

FACTORIES ACT 1961

There are a number of provisions laid down in Part II, ss. 12–56, Part IV, ss. 63–79, and Part V, ss. 80–5. These cover precautions concerning machines, fire risks, lifts, cranes, boilers, floors, tanks, masks and goggles, removal of offensive fumes and dust, some health and welfare requirements, and regulations in dangerous trades. Accidents which result in death or affect pay for more than three days, and specified fires or explosions, must be notified to the factory inspector.

Under Part X a general register is required to record accidents and other aspects of safety. An example of a typical accident report for internal use which would provide sufficient detail for the register and for control purposes is given in Figure 31.

Factories, construction and demolition sites, civil engineering sites, docks, shipyards and electrical stations are covered by the Act.

OFFICES, SHOPS AND RAILWAY PREMISES ACT 1963

Apart from railway workshops, the title of the Act indicates the sites that are covered.

Some of the standards laid down for the working environment do not necessarily agree with those in the Factories Act. A typical example is lighting regulations which conform to modern practice whereas in the Factories Act they are out-of-date.

ALKALI WORKS REGULATIONS ACT 1906

This Act outlines the measures to be taken in the control of emissions into the atmosphere of certain chemicals from specified classes of factories.

AGRICULTURE (POISONOUS SUBSTANCES) ACT 1952

The use of certain specific dangerous substances in agriculture may be regulated by the Minister under this Act.

AGRICULTURE (SAFETY, HEALTH AND WELFARE PROVISIONS) ACT 1956

Standards for washing, lavatory facilities and first aid are laid down.

EXPLOSIVES ACTS 1875 AND 1923, PETROLEUM (CONSOLIDATION) ACT 1928, AND RADIOACTIVE SUBSTANCES ACT 1960

These Acts cover similar broad requirements for use, storage, manu-

ACCIDENT REPORT

Name...............................   Date.......................

Staff/Works........................   Time......................

Clock Number......................   Place.....................

Department........................   Supervisor................

Section............................

Description of Injury:

Cause of Accident

Treatment

Hospital: **Rehabilitation Course:**
Doctor: Date:
Date: Results:

Action to avoid Recurrence

Directive Issued:
Date:
Circulation:
Authority:

Remuneration

Absence: From   Time.............   Date ....
          To   Time.............   Date.............

Reductions:
Compensation:

Records

Entry General Register:
Factory Inspector Notified:
Employee's Record Card:

Circulation: Wages Supervisor.......................

               Safety Officer...........................

               Works Manager.........................

               Personnel Manager......................

Date..................   Signature of Supervisor:................

Fig. 31.—*Accident Report Form.*
An accident report form using this layout provides sufficient details
for the regulation general register and also for safety control purposes.

facture, and labelling of the products, and the licensing of premises within which they are contained.

MINERAL WORKINGS (OFFSHORE INSTALLATIONS) ACT 1971

Installations associated with underwater exploitation and exploration of minerals in waters in and around Britain are covered in this Act which enables regulations to be drawn up for health, safety and welfare.

MINES AND QUARRIES ACT 1954

In addition to the areas in the title, the Act includes buildings on the surface associated with the mine. Certain processes are covered by the Factories Act provided they are not for the purpose of working the mine or for preparation of minerals extracted.

NUCLEAR INSTALLATIONS ACTS 1965 AND 1969

Precise standards are applied to all nuclear reactor sites.

RAILWAY EMPLOYMENT (PREVENTION OF ACCIDENTS) ACT 1900

Rules may be made to cover a number of specific hazards. In addition there are rules produced in 1902 and 1911 which cover shunting arrangements, wagon brakes, lookouts, and wagon labelling.

ROAD TRAFFIC ACTS AND TRANSPORT ACT 1968

Extensive regulations are applied for road transport and railways. Included are vehicle construction, licensing, hours of work, and movement of dangerous goods.

SHOPS ACT 1950

This Act includes shops and similar premises for the purpose of limiting hours of work.

The Health and Safety at Work etc. Act 1974

This legislation is known as an "enabling" Act because it is broad and generalised in nature rather than going into a great deal of detail. Thus powers are given to the Secretary of State for Employment to introduce regulations and codes of practice on specific health and safety matters. He, in turn, acts through the new Health and Safety Commission.

In other words, the Act is a broad framework from which future legislation will be introduced to make up a comprehensive body of legislation (including existing Acts) on health and safety.

Although the Act imposes many extra general duties on employers, it does not cut out, cancel or affect any existing legislation which will continue alongside until new legislation replaces it. Naturally this does not apply to the 8 million employees who are now covered for the first time by the Act.

AIMS OF THE ACT

1. To secure the health, safety and welfare of people at work by involving everybody at the workplace including workers, supervisors and managers in taking responsibility for this task.
2. To protect people other than those at work against any risks to health or safety arising out of or in connection with the activities of people at work.
3. To control the storage and use of explosive or highly flammable or otherwise dangerous substances, and generally preventing the unlawful acquisition, possession and use of such substances.
4. To control the emission into the atmosphere of noxious or offensive substances from prescribed premises.

THE ACT'S APPROACH

To achieve the above-mentioned aims the Act is designed to provide for one, comprehensive, integrated system of law on health, safety, and welfare. The main approaches are as follows.

1. To completely overhaul and modernise the existing law covering health, safety and welfare at work.
2. To create a new Health and Safety Commission.
3. To provide a range of new general duties for employers.
4. To reorganise and unify the various Government Inspectorates.
5. To impose new powers and penalties for the enforcement of safety laws.
6. To establish new methods of accident prevention and new ways of operating future safety regulations.
7. To establish codes of practice instead of regulations whenever possible.

The establishment of codes of practice was an interesting innovation recommended by the Report of the Committee on Safety and Health at Work in July 1972 (the *Robens Report*). The advantages are that codes may be formulated by people in industry with practical knowledge, they may be written in non-legal language which should be more easily understood, and they are easily revised to keep up with changing technology.

The codes will not be statutory requirements but they may be used as evidence in courts of law. Anyone charged with a contravention of a statutory provision will have to prove that the practices used were better than or at least as good as the relevant approved code. Contrary to traditional legal practice, the person will be guilty until proved innocent.

GENERAL DUTIES OF THE ACT

Within the provisions of the Act there are a number of general duties mentioned which apply to employers, employees, and people other than employees. An outline is given below.

Duties to employees

The general duties of employers to their employees are given in s. 2 of the Act.

Section 2(1): "It shall be the duty of every employer to ensure, so far as is reasonably practicable, the health, safety and welfare at work of all his employees."

Section 2(2): further provides that, "without prejudice to the generality of the preceding subsection, the matters to which that duty extends include in particular ..."

Section 2(2)(a): "... the provision and maintenance of plant and systems of work that are, so far as is reasonably practicable, safe and without risks to health." This is a general requirement covering all plant, which the Act defines as including machinery, equipment and appliances used at work. It does not supersede the more detailed and specific provisions covering certain equipment contained in existing legislation, but it goes beyond such provisions in requiring a more wide-ranging assessment of risk.

Section 2(2)(b): "... arrangements for ensuring, so far as is reasonably practicable, safety and absence of risks to health in connection with the use, handling, storage and transport of articles and substances." This subsection is concerned with the materials and articles used at work. "Substance" is defined (in s. 53) as "any natural or artificial substance, whether in solid or liquid form or in the form of a gas or vapour," so that the subsection covers everything used at work and all work activities.

Section 2(2)(c): "... the provision of such information, instruction, training and supervision as is necessary to ensure, so far as is reasonably practicable, the health and safety at work of his employees."

Section 2(2)(d): "... so far as is reasonably practicable as regards any place of work under the employer's control, the maintenance of it in a condition that is safe and without risks to health and the provision and maintenance of means of access to and egress from it that are safe and without such risks."

Section 2(2)(e): "... the provision and maintenance of a working environment for his employees that is, so far as is reasonably practicable, safe, without risks to health and adequate as regards facilities and arrangements for their welfare at work."

Section 2(3): "Except in such cases as may be prescribed, it shall be the duty of every employer to prepare and as often as may be appropriate revise a written statement of his general policy with respect to the health and safety at work of his employees and the organisation and arrangements for the time being in force for carrying out that policy, and to bring the statement and any revision of it to the notice of all his employees." Regulations have since prescribed that all employers with five or more employees must have a written safety policy.

Duties to people other than employees

An employer also has responsibility for protecting other people, such as the public. His duties in this respect are shown in s. 3.

Section 3(1): "It shall be the duty of every employer to conduct his undertakings in such a way as to ensure, so far as is reasonably practicable, that persons not in his employment who may be affected thereby are not thereby exposed to risks to their health or safety."

Section 3(3): places a duty on an employer, in circumstances which will be prescribed, to give to persons who are not his employees information about such aspects of the way in which he conducts his undertaking as might affect their health or safety. Regulations will need to be made prescribing the circumstances and the information required.

Duties relating to premises

Any person who is in control of non-domestic premises where people work who are not their own employees, or where these people use plant or substances provided there for their use, has duties to follow under s. 4.

Section 4(2): "It shall be the duty of each person who has, to any extent, control of premises to which this section applies or of the means of access thereto or egress therefrom or of any plant or substance in such premises to take such measures as it is reasonable for a person in his position to take to ensure, so far as is reasonably practicable, that the premises, all means of access thereto or egress therefrom available for use by persons using the premises, and any plant or substance in the premises or, as the case may be, provided for use there, is or are safe and without risks to health."

The term "premises" is defined by s. 53 and "includes any place and, in particular, includes any vehicle, vessel, aircraft or hovercraft; any installation on land (including the foreshore and other land intermittently covered by water), any offshore installation and any other installation (whether floating, or resting on the seabed or the subsoil thereof, or resting on other land covered with water or the subsoil thereof); and any tent or movable structure."

This is a general provision and the person in control of premises may also have other duties under other enactments, for example with respect to means of escape in case of fire, and general fire precautions, and also with respect to public health.

Duties relating to harmful emissions in the atmosphere

Any person controlling premises which may emit into the atmosphere noxious or offensive substances has certain duties under s. 5.

Briefly, the best practical means for preventing such emissions should be used. This applies also to rendering such emissions harmless and inoffensive.

Duties of employers, etc. concerning articles and substances at work

Section 6 applies to all persons who design, manufacture, import, supply, erect or install any article, plant, machinery, equipment or appliances for use at work, or manufacture, import or supply any substance for use at work. It also applies where research is conducted by designers and manufacturers. The provisions are given below.

Every employer is likely to be affected by these provisions as a purchaser and user of articles or substances and, in addition, many will have duties as a member of one of the classes of persons named in the section.

An "article for use at work" is defined as:

(a) any plant, machinery, equipment or appliance designed for use or operation (whether exclusively or not) by persons at work, and

(b) any article designed for use as a component in any such plant.

A "substance for use at work" is any natural or artificial substance whether in solid or liquid form or in the form of a gas or vapour intended for use (whether exclusively or not) by persons at work.

Section 6(1): "It shall be the duty of any person who designs, manufactures, imports or supplies any article for use at work,

(a) to ensure, so far as is reasonably practicable, that the article is so designed and constructed as to be safe and without risks to health when properly used;

(b) to carry out or arrange for the carrying out of such testing and examination as may be necessary for the performance of the duty imposed on him by the preceding paragraph;

(c) to take such steps as are necessary to secure that there will be available in connection with the use of the article at work adequate information about the use for which it is designed and has been tested, and about any conditions necessary to ensure that, when put to that use, it will be safe and without risks to health."

Section 6(2): "It shall be the duty of any person who undertakes the design or manufacture of any article for use at work to carry out or arrange for the carrying out of any necessary research with a view to the discovery and, so far as is reasonably practicable, the elimination or minimisation of any risks to health or safety to which the design or article may give rise."

Section 6(3): "It shall be the duty of any person who erects or installs any article for use at work in any premises where that article is to be used by persons at work to ensure, so far as is reasonably practicable, that nothing about the way in which it is erected or installed makes it unsafe or a risk to health when properly used."

Section 6(4): "It shall be the duty of any person who manufactures, imports or supplies any substance for use at work,

    (*a*) to ensure, so far as is reasonably practicable, that the substance is safe and without risks to health when properly used;

    (*b*) to carry out or arrange for the carrying out of such testing and examination as may be necessary for the performance of the duty imposed on him by the preceding paragraph;

    (*c*) to take such steps as are necessary to secure that there will be available in connection with the use of the substance at work adequate information about the results of any relevant tests which have been carried out on or in connection with the substance and about any conditions necessary to ensure that it will be safe and without risks to health when properly used."

Section 6(5): "It shall be the duty of any person who undertakes the manufacture of any substance for use at work to carry out or arrange for the carrying out of any necessary research with a view to the discovery and, so far as is reasonably practicable, the elimination or minimisation of any risks to health or safety to which the substance may give rise."

Section 6(6): "Nothing in the preceding provisions of this section shall be taken to require a person to repeat any testing, examination or research which has been carried out otherwise than by him or at his instance, in so far as it is reasonable for him to rely on the results thereof for the purposes of those provisions."

Section 6(7): "Any duty imposed on any person by any of the preceding provisions of this section shall extend only to things done in the course of a trade, business or other undertaking carried on by him (whether for profit or not) and to matters within his control."

Section 6(8): "Where a person designs, manufactures, imports or supplies an article for or to another on the basis of a written undertaking by that other to take specified steps sufficient to ensure, so far as is reasonably practicable, that the article will be safe and without risks to health when properly used, the undertaking shall have the effect of relieving the first-mentioned person from the duty imposed by subsection (1)(*a*) above to such an extent as is reasonable having regard to the terms of the undertaking."

Section 6(9): "Where a person ('the ostensible supplier') supplies any article for use at work or substance for use at work to another ('the customer') under a hire-purchase agreement, conditional sale agreement or credit-sale agreement, and the ostensible supplier:

(a) carries on the business of financing the acquisition of goods by others by means of such agreements; and

(b) in the course of that business acquired his interest in the article or substance supplied to the customer as a means of financing its acquisition by the customer from a third person ('the effective supplier'),

the effective supplier and not the ostensible supplier shall be treated for the purposes of this section as supplying the article or substance to the customer, and any duty imposed by the preceding provisions of this section on suppliers shall accordingly fall on the effective supplier and not on the ostensible supplier."

Section 6(10): "For the purposes of this section an article or substance is not to be regarded as properly used where it is used without regard to any relevant information or advice relating to its use which has been made available by a person by whom it was designed, manufactured, imported or supplied."

Duties of employees

Sections 7 and 8 cover the duties of *all* employees, which implies that managers also come under this heading. These duties are quoted below.

Section 7: "It shall be the duty of every employee while at work:

(a) to take reasonable care for the health and safety of himself and of other persons who may be affected by his acts or omissions at work; and

(b) as regards any duty or requirement imposed on his employer or any other person by or under any of the relevant statutory provisions, to co-operate with him so far as is necessary to enable that duty or requirement to be performed or complied with."

Section 8: "No person shall intentionally or recklessly interfere with or misuse anything provided in the interests of health, safety or welfare in pursuance of any of the relevant statutory provisions."

Charge to employees

Section 9 of the Act states that no employer shall levy, or permit to be levied on any employee of his, any charge in respect of anything done or provided in pursuance of any specific requirement of the relevant statutory provisions.

ENFORCEMENT OF THE ACT

Section 10 establishes two bodies, the Health and Safety Commission and the Health and Safety Executive. The Commission is responsible to the Secretary of State.

Health and Safety Commission

The Commission was established in 1974 and consists of a full-time independent chairman and nine part-time commissioners. The commissioners are made up of three T.U.C. members, three C.B.I. members, two from local authorities, and one independent member.

This body has taken over responsibility formerly held by various government departments and is responsible through the Executive for the new, unified inspectorate.

The Commission is empowered to make agreements with government departments, or others, for them to perform functions on their behalf. It is also responsible for maintaining the Employment Medical Advisory Service which forms the medical arm of the Executive.

The fire authorities and the Home Office are responsible for general fire precautions at places of work, under an amendment of the *Fire Precautions Act* 1971. However, the Commission remains responsible for control over "process" risks which covers those incidents where there is a risk of outbreak of fire associated with particular processes or particular substances.

The Executive

This operational arm of the Commission is responsible for implementing the Commission's advisory functions and for enforcing the relevant statutory provisions. These include the existing legislation, the provisions of this Act and the regulations made under it unless other bodies are specifically made responsible by the legislation for enforcement in certain circumstances.

The Act covers the appointment of inspectors to carry out its enforcement functions through the Executive. Local authorities are also given powers to enforce the legislation in some areas of employment including many covered by health and safety legislation for the first time. These relate broadly to non-industrial activities. Allocation of responsibilities has been made in regulations after consultation.

Although the Executive possesses the main responsibility for enforcement except where local authorities have powers, other organisations may also be given responsibility under the guidance of the Commission. This allows for those particular organisations to continue with their related responsibilities or where expert knowledge is available.

The unified inspectorate

Inspectorates that were previously scattered throughout several government departments are now all under the control of the Health and Safety Executive. They have new powers to enforce the Act which may be grouped into three categories: (*a*) improvement notices, (*b*) prohibition notices, and (*c*) increased fines and the threat of imprisonment.

(*a*) *Improvement notices.* An inspector may serve an improvement notice if he is of the opinion that:

(i) there is a contravention of one or more of the relevant statutory provisions; or

(ii) there has been a contravention in circumstances that make it likely that the contravention will be repeated.

The notice states that the inspector is of that opinion and specifies the provision or provisions contravened. It gives details of the reasons for the inspector's opinion and asks the employer to remedy the situation within a specified time.

(*b*) *Prohibition notices.* An inspector may issue an immediate prohibition notice if he considers there is an imminent risk of serious personal injury. Such a notice requires the work concerned to be stopped immediately. If the inspector does not think the risk of serious personal injury is imminent, he may issue a deferred prohibition notice, which requires the work to be stopped unless the matters are put right within a specified time.

Appeals against both improvement and prohibition notices may be made to an industrial tribunal. An improvement notice is automatically suspended during an appeal. A prohibition notice is only suspended if the appellant applies to the tribunal for suspension and if the tribunal agrees.

(*c*) *Penalties.* An offence is committed if there is non-compliance with these notices. The penalties are a maximum fine of £400 (soon to be increased to £1000) on conviction in a magistrate's court, or an unlimited fine in the case of a trial by indictment (in a court higher than a magistrate's court). A person convicted in a higher court of failure to comply with a prohibition notice may also be liable to up to two years' imprisonment, either in addition to or instead of a fine. There could also be a continuing fine of £100 a day for every day of non-compliance with a notice after conviction.

Powers of inspectors

Under s. 20 power is given to inspectors to enter, at any reasonable time, any premises which may be suspect for the purpose of carrying into effect any of the legal provisions within the field of the inspector's enforcing authority.

The inspector may take with him any duly authorised person and any equipment required. He may take measurements, photographs, recordings and samples. He can require people to provide information and to answer questions, and ask them to sign a declaration of the truth of their answers.

He may require any person to afford him such facilities and assistance, within the person's control or responsibilities, as are necessary to enable the inspector to exercise any of the powers conferred on him.

The power of an inspector is given in writing by his enforcing authority and he must, when invited, produce a copy of his instrument of appointment.

Offences

Under s. 33 of the Act fifteen provisions as to offences are listed:

1. to fail to comply with the general duties under ss. 2 to 7;
2. to contravene s. 8 or 9;
3. to contravene any health and safety regulations;
4. to contravene any requirement relating to the power of the Commission under the Act to direct investigations and inquiries;
5. to fail to comply with any requirement imposed by an inspector in the exercise of his powers;
6. to prevent or attempt to prevent any other person from appearing before an inspector or from answering any question to which an inspector may require an answer;
7. to fail to comply with an improvement or prohibition notice;
8. intentionally to obstruct an inspector in the exercise of his power;
9. to fail to comply with a notice issued by the Commission under the Act and requiring information to be supplied;
10. wrongly to disclose information obtained by the Commission under the Act;
11. to make a statement which is known to be false or recklessly to make a statement which is false when the statement is made in order to show compliance with a requirement or to obtain a document;
12. intentionally to make a false entry in a register or document required by the statutory provisions and to make use of such an entry;
13. with intent to deceive, to forge or use a document issued under the statutory provisions;
14. to pretend to be an inspector;
15. to fail to comply with a court order made under the Act.

Major Aspects for Management

Some of the main measures for management to consider under the Act are as follows.

1. To issue a written statement of safety policy.
2. To establish an organisation and allocate responsibilities for health and safety matters.

3. To train members of the company in health and safety matters as considered appropriate.
4. To ensure that adequate first-aid facilities exist.
5. To provide appropriate fire-fighting equipment and ensure that everyone is familiar with fire drill.
6. To establish a safety committee.
7. To provide appropriate procedures and documents to minimise accidents.
8. To consult with safety representatives appointed under the Safety Representatives Regulations with a view to making and maintaining arrangements which will promote and develop measures to ensure the health and safety at work of the employees, and checking the effectiveness of such measures.

Injury Rates

A considerable amount of information is available on accidents in industry. Various theories on the causes of accidents have been propounded over the years. An interesting theory concerning the importance of minor injuries states that for every one injury causing loss of time from work there are 29 minor injuries and 300 accidents which do not cause personal injury. This theory is based upon the study of many thousands of cases and it follows that by reducing the number of minor injuries a proportionate number of serious and major injuries will be avoided.

Statistical analysis of the immediate cause of injury in a company can indicate the avenues to follow in accident prevention. For example, one industry analysis may show that only one injury in every hundred arises from accidents involving hand- or power-driven machinery, but forty out of every hundred injuries arise from handling materials, and so on.

For control purposes the following two formulae are often used to indicate trends in accidents and to form a standard basis for comparison in industry.

(a) *Frequency rate:*

$$\frac{\text{Number of lost time accidents} \times 100{,}000}{\text{Total man hours lost}} = \text{Frequency rate}$$

The term "lost time accident" refers to one which stops the employee from working at his normal job beyond the day or shift during which the accident occurred. A reduction in the frequency rate indicates less frequency of accidents. A satisfactory figure should be lower than 1.

(b) *Duration rate:*

$$\frac{\text{Total man hours lost}}{\text{Total number of lost time accidents}} = \text{Duration rate}$$

The term duration rate is the average number of hours spent away from the job by an injured person. Naturally, to avoid distortion, fatalities are not included in the calculation.

Another formula often used is given below. Note that all the formulae use 100,000 hours in the calculation as this is thought to be about the average number of hours worked by an employee during his working life.

(c) *Severity rate:*

$$\frac{\text{Number of man hours lost} \times 100,000}{\text{Number of man hours worked}} = \text{Severity rate}$$

If the injured employee is away for more than three days the absence should be reported to the Factory Inspector. The injury is then termed "reportable".

The Supervisor's Role

Although management may ensure that all possible mechanical precautions are taken, the personal aspect of safety precautions rests with the supervisor. His task is to convince employees that safety is mainly a question of attitude and that safety awareness must constantly be kept in mind during working hours.

Occasionally a serious accident occurs; it is then too late to think about the precautions that should have been taken. For peace of mind alone no supervisor can afford to ignore his role in improving safety.

The main aspects of the supervisor's role in promoting safety are described below.

MECHANICAL SAFETY DEVICES

The supervisor should check that safety devices are functioning properly and that operators have not interfered with them in any way. He should encourage employees to suggest improvements and should point out the dangers which are avoided by the use of the devices. He must convince them that the best way of doing a job is the safest way for all concerned and ensure that the use of devices becomes a regular part of the routine. On those occasions when he demonstrates or uses a machine it is essential that he should conform with the precautions, regardless of high skill or any other excuse.

WORK RATE AND FATIGUE

As the rate of working increases, the risk of an accident arises in proportion. Similarly, fatigue also contributes towards higher accident probability. The problem, therefore, is to find a safe working rate, using the best method and the optimum working period to keep fatigue and the accident rate to a minimum.

In order to maintain and improve productivity in these circumstances, it is necessary to apply work study techniques. This subject is discussed in Part 3, Chapters XXI, XXII and XXIII.

PROTECTIVE CLOTHING

The effectiveness of such devices as goggles, gloves, boots and protective clothing depends upon the employee's good sense and the supervisor's watchfulness. The tendency to discard the protection often occurs if it hampers the work, or if the employee considers its use an additional burden rather than a safety precaution. There is always, in addition, the individual who has a false idea of courage and discards the advice to show his prowess. In some instances people simply forget and, inevitably, the lapse coincides with the accident.

The supervisor must try to discipline employees into observing safety routines always, as a personal protection. Periodical campaigns are unsuccessful as the accidents nearly always occur between the periods of enforcement. Continuous checks and appropriate reprimands are essential, although demanding on the supervisor, who is inclined to allow safety to be overshadowed by production problems through pressure of work.

SAFETY ATTITUDE

Most accidents are caused by various forms of neglect, such as careless use of machines or tools, failure to wear protective clothing, taking risks (including horseplay), inconsideration for nearby colleagues, lack of concentration and failure to use safety devices. All these faults amount to a poor attitude towards safety.

Improving poor safety attitudes hinges upon human relations and the supervisor's ability to create a team spirit that encourages employees to work safely. He must set the tone of safety consciousness by insisting on thorough checks for possible hazards on new and existing machinery and on correct methods of working all the time. His attitude towards accident prevention must be clearly demonstrated to subordinates, whom he must train and discipline to observe all precautions.

Working safely is habit forming and rapidly develops into group pride in maintaining accident-free workshops, when operators appreciate the dangers and stupidity of taking risks. Surveys indicate that most accidents could have been avoided by more personal care; therefore, fostering the correct attitudes in employees can reduce the accident rate to a very low figure.

ACCIDENT PRONENESS

The problem employee is invariably accident prone, probably because he has great difficulty in concentrating for any length of time. Those unfortunate people who are suffering with some nervous disorder which manifests itself in periods of moodiness, temperamental outbursts, uncooperativeness, and general anti-social conduct, are often unsuitable for operating machines. They are a menace to nearby colleagues, who may be injured by their sudden lapse of concentration.

Some individuals who suffer with hypochondria are frequent visitors to the sick bay and through their low vitality and general concern over their health, they become accident prone. Whether their complaint is real or imagined is beyond the scope of the supervisor to determine, but he must take action to place such employees in work of a low hazard nature.

The importance of maintaining a regular, careful watch on subordinates is highlighted when considering safety. Naturally the emotionally unstable employee is recognisable in chronic cases through personal contact over a period, but normal people will suddenly change under the stress of a domestic or social problem. A sudden development of emotional instability makes the person very susceptible to accident proneness and he should be removed from a hazardous job until he recovers.

TRAINING

Lack of experience and poor training also cause many accidents. The question of safety and the correct method of performing a task are an essential part of any training scheme. The importance of correcting bad habits as they appear is emphasised from the safety aspect and the supervisor must constantly check new and existing employees. Allowing a newcomer to work on his own before he has reached a suitable level of competence is inviting him to have an accident.

SUPERVISOR'S SAFETY SUMMARY

1. Ensure that all health and safety measures are implemented within the area of his responsibility.
2. Ensure that safe working methods are always used.
3. Insist on the maintenance of good housekeeping.
4. Conduct a daily inspection of the area, machines, tools, ancillary equipment and so on.
5. Issue safety equipment and protective clothing as laid down by management and ensure that they are used at all times.
6. Report all accidents, near misses and hazards.
7. Train subordinates and induct newcomers.
8. Communicate developments and changes in procedures.
9. Liaise with superior on all aspects of safety, health and welfare.
10. Remind employees that they have a duty to take reasonable care to ensure that they do not endanger themselves or anyone else, to co-operate with management and others in meeting statutory requirements and to avoid misusing anything provided in the interests of health or safety at work.

11. Provide any information requested by the safety representative on such things as a substance, process or piece of equipment. If there is any doubt as to the accuracy of the information, make this point clear.

12. Ensure that all staff are aware of all possible fire hazards and are familiar with fire drill and related procedures.

QUESTIONS

1. Give a brief account of the supervisor's responsibility in connection with the safety of his subordinates.

2. How can the supervisor establish a safety-conscious group under his control?

3. You are asked to attend the first meeting of a newly formed safety committee. What topics would you expect to be raised and what suggestions would you put forward?

4. Discuss safety in connection with maintenance of machinery and equipment.

5. What precautions could a supervisor take to minimise the risk of accidents?

6. How would you deal with an employee who refuses to wear goggles when he operates a machine which has a high eyesight hazard?

7. An employee suddenly has two accidents within a few days. What action would you take?

8. Describe the formulae used for control purposes to provide information on the frequency rate and duration rate of accidents.

9. Discuss the employer's liability for safety under common law.

10. Draw up a suitable framework for an accident report form.

11. Why is the Health and Safety at Work etc. Act 1974 known as an enabling Act?

12. Briefly outline the general duties of employers under the Health and Safety at Work etc. Act 1974.

13. What is the Health and Safety Commission?

14. What are the powers of health and safety inspectors?

CHAPTER XIX

WELFARE

THE employee's position has improved beyond recognition over the past century, and workers' welfare is now safeguarded in numerous ways by legislation. The supervisor, however, still plays an important part in ensuring that the employees have adequate and comfortable surroundings at their work, conducive to higher productivity. In addition many concerns offer employees extra benefits, and these are discussed in conclusion.

Legal Requirements

As already mentioned in Chapter XVIII, there are two main sources of law which protect the employee: common law and statute law.

English law may also be considered from another aspect: *civil law* and *criminal law*.

A civil offence does not concern the community; it deals with the relationships between private individuals when redress for grievances is sought legally. The remedies are damages (payment of money), or an injunction (either forbidding or commanding some course of action).

A criminal offence is against the community, and the police may take action even if the victim involved declines. The offender is punished by either imprisonment or fine.

Some offences are both criminal and civil wrongs. For example, an industrial injury may involve a breach of the Health and Safety at Work Act and also provide grounds for damages at *common law*. Under *common law* the employer has an obligation to provide safe working conditions, which include the place of work, machinery, and equipment. This obligation is also reinforced by the Health and Safety at Work Act.

OUTLINE OF LEGISLATION

Considerable legislation has been introduced in recent years to safeguard employees' interests and improve their general position. An outline of the main acts is given below, including those treated more fully in other chapters.

1. Contracts of employment: Employment Protection (Consolidation) Act 1978

This Act lays down provisions relating to contracts of employment previously contained in the Contracts of Employment Act 1972. The following requirements are placed on employers.

1. Give a written statement of the specified terms of employment including commencing date, rate of pay, intervals at which pay is given, hours of work, holiday entitlement and holiday pay, calculation of accrued holiday pay payable on the termination of employment, provisions for sick pay, period of notice, rights to belong or not to belong to a trade union, and rights where an agency shop or approved closed shop is applicable. The statement must also include the name of the person whom the employee may contact to seek redress of any grievance, the method of making such an application, and the sequence of steps he should consequently take.
2. Communicate to the employee within one month any alterations in the terms of employment.
3. Give an employee who has been employed for more than four weeks, but less than two years, at least one week's notice. If employment is over two years, one additional week's notice must be given for each additional year of service, up to a maximum of twelve weeks' notice for twelve years' service or more.

2. Wages Councils Act 1959

In a small and decreasing number of industries no adequate machinery exists to regulate wages; therefore the trend is for remuneration to fall below a reasonable level. In these circumstances the above Act empowers the Secretary of State to establish and operate Wages Councils for fixing the minimum remuneration in such industries where he considers that rates are below standard. A Council is composed of equal numbers of employers and employees in the appropriate industry.

The Department of Employment's Wages Inspectorate assists in interpreting the wages regulation orders for employers and employees and ensures that the employers comply with the orders.

3. Truck Acts 1831, 1837, 1896 and 1940

These Acts protect employees against bad practices connected with the payment of wages, such as paying in kind instead of in cash and forcing employees to spend their money in a particular shop owned by the employer. The Act states the following.

(a) A contract is void if it states that a manual worker is to be paid in any form other than cash (but *see* Payment of Wages Act, below).
(b) Manual workers must be free to spend their money where and how they choose.
(c) No deductions are allowed to be made from wages except those legally enforceable.
(d) An employer must not withhold an advance, or charge for granting it, in those circumstances where it is customary for workers to receive a "sub" before the wages are actually due.

4. Payment of Wages Act 1960

This Act was introduced to bring the Truck Acts in line with modern practice. Employers are permitted to pay wages in the following ways, provided written agreement is obtained from employees.

1. Payment into a bank account.
2. Payment by postal order or money order.
3. Payment by cheque.

5. National Insurance Act 1965 and Social Security Pensions Act 1975

Payment of regular, weekly contributions to the national insurance scheme provides a comprehensive insurance against sickness, unemployment, old age, maternity, widowhood, orphanhood, and death. The insurance benefits are comparatively small; (insurance companies still have adequate opportunities to supplement the payments through private schemes). A married man's contribution includes coverage for his wife and children for certain benefits.

Under the Social Security Pensions Act 1975, retirement, widows' and invalidity pensions will be made up of two parts: a basic pension and an additional pension. Both parts are paid for by national insurance contributions. Employees who are covered by an occupational pension scheme may be contracted out of the additional part of the retirement and widows' pension. In this case insurance contributions will be reduced for both employers and employees.

Pensions are protected against inflation, the calculation being revalued in line with the growth in earnings generally up to the tax year before retirement. After retirement the basic pension will be kept in line with increased earnings (or prices, if better) and the additional pension will be protected against price increases.

Contracting-out relies upon two main conditions. Briefly these are as follows.

1. The personal pension must be based on the employee's final pensionable salary or his average pensionable salary revalued in line with the growth in earnings generally.
2. The pension must not be less than a guaranteed minimum pension; and a guaranteed minimum pension of half that amount must be provided for the widow.

6. National Insurance (Industrial Injuries) Act, 1965

An employee who is injured at work may claim damages from his employer if the employer is negligent; that is, according to the interpretation of the word under the tort of negligence and provided negligence was the cause of the accident.

Often the employer is not to blame for the accident, therefore the employee cannot claim from him and possible hardship may result through loss of wages. These cases were covered under the Workmen's

Compensation Acts 1890, but they were inadequate and eventually replaced by the Industrial Injuries Scheme, 1946, which operated from 1948 and was consolidated in 1965. The scheme provides cash benefits for those who are injured at work, or suffering with one of the prescribed industrial diseases and are unable to work or are disabled. Benefits also are paid to widows and certain other dependants of the casualty. In general it is a compulsory scheme for all employees, except for self-employed and non-employed people.

The rates of contribution and benefits are constantly changing. Current figures are obtainable from the local offices of the Ministries concerned and any queries are settled at the same source.

7. Law Reform (Personal Injuries) Act 1948

At one time an employer could avoid the general rule that he was liable for any tort (civil wrong) committed by an employee if the injuries to an employee were caused by a fellow employee. This was known as the "rule of common employment".

Eventually the Employers' Liability Act was passed in 1880 which limited this right in particular circumstances. In 1948 the right was completely abolished by the Law Reform (Personal Injuries) Act. An employer can no longer use "common employment" as a defence if he is sued by an employee for personal injuries caused by a fellow employee; moreover the Act makes void any provision in a contract of service or apprenticeship which excludes or limits an employer's liability in respect of personal injuries caused by another employee.

In certain circumstances an injured person may claim damages from his employer and from the Industrial Injuries scheme. To prevent this form of double compensation the Law Reform (Personal Injuries) Act states that one half of any industrial injury benefits received for five years from date of injury, must be taken into account against any earnings loss or profits arising from the injuries, if actions for damages for personal injuries are undertaken.

8. Redundancy Payments: Employment Protection (Consolidation) Act 1978

Those employees who are dismissed because of redundancy may claim a lump sum compensation called a redundancy payment. In certain circumstances, employees who are laid off or are placed on short-time for a substantial period may also claim. The lump sum is related to pay, length of service and age of employee.

A Redundancy Fund was established by the original Redundancy Payments Act 1965. Contributions collected with the employer's National Insurance contribution are paid into the Fund which provides a refund to employers, who may claim a rebate of part of the cost. The rebate varies from two-thirds to a little over three-quarters. The industrial tribunals, established under the Industrial Training Act

1964, hear any dispute about entitlement to redundancy payments or rebates from the Fund.

Certain employees are not eligible. Those who are, must have at least one hundred and four weeks continuous employment with their employer, after the age of eighteen years. Any service before the employee's eighteenth birthday cannot be included. The term redundancy, under the Act, is interpreted to mean where the whole or main reason for the employee's dismissal is because his employer's labour requirements have diminished or ceased. An employee who either does not receive a payment or believes he has received an insufficient amount should approach his employer—through the union representative if appropriate. In the event of a disagreement the employee should ask for the necessary application form at the nearest employment office or jobcentre. If the employer is insolvent and cannot pay, the employee should approach the Department of Employment. Arrangements for payment are then made through the Fund and the Ministry claims from the employer as a non-preferential, unsecured creditor.

9. Industrial Training Act 1964

The Act establishes Training Boards for each industry who will plan, supervise, and advise on training schemes and control standards (*see* Chapter XVI, p. 247).

10. Factories Act 1961

This Act covers a wide range of general working conditions. The main sections are as follows.

(*a*) *Health*.   Regulations are laid down concerning cleanliness, overcrowding, ventilation, temperature, lighting, drainage of floors, sanitary accommodation, meals in certain dangerous trades, underground rooms, lifting excessive weights, and lead processes.

(*b*) *Safety*.   Regulations include such topics as fencing, transmission machinery, new machines, hoists or lifts, chains, ropes, lifting tackle and cranes, construction of floors, safe means of access and place of work, cleaning machinery, precautions against gassing, explosions of flammable dust or gas, steam boilers, air receivers, fire, protection of eyes, training of young persons, and notification of accidents and dangerous occurrences.

(*c*) *Welfare*.   This covers such topics as drinking water, washing facilities, accommodation for clothing, facilities for sitting, and first aid.

There are a number of welfare orders which require special facilities for workers in particular jobs where there is a hazard to the skin or where the process is known to be dirty. These orders generally enforce the provision of protective clothing, first-aid facilities, washing facilities to a higher standard than normal, dining rooms, special accommodation for clothing, baths, and drinking water.

(d) *Employment of women and young persons.* Topics included are normal hours of work, overtime, employment outside the factory, prohibition of sundry employment, holidays, two-shift system, van boys and errand boys, exceptions, and certificates of fitness.

11. Offices, Shops, and Railway Premises Act 1963

This extensive Act applies to all offices and shops and to most railway buildings near the permanent way. General requirements include registration of premises and a number of regulations for such aspects as cleanliness, overcrowding, temperature, ventilation, lighting, sanitary conveniences, washing facilities, drinking water, accommodation for clothing, seating arrangements, seats for sedentary workers, eating facilities, floors, passages, stairs, fencing of exposed parts of machinery, cleaning of machinery, training and supervision of persons working at dangerous machines, prohibition of heavy work, and first aid.

The Act also ensures that reasonable fire precautions are taken in premises. Buildings that possess a greater potential fire hazard must be inspected by an expert, who advises on the precautions to be adopted and issues a fire certificate which states certain restrictions dependent upon the fire hazard.

Enforcement of the Act is now carried out under the provisions of the Health and Safety at Work etc. Act 1974 (*see* below and Chapter XVIII).

12. Equal Pay Act 1970

This Act provides that a woman doing the same or broadly similar work to a man in the same employment qualifies for equal pay and conditions of employment. A similar provision applies if she is in a job which may differ from those of men but is considered to be of equal value through the findings of job evaluation. Any disagreements may be referred to an industrial tribunal for a decision.

13. Race Relations Act 1976

This Act replaced the 1965 and 1968 Acts and makes unlawful any discrimination on the grounds of colour, race, or ethnic or national origin. It applies to employment and the provision of goods, facilities and services. Individuals who feel they have been discriminated against in employment may complain to an industrial tribunal.

The Act established the Commission for Racial Equality which replaced the Race Relations Board. The Commission is responsible for promoting the objectives of the Act, for investigating discriminatory practices and for advising the Government on measures to improve the legislation. It also has the power to assist individual complainants.

14. Health and Safety at Work etc. Act 1974

All people at work except domestic servants in private households are covered in this Act. It is an enabling Act imposing a general duty of care on most people associated with work activities. The Act is capable of being changed, expanded and adapted to cope with risks and problems which may arise in the future. The Act's aims, approach and general provisions are dealt with in Chapter XVIII.

15. Employment Protection Act 1975

This Act promotes the improvement of industrial relations through the Advisory, Conciliation and Arbitration Service, and encourages the extension of collective bargaining. New rights and greater job security which were given to employees are now contained in the Employment Protection (Consolidation) Act 1978 (*see* Chapter XVII and below).

16. Trade Union and Labour Relations Act 1974

This Act established for employees (with certain exceptions) the right not to be dismissed unfairly. These provisions are now contained in the Employment Protection (Consolidation) Act. If an employee thinks he has been unfairly dismissed he may seek a remedy by applying to an industrial tribunal (*see* Chapter XV).

17. Employment Protection (Consolidation) Act 1978

This Act brings together under one enactment the provisions on individual employment rights previously covered in other Acts: Trade Union and Labour Relations Act 1974, Contracts of Employment Act 1972, Redundancy Payments Act 1965, and the Employment Protection Act 1975. The rights conferred in those Acts are in no way altered, nor are the corresponding obligations on employers.

The vast majority of sections and schedules which have been consolidated from the earlier Acts mentioned are repealed, with some exceptions. Careful inspection of the various Acts is essential to ensure where each provision is now located.

18. Sex Discrimination Act 1975

Discrimination in employment on the grounds of sex or marriage is prohibited under this Act. Any discrimination regarding training, promotion, short-time working, or dismissal is also unlawful. More details are given in Chapter XV.

19. Employers' Liability (Compulsory Insurance) Act 1969

Section 1 of the Act states that every employer shall insure, and maintain insurance, under one or more approved policies with an authorised insurer or insurers against bodily injury or disease sustained by his employees arising out of and in the course of their employment in Great Britain.

A copy of the certificate of insurance should be displayed at all places of business and in a prominent position where it can easily be seen and read.

Social Responsibilities of Management

WORKING CONDITIONS

In addition to the legal requirements under the various Acts mentioned above the supervisor has a social obligation to insist on adequate working conditions and to maintain a satisfactory standard. The main aspects which require special attention are now discussed.

1. Cleanliness

The workshop should be kept clean by arranging for daily removal of all rubbish and dirt, and regular floor cleaning at least every week. Constant checks are needed to maintain a reasonably clean establishment. A programme for redecoration and general cleaning of walls and ceilings should be drawn up.

2. Overcrowding and ventilation

There must be at least 11.3 cu. m. of space for each employee in the workshop. The calculation should be based upon the capacity of the factory between the floor and a height of 3 m.

Adequate ventilation is also very important to ensure the circulation of fresh air. Tests have shown that high temperature and polluted air have an adverse effect on physical work. The harmful effects on health when no attempt is made to remove dust, fumes, and other impurities from the air are well known. The installation of air conditioning is often worth while because clean air of the correct temperature and humidity encourages better work and improved output.

Layout is also important: subjecting an employee to a draught, or allowing an operator to work in surroundings where rapid temperature changes are occurring, is inviting lower effectiveness. The risk of accidents and sickness is also increased. Many other factors have to be considered, dependent upon the work situation. For example, in a foundry some employees will perspire excessively and require salt tablets to replace the loss.

3. Temperature and humidity

The human body is influenced by the surrounding temperature and the humidity of the atmosphere. These two interacting factors must be considered together, because the heat conductivity of air rises as the moisture content increases. In cold, humid conditions, therefore, the body may lose heat rapidly and the air would feel colder than its actual temperature. A further factor in these conditions is that high humidity will retard the evaporation of perspiration, in which case the cooling process of the body is upset. Thus, warm humid air may feel warmer than the actual temperature.

These facts will explain why the temperature in the workshop may be adequate, but employees may still complain of discomfort. A reasonable temperature for the workshop should be not less than 15°C (60°F). Particular temperatures are recommended for some occupations and, where a major part of the work is carried out in the sitting position, this temperature should be reached by the end of the first hour. Many wet processes must be taken into consideration as these naturally increase the humidity of the atmosphere. Adequate drainage is necessary to minimise this effect.

4. Lighting

The problem of lighting is particularly involved and is often neglected in industry. A thorough knowledge of the behaviour of the human eye and the psychological problems connected with vision is needed before adequate lighting conditions can be determined. Such factors as intensity, wave length and distribution of light are very important and, to some extent, they interact with each other. The services of a lighting specialist are essential, considering the effects on morale and production when poor illumination of workshops is endured. The employee suffers eye fatigue and discomfort which in turn induces irritability. These tensions may cause accidents and errors, and output will be affected. On the other hand, good lighting has a stimulating effect on individuals. This effect is similar to the change in feeling experienced on a sunny day compared with a dull, rainy day.

Some of the common faults in lighting are:

(a) flickering light;
(b) intensity too low;
(c) uneven distribution over the whole visual field;
(d) poor reflecting qualities of walls;
(e) bright spots outside the working area which tend to attract the eyes away from the working area;
(f) glare and intermittent glare from various highly reflective surfaces.

An indication of lighting intensity for various parts of the factory as recommended by the Illuminating Engineering Society is given below.

18.6 lm/sq. ft. (200.2 lx): for corridors, gangways, loading bays, general stores and warehouses.
40 lm/sq. ft. (430.6 lx): for general assembly work and reading large print.

80 lm/sq. ft. (861.1 lx): for close assembly work, reading small print, and drawings.

100 lm/sq. ft. (1076.4 lx): for very fine work.

These rough guides form only part of the over-all lighting conditions, as already stressed. Maintenance of lighting is essential because the light intensity of lamps is considerably reduced after being in operation for some time and coatings of dirt also impair the efficiency of lighting units.

5. Seating requirements

Although there is a legal obligation to provide seating facilities where a reasonable opportunity to be seated exists and where a large portion of the work can be done sitting down, the importance of seating requirements is often overlooked.

According to the medical profession, standing for long periods is tiring and induces tension. Standing causes the muscles of the thighs and calves to contract to keep the body upright, thus energy is used for this purpose. Specialists also are of the opinion that frequent position changes, such as alternate sitting and standing, are beneficial as excessive tiredness is avoided.

Another important factor is the design of the seat. The purpose of the seat is to support the body in such a way that a stable posture is maintained while relaxing muscles which are not used at work. An ergonomically designed seat eliminates discomfort due to unnessary pressure on the underside of the thighs which is recognised often by "pins and needles." Efficient design also allows for varying the position so that the body weight may be shifted during a work period without losing support.

6. Lavatories and washrooms

The bare minimum requirements are laid down in s. 7 of the Factories Act and s. 9 of the Offices, Shops and Railway Premises Act. To provide pleasant and agreeable amenities, however, modern practice is more demanding. For example, two wash-basins instead of one are recommended for every 20 employees, and three instead of two for 21–40 employees. The ratio may be applied to other areas such as cloakroom and toilet facilities.

7. Cloakrooms, etc.

Although provisions for cloakrooms, changing rooms and showers are mentioned in various Acts, there is an element of interpretation involved because such terms as "suitable" and "adequate" are quoted. Some companies, for example, provide baths where people are engaged in hot or dirty work although they are not legally required to.

Another example of interpretation concerns the term "adequate" for clothing accommodation. A High Court decision stated that although there was no absolute obligation to keep clothing safe, the risk of theft had to be considered when deciding whether accommodation was adequate. The Factory Inspectorate gives the following six points as being essential for satisfactory clothing accommodation.

1. Adequate precautions against theft.
2. Adequate space for changing clothes and footwear.
3. Adequate ventilation and lighting.
4. A separate peg or locker displaying the name or works number for each operator.
5. Facilities for drying outdoor clothing and overalls worn in wet processes.
6. A high standard of cleanliness.

8. Noise

Although many employees regard noise only as a nuisance, in fact it is now recognised as a major health hazard. Excessive noise can cause long-term damage to health and it accelerates the normal loss of hearing process through age.

Research findings indicate that prolonged exposure to noise of more than 90 decibels is harmful and when levels above 100 decibels are reached, extensive and permanent damage to hearing can occur. Inexpensive instruments are available to measure the noise level.

The two main ways of reducing noise levels are to deal with it at source or to wear ear defenders. Modifications to equipment such as machine tools, generators and compressors are possible by fitting sound proof shields, baffles or absorbent-lined compartments. The main types of ear defenders are ear plugs, ear valves, and the ear muff. They can reduce the level by as much as 50 decibels.

The Inspectorate's code of practice gives a limit of 90 decibels. Where machines exceed this level they should be masked, prominent warning notices should be displayed and entrance to such areas controlled, and ear defenders must be worn. The code proposes a number of general methods of control, and measures for reducing exposure duration are suggested. These include rearranging work so that part is done in a quiet place, job rotation, and the use of quiet restrooms.

BENEFITS

Most concerns offer benefits, which vary considerably from company to company. In addition, unofficial benefits or "perks" are often received. Employees tend to take these for granted, with or without the knowledge of management. Some examples are petrol from the company's pump, raw materials, components, stationery, and the use of machines and equipment for private purposes. Sometimes the traffic in these "perks" is unbelievably high and loss to the company amounts to very large sums of money.

Official fringe benefits may be divided into the following groups.

(a) *Social facilities.* A wide range of social and recreational facilities is offered in the form of dining rooms, sports clubs, social clubs, outings, and entertainments.

(b) *Financial assistance.* Various forms of assistance are available covering items such as further education, loans for house purchase, discount on purchases of certain products, and reduced prices for company products.

(c) *Insurance schemes.* Various insurance schemes to cover retirement, sickness and injury, are still operated by concerns, but some schemes have been superseded by the National Insurance Scheme described above.

(d) *Payment for non-working time.* Within this category there are various national agreements and legislation which cover holiday pay, including bank holidays. Allowances for part-time day further education, various concessions for visiting sick relatives, funerals, visits to arrange house purchase, and for other legal problems are often given.

(e) *General benefits.* General awards such as gifts for long service, bonuses, free luncheon vouchers, and anniversary payments, which are not directly connected with employee output.

QUESTIONS

1. Discuss the question of "perks" or unofficial benefits.
2. Outline some of the benefits offered to employees under various schemes of welfare.
3. Explain how the law protects the employee.
4. Give a general outline of the Factories Act 1961.
5. What statutory regulations exist concerning wages and conditions of service?
6. Explain the legislation on national insurance.
7. To what extent would you consider that working conditions affect the attitude of employees towards management?
8. Do you think there is any connection between the quality of working conditions and the quality of workmanship in a factory?
9. Is it possible for the supervisor to promote the health of his subordinates?
10. If the social and recreational facilities are poorly supported in a concern what do you think are the likely causes?
11. Outline the legislation which provides for compensation of operators in the event of industrial injury.

PART II: SUGGESTED PROJECTS

1. Attempt an assessment of morale in your concern.
   (a) List all the possible factors which affect morale and investigate each one.
   (b) Draw up a summary of your findings and suggest constructive methods for improving the situation.

2. Write an account of five human problems on the shop floor from your own experience.

Each account should include your personal observations; the opinions of other colleagues wherever possible; the causes of the problem; the actual situation as it arises; the way it is solved; and any after-effects.

Attempt to summarise your work and furnish suitable conclusions.

3. Investigate the operation of the grape-vine in your concern. Classify the rumours; sources; accuracy; and estimate the effects.

Do *not* attempt to trace the *human chain* back to the original source of information.

After an adequate number of cases has been established, attempt to draw conclusions from your work.

4. Carry out a continuous survey for about four months to ascertain the number of occasions when problems or trouble-spots arise through a breakdown in communication.

Classify the causes (such as lack of information, misunderstandings) and summarise the findings, making suitable recommendations.

5. If the concern's personnel policy is publicised, investigate the effectiveness of its operation in practice.

Choose a group and study each individual's reactions and problems within the province of personnel policy.

Tabulate and explain your findings with a view to constructively criticising the policy, its interpretation by management and the reactions of employees.

6. Prepare and maintain a record of negotiations between management and the trade union in your concern. Include such aspects as date; subject; negotiations; results; and follow up.

Attempt to assess the effectiveness of the talks and the possible causes of disagreements when they arise.

7. Maintain a record of negotiations between yourself and the shop steward. The report should include all relevant details of the talks and each disagreement or problem should be amplified to show the possible causes and the opinions of both sides.

Prepare a summary of your conclusions, indicating some of the basic problems or difficulties encountered and how you would overcome them if given the opportunity.

8. Attempt to assess the importance of welfare in your company. Make notes on individuals' reactions to welfare facilities; their complaints concerning welfare; whether schemes are supported; and the general attitude towards welfare.

Write a comprehensive report and include your recommendations.

9. Examine the jobs of five employees who have the reputation of being lazy. Consider whether or not they would benefit if the jobs were enriched.

10. Study the job structures in your section and attempt to enrich them.

PART THREE

CONTROLLING THE WORK

CHAPTER XX

THE NATURE OF CONTROL

Importance of Control

THE term "control" has many meanings: power of directing; ability to restrain; means of restraint; standard of comparison for checking inferences deduced from experiment; or as a verb, to dominate; and to regulate. Any term which has a variety of meanings leads to confusion in practice unless the meaning intended is carefully detailed. Control as applied to business may be defined as the direction of activities to achieve an objective, according to predetermined plans and standards.

A Basic Control Procedure

The ability to control effectively requires a sound understanding of certain logical steps which form a basic procedure. Three steps are essential to ensure that everything has occurred in accordance with the plan; the basic procedure is to:

1. set standards;
2. check performance;
3. correct deviations.

This simplification of procedure does not indicate the logical sequence involved in a control cycle, for Step 2, "Check performance", covers the whole process of feedback of information and comparison of the actual with the standard. The procedure for starting a machine forms a simple example:

Cycle	Observation
1. Instruction and Action:	Press starter button.
2. Feedback of Effect:	Machine refuses to start.
3. Information:	Electric power switch is off.
4. Adjustment:	Switch on power.
5. Instruction:	Press starter button.

This concept of a control cycle as applied to starting a machine is illustrated in Figure 32, which should be studied carefully. Cycles of action are represented as loops. A fault is corrected by means of the *transient loop*, and the *terminal loop* is only completed when the action taken to start the machine is successful, i.e. only one terminal loop can be made for each event. This means that after one loop is completed to start the machine the next terminal loop may be to feed the machine, and the next to switch it off. The transient loop, however,

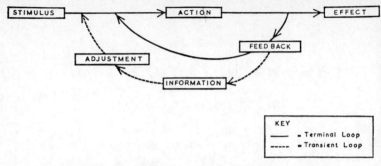

Fig. 32.—*Terminal and Transient Loops in Control.*
An effective control cycle must contain a *transient* loop to provide: 1. Feedback (notify failure to achieve desired result); 2. Information (cause of failure); 3. Adjustment (rectify fault); this is repeated until the *terminal* loop is successful, providing: 1. Action (repeat instruction); 2. Feedback (notify success).

must be repeated in the same sequence until the action is successful; that is, until the machine is finally started.

Under normal conditions a transient loop must be followed by a terminal loop before a stimulus (instruction) is satisfied. If an action fails to achieve its purpose, a sequence of five steps is necessary. Firstly, the transient loop operates through three stages:

1. feedback, which notifies the controller of the failure;
2. information, which provides a reason for the failure;
3. adjustment, which should rectify the fault.

Secondly, the terminal loop must follow by:

4. repeating the original instruction; and
5. feedback, which notifies the controller that the desired effect is achieved.

If the transient loop is unsuccessful, the five steps are repeated until the terminal loop is completed.

The waste of time and frustration may be considerable when transient loops continually occur through lack of adequate control, such as faulty feedback of information and ill-considered adjustments.

It must be appreciated that control is essentially a *continuous process of adjustment* to situations, like steering a vehicle which is constantly deviating from a straight course.

This aspect of control is illustrated diagrammatically in Figure 33. The input factors are those variables which may be altered by the controller when corrections are necessary. These factors—when properly manipulated—can alter the output variables according to need in the particular circumstances. Take a simple example such as riding a

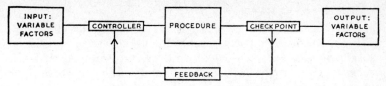

Fig. 33.—*Basic Control Procedure.*

Control is a *continuous* process of adjusting input variables in order to produce the desired output effects. These variable factors, or variables, are also termed "parameters."

bicycle. The input variables such as steering, rate of pedalling and use of brakes, are manipulated by the rider to adjust the output variables—direction and speed—according to desire and conditions.

CONTROL APPRAISAL

From the three basic steps of control (set standards; check performance; correct deviations) a more elaborate appraisal of the organisation of production can be built up, which is essential before any effective system of control can be applied. This appraisal may take the form of a number of control questions and these are listed below, together with the various functions which provide a means of answering them.

Control questions

1. Who is responsible for each section of the work and for doing the work?
   Organisation plan—division of responsibility and delegation.
2. What is the work content?
   Job description.
3. How is the work to be performed?
   Method study.
4. How long should the work take to perform?
   Work measurement.
5. Where should the work be performed?
   Method study and layout.
6. When should the work be performed?
   Planning and scheduling.
7. What is the cost of performing the work?
   Accounts and costing.
8. How is work performance regulated?
   Human relations; motivation; cost reduction; progress.
9. How is quality of work checked?
   Quality control.

These questions indicate the complexities of control as an aspect of production, its difficulties and the demands it makes on supervision and management.

PROBLEMS OF CONTROL

Many problems arise in the final stage of correcting deviations. The ability to correct effectively depends upon knowledge, experience, imagination, and judgment; all of which can be overshadowed by an unexpected occurrence such as a power cut, machine breakdown, or an accident.

The problem of size may easily defeat control with such obstacles as feedback delay, the excessive growth of information flow, the general haze over operations which increases with size and complexity, human problems, and lack of time to think.

These problems of control are multiplied considerably at higher levels of management, where additional external factors and uncontrollable variables impede decision-making, often at a time when speed is essential.

Criticism of any person who is controlling is exceptionally easy, because immediately some form of action is taken, the situation is changed, requiring further adjustments which may appear illogical or contradictory to someone not knowing all the facts. Constructive criticism is far more difficult.

The main aspects of control to be discussed are listed with chapter references below.

Establishing standards of control (XX).
Work study (XXI–XXIII).
Use of statistical methods (XXIV).
Production planning and control (XXV).
Quality control (XXVI).
Financial aspects (XXVII).
Costing aspects (XXVIII–XXIX).
Cost reduction and maintenance (XXX).

Effective control is achieved by integrating the various control aspects.

Establishing Standards

Scientific control is not possible unless most of the variable factors involved in a process are measured and standards are established. Standards may be set for factors such as methods, performance, quality, forms, equipment, working conditions, grading individuals, work batches, layout, materials, and tools.

Some supervisors are very reluctant to set standards, possibly because they fear that their estimate will be very inaccurate. This possible error is of no importance. The vital point is to provide some basis against which the actual figure may be measured, so that the reason for the deviation may be ascertained, and corrective action taken if necessary. If the actual figure is justified after investigation, the standard is revised, and no harm is done; in fact, the process of scientific control has commenced.

Naturally, the burden on the supervisor of setting standards largely disappears where a work study specialist is available. The development and application of work study is described in the next chapter, followed by discussion of work study techniques in Chapters XXII and XXIII.

QUESTIONS

1. What is "feedback" and why is it so important in connection with management control?

2. Define control and give an example of its meaning as applied to a machine.

3. What is meant by a terminal loop and a transient loop in control theory?

4. Outline a simple basic control procedure.

5. Discuss the basic steps which are necessary to set up control of a plan.

6. What is meant by control appraisal?

7. State the main aspects of control in a business and give a brief account of each one.

8. "Control may be said to be a continuous process of adjustment." Discuss this statement.

9. "Control is an essential part of supervision." Give a reasoned account of this statement.

CHAPTER XXI

INTRODUCTION TO WORK STUDY

The Function of Work Study

BRITAIN has suffered severe economic setbacks during the last half century, partly because of the inability of large groups of employers and employees to recognise the importance of work study in productivity drives. The reasons and excuses for this oversight, such as complacency, lack of information, resistance from trade unions, suspicion of managements' intentions, are incidental.

Work study now is generally recognised as an essential, specialised function to increase productivity and maintain an effective business. No company can afford to ignore work study today in the face of swiftly increasing competition from other countries, some of whom are already far advanced in this field.

Admittedly, management must bear the responsibility of appreciating the situation and taking appropriate steps such as setting up a work study department, using an industrial consultant, or training employees in work study, according to the size of the company and circumstances. The supervisor, however, still remains at the critical position between operatives and management. Unless he is genuinely convinced of the vital need for work study and is prepared to support the specialist, most of the improvements suggested will be neutralised through lack of support from operatives.

Once operatives can be persuaded to change their routine and try out new proposals, the advantages are soon appreciated and accepted. The barriers of suspicion and resistance to change can be removed by the supervisor who is convinced of the need for work study and imparts his enthusiasm to the operators. He must also possess sufficient knowledge of the subject to apply it and explain the purposes of each technique adequately.

DEFINITION OF WORK STUDY

Work study may be broadly described as a scientific study of any form of work. It involves the study of such factors as people, machines, equipment, tools, materials, and layout, with a view to increasing productivity by improving the effectiveness of each factor involved.

Cruder forms of work study naturally commenced at a time when a human being first used his brain to reason out a better way of performing a task, such as trapping an animal for food. Today work study is highly sophisticated and continually expanding into a number of techniques which involve complex scientific calculations and the use of an electronic computer. All these modern techniques are not concerned with increasing the speed of processes. They are aimed at locating the optimum utilisation of individuals, machines, processes, materials, equipment, space, and any other factors which are involved in the particular work under investigation.

The usual interpretation of the phrase "optimum utilisation of individuals", is that people must work harder to increase productivity. This must be expected not only because people confuse the word *optimum*, the best, with *maximum*, the greatest, but also because it is not unusual to see numbers of employees idle—often through no fault of their own—while others are working well beyond a normal rate. The fact remains that forcing people beyond a natural or normal rate of working under supervision, does not largely increase output. The aim—as the word *optimum* implies—is to create the most favourable utilisation of individuals, which includes minimising fatigue and ensuring that all concerned perform a normal day's work.

Far greater savings are possible by improvement of methods, more detailed planning and control of work, and effective utilisation of machines and other facilities, than by driving operators at too high a rate.

The definition of work study by the British Standards Institution is:

"a generic term for those techniques, particularly method study and work measurement, which are used in the examination of human work in all its contexts and which lead systematically to the investigation of all the factors which affect the efficiency and economy of the situation being reviewed in order to effect improvement."

THE AIMS OF WORK STUDY

1. The most effective use of economic resources available to the concern, i.e. people, machines, space, equipment, and capital.

2. A more even spread of work among employees.

3. Improved standard procedure for more effective control.

4. Improved planning by the provision of standard times and procedures.

5. Fairer wages schemes, through the careful assessment of job values.

6. A more contented working force. The streamlining of production should eliminate many sources of frustration and tension, provided that management does not neglect the human element when introducing changes.

7. Increased productivity. This should help to bring economic benefits both to the concern and to the community as a whole.

THE SCOPE OF WORK STUDY

For the purpose of explanation only, work study is divided into two main categories.

1. *Method Study:* to find better ways of performing jobs with available facilities.
2. *Work Measurement:* to determine the time a proficient operator takes to perform a specified job, based upon a given level of performance.

In practice the two categories are closely integrated, but generally method study comes first, followed by work measurement, which is based upon the revised method. Often the practice of measuring the work reveals further improvements which are incorporated in the standard method originally devised.

The field of work study is expanding continually and is resulting in some degree of overlap in new terms and techniques as they emerge from the study of various aspects of the function. For example, there are many terms meaning more or less the same as work study, such as production engineering, organisation and methods, methods engineering, and operational research.

The function of work study as a service department has broadened from the study of work on the shop floor to include the study of a vast range of managerial activities. This critical, analytical and scientific approach to problems is now applied to: new projects, all main and sub-functions within the organisation, the organisation itself, and all managerial activities, with particular emphasis on planning, control, and general and operational policies.

The diagram in Figure 34 attempts to show the modern extent of work study and to indicate its complex developments, with overlapping of techniques and terms.

Attitudes to Work Study

THE WORK STUDY PRACTITIONER

The supervisor should possess some knowledge of the qualities of a good work study practitioner and what he hopes to achieve. The object is not to be critical of the engineer's shortcomings, but to help him achieve his purpose, which, like all specialists, is to help the supervisor and his operators.

The work study engineer's reputation rests entirely with the supervisor and subordinates—they can make his proposals work well or ruin them—and most engineers are aware of this fact.

Inevitably he needs the supervisor's help and the assistance and suggestions of operators. Any supervisor who deliberately forestalls and attempts to create the wrong atmosphere between the engineer and operators, is hindering both parties and openly displaying his ignorance and conceit.

THE INDIVIDUAL AND WORK STUDY

Unfortunately there is an inherent belief, whether the person is a

EXPANDING FIELD OF WORK STUDY

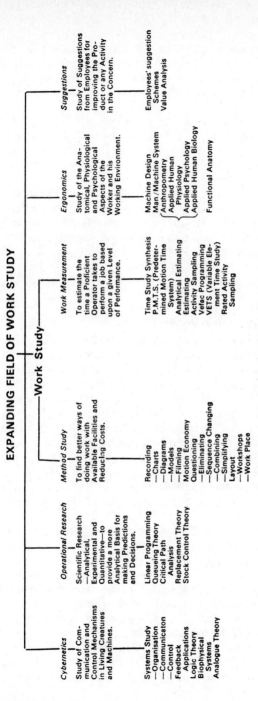

Fig. 34.—*Expanding Field of Work Study*.

This chart indicates not only the modern extent of work study, but also the complexity of its development in various directions.

manager, supervisor, or operator, that any suggested change in the way he (or even his subordinate) performs his work is a direct reflection on his own ability. This natural resistance can be overcome by sound explanations of the need for improvements, when people realise that work study is only an extension of the specialist function, is very time-consuming, and is not a personal criticism of their methods.

Redundancy and wages are two problems which management must be prepared to face squarely if the recommended changes are to be successful. Guarantees that employees will be absorbed into other jobs and retrained, or planned reduction of numbers through normal labour turnover, are essential if employee co-operation is to be achieved. The wages system also needs reconsideration on matters such as incentives and—if productivity is improved—the employees' share of savings. Solutions must be acceptable otherwise fresh problems will emerge and more than offset the improvements.

The full support of employees is essential in work study. Management must provide information and guarantees, while supervision must create the desirable atmosphere and achieve co-operation from operators.

THE SUPERVISOR AND WORK STUDY

The results of work study provide the supervisor with improved standard procedures, standard methods of performing jobs and established performance times for operations. All this is vital information for purposes of planning and control which, with intelligent application by supervisors and managers, should improve productivity.

Whether the improvement in productivity will reach the targets set by management and the work study specialists depends largely upon the supervisor. He may not have sufficient faith in the effectiveness of the new methods to take full advantage of them. On the other hand, he may become so engrossed in procedure and methods, in timing, recording, and controlling work flow—all elements of production—that he neglects the operators who must put the new methods into practice.

The full implications of motivation and human relations have been stressed in previous chapters. The supervisor, therefore, has to achieve a balance: he must pay sufficient attention to production details to gain the benefits of work study findings, at the same time providing his subordinates with guidance and encouragement, to maintain their morale and to achieve maximum results from the new methods.

To summarise, an effective supervisor does not allow production tasks to over-ride the human element.

Usually operators are inclined to wait for the supervisor to propose better ways of doing the work, although some take the initiative and develop their own short cuts. Probably they think it is the responsibility of supervision, or perhaps suggestions have been ignored in the past and, as a result, a general apathy has developed.

There is also the attitude that new methods mean more work and job changes may mean redundancy. People are not inclined to take the risk of bringing about changes, especially if they are already happy and secure in their jobs. This natural resistance to change is understandable. The supervisor must accept the problem as a challenge to convince operators of the necessity for progressive thinking and the dangers of lagging behind in productivity.

The case for work study is strengthened if the supervisor remembers that usually individuals are disinclined to ask for more work. Generally, people do the work allocated to them and they manage to spread it very accurately over the time available.

The ability to assess a reasonable time for a given work load is a distinct advantage to the supervisor. He will become more aware of those who are slacking and can apply appropriate pressure. He can also avoid putting unnecessary pressure on those who are working at a reasonable speed. The latter point is very important: the conscientious employees are fully aware of the slackers and grow resentful if they seem to be treated no better. In addition, timing the work load to keep people fully occupied has a stimulating effect on output, as there is less tendency to slacken off when the end of a load is in sight.

Finally, when jobs are measured the standards set provide a good indication of quality and output requirements to operators who appear to prefer working with clearer objectives in mind. This allows the supervisor to relax very close control over an operator, who then has, where practicable, the opportunity to work at his own variations of speed to suit his personality and enjoy more freedom in his work generally.

The Application of Work Study for the Supervisor

In many concerns the supervisor will be without the services of a work study specialist and will have to rely upon his own resourcefulness and energy to attempt improvements. The main fields of improvement which do not involve capital expenditure and, therefore, come within the scope of the supervisor are as follows.

1. Workshop layout.
2. Work flow.
3. Individual workplace layout.
4. Use of machines and equipment.
5. Method of work.
6. Measuring the work.

Each aspect should be examined critically and in accordance with method study procedure, which is explained in the next chapter. Some degree of improvement is always possible if time is spent examining the situation and possible rearrangements are carefully considered. Operators always have ideas for improvements as they are most closely concerned. The problem is persuading them to give their opinions and to co-operate during and after the changes.

1. Workshop layout

Gradual and subtle changes occur in many workshops all the time; a cabinet may be moved to accommodate a supply of materials, a bench moved nearer to an electrical point, and so on. As processes and output change, some rearrangement occurs and, unless the supervisor maintains a constant check and plans ahead, even the best layout gradually deteriorates into a muddle, especially if individuals are allowed to move equipment without permission.

It pays to carry out periodical surveys of workshop layout. The problems of storage, clear gangways, maximum use of overhead space, locker location, siting of benches, machines, and equipment, should be listed and possible solutions noted. The question of safety and the existing locations of supply lines such as air, electricity, water, and gas, must be considered. Workshop layout is naturally closely allied with work flow which must be considered at the same time.

One useful method of trying out ideas is to make scale models of all the workshop furniture in the form of cardboard cut-outs and locate them on a scale plan of the workshop. All the essential supplies should be marked in. Various layouts can be arranged quickly and the snags noted until the most suitable layout is found.

2. Work flow

The main principles to apply are: no crossing flow lines; no backtracking; clear points for materials feeding in to the line at appropriate places to avoid congestion; due allowance for testing and inspection points; and correct sequence of operations, arranged to minimise movements of materials and assemblies through each process.

Transporting is expensive; therefore, each unnecessary movement of materials or assemblies must be eliminated. Carefully-planned work flow can avoid bottlenecks at the junctions of gangways, the loss of time and temper which such delays cause, and the danger of accidents.

3. Individual workplace layout

Some of the reasons for poor workplace layout are: lack of forethought; overcrowding; changes in job content; untrained employees; and disregard for new work study techniques.

A number of advantages may be gained by attending to this problem. Employee fatigue and accident risk should be reduced, and work quality and output should improve.

Like workshop layout, the layout of the individual workplace must be considered in relation to the work flow and many of the same principles apply. Such fundamental items as the points of arrival and departure of materials and assemblies on the bench; the positioning of jigs and fixtures; and the siting and use of the most appropriate tools for the job, are too easily accepted without question. Other techniques applied in the improvement of workplace layout are ergonomics (study of man's physical abilities in relation to his working environment) and motion economy (eliminating unnecessary, awkward and fatiguing movements). The importance of general working conditions, such as lighting and ventilation, was discussed earlier (Chapter XIX).

4. Use of machines and equipment

The inadequacies of existing machinery which may be obsolete or to some extent unsuitable are frustrating, but the importance of making full use of machines and equipment must not be ignored. Precious capital has been spent on these items and unless they are fully utilised the concern will suffer a loss. Idle time on machines is an irrecoverable loss, and therefore it must be kept to a minimum by careful planning. It is the supervisor's responsibility to make the best possible use of existing facilities, and he cannot excuse himself on the grounds that his predecessors or management have purchased unwisely.

The supervisor may make recommendations for replacements and additional mechanisation, but these must be justified in terms of savings in time and labour, and improved quality. Capital expenditure is a complex and risky part of management's job. One major error of expenditure in a small concern may result in the eventual liquidation of the company. A certain amount of sympathy and understanding is essential in such cases where the need for expenditure seems obvious, but management is inclined to be cautious for no apparent reason.

5. Method of work

A critical study of the operations performed in a job is an essential part of the technique of method study. The supervisor must adopt a questioning attitude towards each activity in the work with a view to either eliminating, combining, changing the sequence of, or simplifying various activities. Most jobs can be streamlined in this way and, coupled with the application of the principles of motion economy, productivity should improve through quicker and less fatiguing methods.

6. Measuring the work

Unless the supervisor has a fairly accurate assessment of the time jobs take to perform, the effectiveness of planning and control is considerably reduced.

The supervisor does not have to be an expert to time a job within reason. His experience of the work and knowledge of subordinates who are performing the operations should enable him to make a fair assessment, in the absence of a specialist.

Sound planning and control is now possible, but naturally the set times must be acceptable to employees before they can be utilised for incentive schemes.

O. & M.

The application of work study in the clerical field is called O. & M., in full, Organisation and Methods.

Problems of supervision encountered in offices are very similar to those on the shop floor. Managers and supervisors are forced to spend most of their time running the departments while the question of improvements tends to fall into the background. The employment of an O. & M. officer provides the concern with a specialist, who concentrates on this activity, keeps up to date, and advises and helps to introduce more effective clerical systems, based on work study techniques.

QUESTIONS

1. Discuss the importance of work study in connection with higher productivity.
2. How would you convince an employee of the necessity for work study?
3. Define work study and give a brief outline of its scope.
4. Explain the terms *method study* and *work measurement* and show their interrelationship.
5. What are the main problems which confront the work study engineer during the normal course of his duties?
6. How can the supervisor assist the work study engineer?
7. What part must management play if the suggestions for improving work are to be successfully employed?
8. Discuss the reactions from employees that should be expected by the supervisor when they are informed of the proposed visit of a work study engineer.
9. How can the supervisor ensure that the proposed improvements made by the work study engineer are successfully installed?
10. What should the supervisor do if an employee strongly objects to the presence of a work study engineer at the workplace?

CHAPTER XXII

TECHNIQUES OF WORK STUDY I: METHOD STUDY AND MOTION ECONOMY

Introduction

THE supervisor should at least have an appreciation of the most common techniques of work study. He will then be able to speak intelligently with work study specialists when the occasion arises and understand their reports and diagrams. He can also participate more effectively during investigations and meetings, when his opinions and ideas are required.

For the purpose of clarity the techniques are divided as follows.

Main techniques:
1. method study, including motion economy;
2. work measurement.

Ancillary techniques:
1. cybernetics;
2. operational research;
3. ergonomics;
4. value analysis

This chapter discusses method study and motion economy. Work measurement and other techniques are the subject of Chapter XXIII. Whenever possible the terms used in describing the various techniques conform to the definitions in the *Glossary of Terms in Work Study*, issued by the British Standards Institution (B.S.I.), and are reproduced with their kind permission.

Definition of Method Study

The British Standards Institution's definition of method study is:
"The systematic recording and critical examination of existing and proposed ways of doing work, as a means of developing and applying easier and more effective methods and reducing costs."

Method Study Procedure

A logical sequence for applying method study is in five steps.

Stage I: Select the job to be studied.
Stage II: Record all the appropriate facts.

Stage III: Critically examine the facts.
Stage IV: Develop a new method.
Stage V: Install and maintain the new method.

Each step is now dealt with in turn, illustrating the main techniques where necessary.

STAGE I: SELECT THE JOB TO BE STUDIED

Generally, selection is based upon economic considerations. Where costs are abnormally high there is a good opportunity to make considerable savings.

The signs which reveal likely areas for investigation are trouble-spots, bottlenecks, low and erratic output, poor quality work, excessive scrap, high accident rate, excessive overtime, high fatigue, high labour turnover, and a high number of complaints and grievances.

STAGE II: RECORD THE FACTS

A clear picture of all the existing operations and flow of work provides a sound basis for examining the system followed and stimulates ideas for improvement, often not apparent until the over-all scene is portrayed. Faults become more obvious when operations are recorded.

The recording techniques may be grouped into four categories.
1. Charts.
2. Diagrams.
3. Models.
4. Filming.

1. Charts

(a) *Process charts*. A sequence of events is portrayed diagrammatically by means of a set of process chart symbols. There are various types of process chart. The main ones in use are: the *Outline Process Chart* which gives an over-all picture of one job by recording in sequence the main operations and inspections; the *Flow Process Chart* which sets out the sequence of the flow of a product, or a procedure, by recording all the events under review; and the *Two-Handed Process Chart* which records the activities of an operator's hands or limbs, in relationship to one another.

The Flow Process Chart may be drawn up to record what the operator does (man type), or what happens to material (material type), or how the equipment is used (equipment type).

There are two sets of process chart symbols in common use, but the trend is to use the symbols developed by the A.S.M.E. (American Society of Mechanical Engineers) in preference to Gilbreth's, which are given on the right as alternatives:

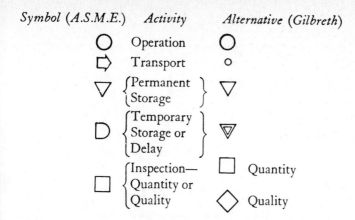

Symbol (*A.S.M.E.*)	Activity	Alternative (*Gilbreth*)
◯	Operation	◯
⇨	Transport	○
▽	{Permanent Storage}	▽
D	{Temporary Storage or Delay}	▽
□	{Inspection— Quantity or Quality}	□ Quantity ◇ Quality

Examples of an outline process chart and a flow process chart, material type, are given in Figures 35 and 36.

(*b*) *Time scale charts.* There are three time scale charts used for recording the activities of more than one subject at once and for recording all the movements taking place in an operation. These are as follows.

(*i*) *Multiple Activity Chart:* this chart records the activities of two or more subjects, which may be operators, machines, or equipment, on a common time scale to show their inter-relationship.

(*ii*) *Simo Chart:* this abbreviated name for a *Simultaneous Motion Cycle Chart* is often based upon film analysis. The chart records simultaneously, on a common time scale, the *therbligs* or groups of therbligs performed by various parts of the body of one or more workers. The name 'therblig" was given by Frank Gilbreth to each of the specific divisions of movement, according to the purpose for which it is made. (The name was coined by the reversal of his surname.) They cover movements, states of being, and pauses, e.g. select, grasp, assemble, inspect, transport loaded, rest, plan, delay. Each therblig has a specific colour symbol and letter for recording purposes.

(*iii*) *P.M.T.S. Chart:* the *Predetermined Motion Time System Chart* is used to record all the movements taking place in any operation by means of one of the predetermined motion time system codes. These codes represent, through combinations of figures and letters, basic human motions and qualifying conditions with corresponding time values.

2. Diagrams

Effective indication of movement is achieved by using diagrams of various types. A *flow diagram* shows the location of specific activities carried out and the routes followed by operations, materials, or

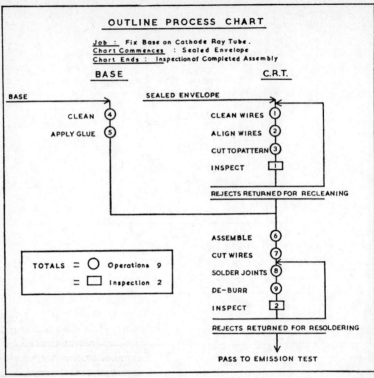

Fig. 35.—*Outline Process Chart.*

This gives an over-all picture of a job—to fix the base on a cathode ray tube—recording in sequence the main operations and inspections. Various symbols are used for different operations (*see* p. 339 and Fig. 36).

equipment, in their execution. A *string diagram* is a scale plan or model on which thread is used to trace and measure the path of operators, materials, or equipment, during a specified sequence of events.

In addition, there are various photographic means of recording movement by attaching a light source to the moving object and recording the path taken. These devices are called *cyclegraphs* and, when timed, *chronocyclegraphs*.

3. Models

A more expensive method of recording is the preparation of three-dimensional models. They have the advantage of being easily understood, and proposed changes may be visualised more accurately.

A more popular method is the two-dimensional model which is drawn to scale; cut-outs or loose templates are used to indicate the positions of machines, benches, and equipment.

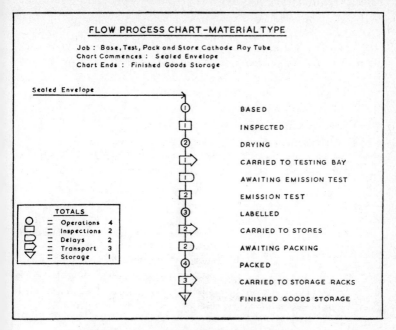

Fig. 36.—*Flow Process Chart, Material Type.*

This chart shows the sequence of flow of a simple product, recording each step in the procedure. The symbols used are those developed by the A.S.M.E. (*see* p. 339).

4. Filming

Recording operations by ciné film, or still film, provides a permanent record and is unobtrusive in operation. The main techniques are as follows.

(*a*) *Micromotion analysis:* a frame-by-frame analysis of a ciné film prepared in the form of a simo chart.

(*b*) *Film analysis:* a frame-by-frame examination on a ciné film of an operation to determine the state of activity of the subject during each exposure.

(*c*) *Memomotion photography:* a form of time lapse photography which records activity by a ciné camera adapted to take pictures at longer intervals than normal. This method makes it possible to record activities continuously over a long period.

STAGE III: CRITICALLY EXAMINE THE FACTS

An objective attitude is essential for the examination of any work if a new method is to be satisfactorily evolved. Any personal bias towards people or the work must be forgotten in favour of a broad outlook, free of narrow viewpoints; painstaking attention to detail and an analytical and logical approach to the problem are also vital.

The critical examination of the recorded operations is conducted by means of the questioning technique. Each activity in turn is subjected to a systematic and progressive series of questions.

There are two stages in this technique.

1. Primary questions

The first stage queries the fundamental need for the performance, place, person, sequence, and means of every activity recorded. The main headings for the primary questions, therefore, would be as follows.

> The purpose: Is the work needed? What is achieved? Why is it needed?
> The place: Where is the work done? Why is it done there?
> The person: Who does the work? Why does that particular individual do it?
> The sequence: When is the work done? Why is it done then?
> The means: How is the work done? Why is it done in that way?

If all these questions are answered correctly a thorough understanding of the existing method should result and, at this stage, clear indications of improvements in various sectors should be seen.

2. Secondary questions

The second stage subjects these answers to the primary questions to further inquiry. These secondary questions determine whether possible alternatives of place, people, sequence, and means, are practicable and preferable as a means of improving the existing method. Some typical questions would be the following.

> Purpose: Could the work be altered or eliminated in any part? Is the whole operation needed?
> Place: Are there other places available? Is there a more convenient place?
> Person: Who else could do the work? Could a person with lower skill do the work, with some alterations?
> Sequence: When else could it be performed? Would it be cheaper if performed earlier or later?
> Means: How else could the work be done? Are the principles of motion economy used? Are the most suitable machines and tools used? Could the working environment be improved?

STAGE IV: DEVELOPING THE NEW METHOD

Developing the new method from the answers hinges on four factors for improving an operation. These are:

1. elimination;
2. change of sequence;
3. combination;
4. simplification.

1. Elimination

The first consideration should be whether or not the operation can be dispensed with entirely. The operation may appear necessary, until a more searching investigation reveals that it no longer serves any purpose in the end product.

2. Change of sequence

When satisfactory proof of the need for the operation has been found, the merits of the existing sequence can be considered. A change of sequence may be justified by an improvement of work flow and the removal of unnecessary or duplicated work. For example, an assembly may be carefully cleaned at one stage, receive dirty treatment at the next, and then be cleaned again. A more glaring type of sequence fault occurs when an assembly must be partly dismantled to fit a component and then re-assembled.

3. Combination

The possibility of combining operations is the third consideration. Can any time be saved by eliminating unnecessary movements between operating points or by cutting down operation time? For example, sometimes work is performed in two places when one place would be sufficient; perhaps operations can be combined by slight modification; perhaps tools and machines can be more fully utilised through combination. The gains may be considerable and time is well spent in exploring these possibilities.

4. Simplification

The fourth consideration is probably the most important way of improving the essential operation. Invariably there are easier ways of performing an operation. The problem can be approached from a number of aspects. Some are described below and include motion economy, materials, the operator, design, power, handling, tools, machines, and equipment.

(a) *Motion economy*. The principles of motion economy should be used to save time and reduce fatigue. They are described later in the chapter.

(b) *Materials*. Often a different material which is easier to work with can save time. Perhaps a cheaper material is available which will not affect the quality of the finished product, or a lighter or heavier gauge could be used to advantage. The possibility of using waste or rejects should be examined. Another factor is whether the most economical lengths or sizes are being purchased; cutting can often be avoided by wiser purchasing thus reducing scrap costs.

(c) *The operator*. The suitability of a particular operator is often overlooked. Details such as height and weight may interfere with the work; for example, a tall operator may be at a disadvantage and suffer from fatigue quickly if he is working in a confined space inside an aircraft. The principles of ergonomics, or "fitting the job to the worker" (*see* Chapter XXIII), should be applied to avoid unnecessary fatigue.

(*d*) *Design*. Unfortunately, designers do not always manage to create the simplest designs. Various short cuts are possible and these small rearrangements result in large savings. Tolerances can often be opened without loss of quality, and standardisation of parts simplifies assembly. Methods of reducing the number of parts in an assembly through redesign are often obvious to the operator.

(*e*) *Power and handling*. Greater use of power for assembly and materials handling is recognised as making work easier, but not always applied for reasons such as lack of capital, lack of interest or dislike of changes and inconvenience. A careful choice of equipment is essential to achieve substantial economies, otherwise the expenditure will cancel out the saving.

(*f*) *Tools, machines, and equipment*. Although these aspects overlap with power and handling they are treated separately from the operating viewpoint. A vast number of questions could be raised about these items, such as: positioning? running speeds? location of controls? sequence of use? loose or fixed tools? combination tools? use of jigs and templates? could automatic feed be used? Imagination and the questioning technique can produce large savings.

STAGE V: INSTALL AND MAINTAIN THE NEW METHOD

Studying the system and evolving a new method is only half the work. Installing the new method requires great care, detailed planning, and the co-operation of everyone concerned with the change.

Naturally the magnitude of the change must be a major consideration. A small rearrangement is comparatively easy, but when transfers of operators, retraining, and rearranged layouts of workplaces and workshops are involved, the disruption of production is obviously considerable and timing becomes important. Detailed planning must include giving adequate information to all concerned, who must support the change wholeheartedly if the scheme is to be successful.

Periodic review of the new method is needed to check on and correct any deviations from the procedure. During these reviews the effects of the change should be noted for future improvements and resistance points examined more closely to find the cause.

The supervisor has a heavy responsibility during the period of installation and in maintaining the new method. His acceptance of change and ability to arouse enthusiasm and confidence in his subordinates are the key factors for successful operation of the revised scheme.

Motion Economy

The principles of motion economy are a fundamental part of method study. Any movements in an operation which can be eliminated, reduced, or made easier, will reduce fatigue and wasted time. Motion economy makes some contribution, therefore, towards increasing the effectiveness of the operator.

Economy in human movement was studied by Gilbreth, who classified the principles of motion analysis to form a foundation for construction layout of workplaces and patterns of movement. Observation of working movements quickly highlights those principles which are being abused and, in many instances, improvements can be made by minor rearrangements.

The seven principles of motion economy given below are only indications or guides and, as stressed in other chapters, much depends upon particular circumstances in deciding upon courses of action.

THE SEVEN PRINCIPLES OF MOTION ECONOMY

1. Minimum movements
All materials, tools, and equipment should be arranged so that the minimum amount of movement is necessary for their use. The degree of movement necessary to carry out an operation was classified by Gilbreth into five groups.

(*i*) Finger motions only.
(*ii*) Fingers and wrist movements.
(*iii*) Fingers, wrist and forearm.
(*iv*) Fingers, wrist, forearm and upper arm.
(*v*) Fingers, wrist, forearm, upper arm, and shoulder.

The use of the first three classifications constitutes the *normal working area*. The inclusion of the last two classifications provides the boundary for the *maximum working area* which will have to be used if all the tools, materials, and equipment cannot be accommodated within the normal working area.

The aim is to reduce the movements of the upper arm and shoulder (classifications (iv) and (v)) to a minimum. The natural sweep of the arms at each side of the body produces areas in the shape of arcs in the horizontal and vertical planes; these are illustrated in Figure 37 and form the working areas described.

Items used most frequently should be placed as close to the assembly area as possible and workplaces should be planned in accordance with the natural arc of working area.

2. Simultaneous movements
When different limbs are working at the same time they should be balanced by synchronising the movements, e.g. stretching out both

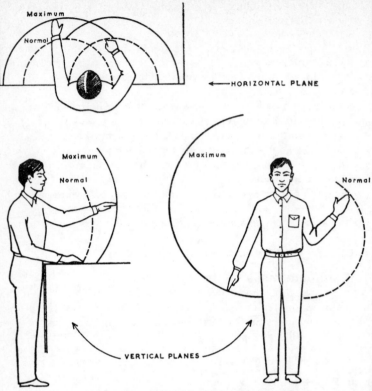

Fig. 37.—*Normal and Maximum Working Areas*.
The normal working area is covered by movements of the fingers, wrist and forearm, in both horizontal and vertical planes. The natural sweep of the arms forms arcs around the body. The maximum area is covered by bringing in movements of the upper arm and shoulder as well.

hands at once to pick up a bolt and a nut. This principle is very important because balance is achieved, less effort is required as concentration is reduced, and learning is easier. Fatigue is reduced because the natural reaction of a body is to divide exertion evenly between the left and right sides. Thus, when the left hand is moved, the right hand tends to move in a similar fashion.

3. Symmetrical movements
A further refinement—closely associated with simultaneous movements—states that movements should be balanced by performing them on the left and right-hand sides of the body about an imaginary line through the centre of the body. A common example of the combi-

nation of simultaneous and symmetrical movements is the range of physical exercises which involve both arms and a swinging motion.

4. Natural movements

Natural movements are those which make the best use of the shape and design of the body. The use of the feet, for instance, is often overlooked. They can be used either to perform an operation if they are more suitable than hands, or as an additional function when the hands are occupied. For example, if an assembly is held in a particular position for drilling by the hands, a foot may be used to operate the machine.

5. Rhythmical movements

Movements should be so ordered as to induce a natural rhythm in the cycle of operations. Regular repetition of movement develops speed and reduces mental and physical fatigue.

6. Habitual movements

This principle is closely associated with rhythmical movements. Precise repetition is habit forming and, as mental effort is reduced, the movement nears that of a reflex action.

Habitual movements are not possible unless conditions such as layout, supply of materials, and placing of tools, are standardised. Any slight alteration will defeat the object because extra mental effort is introduced to locate the item and the automatic movement is wasted.

7. Continuous movements

Any acute change in direction of a limb causes it to slow down, stop, and have to accelerate back to the original speed. Such action involves extra muscle movement and tension; therefore, it is more fatiguing compared with movements which are smooth and curved. Layout should be planned with this principle in mind.

THE SUPERVISOR AND MOTION ECONOMY

Although a detailed study of an operation may require the services of a specialist, there are often many obvious faults which the supervisor can easily improve.

Some of the glaring faults are as follows.

1. Cramped and dangerous positions of working.
2. Poor siting of tools, materials, machines and equipment, which require extra and awkward movements to use them.
3. Long stretching movements.
4. Using unnecessary force such as pulling excessively, levering, hammering and ramming.
5. Eye-strain and groping movements.
6. Loss of control of the operation.

7. Unnecessary movements such as changing the position of tools and materials, and walking round to various positions.

8. Lengthy adjustments.

9. Long pauses where fatigue is indicated as the cause.

10. Inadequate tools.

With a little ingenuity, the supervisor can eliminate many of these faults. The use of the principles of motion economy described above and small mechanical aids (e.g. simple transportation devices such as gravity feed containers and rollers, drop deliveries into bins, and quick release clamps), are a few of the methods of improvement.

QUESTIONS

1. For what purpose should a supervisor have a reasonable knowledge of work study techniques?

2. Outline a logical sequence for applying method study.

3. Illustrate by examples the main recording techniques in method study.

4. What is meant by the "questioning technique" in method study?

5. Explain and give examples of four main factors for improving an operation.

6. How can the supervisor ensure that a new method is installed and maintained with the minimum of disruption?

7. Discuss methods of reducing operator fatigue.

8. State and explain the seven principles of motion economy.

9. Describe some of the glaring, common faults that the supervisor can eliminate easily.

10. Discuss the uses of three time scale charts including a brief description of each chart.

CHAPTER XXIII

TECHNIQUES OF WORK STUDY II: WORK MEASUREMENT AND ANCILLARY TECHNIQUES

Work Measurement

THE B.S.I. definition of work measurement is:

"the application of techniques designed to establish the time for a *qualified worker* to carry out a specified *job* at a defined level of performance."

APPLICATION OF WORK MEASUREMENT

Sensible application of work measurement provides essential information for effective planning and control of production and other main functions. It is also used for improving systems of wage payments, more accurate costing, improving work loads through more accurate budgeting, and more accurate estimates.

Standard time

Human work can be divided into physical work, which is measurable, and mental work, which can only be estimated. Machine work must also be considered in work measurement, but in this case the work can be calculated easily and presents no problems of developing techniques.

People vary considerably in their rate of working; therefore, the time determined by work measurement is the average time a number of operators would take to perform the operation, without feeling more than healthily tired at the end of each day. This value is known as the *standard time* for a job.

Procedure

A typical procedure for applying work measurement is described below.

(*a*) *Select the work to be measured.* A similar investigation for selection should be carried out as in method study (Chapter XXII) to ensure that work is studied on a priority basis.

(*b*) *Record all the relevant information.* All available data on the job should be collected and recorded. Such sources as production schedules, inspection records, and drawings provide useful information.

(*c*) *Define the job in detail.* A job analysis should be carefully carried out, breaking the work down into elements or distinct parts, convenient for observation, measurement, and analysis.

(d) *Measure the work.* Measurement of the work is conducted by using one of the techniques described below.

TECHNIQUES OF WORK MEASUREMENT

The main techniques of work measurement are as follows.

1. Time study.
2. Synthesis.
3. P.M.T.S. (predetermined motion time systems).
4. Varifactor sampling.
5. Activity sampling.
6. Rated activity sampling.

1. Time study

The basic technique is time study, a direct observation of the job while it is being performed by the operator. The observer must possess an adequate job breakdown, the ability to estimate the rate of working, and a stop-watch to measure the elements accurately.

(a) *The rating.* The operator's rate of working is given a numerical value. The observer must judge the rate relative to a standard rating scale which runs from zero to 100, based upon the B.S.I. recommendation.

Standard performance is represented by 100 and is defined as: "the rate of output which *qualified workers* will naturally achieve without over-exertion, as an average over the working day, provided they know and adhere to the specified method, and provided they are motivated to apply themselves to their work" (B.S.I.). Other rating scales use 80 and 133 in place of 100.

(b) *The basic time.* Given the rating and the actual time taken to perform an element of the job, the basic time for that element can be calculated.

For example, if the observed rating is 90, the observed time is .10 minutes, and the standard rating is 100, this would appear as:

$$\text{Basic time} = \frac{90 \times 0.10}{100} = 0.09 \text{ minutes}$$

(c) *Relaxation allowance.* An addition to the basic time is provided, to allow for the general physiological and psychological effects of performing the work and to allow for attention to personal needs. The time allowed varies, dependent upon the nature of the job.

2. Synthesis

Many jobs contain some elements which are common to all of them. Therefore, a saving in time study is possible by building up a range of element times which can be referred to when required in a particular job. Ultimately a sufficient range of element times may be accumulated to provide the correct time for the whole job even before the job is performed.

The process of building up a stock of synthetic data may be accelerated by planning a series of studies to cover a wide range of elements. This is a long-term scheme and the question of whether it is economic must be considered.

3. Predetermined Motion Time Systems (P.M.T.S.)

Whereas the synthetic data in synthesis are established by observation of the separate elements of a job, the data obtained by predetermined motion time systems are calculated from standard times for basic human motions. These times are classified according to the nature of the motion and the conditions under which it is made.

The purpose is to remove the factor of human judgment and, briefly, the basis of the technique is that all work in an industrial environment consists of various combinations of a relatively small number of basic human motions. Times for these are measured from high-speed films and scaled to allow for circumstances, e.g. a heavy weight takes longer to lift than a light weight. The specialist analyses the job into its basic movements in detail, and then computes the times required from special tables, to find the total for the job, plus any allowances to be made.

The two main systems are known as "Work-Factor" and "M.T.M." or Methods-Time Measurement. The "Work-Factor" system originated in the U.S.A. in 1934; later a similar system was introduced by the Methods-Time Measurement Association.

4. Varifactor Synthesis

This heading may be subdivided into four specific techniques.

(a) *Estimating*. The B.S.I. defines estimating as:
"a means for assessing the time required to carry out work, based on knowledge and experience of similar types of work, without a detailed breakdown of the work into *elements* and their corresponding times at a defined level of performance."

(b) *Analytical estimating*. Some types of non-repetitive work, such as maintenance jobs, do not lend themselves to complete synthesis of all the elements involved by observation alone. This problem is overcome by analytical estimating which is a development of estimating. In analytical estimating the time required to perform elements is estimated from knowledge and experience of the elements concerned. The degree of accuracy depends largely upon the ability of the estimator.

(c) *VeFAC Programming*. VeFAC Programming (formerly known as Variable Factor Programming) is a technique developed by WOFAC Corporation of America for reducing and controlling payroll costs in such areas as clerical work, data processing, drafting, inspection, maintenance, packaging, sales, and design; the scope being virtually unlimited. Briefly the steps are: collection of the facts, preliminary reporting, developing Target Times (from WOFAC Prime Work Time Data), establishing work schedules, and periodic reporting.

VeFAC Programming is not a speed-up, but a way of encouraging workers to use their time more productively.

(d) *Variable Element Time Study (VETS)*. This procedure was introduced by Dr. Whitmore in his book, *Work Study and Related Management Services* (*see* Bibliography). It is a method of setting time standards for non-repetitive jobs and is based on calculating *average* times for complete jobs. Rating is employed using four multipliers corresponding to slow (0.5), average (0.8), fast (1.0), and very fast (1.2), rather than on the detailed rating scales used in time study.

A maintenance engineer, for example, may spend time on cleaning machines, repairing them, replacing assemblies, building special equipment, writing reports, visiting dispersed areas, and installing new machines. He may be observed cleaning machines, the average time to clean (per machine) being determined by timing with a watch. The rating multiplier is applied (say, 0.8 if he is working at an average rate). If the average time is eighteen minutes for cleaning each machine the time allowed would be:

$$18 \times 0.8 = 14.4 \text{ minutes for each machine.}$$

Although it may be argued that the time to clean individual machines will vary according to size, if the average time determined is a good average for all machines, the time lost while cleaning complex machines will be regained when dealing with simple ones. This system does not give precise measurement, but the times will be sufficiently accurate to provide reasonable control of indirect labour (*see* Elements and Methods of Costing, Chapter XXVIII).

5. Activity sampling

The work content of some jobs is so varied that normal techniques of work measurement cannot be effectively applied.

When a reasonable assessment is required for these jobs a form of statistical sampling is used which assesses the results of a few samples of work content or individual movements. The samples are selected at random intervals from an appropriate period. Each observation records the work occurring at that instant and is expressed as a percentage of all the observations which record that particular activity. This provides an indication of the percentage of time spent on that particular activity.

6. Rated activity sampling

This technique is an advanced form of activity sampling where each work element is rated to determine the work content, in addition to the percentage of time spent on the activity.

Ancillary Techniques

CYBERNETICS

The study of communication and control mechanisms in machines and living creatures is known as cybernetics. The subject harbours a field of research with an enormous potential for improving the effectiveness of industry.

The science of cybernetics is complex and extensive. Briefly, the cybernetic attitude adopted towards industry accepts it is actually living, or working as if it were living.

Considerable progress has been made since a group headed by Norbert Weiner, the American mathematician, called this science "cybernetics" in 1947. This group of scientists had been working together for about five years on the problems of control. They realised that common ground existed between control systems in a number of different sciences. Thus, a number of eminent statisticians, mathematicians, biologists, sociologists, logicians, psychiatrists, engineers, and other specialists, commenced research with a common aim.

The engineers were particularly interested in applying this new science to automation and computer sciences and considerable progress has been made in this direction. The basic notions of cybernetics are outside the scope of this work but additional reading on this subject—which will probably influence the future of industry—may be found in the book, *Cybernetics and Management*, by Stafford Beer.

OPERATIONAL RESEARCH

Although operational research is difficult to define accurately in the space allowed, it may be briefly termed the application of scientific analysis and careful reasoning to provide a quantitative basis for measuring possible courses of action, thus assisting management in decision-making. There is no limit to its breadth of application in industry and as a general aid to decision making.

The term operational research (O.R.) was coined at about the beginning of World War II, when various specialists were grouped to study wartime operations such as setting up radar systems and fuse setting for depth charges. Since then a number of large concerns have introduced O.R. teams to study such problems as the optimum loading of machines, efficient use of staff, economic methods of transportation, stores congestion, effective maintenance schemes, and optimum stock levels.

To-day, operational research is applied throughout industry and other fields in many countries. O.R. societies have been established and international conferences were held in 1956 and 1960.

The main techniques are: linear programming; queueing theory; critical path scheduling; replacement theory; and stock control theory. Many books describing these techniques are available, including one called *Some Techniques in Operational Research*, which was prepared by the O.R. group of the National Coal Board and edited by B. T. Houlden.

ERGONOMICS

The study of human capabilities and performance in relation to the demands of the job is known as ergonomics. The knowledge accumulated by biological scientists in their study of the operator and his working environment is now—after many years of neglect—being applied considerably more in industry.

For many years designers in industry have concentrated on machine design because it was the limiting factor, but in recent years the operator has been overtaken by the machine. He, in turn, has now become the limiting factor. The result is the study of the anatomical, physiological, and psychological aspects of the operator, who must now be viewed as an integral part of the machine, i.e. as part of one unit (man/machine).

Operators are subjected to new stresses and strains of a mental as well as a physical nature as they become machine minders. The various aspects of ergonomics dealt with below, which are becoming very important in reducing mental and physical fatigue, were shown in Figure 34.

Anthropometry

Anthropometry is the measurement of the physical dimensions of the human body. The findings of anthropometric study are essential for the correct design of seats, benches, machines, and other equipment used by people. The British Standards Institution Advisory Committee on Anthropometrics has recommended dimensions which are published in a booklet called *Anthropometric recommendations for dimensions of office machines, operators' chairs, and desks*, No. BS 3404.

Conventional seating is a typical example of incorrect practice which results in unnecessary fatigue and, therefore, must affect operator performance. The so-called conventional height for seats is 18 in. (457 mm) which—according to specialists—is too high for about 50 per cent of the working population. The mean lower leg length for the male is 17 in. (432 mm) and for the female 15 in. (381 mm), therefore, the maximum suitable height should be no more than 17 in.

Applied human physiology

The study of applied human physiology reveals that considerable improvements are possible in the general working environment. This science studies the function of the body in relation to applied forces and the tolerances it can stand in various surrounding environments.

Such factors as noise, heat, light, vibration, and heavy physical effort, are measured and the effects recorded.

Numerous booklets are available which give adequate information on maximum and minimum levels for each factor (*see* Bibliography). In addition, the use of kinetics in handling and lifting activities is essential to avoid strain and injury. The Royal Society for the Prevention of Accidents (RoSPA) conducts courses and issues leaflets and posters illustrating the essential points for smooth and easy handling of all kinds. The main aspects are: the correct methods for drum and cylinder handling, pushing and pulling, and stowing and stacking.

Applied psychology

A study of the operator's ability to receive information in various forms through the different senses, to process the information, and to take appropriate action, is termed "applied psychology".

The importance of this science and its application is illustrated by an experiment conducted during World War II on the ability of a radar operator to concentrate on the radar screen for long periods. Tests proved that concentration was lost after thirty minutes: clear signals were not seen after that time lapse because of monotony and mental fatigue. Similar dangers exist today where critical processes and procedures demand long periods of concentration.

The design of dials provides a further example. Visual displays of information can confuse and easily be misinterpreted unless careful attention is given to these problems. Control movements connected with visual displays can cause a serious error if they do not conform to expected standards, e.g. turning a wheel in a clockwise direction resulting in the movement of a pointer to the right, or pushing a lever forward resulting in a pointer moving forward or upward. (A clockwise turn is also anatomically more natural for a right-handed person.)

Some confusion occurs when movements are learned or made through experience; e.g. in Britain a downward movement switches *on* the light, whereas in the U.S.A. a downward movement switches *off* the light. An imported American machine can confuse and irritate a British worker unless the switch system is adjusted.

Applied biology

The scientific design of visual displays, the established optimum rate at which an operator can receive information, and the planning of suitable surrounding conditions, are partly based upon a knowledge of applied biology.

The study of human beings in terms of physical structure and capacity includes the following topics: an understanding of the bone structure; the physical effects when work is performed; the production of energy and the disposal of resultant waste; the receptors (nerves) which feed in information to a central control mechanism that processes and takes decisions, which are transmitted through the motor system (nerves and muscles) to appropriate points of action; the self-governing system that automatically controls the heart, glands, and other parts of the body which function without conscious effort.

VALUE ANALYSIS

This technique is a more sophisticated approach to the old problem of cutting costs. Although many concerns review their products and costs periodically, a much smaller number actually approach the project in a wholehearted or thorough manner.

Value analysis is a psychological, questioning attitude towards the product and each component part, as to its function and whether it could be performed in a cheaper way.

The success of this technique depends largely upon providing sufficient time to study each component, and the ability of the people involved to use their imagination and come up with new ideas or suggestions, regardless of how absurd they may seem at the time. The next step is to investigate and experiment with the suggestions. Invariably savings occur, either by changing the method of producing the component, redesigning it, or dispensing with it entirely by redesigning other components. The public should also benefit from a better-designed product.

QUESTIONS

1. What are the objects of work measurement?
2. Explain the term "standard time" in connection with work measurement.
3. Outline a typical procedure for applying work measurement.
4. Briefly describe the main techniques of work measurement.
5. Give an account of time study, including the rating and calculation of the basic time.
6. Explain some of the newer techniques in work study, including cybernetics.
7. How can a knowledge of ergonomics assist the supervisor?
8. Explain the term "value analysis".
9. Give a brief definition of operational research mentioning the main techniques included in this term.
10. Describe the various aspects of ergonomics.

CHAPTER XXIV

STATISTICAL METHOD

Introduction

STATISTICAL method may be defined as various ways of abstracting, classifying, and comparing information for control purposes. From this definition the stages in a statistical investigation would be as follows.

1. Define the reasons for the investigation.
2. Collect the information required.
3. Collate the data.
4. Analyse the data by using one or more of these methods:
    (a) graphical representation;
    (b) tabulation;
    (c) numerical methods.
5. Interpret the results.
6. Use the information.

This chapter deals with stage 4, the analysis of data by the methods listed.

The use of statistics in industry is essential for effective control. In such fields as stock control, production control, quality control, market research, sales, finance, and most other functions, a high degree of control is not possible without full use of statistical method.

Two sets of figures can only be accurately compared when they are measured in the same units (such as value in pounds sterling, weight in kilogrammes, percentages, etc.) and are expressed in similar terms (such as pounds sterling in pounds and pence, or fractions of a pound).

Before discussing the main ways of analysing data, a short introduction is given to the use of percentages, decimals, and the methods of stating accuracy.

Percentages

A reminder of the three ways of using percentages is given below.

(a) Calculation of a number expressed as a percentage of a total. For example, if 250 working hours were lost and 15 per cent of this total was due to absenteeism, the calculation would be expressed as:

$$\frac{250}{1} \times \frac{15}{100} = 37.5 \text{ hours lost.}$$

(b) Calculation of a number to be expressed as a percentage of another number. For example, if 250 working hours were lost and 75 hours lost were due to sickness, the percentage would be:

$$\frac{75}{250} \times \frac{100}{1} = 30 \text{ per cent.}$$

(c) Calculation of an increased, or decreased percentage of an original number. For example, if the working hours lost dropped from 250 in 1971, to 200 in 1972, the percentage decrease would be:

$$
\begin{array}{r}
250 \ (1971) \\
- \ 200 \ (1972) \\
\hline
50
\end{array}
\qquad
\frac{50}{250} \times \frac{100}{1} = 20 \text{ per cent decrease.}
$$

Care is needed in assessing the value of a percentage; until the original number is known the percentage may be misleading; for example, serious accidents may be said to have increased by 100 per cent in 1972 in a particular company; in fact the number of serious accidents in 1971 was one and in 1972 it rose to two.

Decimals
The change to decimal currency has achieved an increasing awareness and understanding of this system.

(a) To convert fractions to decimals the bottom figure is divided into the top figure which gives the decimal equivalent directly. For example:

$$
\frac{5}{8} = 8)\overline{5 \cdot 00} \ \begin{array}{l} 0 \cdot 625 \end{array} = 0 \cdot 625
$$

$$
\begin{array}{r}
0 \cdot 625 \\
8)\overline{5 \cdot 00} \\
\underline{48} \\
20 \\
\underline{16} \\
40 \\
\underline{40}
\end{array}
$$

(b) To convert decimals to fractions the figure 1 is placed under the decimal point, zeros are added under each figure, the decimal point is then ignored, and the figures are cancelled out into their lowest form. For example:

$$
\frac{0.625}{1000} \rightarrow \frac{625}{1000} = \frac{5}{8}
$$

METHODS OF STATING ACCURACY
Invariably errors will occur in passing and processing information. Misreading of figures and miscalculations may be reduced by super-

vision and checking, but complete elimination can be very expensive and often not worth the high degree of accuracy, dependent upon the purpose of the figures.

Biased and unbiased errors must also be considered. Rounding off figures causes these errors, which are *biased* if figures are raised or lowered to a particular number, or *unbiased* if they are rounded off to the nearest particular number. The errors may be expressed either as *absolute*, which is the difference between the actual figure and the estimated figure; or *relative*, which is calculated by placing the absolute error over the estimated figure as a fraction. An example is given below:

Actual	*Working Hours Lost* Biased (lower hundred)	Biased (upper hundred)	Unbiased (nearest hundred)
100	100	100	100
230	200	300	200
360	300	400	400
190	100	200	200
200	200	200	200
1080	900	1200	1100

Absolute Error =	-180	$+120$	$+20$
Relative Error =	$\dfrac{-180}{900}$	$\dfrac{+120}{1200}$	$\dfrac{+20}{1100}$
	$\simeq -20\%$	$\simeq +10\%$	$\simeq +2\%$

Absolute error. Allowance for absolute error may be expressed in the following ways. True value is:

(*i*) the estimated figure plus or minus the absolute error:
$$2980 \pm 10$$
(*ii*) somewhere between the estimated figure less absolute error and the estimated figure plus absolute error:
$$2970 \text{ to } 2990$$
(*iii*) it may also be written as 2980^{+10}_{-10}.

Relative error. Allowance for relative errors may be expressed as:

(*i*) estimated value correct to relative error:
$$2980 \text{ correct to } 0.3 \text{ per cent;}$$
(*ii*) 2980 correct to 3 per mille (or parts per thousand).

Where estimates are used, the supervisor should state the limits within which the true number should fall and he should remember that biased figures produce a greater error compared with unbiased figures.

Analysis of Information

There are three main classifications for data analysis.

Graphical representation.
Tabulation.
Numerical methods.

GRAPHICAL REPRESENTATION

When information should be presented in the simplest and most easily understood manner, the pictorial form of representation is most effective. The following charts come under this heading.

1. Bar charts

The three main types, which are illustrated in Figure 38, are:

(a) Simple. The height or length of each bar indicates the value represented.

(b) Multiple. Separate components of the total are shown as separate adjoining bars.

(c) Component. The bars are subdivided into the different components of the total, represented either as actual figures or as percentages.

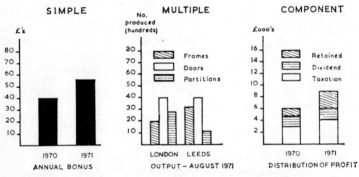

Fig. 38.—*Simple, Multiple and Component Bar Charts.*
The bar chart represents information in easily understood, pictorial form (*a*) Simple bar chart: the height of each bar indicates the value represented. (*b*) Multiple bar chart: separate components of the total are shown in separate bars. (*c*) Component bar chart: the bars are subdivided to show their different components.

2. Pie charts

This type of diagram creates a quick impression of the structure of the total information presenting the parts as sectors of a circle. Often the percentages or values are entered in each sector. The angle of the sector is calculated by multiplying the percentage by 3.6 (e.g. 20 per cent is represented by $20 \times 3.6 = 72$ degrees).

Accurate comparison of segments is difficult where there is little variation, but where obvious comparisons can be illustrated, such as in Figure 39, their use is ideal for immediate effect.

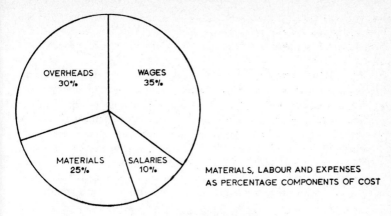

Fig. 39.—*A Pie Chart.*

This is a method of presenting the different parts of a total instantly. It is clearly more useful for making obvious comparisons than for providing detailed analysis.

3. Pictograms

These pictorial charts are very easy to understand provided the symbols, representing a particular quantity, are simple and the quantity clearly stated. Smaller quantities are represented by fractions of the symbol and larger quantities by a number of the symbols. If the symbols are arranged in line, the effect is similar to a bar chart. Figure 40 illustrates a typical arrangement.

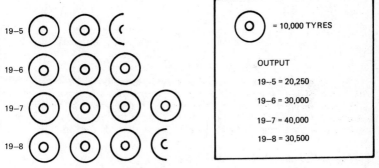

Fig. 40.—*A Pictogram.*

This method uses a symbol to represent a certain quantity and fractions of the symbol to represent smaller amounts. As with the pie chart, its accuracy is limited.

4. Graphs

The graph or line chart conveys the relationship between two variables by plotting a curve or straight line. A graph is constructed by drawing two lines at right angles which represent the variables, one being the dependent variable which is plotted on the Y or vertical axis, the other being the independent variable which is plotted on the X or horizontal axis. Figure 41 illustrates the layout of a graph. When data are classified chronologically, the time series is plotted as an independent variable on the X axis. For example, output per month would be portrayed by drawing the months on the X axis and the range scale of output on the Y axis (*see* Fig. 41). The scale should commence at zero for the dependent variable to avoid distortion. Attention to detail is important when preparing a graph otherwise it will not convey the correct impression. Details must be remembered such as inserting a title, the source of data, the key to co-ordinate lines if more than one is used, and naming the variables clearly with sufficient information.

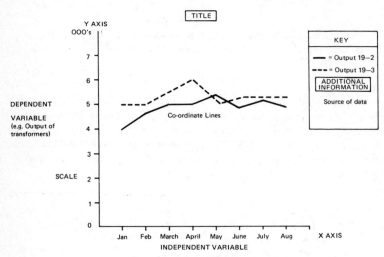

Fig. 41.—*Graph Layout*.

The graph, or line chart, conveys the relationship between two variables. The dependent variable is plotted on the *y* axis and the independent variable on the *x* axis. It is important to remember to provide full details, such as a title and a key, and to name the variables. The scale on the *y* axis normally begins at zero to prevent distortion.

5. Trend Charts

A fundamental problem of control is the fluctuation in demand for production caused by seasonal market conditions. The use of line graphs which give current output figures of set periods, such as weeks or months, can be misleading and difficult to interpret on a comparison basis of one year with another. Figure 42 illustrates this problem: at any time during 19–3 an estimate of the trend compared with 19–2 is likely to be inaccurate.

This problem may be overcome by thinking in terms of annual

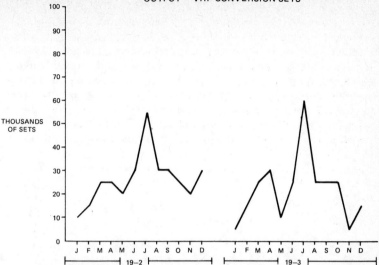

Fig. 42.—*Graph Illustrating the Difficulty of Comparing Output Visually.*

Graphs showing output figures for set periods are very difficult to interpret comparatively, especially when seasonal fluctuations are involved. It is impossible to estimate the over-all trend at any time in 19–3 compared with the previous year from these two graphs.

OUTPUT TREND – VHF CONVERSION SETS

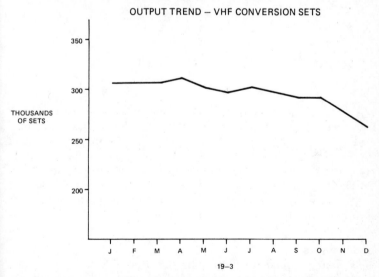

Fig. 43.—*Trend Chart Illustrating the moving Annual Total.*

The moving annual total of trend is calculated by deducting the monthly figure for the previous year from that year's total and adding the current monthly figure. The resultant figure is plotted and used for the next month in place of the annual total. This graph is drawn from the same figures as the graph in Fig. 42. All the data are given on p. 364.

figures for comparison and plotting the moving annual total (M.A.T.) or trend. The trend line dispenses with seasonal fluctuations and gives a clear indication of the true position compared with the previous year.

The M.A.T. or trend is calculated by deducting the monthly figure for the previous year from the annual total and adding the current monthly figure. The resultant figure is plotted and used for the next month to replace the annual total; a similar deduction and addition being made for the next month, and so on. This is illustrated below with the figures which are the basis of the graphs in Figures 42 and 43.

Total 19–2	=	315		Trend Jan. 19–3	=	310
Less Jan. 19–2	=	– 10		Less Feb. 19–2	=	– 15
		305				295
Plus Jan. 19–3	=	+ 5		Plus Feb. 19–3	+	15
Trend Jan. 19–3	=	310		Trend Feb. 19–3	=	310

Month	19–2	19–3	Cumulative Totals	Moving Annual Total
January	10	5		310
February	15	15	20	310
March	25	25	45	310
April	25	30	75	315
May	20	10	85	305
June	30	25	110	300
July	55	60	170	305
August	30	25	195	300
September	30	25	220	295
October	25	25	245	295
November	20	5	250	280
December	30	15	265	265
	315	265		

A comparison of the trend chart in Figure 43 with the graphs in Figure 42 illustrates how graphs showing monthly figures can be misleading when comparing the two years. The output trend chart in Figure 43 indicates a gradual fall from July, which accelerates from October to December. The purpose of this example is to show that the effect of relatively small changes in monthly figures is hidden in graphs showing current figures whereas in trend charts the effect is seen immediately.

6. Z charts

This chart is useful for illustrating the over-all picture of current figures (say, monthly), the moving annual total, and the cumulative total. The effect of plotting these three lines resembles the letter Z, as shown in Figure 44. The data are prepared in the same manner as for trend charts, the cumulative total being calculated by adding each monthly figure to the total of the previous months.

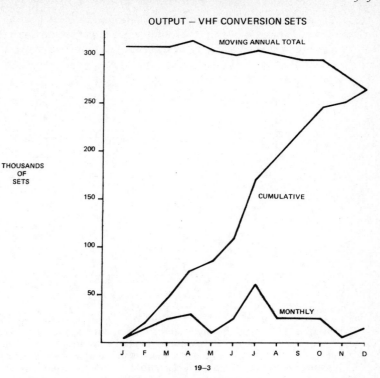

Fig. 44.—*The Z Chart*.

The form of chart produced when the figures (e.g. monthly), the moving annual total and the cumulative total are plotted on the same graph. The data are prepared as for trend charts (p. 363): the cumulative total is reached by adding each monthly figure to the total of the previous months.

7. Frequency distributions

Frequency distributions are a method of presenting a mass of data more simply and more meaningfully. Basically, frequency distributions give all the data and the number of times each piece of data occurs. The data are usually further grouped into classes, so that the frequency pattern is more clearly seen. (The total number of frequencies must always agree with the total number of occurrences.)

The variables (i.e. the factors being measured, represented by the data) may be either discrete or continuous. *Discrete* variables are measured in whole numbers only (e.g. 11 operators, 17 machines), whereas *continuous* variables are measured in quantity or extent (e.g. operator's height, 1.7 m, a load of cement, 7.23 tonnes), and can be expressed in fractions of a number. This is important when deciding the class limits. Working groups can be classed according to numbers,

1–4, 5–9 operators, etc., but if, for example, lengths of steel rod were classed in this way, no provision would be made for lengths which were more than 1.25 m, say, and less than 1.5 m. Figure 45 shows a discrete frequency chart.

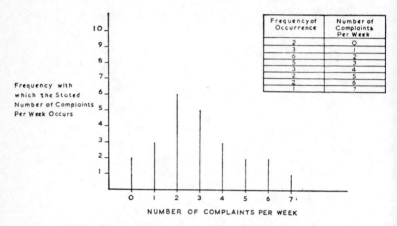

Frequency of Occurrence	Number of Complaints Per Week
2	0
3	1
6	2
5	3
3	4
2	5
2	6
1	7

Fig. 45.—*Discrete Frequency Chart.*

This frequency distribution gives all the data and the number of times each piece of data occurs. It is only suitable for variables which are *discrete* (i.e. measured in whole numbers only) whereas *continuous* variables are measured in quantity or extent and are plotted in class intervals as in Figure 46 below.

8. Histograms

A diagram illustrating the frequency distribution of a continuous variable is known as a histogram (*see* Figure 46). Class intervals are plotted along the X axis, and distribution is shown in the form of rectangles, measured against the frequency scale on the Y axis. The area of the rectangle representing each class is also proportional to the frequency in that particular class. The histogram should not be confused with bar charts, which show magnitude.

9. Frequency polygons

Frequency distributions can also be plotted as frequency *polygons*. These are drawn by coupling the centre points of the tops of each rectangle in a histogram and extending the line to the X axis at each end of the histogram, as shown in Figure 46. The line can only be plotted when the class intervals are equal. Where the class intervals are very small this will produce a frequency *curve*. The area enclosed by the frequency curve or polygon should be equal to that of the histogram.

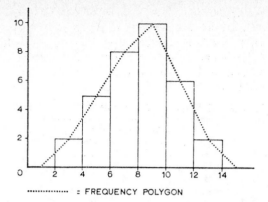

······· = FREQUENCY POLYGON

Fig. 46.—*Histogram Illustrating a Frequency Polygon.*
A histogram is a graph of a frequency distribution. It is *not* a bar chart; the *area* of each rectangle should be proportional to the number of observations in its class. A frequency *polygon* is constructed by plotting a curve through the halfway points at the top of each rectangle, i.e. of each class interval. The curve should extend to the axis, half a class interval beyond the end classes.

TABULATION

Classifying and tabulating information is essential before a reasonable impression of data is possible. Information is presented in the form of a table which should contain all the essential details such as a title, appropriate headings for each column, footnotes where further explanation is needed, and clear rulings between sections. The data should be arranged in logical sequences and missing information marked not available (N/A). Tables may be used to collate and present information, and to provide details for graphical presentation and numerical calculation. The information normally includes the subject, how it is divided into groups, the characteristic of each group, and the values of each characteristic.

The type of table depends upon the complexity and nature of the data. The main types are as follows.

1. Simple tables

When the subject is divided into groups by using one characteristic only, this forms the basis of a simple table as shown in Table X. The subject of this table is machine maintenance costs, divided into groups according to the type of machine.

2. Complex tables

When the subject is split into two or more characteristics which are arranged to show the relationship between them, a complex table is formed. The example of a simple table may be extended to form a hierarchical complex table by introducing a further characteristic such as the range of models for each type of machine, which is illustrated in Table XI. A further example is given in Table XII, illustrating a breakdown of machine costs for a number of workshops based upon one type of machine. This type of table is known as a cross-classification complex table.

Table X—*A Simple Table for Machine Maintenance*

Maintenance costs (year ending 31st December 19–1)	
Type of machine	£
Lathes	1050
Drills	500
Saws	750
Presses	2500
Total	£4800

Table XI—*A Complex Table—Hierarchical*

Maintenance costs (year ending 31st December 19–1)		
Type of machine	Model	£
Lathes	A	250
	B	350
	C	450
Drills	A	50
	B	75
	C	25
	D	350
Saws	A	600
	B	150
Presses	A	600
	B	1000
	C	300
	D	600
Total		£4800

3. Frequency tables

A frequency table classifies characteristics into mutually exclusive groups. For example, if a table is prepared showing the number of new employees engaged for Workshop A each year, this would represent a frequency table, but if the table only indicates the number of employees working in Workshop A for each year, this would not be a frequency table. An illustration of such a frequency table is given in Table XIII.

Table XII—*A Complex Table—Cross-Classification*

Maintenance costs (*year ending 31st December 19–1*)

Workshop number	Lathes						Total £
	A	£	B	£	C	£	
1	12	250	18	350	25	450	1050
2	12	170	12	200	18	280	650
3	3	25	6	70	6	50	145
Totals	27	£445	36	£620	49	£780	£1845

Table XIII—*A Frequency Table*

WORKSHOP A

Year	Number engaged
19–8	10
19–9	17
19–0	21
19–1	26
Total	74

NUMERICAL METHODS

1. Averages

Although tabulation classifies information into logical groups and characteristics, the problem of analysis remains because of the difficulties involved in being able to perceive the true significance of a number of figures. By using various statistical formulae, the information is condensed into a more easily assimilated form which clearly shows the critical relationships. These formulae are known as averages or measures of central tendency. They provide the measurement of location for the central group in a distribution around which other groups are gathered. The arithmetic mean, the median and the mode are the main types of location or average, and these are discussed below.

(*a*) *The arithmetic mean.* The arithmetic mean may be defined as the sum of a number of values, divided by their number. This average or mean is important when comparing the same characteristic in two groups of a similar nature. For example, if the mean weekly output of group A assembly operators is 200 parts, whereas group B which consists of a similar number of operators is 180 parts, the significance is obvious.

A quick way of finding the mean of long numbers is to guess at an average by visual appraisal, add up the variances between the assumed average and the actual numbers and divide by their number. This average variance plus or minus the assumed average is the true mean. A simple example is given in Table XIV.

Table XIV—*Quick Way of Averaging Large Numbers*

Values	Assumed Average	Variance
230	235	-5
241	235	$+6$
238	235	$+3$
231	235	-4
240	235	$+5$
		$+5$

$$\text{Average of variances} = \frac{+5}{5} = +1$$
$$\text{True Mean} = 235 + 1 = 236$$

(b) *Weighted mean.* The common or simple average assumes that each group is of the same importance. Often groups vary in loading, however, and to overcome this distortion factor an appropriate weight based on the distortion factor is calculated. The data for each group are multiplied by the appropriate weight, all the resultants are totalled, and then divided by the total number of weights. The example below (Table XV) illustrates the procedure. The simple mean idle time for

Table XV—*Weighted Arithmetic Mean*

		IDLE TIME—SEPTEMBER 19–1	
Group	Hours	Weight Factor (Number of operators in each group)	Resultant
A	10	1	10
B	12	4	48
C	14	4	56
D	16	2	32
E	18	8	144
F	20	2	40
	90	21	330

$$\text{Weighted Mean} = \frac{330}{21} = 15.7 \text{ hours}$$

the six groups is 15 hours (90 ÷ 6), but the groups differ in size. Therefore the number of operators in each group is taken as the weight.

The weighted average is larger than the simple average because of
the larger proportion of operators in the 18 hours group.

There are other methods of calculating the arithmetic mean by
using approximate weight, the moving average, and a more involved
method for grouped frequency distributions.

The mean uses all the data and is easy to understand, but it can
give a distorted value when extreme values influence the average
excessively.

(c) *The median.* The median is the value of the middle item of an
array of data (i.e. data arranged in order of magnitude from lowest
to highest). This mean point is easily found by using the formula,
$\frac{n+1}{2}$, n standing for the number of items in the array.

Thus in the series: 15, 16, 17, 18, 19, 20, 21, 22, 23, 24, and 25, the median
is 20. By inspection there are five numbers below and five above 20; or by
formula: $\frac{11+1}{2} = 6$ therefore, the 6th number, 20, is the median.

The median is useful in those circumstances where difficulty is experienced in measuring particular qualities, or where the control point
is required in order to correlate and compare sets of data. For example
if time lost through absenteeism is arranged in order of magnitude
and amounts to 20 hours for the median employee (26th) in Workshop
A, which has 50 employees, but in Workshop B 20 hours absenteeism
does not occur until the 42nd employee, the situation in Workshop
A obviously requires investigation.

(d) *Median of a discrete distribution.* When a frequency distribution
is non-continuous or discrete, the location of the median is calculated
again by applying the formula $\frac{n+1}{2}$. In Table XVI the number of
operators (n) is 117, therefore, the calculation is $\frac{117+1}{2} = 59$. The 59th
operator comes in the 3-year group, as inspection of the cumulative
frequency column shows. The median, therefore, is 3 years.

(e) *Median of a grouped distribution.* The formula for calculating
the median of a grouped distribution is $\frac{n}{2}$. Thus in Table XVII the
total number of operators is 130 and the median is therefore $\frac{130}{2} = 65$.
Inspection of the cumulative frequency column reveals 65 as lying
between 37 and 69, in the group 30–35 years. To find the value of
the median, i.e. the median age, further deductions are necessary. The
value of the 37th operator is 30 years, therefore, the median must be
65 less 37, which equals 28, making it 28 items more than 30 years.
In the group containing the median there are 32 items equally

Table XVI—*Median of a Discrete Distribution*

LENGTH OF SERVICE—OPERATORS

Number of Years	Number of Operators	Cumulative Total
1	30	30
2	28	58 ← 59
3 (Median)	20	78
4	17	95
5	9	104
6	5	109
7	5	114
8	3	117
	117	

distributed between 30–35 years, which increase continually until the age of 35 years is reached; therefore, the last one is 5 years older than the first. In these circumstances the median can be found by placing the increase in items (28), over the number of items in the group (32), and multiplying by the age range of 5 years. $\frac{28}{32} \times 5$ years = 4.4 years. The median is, therefore, 30 years + 4.4 years = 34.4 years.

Table XVII—*Median of a Grouped Distribution*

AGE GROUPS OF OPERATORS

Ages	Number of Operators	Cumulative Total
15 and under 20	6	6
20 ,, ,, 25	5	11
25 ,, ,, 30	26	37 ← 65
30 ,, ,, 35	32	69
35 ,, ,, 40	16	85
40 ,, ,, 45	28	113
45 ,, ,, 50	4	117
50 ,, ,, 55	4	121
55 ,, ,, 60	7	128
60 ,, ,, 65	2	130
	130	

The median is unaffected by extreme values, is easy to understand, and it can be calculated without all the data, provided the middle values are given and even weighting appears on either side. A comparatively large number of items is necessary for accuracy, which may be time-consuming to assemble.

(*f*) *The mode.* The value of the variable which occurs most frequently is known as the mode. In other words it is the position of largest density in a group and is useful in industry, for example, to indicate to manufacturers which size of a component or material is in greatest demand. An illustration would be as follows:

S.W.G. Sheet Steel = 10, 12, 14, 16, 18, 20, 22.
Frequency   = 3, 4, 9, 12, 16, 8, 3.

The mode is 18 S.W.G. because it has the greatest frequency in the distribution.

In general usage the mode is often described as the average, such as "the average teenage girl uses make-up", which means the majority or that a larger number of girls use make-up than those who do not.

The mode of a discrete variable may be located by inspection as indicated in the example above. For a continuous variable the following formula is used:

$$xl + \frac{(f_1 - f_0)h}{2f_1 - f_0 - f_2}$$

Notation
xl = Lower limit of modal class.
xu = Upper limit of modal class.
f_1 = Frequency in modal class.
f_0 = Frequency in next lower class.
f_2 = Frequency in next higher class.
h = Class interval (difference between xl and xu).

The histogram in Figure 47 clarifies the notation and shows how the mode may be located graphically. The calculation with values from the histogram would be:

$$150 + \frac{(50 - 30)50}{2(50) - 30 - 40} = 150 + \frac{1000}{30}$$
$$= 150 + 33.3 = 183.3 \, \text{kWh}$$
$$\text{Mode} = 183.3 \, \text{kWh}$$

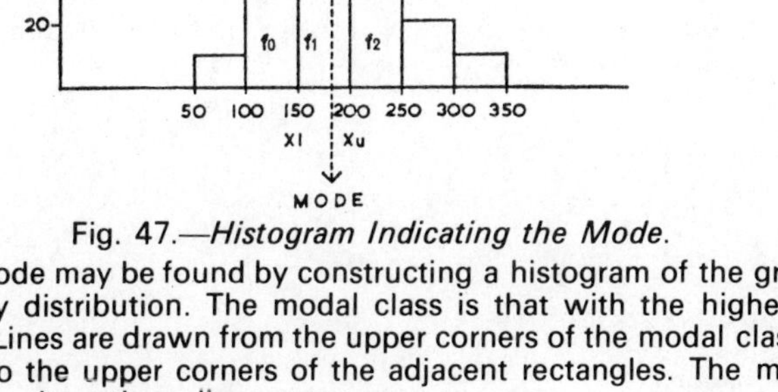

Fig. 47.—*Histogram Indicating the Mode.*

The mode may be found by constructing a histogram of the grouped frequency distribution. The modal class is that with the highest frequency. Lines are drawn from the upper corners of the modal class diagonally to the upper corners of the adjacent rectangles. The mode is the point where these lines cross.

The mode is unaffected by extreme values and is easy to understand. Only the middle items are needed for calculation, but arranging the information can be a lengthy process.

2. Dispersion

Although averages are useful as measures of central tendency when groups of numbers are concentrated around a central point, they lose their value when the groups are widely dispersed. The importance of assessing the form of the whole distribution is apparent in these circumstances, otherwise a distorted position will be given. The measures which show the extent to which the groups spread around the central point are known as dispersion, and these may be divided into the following.

(a) The range.
(b) The mean deviation.
(c) The quartile deviation.
(d) The standard deviation.

(a) *The range.* This measure is the difference between the largest value and the smallest value in a distribution. A simple example would be:

$$7, 19, 25, 31, 39, 52.$$
$$\text{Range} = 52 - 7 = 45.$$

Naturally the range is considerably affected by outlying values and may be misleading for comparison purposes because it does not indicate the level at which the range occurs. For example the price range of products A, from £5 to £10 is £5; and for products B, from £50 to £55 is also £5; but the comparison between the two ranges of products is lost if the range is taken as a basis of comparison.

(b) *The mean deviation.* This measure of dispersion is the mean or average of all the absolute values (value ignoring the mathematical sign) of deviations from the mean. The sum of the deviations from the mean is obviously zero as illustrated in the example below therefore, the signs of the deviations are ignored.

The measure is useful for comparing the relative tendency of groups to gather around the central point, or to spread themselves throughout the range of the distribution.

EXAMPLE:

4, 7, 12, 14, 18.

The Mean $= \dfrac{55}{5} = 11$

Deviations from the mean $= -7, -4, +1, +3, +7.$
$$= 0$$
Total (ignoring signs) $\quad = 22$

Mean Deviation $\quad = \dfrac{22}{5} = 4.4$

(c) *The quartile deviation.* This measure is used to indicate the range of only a restricted group of values in the distribution by measuring the dispersion of the series that lie between the lower and upper quartiles, i.e. the items which, with the median (the central quartile), divide the array into quarters. The lower quartile (Q_1) is $(n+1) \div 4$ and the upper quartile (Q_3) is $3(n+1) \div 4$.

The formula for the quartile deviation is:

$$(Q_3 - Q_1) \div 2$$

Another name for this measure is the semi-interquartile range. The degree of dispersion is restricted to within the limits of the two quartiles.

(d) *The standard deviation.* This measure of dispersion is more accurate than the other measures and is the best way of assessing the form of the whole distribution. The calculations are more involved and the method may be defined as the square root of the mean of the squares-of-deviations-from-the-arithmetic-mean. The formula and an example are given below:

$$\text{Standard deviation (S.D.)} = \sqrt{\frac{\Sigma f d^2}{n}}$$

Notation
f = Frequency in each value.
d = Deviation from the mean.
n = Total number of items.

Value	Frequency	Value × Frequency	d	fd²
10	1	10	−5	$1 \times 5^2 = 25$
12	3	36	−3	$3 \times 3^2 = 27$
15	5	75	0	$5 \times 0^2 = 0$
16	4	64	+1	$4 \times 1^2 = 4$
20	2	40	+5	$2 \times 5^2 = 50$
	15	225		106

$$\text{Weighted Mean} = \frac{225}{15} = 15$$

$$\text{S.D.} = \sqrt{\frac{106}{15}}$$

$$= \sqrt{7 \cdot 07}$$

$$= 2 \cdot 66$$

A rough check on the standard deviation may be carried out in most large normal distributions of the single peaked type by multiplying the S.D. four to six times, which should approximately equal the range. The S.D. decreases in value as dispersion decreases until nought is reached, which is equivalent to no dispersion.

3. Measures of skewness

The measures of dispersion already described indicate the variation or dispersion of frequencies throughout the range. A further measurement of variation illustrates the degree of symmetry of a distribution, when shown as a curve of frequency on a graph. Curves which are not symmetrical are called skewed or asymmetrical, and most frequency curves come under this category. This fact explains why the mean, median, and mode have different values. If the curve is symmetrical, these three averages are equal. Thus, skewness measures the divergence of the three measures of central tendency. The formula devised by Professor K. Pearson to calculate skewness is:

$$SK = \frac{mean - mode}{S.D.}$$

Other measures are known as the quartile measure of skewness and the third moment of skewness, both of which involve more complicated formulae.

QUESTIONS

1. How would you conduct a statistical investigation?
2. Discuss the problem of analysing data and name the main classifications that may be used for this purpose.
3. State the essential requirements in the preparation of a graph and give six examples of its use as a means of control.
4. What is meant by the term "trend chart"? Explain its advantages compared with a line graph.
5. Draw up a Z chart and indicate its uses.
6. Briefly describe a histogram and a frequency polygon, illustrating your answer with suitable diagrams.
7. Outline the main forms of tables used in tabulating information.
8. Name and briefly explain the four main types of location or average.
9. How would you make use of the median and the mode?
10. Give a brief description of the four measures of dispersion.

CHAPTER XXV

PRODUCTION CONTROL

Types of Production

THE broad types of production fit conveniently into three groups on the basis of quantity manufactured. The volume of production is a most important factor for a number of reasons which are discussed below under each type of production.

In general, the longer the run of production, the wider the spread of fixed costs (those that do not tend to fluctuate in sympathy with production) thus making greater economies possible. Longer runs are desirable, but unfortunately not always possible because of market restrictions and other reasons.

The question of preparation costs also plays a dominant part. If a variety of products is manufactured—all consisting of short runs—the extra costs attributed to design, drawings, specifications, tooling, and scheduling, tend to raise the price of the product. In short runs, the costs of these preparations cannot be spread effectively and the cost per unit is naturally higher.

Such factors as the length of runs and the variety of goods must be carefully considered when deciding upon production policy. Closely coupled with these factors are the three types of production which can be used:

Job production.   Batch production.   Flow production.

JOB PRODUCTION

All products of the "one-off" type, such as a bridge, an office block, an ocean liner, a special purpose machine, or a very large transformer, come under this heading, often known as "jobbing". A large proportion of small concerns and some very large companies are engaged upon this type of production, mainly by contract, but not always. For instance, a large tanker may be constructed before a buyer is found.

The usual procedure is for prospective buyers to advertise or to approach companies for a tender or quotation, being an estimate of the cost, quality, and delivery date of the job. Drawing up the estimate can be costly for large products. The design and pre-planning may take considerable time and effort to compile, and must be reasonably accurate considering the large sums of money often involved and the profit margins. The element of competition is always present. Invariably at least three tenders are required by the prospective buyer to assess the value of each one and to make a choice.

When the contract is received it is usual to place an engineer in charge who schedules the work. Special requirements for this type of work depend upon whether the product can be manufactured in the factory, on the site, or a combination of the two. Site engineers must be of high calibre and the supervisory staff under them play an important part in controlling the job. The operators must be highly skilled with a wide range of experience in many cases; often specialised operators are needed for short periods. Machinery must be versatile, therefore general-purpose machines are used in conjunction with equipment of a similar nature.

Materials can be a problem unless they are ordered to a set schedule, which allows for delays in delivery and the time required for usage. A missing piece of material or component can cause an expensive hold up for days. Storing materials must be considered. For example, a large storage site near to the work would be necessary to house the many assemblies for constructing a suspension bridge. Site workshops would also be required on many projects.

Products which can be manufactured in the factory include a variety of equipment and assemblies for industry. Examples are special-purpose machines, castings, and tools. These general engineering items are essential from the industrial point of view.

BATCH PRODUCTION

When a range of products is manufactured in quantities that do not justify the continuous flow line method, batch production is adopted. General-purpose machines can be used and scheduled to ensure that the maximum possible machine utilisation is achieved. This principle of machine utilisation, meaning that each machine may be performing operations on a number of different components, illustrates the main distinguishing feature between batch and flow production. The diagram in Figure 48 shows the difference between the two types. It should be noted that in batch production the machines are grouped in types to suit the particular function, which involves specialist supervision, tooling, and inspection; whereas in flow production the machines are laid out in strict operation sequence, each machine performing a particular job at maximum efficiency while the flow line is in operation. A combination of the two types may be seen in many large concerns. The majority of products which are manufactured in quantity come under this heading: for example, ready-made suits, paint brushes, watches, books, lamp-shades, mirrors, furniture, and plain bearings.

The batch production of components feeding a flow line within the same factory is often seen. For example, in motor car manufacture the flow line will be fed with batch-produced engines, wheels complete with tyres, and back axle assemblies. This combination of types is known as *batch/flow production*.

To produce an economic batch size, the amount is often increased

BATCH PRODUCTION

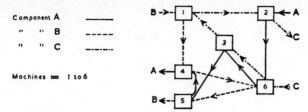

Component A ———
" " B - - - - -
" " C —··—··—

Machines = 1 to 6

FLOW PRODUCTION

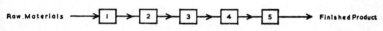

Raw Materials ———▸ 1 ▸ 2 ▸ 3 ▸ 4 ▸ 5 ———▸ Finished Product

Machines = 1 to 5

COMBINATION OF BATCH AND FLOW PRODUCTION

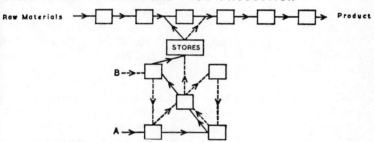

Raw Materials ———▸ □ ▸ □ ▸ □ ▸ □ ▸ □ ▸ □ ▸ Product

STORES

B—▸
A—▸

Fig. 48.—*Machine Layout, Batch and Flow Production.*

In flow production the machines are laid out in strict operational *sequence* whereas in batch production, the machines are grouped according to *function*. Each machine may perform its particular operation on a number of different components.

above the actual orders received, the balance being placed in stock; hence the alternative name, "stock order" production. Design of the product is intended to satisfy a specific market, but it is not unusual for concerns to modify the product to suit particular requirements. Work-in-progress tends to become excessive because of the essential need to provide queues of work to maintain high machine utilisation. This often leads to setting up work-in-progress stores which must be controlled in conjunction with scheduling, otherwise over-stocking may tie up an excessive amount of working capital. Working capital is explained in Chapter XXVII on Financial Aspects. The importance of production control is easily overlooked in batch production. Effective scheduling, which can be very complex in many ways, really decides the efficiency of production.

FLOW PRODUCTION

In flow production each batch of work is manufactured in strict operation sequence. Reference to Figure 48 illustrates the principle in which machines are aligned (not necessarily in straight lines) in order of operation.

Speed of manufacture is governed by the slowest operation as each batch or assembly must adhere to the flow-line sequence; consequently no scheduling is required for each operation, but batch sequences must be scheduled. Compared with batch production the amount of work-in-progress is negligible. Little or no queueing between operations is necessary.

Examples of flow production goods which generally incorporate batch production assemblies are motor vehicles, washing machines, and refrigerators. Other items such as petrol, gas, and many chemicals, are produced by process production which follows a purer form of flow production.

Some of the advantages of flow production are that, when careful planning is completed, the problem of production control is not so complex, breakdowns and faulty workmanship are immediately apparent, and corrective action can be concentrated on the fault. Full utilisation of special-purpose machines produces large savings. Floor space is used more economically mainly through the reduction of work-in-progress.

Effective planning in minute detail before production commences is essential. The market must be carefully analysed and sounded periodically to ensure adequate sales of the large output levels.

Heavy losses occur when the plant is shut down through labour troubles or lack of materials. Similarly, when a new line is introduced, change-over time is costly and must be reduced to a minimum.

Production Planning

A detailed programme of all the operations necessary to complete the product is essential before production and effective control can commence.

The first stage of planning involves gathering information on the product in the form of drawings, specifications from the designers, and drawing office records. When a clear picture is drawn up of all the processes involved, further investigation of work content and reference to past production records provide information for deciding whether to purchase components or assemblies from outside, or to produce them internally.

The next stage involves more detailed problems of setting up stock lists and parts lists, determining the availability of jigs and tools, preparing supplies of drawings and specifications, together with many other general jobs, to ensure that a complete planned programme is presented to production control.

It is now possible, with the aid of information on existing machines and equipment available for production, to produce *process layout instruction sheets*. An example of one is shown in Figure 49. A *detailed process operation study* given in Figure 50 illustrates how the time allowed is calculated by setting out all the elements in an operation.

A master plan may be drawn up for a new product to show the dates when each production stage must be ready and each phase completed so that the delivery date agrees with the estimate. The type of chart which is most suitable for this control function was developed by Henry L. Gantt and is known as the *Gantt chart*. Each part of the plan is subjected to an estimated time which is plotted. The actual time taken is also plotted underneath the estimated or standard time, thus clearly indicating the true position in relation to time and subject.

PROCESS LAYOUT INSTRUCTION							
PART NAME : PART No. : DATE : MATERIAL/UNIT : TIME / 100 PARTS : WEIGHT / 100 PARTS :				No. OF SHEETS : SHEET No. : DRAWN BY : CHECKED BY : STANDARD ORDER QUANTITY :			
DEPT.	OPERATION	OP. No.	TIME ALLOWED	SET UP TIME	MACHINE	TOOLS	SPECIAL EQUIP'T

Fig. 49.—*Process Layout Instruction Sheet*.
This is used to record in sequence each operation needed to produce a part.

DETAILED PROCESS OPERATION SHEET					
PART NAME : PART No. : TIME ALLOWED :			OPERATION : MATERIAL/UNIT : DATE :		
No.	ELEMENT	TIME ALLOWED	No.	ELEMENT	TIME ALLOWED

Fig. 50.—*Detailed Process Operation Sheet*.

The Gantt chart is versatile as it can be adapted to any control system where a number of functions are allied to the time factor. Figure 51 illustrates a simple Target Date chart using the Gantt chart principle. There are certain disadvantages, however, particularly in showing interrelationships between activities. More advanced systems involve the use of critical path or network analysis (*see* Bibliography).

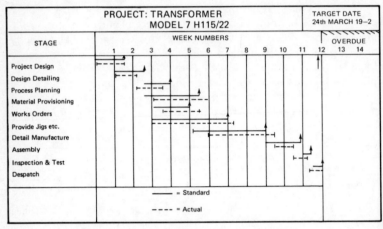

Fig. 51.—*Gantt Chart, Production Project.*

This is a simple target date chart using the Gantt chart principle. As a master schedule it controls the production of a new transformer from initial design through to delivery. Actual production progress is measured against estimated "standard" times for achieving delivery by the target date.

Production Control

The purpose of production control is to ensure that the correct quantity of a product is manufactured at the right time, at the required quality, by the most economic method.

Production control may be defined as the direction of all production activities, according to the planned programme, and fully utilising available facilities in the most economic way.

There are six main aspects of production control, discussed more fully below (*see* p. 385).

1. Scheduling—when the work is to be done.
2. Machine and labour utilisation—loading the capacities of departments.
3. Manufacturing order control—authority to proceed.
4. Stock control—material provided on time.
5. Despatching—assignment of work.
6. Progressing—recording and chasing of work.

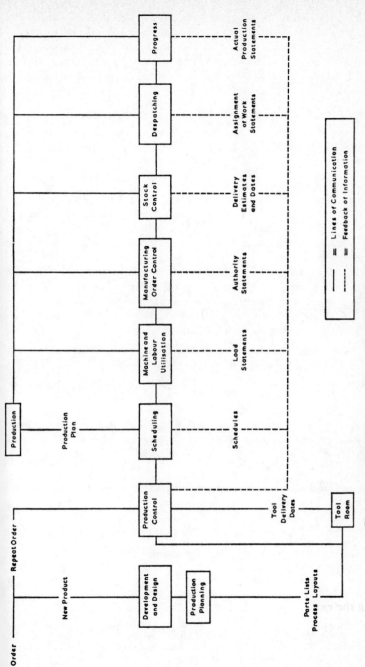

Fig. 52.—Simplified Diagram of Production Planning and Control.

Planning and controlling production depend upon many factors peculiar to the particular industry and the products being manufactured. Basic principles apply and can be discussed and borne in mind when building up a practical system within the particular concern.

A simplified chart showing the main aspects of production planning and control is shown in Figure 52.

THE BROADER CONCEPT OF PRODUCTION CONTROL

There are a number of activities undertaken outside the production control department, which nevertheless form an essential part of this function. These activities are as follows.

1. Sales forecasting and sales orders.
2. Specifications and drawings from the drawing office.
3. Financial accounting as regards the purchase of capital equipment, which in turn affects the economic batch size of production; and the purchase of materials in certain quantities, dependent upon availability of funds and storage space.
4. Capabilities of the tool room to produce requirements such as jigs, fixtures, special tools, and other equipment.
5. Storage of finished goods and partly finished goods.
6. Materials control: this is sometimes treated as a separate activity outside production control.

The few activities mentioned above should indicate sufficiently the breadth of production control in practice. The problems faced by the production controller often originate from services over which he has no control; therefore, he must rely upon the flexibility of the control system to overcome difficulties.

A composite outline of production planning and control is shown below, giving the main activities likely to be encountered and indicating the executive responsible for each activity:

Responsibility	Activity
Chief Designer	Design of product
Production Manager	Prototype built.
Chief Designer	
Chief Designer	Tested and approved.
Chief Inspector	
Sales Manager	Selling price fixed.
Chief Accountant	
Cost Accountant	
Sales Manager	Sales enquiries.
Chief Accountant	Capital expenditure.
Chief Planner	Planning for production: (Tool requirements,
Chief Draughtsman	parts lists, production drawings, process
Production Manager	layout, process operations, batch size, general
Work Study Engineer	services)
Purchasing Officer	

Responsibility	*Activity*
Sales Manager	Sales orders.
Production Manager	Authority to produce.
Production Controller	Production Control: (Scheduling, machine and labour utilisation, manufacturing order control, stock control, despatching, progress).
Chief Inspector	Testing and inspection.
Sales Manager	Packaging.
Stores Manager	Despatch.
Transport Manager	

ASPECTS OF PRODUCTION CONTROL

The six aspects of production control listed on p. 382 are now discussed.

1. Scheduling

This activity covers the following areas. *Firstly*, the work of listing all the items required for production. These items include raw materials, components, and sub-assemblies, which may be purchased or produced internally. *Secondly*, placing them in a convenient sequence for production, considering such problems as time taken to produce, time taken to deliver from supplier, time required on the production line, the production cycle, and allowance for scrap and waste. *Thirdly*, routeing the materials and assemblies from section to section, so that the plan of production illustrates to everyone concerned the whole sequence of operations from commencement to completion of the programme.

Scheduling presents a workable programme of production in workshop language. The sequence of manufacturing and the quantities will depend upon sales orders, economic batch size, manufacturing time and delivery dates.

On this basis the information required for effective scheduling includes the following.

(a) Sales orders.
(b) Promised delivery dates.
(c) Planning layout.
(d) Parts lists.
(e) Machine load statements.
(f) Labour utilisation estimates.
(g) Supply details for tools, equipment, materials, items from subcontractors, components from suppliers, and jigs and fixtures.
(h) Scrap and waste statements.
(i) Information from progress section as work proceeds. Schedules are revised as feedback from progress is compared with estimates.
(j) Information on finished goods storage facilities and despatch.

The main types of schedule are the master schedule, the production schedule, and the workshop schedule.

The *master schedule* generally provides a weekly or monthly indication of requirements over a period of say a quarter, half year, or year. The schedule indicates plant capacity; as orders are received they are entered and the resultant capacity calculated for the period. When capacity is filled, orders are either carried forward to the next period, or arrangements made to increase capacity for that period. This scheme shows immediately the current position to be noted, the basis for increasing output to accommodate delivery dates, and the over-all loading of plant in the factory.

An outline of the main requirements of a master schedule is given in Figure 53. Production schedules (Figure 62) and workshop schedules (Figure 63) are discussed later in this chapter.

Master Schedule													
Component: Helical Spring **Component No:** 6 : 8940						**Maximum Run:** 7000 **Minimum Run:** 2000							
Production	*Quarter (in week No's.)*												
	1	*2*	*3*	*4*	*5*	*6*	*7*	*8*	*9*	*10*	*11*	*12*	*13*
Scheduled Below Schedule Above Schedule Total													

Fig. 53.—*Master Schedule.*

2. Machine and labour utilisation

The purpose of this aspect of control is to organise the loading of machines and labour so that idle time is reduced to a minimum and co-ordination is achieved. The activities within this function include: maintenance of accurate records of plant capacity; preparation of statements which compare the current loading with the maximum capacity available; compilation of machine and labour records, indicating the actual and possible utilisation.

Information for preparation of these records may be obtained from plant records, planning sheets, operation layouts, work study department records, and previous records of machine and labour utilisation. The uses of this information are to provide management with efficiency ratios and production shops with schedules, and to feed back information to scheduling for revision purposes. Examples of a labour utilisation chart, a labour utilisation summary sheet, and a machine loading chart are shown in Figures 54, 55, and 56.

LABOUR UTILISATION						
DEPARTMENT: ASSEMBLY D					WEEK COMMENCING 20th Sept 19—2	
NAME	CLOCK No.	MONDAY	TUESDAY	WEDNESDAY	THURSDAY	FRIDAY
WHITE. R.	232	72 ⊢ A	76	82 ⊢ 84		
		72 \76\\\\\\\\	\\\\\\82\	84\\\\\\\\\	90\\\\\\	
CASTLE. S.	233	M ⊢	83	85		
		83\\\\\\\\\	\\\\\85\	\\\\\\86\	\\\\\\\\\\	\\88\\\\\\
OLIVER. R.	234	73 ⊢ B	74	75		
		73\\\\\\\\	74\\\\\\\	75\\\\\\\\\	77\\\\\\\	
ROBIN. S.	235	101 ⊢ I		102		
		101\\\\\\\		102\\\\\\\	103\\\\\\	
DARE. T.	236	110 ⊢ T	111			
		110\\\\111\	\\\\\\\\\\\	\\115\\\\	\\\\\\\116	\\\\\\\\\\\
ASTER. W.	237	103 ⊢ L	104			
		103\\\\\\\\	\\\\104\\\	\\\\\\\\\\\	105\\\\\\\	
ETC.						

76\\\	= Capacity Allocated	I	= Idle Time
⊢——⊣	= Work Done	A	= Absent
⊢ 76	= Job Not Completed	B	= Machine Breakdown
⊢76⊣	= Job Completed	L	= Labour Problem
76	= Job Number	M	= Materials Delay
		T	= Tool Problems

Fig. 54.—*Gantt Labour Utilisation Chart.*
The chart shows the current job-labour ratio at any given time.

Many different types of production control board, using discs, pegs or rotary devices to display information, are also available. Set-up time for these control boards is much quicker, and the current situation is more easily seen than from a chart which needs to be read.

NOTE: Some ratios of efficiency are:

$$\text{Labour Utilisation} = \frac{\text{Net machine running time}}{\text{No. of operators} \times \text{average hrs. worked per wk.}} \times 100$$

$$\text{Machine Effectiveness} = \frac{\text{Net machine running time}}{\text{Net machine running time} + \text{stoppages}} \times 100$$

$$\text{Machine Utilisation} = \frac{\text{Net machine running time} + \text{set-up time}}{\text{Total working hours of machine section}} \times 100$$

LABOUR UTILISATION

Department.................   Week Ending...............

Name	Clock No.	Hours							
		Work Completed	Idle Time	B	L	M	A	T	Total Time Lost

Fig. 55.—*Labour Utilisation Summary Sheet*.
This chart shows a breakdown of total time lost on a particular job.

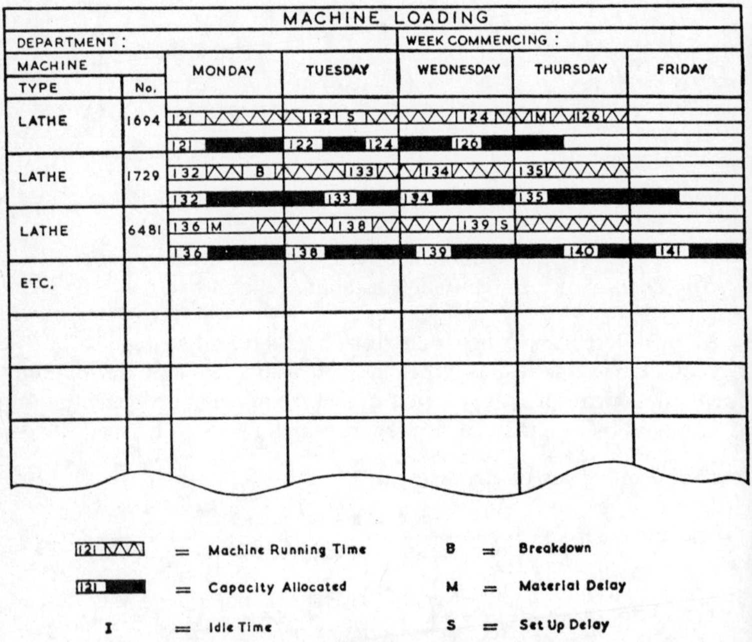

Fig. 56.—*Gantt Machine Loading Chart*.
This chart shows allocated work, running time and lost time for each
machine.

3. Manufacturing order control

The provision of documents which give authority to the production shops to produce (according to the schedule and the plan) is known as manufacturing order control. This clerical function controls all activities requiring the issue of paperwork, such as the movement of materials from stores to the first operation point and from operation to operation, until the product is completed. Similar controls are applied to the preparation of tooling, jigs and fixtures, and their movement from process to process; commencement of work on each operation; and recording progress of the job through the production shops.

The system varies widely, dependent upon the size of the organisation and the type of product. The information normally required to operate the procedure is obtained from process layout sheets, schedules, and details of scrap and shortages. Documents are prepared to cover all the activities connected with manufacturing the product. A typical list of these documents and schedules—in sequence of use—is given below:

Production Factor	Paperwork	Operation
(a) Operator	Labour Loading Schedule	Operator allocated
(b) Machine	Machine Loading Schedule	Machine allocated
(c) Materials and drawings	Material Requisition	Issued
(d) Tools	Tools Requisition	Issued
(e) Authority to produce	Works Order	Carry out operation
(f) Identity	Identity Label	Affix to assembly
(g) Inspection	Inspection Order	Inspection—passed/rejected
(h) (i) Move to next operation	Authority to move	Transport
(ii) Move to scrap	Reject order	Transport
(i) Control	All copies of documents	Complete and despatch to control
(j) Costing	All copies of documents	Complete and despatch to Costing Dept.
(k) Wages and bonus	Works Order copy	Complete and despatch to Wages Section.

The main types of manufacturing order are: firstly, single cards which have all the information on the front and act as identity labels; secondly, multi-copy orders which reduce writing to a minimum; thirdly, single copy tear-off orders which have perforations dividing each section. Figure 57 shows an example of the single card type.

If the product is manufactured in one department a job card is generally raised with works orders attached for each operation. When more than one department is involved, a route card travels with the assembly from department to department.

Manufacturing Order

Order No.	Batch No.	Quantity	Part Name	Part No.

Materials	Quantity	Date Required

Tools	Quantity	Date Required

Operator	Clock No.	Machine	No.	Part No.	Quantity		Standard Time	Actual Time
					Passed	Rejected		

Signature Inspection: ....

Signature Foreman:..................

Date......................................

Fig. 57.—*Manufacturing Order.*

This single-card type of manufacturing order provides a record of the progress of a production job from the initial order to produce to the final inspection.

4. Stock control

The two main aspects of stock control are materials control and stock control proper. *Materials* control covers the purchasing and cost of materials, and the organisation of material flow within the company. *Stock* control is the means of controlling the quantity and quality of materials and components, in accordance with the production plan.

The purposes of stock control are to ensure, by using clerical procedures, that:

(*a*) material required for production or other uses is available on time, in the right quantity and quality;
(*b*) information is provided for financial control;
(*c*) stock is safeguarded;
(*d*) accurate stock records are maintained.

The clerical nature of stock control allows the function to be carried out in a section other than the Stores where the physical movement of stock actually occurs. The various records include job analysis sheets, purchase requisitions, manufacturing orders, goods received notes, and material requisitions. A record card for each type of material may contain details such as description of material, part number, location in stores, reordering level, maximum and minimum quantity levels, quantities on order, receipts, issues, balance, any quantity appropriated, and the price.

Usually stock levels are reviewed regularly to dispense with obsolescent and obsolete materials; physical stock checking is essential to prove the accuracy of the stock records.

There are two main ways of stock checking.

(*a*) By *annual stocktaking*, which involves suspending the movement of all materials during the count.

(*b*) By *perpetual inventory*, along with continuous stocktaking, which avoids the suspension of all material movement. This method operates through a reliable individual who is fully employed checking physical stocks against stock records throughout the year. He maintains a register of all the counts and variances. This record is acceptable by the auditors who must certify its accuracy for entry in the Balance Sheet, under the Companies Act.

5. Despatching

This activity may be defined as the act of authorising the operator to carry out work allocated to him, in accordance with the standard method, by using the allocated tools, drawings and scheduled information. The Despatching Section is responsible for:

(*a*) Assigning the work to the workplace, or machine.
(*b*) Preparing, assembling, and issuing the materials, tools, fixtures, and gauges for production.

(c) Releasing works orders and production sheets.

(d) Co-ordinating the movement of work in progress, by using a recording procedure.

Despatching may be decentralised or centralised. A description of each system is given now, together with its advantages and disadvantages.

Decentralised despatching. The orders are issued in a batch to the despatcher, or to the supervisor, in each department. His responsibility is to decide upon the most suitable sequence for issuing the orders and to ensure that materials, tools, and the manufacturing orders arrive on time to each operator or machine. The advantages of this scheme are that the supervisor has more control of production activities within his section; there should be more flexibility of operation, and paperwork is reduced considerably. The capabilities of the supervisor or despatcher decide the success of this arrangement, and probably maximum machine utilisation is more difficult to achieve.

Centralised despatching. Orders are despatched directly to operators or machines from a centralised office where records and charts are kept of capacities, any backlog, and loadings of operators and machines. Greater control of production is claimed for this method, which gives more over-all flexibility when operating near the optimum level of production.

Unfortunately, it is said that the foreman or supervisor merely runs the machines to produce in the sequence outlined; therefore, he is not responsible for all the production aspects of his section. Further disadvantages are that there is more red tape, a duplication of effort, and that quick action is difficult, although the supervisor can object to an order if he feels justified.

6. Progressing

The Progress Section provides the means for co-ordinating the production programme by revealing and, if possible, eliminating or correcting, any deviations from the schedule.

Regulating the progress of materials and parts through the various production processes is known as *expediting*. Other names given to this task are progress chasing, stock chasing, and follow-up. This difficult task is carried out by the following procedure.

(a) Taking responsibility for all production orders, after they have been issued.

(b) Co-ordinating the production activities to produce work in progress at the correct time, at the right place, in the right quantity, and quality.

(c) Investigating and reporting variances from the schedules.

(d) Providing alternative routes for production processes when breakdowns or bottlenecks occur.

(e) Recording and analysing progress records of production, for comparison between planned and actual output at each stage.

There are two methods of expediting.

Unit expediting. This method gives the expeditor responsibility for progressing a unit or contract from the commencement to the final stage of production. Slow moving and complex products and long runs are suitable for this method, as all the problems connected with the unit are centralised through one person who is fully aware of the whole situation. Unfortunately, this often results in a number of expeditors who are all dealing with one foreman in each department, which adds to the problem of over-all control.

Departmental expediting. When the expeditor is responsible for all work passing through a department, the method is called departmental expediting. This scheme is suitable for fast moving products, but it can cause control problems. The supervisor must be prepared to pass to the expeditor the responsibility for production progressing, otherwise a conflict will result.

SOME TYPICAL CAUSES OF PRODUCTION DELAYS

Innumerable factors can cause considerable delays in production, although many of these delays could be avoided with a little more care and forethought.

(a) *Personnel problems:* absenteeism; labour turnover; disputes; poor selection; lack of training.

(b) *Machines:* breakdowns; poor maintenance; bottlenecks (through lack of duplication of vital pieces of equipment); inefficient operation; loading errors or oversights; unsuitable machines.

(c) *Materials:* overdue deliveries; inefficient ordering; poor quality materials; poor stores handling and transportation.

(d) *Design:* poor design creating production difficulties; unsuitable materials recommended; accuracy required is too high for equipment available; tolerances and allowances too tight, without good reason.

(e) *Equipment:* lack of correct tools, jigs and fixtures; delay in delivering equipment.

(f) *Planning:* excessive set-up times due to uneconomical batch sizes; poor estimates of work content.

(g) *Inspection:* inadequate, causing excessive scrap at later stages.

The Supervisor and Production Control

The supervisor must avoid looking upon production control as another attempt to reduce his status and responsibility. Production control assists the supervisor by relieving him of the numerous routine activities necessary to control production. These may be successfully carried out by individuals who can devote all their energies to ensuring that the various factors of production, such as loading, materials and tools movement, authority to proceed, inspection, costing and wages control, drawings, and chasing, are dealt with effectively. The supervisor may now devote more time to his true role of supervising the department.

In the small concern this concept of relieving the supervisor of routine is not possible. As the concern grows, however, the opportunity is open to relieve him gradually of these tasks and allow him to develop into a specialist who concentrates on directing, ensuring that individuals become fully productive. His influence should be increased rather than lessened as he becomes the link between his subordinates and management. In addition, he has the important task of co-ordinating the many separate activities which will develop as the company grows. These activities include production planning and control, costing, inspection, materials control, and preparation of wages and bonuses. Successful co-ordination depends upon the supervisor's knowledge of the systems. He will not be able to appreciate fully the other person's point of view unless he clearly understands what the person is doing, his responsibility, and the environment under which he operates. This concept elevates the supervisor's job to one of higher responsibility and importance.

Production Control in the Small Concern

Organised production control is often non-existent in the small company. The works foreman controls by keeping most of the relevant activities in his head and making arbitrary decisions as the problems arise. This lack of method is usually demonstrated by impracticable estimates (e.g. of delivery dates) and general inefficiency. If the works foreman is sick, chaos quickly develops.

A guide is given now illustrating a simple production control system which can be elaborated or rearranged to suit the particular workshop. This scheme is divided into the following aspects.

1. Information from the office.
2. Information from the workshop.
3. The estimate.
4. The production schedule.
5. The workshop schedule.
6. Additional records.

1. Information from the office
The supervisor or works foreman should receive the following information.

(*i*) Orders received.
(*ii*) Promised delivery dates.
(*iii*) Any special information on orders.

   (*iv*) Revised delivery dates.

    (*v*) Urgent orders—delivery required as soon as possible.

   (*vi*) Materials and equipment received.

  (*vii*) Promised delivery dates for materials and equipment.

2. Information from the workshop

The supervisor should keep a check on these matters and also report them promptly to the controlling office.

    (*i*) Progress of work through each stage of manufacture.

   (*ii*) Any breakdown of plant.

  (*iii*) Shortages of materials, components, and assemblies.

  (*iv*) Any other reasons for stoppages.

The transmission of this information may be conducted in many ways. Written forms of feedback to various control points (e.g. the cost office, wages section, progress section, and the supervisor), are often essential, but in the very small concern they may be dispensed with entirely. The three main records in use are the *operator's work ticket*, the *job card*, and the *detachable ticket*. A brief description of each one is given below.

(*a*) *Operator's work ticket.* Generally this ticket is a simple document used by the operator to record his output. When completed, the form is passed to various sections for calculating wages or for costing purposes. An example is given in Figure 58.

WORK TICKET			
Operator's Name.................. Week Commencing.........			
Clock No.			
Section			
Operation	*Quantity Produced*	*Total*	*Checked*
Operator's Signature			
Supervisor's Signature.................... Date			

Fig. 58.—*Operator's Work Ticket.*

This record of the operator's output is used for calculating wages or costs.

(b) *The job card*. This document states the work to be performed by the operator. Generally the cards are completed and collected on a daily basis, and the information is used for making entries in the Workshop Schedule. Figure 59 illustrates the type of card which can be used for this purpose. The card may be designed to include details of bonus schemes, and any other information required.

			Time			Passed	Rejected
Date	Operator's Name	Clock No.	Commenced	Finished	Total		

JOB CARD

Job No. .... Date Job Required ....

Operation .... Operation No. ....

Section ....

Fig. 59.—*Job Card*.

This states the work to be performed by the operator. A card like this one can be completed daily and used to make up the workshop schedule.

JOB NO.

	Hrs.	Mins.
Operation 1 =	:	
2 =	:	
3 =	:	
4 =	:	
5 =	:	
6 =	:	
Total Time =	:	

Passed / Rejected

Inspector ....

Storekeeper ....

Date ....

Operation 5	Operation 3	Operation 1
Op. Clock No.	Op. Clock No.	Op. Clock No. ......
Job No.	Job No.	Job No. ....
Time	Time	Time ....
Date	Date	Date ....
Operation 6	**Operation 4**	**Operation 2**
Op. Clock No.	Op. Clock No.	Op. Clock No. ......
Job No.	Job No.	Job No. ....
Time	Time	Time ....
Date	Date	Date ....

Fig. 60.—*Job Ticket*.
The perforated sections are torn off as each operation is completed.

(c) *The detachable ticket.* A ticket may be designed with a number of perforated sections containing information on each operation. As each operation is completed in sequence, a section is torn off and signed by the operator, who places it in a box which is emptied daily. Generally, the ticket is tied to the assembly and each section bears the job number, the operation, and any other relevant information. Figure 60 gives an example.

3. The estimate

The estimate must be based upon the production schedule and the capacity of the workshop, to provide an adequate delivery date. The

---

ESTIMATE

Internal Use Only

Customer   Est. No..............

Name..   Date ....

Address.......................................

        ....

Job ....

        ....

        ....

Price........................

Date Estimate Despatched ....

Closing Date for Acceptance ....

Accepted/Rejected........................... Date ....

Job No. ....

Drawings ....

Tools ....

Manufacturing Order No..

                    Signature........................

Fig. 61.—*An Estimate.*
This is the type of form used for internal circulation.

question of costing is covered in Chapters XXVIII and XXIX. Although the estimate is closely related to the order, which is dealt with in the office, the foreman may have to prepare the estimate himself. The type of form which would be circulated internally is shown in Figure 61.

4. The production schedule

This schedule records the progress of each manufacturing order which is raised when the estimate is accepted. The schedule should be located in a convenient place for easy access. The example of a production schedule in Figure 62 shows the information generally recorded.

5. The workshop schedule

This schedule indicates the jobs to be undertaken by the workshop and provides information for the supervisor, or progress chaser, to expedite the work. A refinement of this system would include a weekly summary, or an arrears schedule, to facilitate the preparation of the revised workshop schedule. A diagram of a typical workshop schedule is given in Figure 63. The information in this diagram is only intended to indicate the standard framework, which may be varied to suit particular requirements.

6. Additional records

In some establishments further records may be necessary, owing to such factors as the complexity of the operations and the size of the stores. For example, if a large number of operations and machining is necessary, the use of loading charts and additional progress sheets would be worth while. The size of the stores is another example. In some concerns the range of materials is small; therefore, visual inspection may be sufficient for reordering purposes, especially if the materials are commonplace and present no problem of delivery delays. The other extreme may warrant the use of stock records, material requisitions, and a strictly regulated reordering system. In conclusion, it must be stressed that good sense and a thorough grasp of the particular requirements of the work situation must over-ride stereotyped systems. They are intended to act as guides and provide basic principles upon which a sound production control system should be based.

The tendency is to create unnecessary paperwork and controls. Each proposed document, and each existing document, should be subjected to a stringent test for its usefulness before it is printed. Such answers as "It may be useful", "We should really keep a record", do not justify its existence. Paperwork is very expensive and a definite reason for raising a document is essential.

PRODUCTION SCHEDULE

Manufacturing Order No.	Date Received	Job Description	Job No.	Cost Code	Quarter (in Week Nos)												
					1	2	3	4	5	6	7	8	9	10	11	12	13

Fig. 62.—*Production Schedule.*

It records the progress of each manufacturing order raised when the estimate is accepted.

WORKSHOP SCHEDULE

Department.................

Week No..................

Manufacturing Order No.	Job Description	Job No.	Cost Code	Date Req'd	Date Completed	Operations											
						A		B		C		D		E		F	
						No.	Time	No.	Time	No.	Time	No.	Time	No.	Time	No.	Time

Fig. 63.—*Workshop Schedule.*

This standard framework can be varied to suit particular conditions. The schedule should indicate the jobs to be done by the workshop and provides information for expediting.

QUESTIONS

1. Explain the importance of production planning to the supervisor.
2. Describe the Gantt chart and draw up a simple example of one.
3. Give an account of the various stages of planning production.
4. What is the purpose of production control and how is it achieved?
5. Outline the main aspects of production control and illustrate the purpose of each aspect.
6. Describe the activity of scheduling.
7. Discuss machine and labour utilisation, illustrating some efficiency ratios which may be used to control these activities.
8. Outline the purpose of manufacturing order control in a production control system.
9. Discuss the two main aspects of stock control.
10. What are the purposes of stock control and how are they achieved?
11. Give a detailed account of the purposes of despatching and expediting in a system of production control.
12. Give an account of the typical causes of production delays. Illustrate, wherever possible, with examples from your own experience of this problem.
13. "The supervisor must adopt the right attitude towards the production control department." Explain this statement thoroughly.
14. Explain the three main types of production and give examples of products manufactured under each type.

CHAPTER XXVI

QUALITY CONTROL

Introduction

QUALITY control may be defined as the scientific control of all the chance and assignable variables which affect the processes of production and interfere with the excellence of the manufactured product. The essential aspects are: continued recording of quality levels, comparing with established standards and specifications, rejecting goods outside the set limits, and indicating that adjustment is necessary to production process variables as they become unacceptable. Each aspect is discussed shortly.

Control of quality in a manufacturing concern is essential for two main reasons.

(*a*) *Influence of competition.* The product must conform to certain standards of quality, which are impressed upon the consumers' minds by advertising and by direct contact with the product.

(*b*) *Technical necessity.* Often manufacturing processes are made less costly by using interchangeable parts which may be selected at random and, when assembled, conform to the standards laid down. This practice means that designers must open tolerances as far as possible without interfering with set standards of quality; and that inspection must be adjusted to allow permissible variations from the standard to pass, within set limits.

Main Activities of Quality Control

The main activities of quality control fall conveniently into three groups.

1. Establishing standards and specifications.
2. Inspection.
3. Statistical quality control.

ESTABLISHING STANDARDS AND SPECIFICATIONS

The establishment of standards and specifications makes it possible to ensure that the product conforms to the requirements. The standard is set by top management in conjunction with production engineering, which assesses the feasibility of the proposed standard. The sales department assesses the market requirements. The purchasing department provides information on standards of material available, and the production department then gives an indication of the feasibility of manufacturing at the proposed standard within a proposed cost.

Perfect standards in production are both costly and difficult to achieve. The basic standard, for a product to sell effectively, must conform to the consumers' minimum standards, at a selling price which is acceptable for that level of quality. Naturally there is an area of acceptability, which allows for slight variations that do not drastically change the performance of the product. These variations are caused by chance variables and assignable variables.

(a) *Chance variables.* These are inherent in the production processes; e.g. machine limitations, material imperfections, limitations of inspection equipment, and human error.

(b) *Assignable variables.* These are external influences, such as incorrect operation of machines, misuse of equipment, incorrect sequence of operations, worn and faulty machines, worn inspection equipment and variations in working conditions, including humidity, temperature, and vibration.

INSPECTION

The purpose of inspection is to separate defective goods from those conforming to the standard of accuracy laid down by management. This important aspect of quality control attempts to ensure that only goods of adequate quality pass to the consumer; and that faults are located in materials, components, work in progress, and finished goods. The Inspection Department often supervises the task of salvaging rejected work, or the disposal of scrap, to reduce the possibility of defects returning accidentally (or sometimes intentionally) to the production line. The Department is also responsible for the general control of all inspection devices.

Inspection also provides information for statistical quality control, but setting quality standards is outside its function. Quality standards must be measurable, reasonable, and understandable; therefore, they must be in writing. Rigid inspection is uneconomic, since it tends to increase scrap by rejecting anything that does not conform exactly to the drawing, whereas reasonable inspection is flexible and allows a degree of departure from the drawing, provided that adequate operation of the product is not impaired and quality standards are maintained. Quality control provides these limits within which inspection can operate effectively.

Inspection methods

There are two methods of inspection: 100 per cent inspection method and the sampling method.

(a) *100 per cent inspection.* This method entails the inspection of every single item in a batch or process, which is costly, difficult to carry out satisfactorily because of human error and, in general, is avoided whenever possible. This method is justified for large and complex products with critical stages of production, which would involve heavy losses if faults were not discovered in the early stages.

(*b*) *Sampling method*. The sampling technique involves selecting at random a given number of pieces for inspection. Statistical tables provide the appropriate sample size for the total number involved at a set level of quality. The number of rejects gives a fair indication of the quality level for the whole batch.

STATISTICAL QUALITY CONTROL

This approach to quality control uses statistical method to provide information for supervisors and operators to maintain control of the actual processes.

This method (using the theory of probability) establishes a set of control limits for each process by determining the range within which the chance variables are likely to occur. When these limits are exceeded, an immediate indication is given that some action must be taken to correct an assignable variable which has forced the process over the specified limits. The physical side of process control involves sampling at regular intervals and the plotting of results on the chart as quickly as possible to show the current trend. Figure 64 shows such a chart.

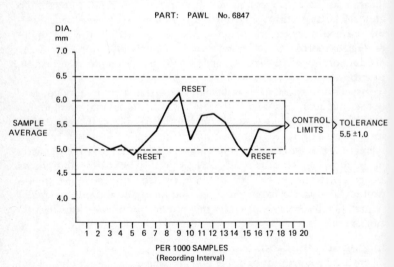

Fig. 64.—*Statistical Quality Control Chart.*

Control limits are set for each process. Results of sampling are plotted on a graph to show trends. Corrective action can then be taken at an early stage, whenever trends indicate that the control limits are in danger of being exceeded.

Control charts of this nature are provided for each process and a running record is maintained. When the plot falls outside the limits the incident is reported and an immediate investigation follows to find out why the deviation has occurred. Remedial action must be taken to steer the process back to within the limits specified. After some experience it becomes more obvious when the process is veering away towards the limits and corrective action may be taken earlier. Thus a greater percentage of the product is manufactured within the specified limits.

This emphasis on controlling the process which ensures increased quality in the early stages of production, also results in higher machine utilisation in later stages, less possibility of damage to machines, and a reduction in further processing of faulty work.

The concept of statistical quality control has been over-simplified here for the purpose of explanation. The method can be very successful when correctly applied in suitable circumstances. The need for consistently good quality is vital in a competitive market.

The Supervisor and Quality Control

Although the supervisor is assisted by the quality controller, inspector, and other specialists who perform functional duties within his department, he is still responsible for the quality of the work. His responsibility may be considered from three aspects—operators, materials, and machines—which are now discussed.

1. Operators

The supervisor should encourage operators to be quality-minded and conscientious. They ought to be proud of the product and the company and their enthusiasm must be aroused by dynamic leadership. Most employees are basically conscientious and take pride in their workmanship, therefore the supervisor should constantly counteract any undesirable pressures that tend to change this outlook.

Other important factors affect quality. If operators are not fully aware of the standards set for each process they can hardly be expected to aim for high quality. Similarly, if operators are not fully trained or familiarised with better methods of performing operations, quality will suffer. Careful selection also is important otherwise employees will be misplaced, and those who lack the necessary ability to work without set standards will naturally produce inferior parts. Finally, there is the problem of dealing with careless operators who, for various reasons, have difficulty in concentrating. Scrap is very costly, so it is essential to deal firmly with these careless employees.

2. Materials

If materials are reported to be faulty, or the wrong type, the supervisor should report the fact together with recommendations to his superior. The cost of production rises as more time is spent on unsuitable materials and every effort must be made to rectify this situation.

3. Machines

If a machine develops a fault, the supervisor must either order the machine to be stopped to avoid excessive scrap or report the defect immediately to his superior, according to circumstances. The servicing of the machine and the rearrangement of the production programme should follow as a natural sequence of control.

Summary

The achievement of high quality is dependent upon a number of factors, all equally important. One neglected factor may ruin the combined effect of all the rest. These factors in maintaining quality are: statistical quality control; fully trained operators; high morale; pride in workmanship; suitable materials and machines; carefully maintained machines; adequate equipment; good design; good supervision.

QUESTIONS

1. What is meant by the term, "quality control"?
2. Explain the purposes of quality control and its importance to the supervisor.
3. Describe the three main activities of quality control.
4. How can the supervisor develop a quality-conscious attitude in operators?
5. Discuss the various factors that help to achieve high quality.
6. Explain the difference between chance variables and assignable variables in quality control and give examples of each.
7. What is the purpose of inspection?
8. What is meant by 100 per cent inspection and the sampling method of inspection? When would you be able to justify the former method?
9. Discuss the nature and uses of statistical quality control.
10. The supervisor's responsibility for quality may be considered from three aspects—operators, materials, and machines. Discuss each aspect.

CHAPTER XXVII

THE FINANCIAL FUNCTION

Financial Management

FINANCIAL control of a concern is obviously a critical function; serious errors may lead to bankruptcy or liquidation of the business. Careful recording of all financial transactions is necessary as a measure of control, and to satisfy certain legal requirements.

Actual control is achieved by measuring expenditure and income, ensuring that a reasonable balance is kept in hand and sufficient cash flow is maintained. The business must be able to pay its debts, allow for replacement of its fixed assets such as machines, equipment, and vans, and build adequate reserves for expansion programmes.

Important decisions have to be taken on the capital structure of the business; the acquisition of funds; the determination of dividends; the degree of liquidity; short, medium and long-term investments; and in areas associated with mergers and take-overs.

In view of these aspects the financial function will vary in operation, dependent upon the circumstances and size of the company. In a small company it may be possible to calculate the profit or loss on each transaction. As a company grows the recording of all financial activities increases. Difficulties arise unless sound, basic principles are established and followed by all employees. Essential guide lines ensure realistic recording and valuation of activities and assets to arrive at a reasonably accurate profit or loss. Problems of controlling expenditure also increase with growth.

Often personnel do not appreciate the importance of adhering to financial procedures. As a result the quality of accounting data is reduced and management's decisions based upon such data are impaired. Financial accountancy is essentially a *tool* for use by managers, employees, and shareholders.

Problems of Financial Accounting

The purpose of both financial and cost accounting is to record all transactions and analyse them so that information is presented in the most suitable form for various purposes. The four main problem areas which usually arise are associated with debts, legal requirements, managerial requirements, and social obligations.

DEBTS

The launching of a product from the idea stage to the sale is generally a slow process. This time-lag often causes problems as expenditure may commence with the purchase of various assets such as buildings, plant, materials, and continue with the payment of wages and a variety of other expenses, as plans are developed.

A considerable period of time may elapse before any income is received but during this time funds must be found to pay all the debts.

The degree of indebtedness of a company is important and it is the responsibility of the accountant to provide accurate evidence on this item. In addition banks and other financial institutions will require such evidence, along with other information, to calculate the risk involved in granting a loan. Thus creditworthiness may be established considering the orders in hand, profits over the years, the value of fixed assets, and other liabilities outstanding.

LEGAL REQUIREMENTS

The accounting requirements of the Companies Acts 1948/1976, are intended to protect and safeguard the investor. Every company must keep proper books of account, as laid down in a comprehensive schedule of detailed requirements, covering all the important items in the Balance Sheet and Profit and Loss Account. A copy of these statements is sent annually to the Registrar of Joint Stock Companies; they may be seen by any individual on payment of a small fee.

The Acts also increased the rights and duties of auditors, to include a report on the Profit and Loss Account as well as the Balance Sheet and any group accounts. The report must conform to a stringent list of requirements in the schedule; furthermore, only those who possess the qualifications stated in the Acts may be appointed as auditors.

The accounts must give a true and fair view of the company's activities and state of affairs. They must also be acceptable to the Commissioners of Inland Revenue who require a copy for taxation calculations.

MANAGERIAL REQUIREMENTS

Unfortunately conventional accounting procedures for the preparation of final accounts and records do not provide information in its most suitable form for managers to become more effective. The exercise of managerial skills demands complex analysis of external economic affairs and internal business activities. The use of cost accountancy, budgetary control and other forms of management accountancy is essential for this purpose.

The management accountant needs considerable expertise to provide all relevant information to managers who may then use their skills with a thorough knowledge of possible consequences.

SOCIAL OBLIGATIONS

The modern approach is for a company to recognise that there are obligations to its employees, shareholders, the community and trade unions. Today these social obligations tend to be based upon the concept of adequate reward for all social groups rather than the maximisation of profits alone. Probably this change was caused by the reduced influence of shareholders, the increased power of trade unions, and the strengthening of the bond between the company and employees/consumers.

Another trend is the increased emphasis on long-term stability and growth in view of the risk undertaken by the shareholder and the overall effect on the community. Naturally a person who invests in a company expects an adequate return on the capital invested. How much dividend should be expected is another question. Certainly the investor does not expect management to take extreme risks unless he is a gambler who chooses to invest in a concern where the dangers of collapse are recognised.

To satisfy these obligations companies generally produce interim and final accounts which give considerable detail. The annual report is usually particularly informative; explanations on financial matters are included along with photographs of the products and factories. Most companies allow visitors to tour the premises and talks are often arranged on specific financial topics.

Employment of Capital

A company seldom stagnates, it is either expanding or contracting. Healthy expansion demands adequate supplies of cash and careful planning of expenditure. The amount of cash required is very difficult to assess considering the large range of expenditure involved. The financial requirements of a business may be divided into two main groups: *fixed* or permanent capital, and *circulating* or working capital.

FIXED CAPITAL

All fixed assets, such as land, factory and office buildings, plant and machinery, furniture and fittings, vans and cars, come under this heading. They contribute to profit by their use in the business, therefore a charge for depreciation is included as an expense in the annual accounts. Many fixed assets depreciate in value through use, age, and obsolescence. Eventually they must be replaced and, in the case of machines, it may be more economic to scrap and sell a model which has been superseded by a more efficient type. Some fixed assets, such as vans and tools, have a very limited life, and provision is needed for replacements. Inevitably the prices of new fixed assets tend to rise, so replacement plans must include this factor.

The prudent company also keeps reserves for unexpected occurrences such as legal costs, accidents, and damage. Some fixed assets actually appreciate in value, land being a typical example. Intangible assets such as goodwill, patents and trade marks may be of considerable value within a prosperous company. These also are regarded as fixed or permanent capital.

CIRCULATING CAPITAL

Current assets continually change their form and are not retained in the company for any long period of time, unlike fixed assets which remain for a number of years. The money used to acquire current assets is known as circulating capital. Such items as raw materials are purchased; salaries, wages, and expenses are paid; and the finished goods are sold. Although salaries and wages are paid in cash or by cheque, the other items may involve credit transactions. The length of the credit period also affects the amount of cash required at any time. Briefly, cash changes its form into goods through various processes and returns to its original form when products are sold, hence the name circulating capital.

All current assets are sometimes called working capital, but it is more realistic to deduct current liabilities from the current assets to arrive at a figure which represents the actual cash available as working capital.

The term, current liabilities, refers to all current debts owed by the concern which would include creditors, a bank overdraft, and short-term loans. These debts are current in the sense that they must be paid in the near future, that is within one year.

BALANCE OF CAPITAL

Establishing and maintaining a correct balance between fixed and working capital is an important factor in financial control. If too much cash is spent on fixed assets, the situation will develop where insufficient working capital is available to utilise fully the plant and machines which have been purchased. On the other hand, insufficient allocation of cash to fixed assets indicates either surplus cash lying idle in the bank, or inefficient use of working capital. Effective use of working capital is vital for growth.

Forecasting and Budgeting

Forecasting the financial activities of a company is based upon previous financial records of income and expenditure, and on predictions of the trends in sales, production costs, and general expenses. The difficulties of forecasting are aggravated when markets are unstable, or when there are no previous records to indicate trends, as in the case of a new business.

Forecasting the future is naturally guesswork and the correct attitude towards the forecast is to be ready for the unexpected. Precautions and a degree of flexibility in plans based on forecasts are essential.

The forecast or estimate is used to plan the financial budget, which is adjusted to make the best use of available cash. Such adjustments include decisions on cash requirements or cash investments if there is a surplus, and consideration of the choices of expenditure. Budgeting for cash flow in the form of income and expenditure is essential as an indication of events; but financial controls must check continually and promptly on the *actual* cash flow to make corrections and revisions of the budget as the situation changes.

Sources of Capital

The ways of raising capital depend upon the type of business and its reputation. The one-man business or sole proprietor is very restricted; when he wishes to start his business no reputation exists in most cases; therefore, he must depend upon his own resources and loans from friends and relatives.

A similar situation exists with partnerships. As the business develops and appears to be stable and thriving, the opportunity to increase its credit will be established. If the creditworthiness of the business is acceptable, suppliers will deliver more goods at longer credit terms. Banks will also allow overdrafts and loans on this basis. Other ways of raising money are to sell property already owned and lease it back or to raise a mortgage on property owned. Indirect methods are to buy assets on hire-purchase or hire on a rental scheme.

Continued expansion of the concern often demands large sums of cash, more easily raised by forming a private limited liability company.

Further expansion may mean inviting the public to invest, which involves conversion to a public limited company. Conversion is conducted by an issuing house or, if the company is very secure and of high reputation, it may make a direct issue to the public. The issuing house will handle all the requirements, including capital gearing (proportion of ordinary and preference shares and loans), advertising, and legal aspects.

SHARES AND DEBENTURES

Certain responsibilities rest with the concern when capital is raised, and these cannot be shrugged off as unimportant; investment must be paid for in various ways, such as interest and dividends.

There are two main types of shares offered by a public limited company to the general public. These are ordinary and preference shares. They should not be confused with debentures, which are loans. All three, however, form the permanent capital of a concern.

The ordinary share or "equity share" normally carries voting rights; therefore, the holders have a degree of control over the running of the business. There is more risk attached to this type of share because the amount of dividend depends upon the prosperity of the business. Before any dividend is payable, both preference shareholders and debenture holders must receive their fixed rate of dividend or interest respectively. A share of the surplus profit, if any, is then divided among the ordinary shareholders.

The preference shareholders are entitled to a fixed rate of dividend, as the name implies, in preference to ordinary shareholders. With cumulative preference shares, the amount of dividend due may accumulate annually if no dividend is declared in one year or in a number of years.

Debentures are loans and they do not form part of share capital. The holders are creditors of the concern; therefore, the fixed interest rate is payable regardless of profit or loss. Debentures are safer than shares and—in some cases—mortgage debentures are issued, which means that the loan is secured by a fixed charge on the concern's assets.

THE STOCK EXCHANGE

The raising of permanent capital through the issue of shares is safeguarded by the Council of the Stock Exchange. The Council is aware that any investor who is prepared to subscribe to a new issue may not wish to leave his money indefinitely in the company; therefore, he needs an assurance that the shares will be negotiable through the Stock Exchange. This does not mean that when the shareholder sells his shares the cash is withdrawn from the company and then replaced. Only the shares change hands and often the shares are bought and sold several times over a short period before the share certificate is issued by the company to the eventual new holder.

Permission to deal in a company's shares, or a quotation, must be obtained from the Council, which insists on very stringent requirements before agreeing. Unless the Council is satisfied with its investigations it will not grant a quotation or permission to deal in the particular shares and, in these circumstances, it is doubtful whether many prospective subscribers would be interested in buying them.

A further legal precaution is embodied in the Companies Acts 1948/1976, which states that if a company implies that an application has been made to the Council for a quotation, and the application is refused, all application cash must be returned to the investor and all allotments of shares are void.

The main function of the Stock Exchange is to provide a market for stocks and shares which can be bought and sold in a fair and straightforward manner.

According to estimates presented by the Royal Commission on the Distribution of Income and Wealth (1975), the outstanding feature of ownership of equity capital is the trend over the past ten years away from individual share ownership towards shareholding by institutions. In particular pension funds and life assurance funds have shown considerable growth.

Individual shareholdings fell from 59 per cent (1963) to 42 per cent (1975). In the same period the holdings of pension funds and insurance companies increased by about 10 percentage points to 28 per cent.

The Royal Commission distinguished three main groups of individuals who benefit, directly or indirectly, from dividends:

1. 2.1 million taxpayers who receive dividends directly on personal holdings of shares and stocks;
2. up to 11 million members of occupational pension schemes and 2.25 million taxpayers receiving occupational pensions;
3. 14 million taxpayers who save through life assurance.

Approximately one-half of dividends paid by quoted companies appear in group 1 above and more than one-third to groups 2 and 3 together.

The community also invests in other concerns which in turn directly invest in shares. For example in 1973 charities and non-profit-making bodies accounted for 4.4 per cent, investment trust companies 6.5 per cent, unit trusts 3.4 per cent, banks and other financial institutions 3.3 per cent, non-financial companies 4.3 per cent.

The prices of shares are controlled by supply and demand, *not* by the Stock Exchange. If there are more buyers than sellers for shares in a particular company, the price rises; if sellers predominate then the price falls.

Some idea of the importance of the market may be imagined when it is estimated that around four-fifths of industry and commerce in Britain is conducted by companies with capital owned by the public. The total value of securities officially quoted is about £50,000,000,000.

Although people are inclined to speak of the Stock Exchange located in London, there are twenty-two stock exchanges throughout the country which collectively form the Stock Exchange. They are strongly bound together by common regulations and connected with each other by private telephone lines, or teleprinters, so that information is immediately available at all centres.

Profit and Accounts

Although the object of a business may be to provide goods or services for the community, the achievements of a concern are based upon its ability to run the establishment at a profit.

Owing to sociological change, the amount of profit has become an important factor in managerial policy. The surplus must be sufficient to pay shareholders and to provide adequate sums for replacement of capital equipment and expansion programmes. Excessive profits, however, should be avoided because of the social obligations towards the community to provide quality products at a fair price. Management must also consider the question of high productivity and its part in the national economy (e.g. the need for competitive prices in the export market).

In general terms, it may be said that the consumer will only buy within a price range that is considered adequate for the quality of the goods; this fixes the upper limit of the price range. The supplier will attempt to market a product of his choice which provides sufficient return to pay for all expenses and provide a suitable amount of profit.

ACCOUNTING FOR PROFIT

At this point two terms should be considered: "trading profit" and "net profit". *Trading profit* is calculated by deducting all the costs directly connected with production from the total sales. *Net profit* is arrived at by deducting all the indirect expenses from the trading profit. In other words, net profit is the amount remaining after all expenses for a period have been deducted, as indicated in the accounts in Figure 65.

In financial accounts, trading profit and the direct expenses involved in production appear in the Manufacturing and Trading Account, while the net profit and indirect expenses appear in the Profit and Loss Account.

Finally, the net profit is appropriated, or divided, into three main groups: income tax, dividend, and general reserve. The general reserve, or undistributed profit, is the amount previously mentioned which is retained by the company for replacement of capital equipment or fixed assets, and for expansion programmes. The appropriation of profit to reserves is known as "ploughing back the profits". How the profit is divided depends upon such factors as the total amount of surplus, commitments towards shareholders, and the prudence of the concern in establishing adequate reserves for future plans.

An example of each account is given in Figure 65, outlining the main items of expense likely to be seen.

The profit and loss account produced for public companies may be a summary of the complete account. There is no need to disclose all the information so long as the provisions of the Companies Acts are met. Many companies, however, issue full accounts to satisfy their obligation to shareholders. A pro-forma example is given in Figure 66. To avoid excessive length a number of notes are usually given at the end of the report which give greater detail and explanations where considered necessary.

THE BALANCE SHEET

The Balance Sheet is a statement of all the assets and liabilities at a certain date, which is normally the last day of the financial year. The liabilities are located on the left-hand side and are divided into two

P.W.B. Company Limited

Manufacturing and Trading Account
for year ended 31st December 19–9

Items directly connected with production	£	Income	£
Wages & Salaries	10,500	Sales	40,000
Raw Materials	7,000		
Expenses	2,500		
Trading Profit	c/d 20,000		
	£40,000		£40,000

Profit and Loss Account

Items not directly connected with production	£		£
Rent	800	Trading Profit	b/d 20,000
Rates	300		
Depreciation	700		
Insurance	130		
Salaries	6,400		
Directors' Fees	500		
Stationery	520		
Interest on Loan	80		
Telephone	170		
Lighting & Heating	400		
Net Profit	c/d 10,000		
	£20,000		£20,000

Appropriation Account

	£		£
Income Tax	4,500	Net Profit	b/d 10,000
Dividend	2,500		
General Reserve	3,000		
	£10,000		£10,000

Fig. 65.—*Layout of the Annual Accounts.*
Trading and net profit are clearly shown in these accounts.

main groups called fixed and current liabilities. Fixed liabilities include capital, reserves, and any debentures or long-term loans. The capital is generally shown as the amount authorised and the amount issued; authorised capital being the amount that the company has power to issue, stamp duty being already paid on the sum quoted, whereas issued capital is the sum offered by the company and subscribed by shareholders.

The assets are shown on the right-hand side and are divided into

Profit and Loss Account for the Year Ended 31st December 19–8	19–8 £	19–7 £
1. *Turnover* Deduct: Trading and manufacturing expenses Wages and salaries Materials consumed Overhead costs		
2. Total expenditure	£	£
3. Gross profit (1–2)		
4. *Deduct:* Depreciation on cost		
5. *Trading profit* (3–4)	£	£
6. Income from investments		
7. *Profit before taxation* 5+6)		
8. Taxation		
9. *Profit after taxation* (7–8)		
10. Minority interests		
11. Extraordinary items		
12. *Net profit* (9–10–11)	£	£
Appropriation Account		

1. *Net profit*
Deduct:
   Dividends
   Transfer to fixed assets replacements fund
   Transfer to debenture redemption reserve
   Transfer to preference share redemption fund		

2. *Total appropriations*	£	£
3. Profit and Loss Balance (1–2) Add: P. & L. Balance from previous year		
Balance of profit carried forward	£	£

Fig. 66.—*Pro-forma Profit and Loss Account.*

two main groups called fixed and current assets. The fixed assets are listed first, followed by current assets. Intangible assets such as goodwill and patents may be shown separately. The traditional form of Balance Sheet is shown in Figure 67, but several variations are common.

NOTE: For example, the capital employed may be shown on the left-hand side (which amounts to all the fixed liabilities) and on the right-hand side, the fixed assets are followed by current assets *less* current liabilities, which gives the work-

P.W.B. Company Limited

Balance Sheet as at 31st December 19–9

Fixed Liabilities	£	Fixed Assets	£
Capital	45,000	Land & Building	18,000
General Reserve	5,000	Plant & Machinery	12,000
Loans	5,000	Vans	4,000
		Furniture & Fittings	3,000
Current Liabilities		Current Assets	
Creditors	11,700	Stock	11,500
		Debtors	14,500
		Cash in hand	3,700
	66,700		66,700

Fig. 67.—*Layout of a Balance Sheet*.

This is the traditional form of balance sheet showing liabilities on the left-hand side and assets on the right.

ing capital. Thus, the capital employed on one side, equals the employment of capital on the other side, consisting of fixed capital (or fixed assets plus working capital).

Many companies now issue a vertical balance sheet, an example of which is given in Figure 68. In practice a number of notes would be appended explaining each main item in more detail. In this example ordinary shares and cumulative preference shares have been included to show a typical layout.

INTERPRETATION OF ACCOUNTS AND STATEMENTS

From management's viewpoint, the ability to interpret the accounts and statements greatly assists control and co-ordination, and provides trends for forecasting and planning. Unfortunately, incorrect impressions are easily created by studying the figures. To aid management "accounting ratios" are available which provide a guide. The British Institute of Management and the British Productivity Council established the Centre for Inter-firm Comparisons in 1959. This Centre is an independent body that acts as a data collection point, compares the results of a number of firms who contribute, and indicates achievements and weaknesses.

The investor is interested in the true financial position of a concern and its prospects. These are often very difficult to assess. For example, the current value of fixed assets may not be indicated, and the progress of research and development schemes is naturally not revealed. Predicting the future of a company is as hazardous as picking the winner of the Derby, with just as many variables involved which affect the result. Reasonable guesses can be made on the possible progress of

Balance Sheet at 31st December 19–8

CAPITAL EMPLOYED (*sources of funds*)

			19–8	19–7
1. *Ordinary share capital*	*Authorised*		£	£
	19–8	19–7		
	£	£		
Ordinary shares of 50p each				
'A' Ordinary shares of 50p each				

2. *Capital Reserves*
   Share Premium Account
   Debenture Redemption Reserve
   Capital Redemption Reserve Fund
   Fixed Assets Replacement Reserve
   Preference Share Redemption Fund
3. *Revenue Reserves*
   Profit and Loss Account Balance
   General Reserve
4. *Deferred Taxation*

	19–8	19–7
TOTAL EQUITY CAPITAL	£	£
Asset value of ordinary share		

5. *Preference Share Capital*	*Authorised*			
	£	£		
	19–8	19–7		
7½% Cumulative Preference shares				
8¼% Cumulative Preference shares				

6. *Preference Capital*
   Interest of Minority Shareholders
7. *Minority Interest*
8. *Loans*

	19–8	19–7
TOTAL CAPITAL EMPLOYED (1 to 8 added)	£	£

EMPLOYMENT OF CAPITAL (Employment of funds)

			NET	
			19–8	19–7
Fixed Assets	*Cost*	*Aggregate depreciation*	£	£
Freehold Property				
Leasehold Property				
Plant, Machinery, Furniture				
1. Total Fixed Assets			£	£
Investments				
Trade investments				
Associated companies				
Interests in subsidiaries				
2. Total Investments			£	£
Current Assets				
Stocks				
Debtors				
Bank balances and cash				
Marketable short-term securities				
3. Total Current Assets			£	£
Deduct: Current Liabilities and Provisions				
Bank overdrafts				
Creditors and provisions				
Taxation				
Fixed dividends				
4. Total Current Liabilities			£	£
5. Net Current Assets (3−4)			£	£
TOTAL CAPITAL EMPLOYED (1+2+5)			£	£

Fig. 68.—*Pro-forma Vertical Balance Sheet.*

a concern by studying the reputation of the managing director, the trend of the particular market, and the efficiency of the organisation, though hidden factors can still influence appearances. If the market trend is sufficiently favourable and there is a strong demand for its product, a concern may prosper in spite of inefficiency and mis-management. It is easy to be misled in such ways, even with inside knowledge of a business.

The over-all trend in a group of companies can be very misleading when a variety of products is manufactured; an individual may be employed in a division where prosperity is high, but another division may fare so badly that it is sufficient to reduce over-all profit to a level which immediately affects the share value when the results are dis-closed.

These examples should give an indication of the complex problem concerned with assessing the prospects of companies. There is always some contributory factor which is unknown, whether to management or to prospective investors.

QUESTIONS

1. Discuss profit and loss and how they affect the business.
2. Outline some of the common risks that a concern will have to face.
3. Give your opinion of a sound financial policy for a company.
4. What are the objects of an accounting system?
5. Why is financial control so important?
6. How may capital be raised in a concern?
7. What is the purpose of the Balance Sheet and Profit and Loss Account?
8. State how you would explain to an employee the problems involved in dividing up profit among shareholders and for other purposes.
9. How would you explain to an employee the need to make a profit?
10. What forms of protection are afforded to shareholders in a public limited company and what facilities are available if an investor wishes to sell his shares?
11. What is meant by the terms *fixed* and *circulating capital*?
12. Give a brief account of forecasting and budgeting.

CHAPTER XXVIII

ELEMENTS AND METHODS OF COSTING

Introduction

THE previous chapter outlined the organisation of business finance and discussed the items shown in the statements on the general financial position of the concern; but these statements do not provide more detailed information for effective control of processes and operations within the concern. For this purpose and others mentioned shortly, cost accounting provides the answer.

Control depends upon feedback of information from *all* points where deviations occur. These variances must be measured and compared, otherwise true control is non-existent. Cost accounting, therefore, should measure and compare the costs of each product, each process and operation, every item of expense, and so build up a complete picture for control and policy decisions.

The costing function provides a means of scientific control over all expenditure in the concern, which is vital for directing its activities, for estimating accurately and for assisting in establishing the selling price. Neglect of costing and its uses places a concern in a vulnerable position. Although a company may escape repercussions for a number of years, eventually keener competition from home or abroad will force the issue.

Costing may be regarded as a service or maintenance programme of expenditure; e.g. it is wise with machine maintenance to plan a programme of careful assessment and preventive maintenance than to wait until machines break down, thus causing upheavals, delays, and heavy losses. The same applies with control of expenditure.

The expense of effectively running a costing system which checks and provides information for control purposes is negligible, compared with the savings and lessened risks, which otherwise remain hidden and are difficult to assess. One fact should be sufficient to indicate the strong need for costing: many firms fail to estimate accurately the cost of a job and therefore suffer a considerable loss.

The clerical aspect of costing can be time-consuming for the supervisor, who may feel that the burden is not worth while. Clerical assistance is necessary to relieve him of this problem thus allowing more time for controlling the variances (which are explained later). Although the supervisor is mainly concerned with the control aspects of costing he should understand the *costing environment* within which he operates. Unless he appreciates the type of system or techniques in operation, he may fail to grasp the significance of procedures and activities which seem totally unnecessary.

A review is now given of costing systems and methods, the elements of cost, allocation and apportionment, and a short survey of estimating. A more detailed description of standard costing, budgetary control and marginal costing is given in Chapter XXIX.

DEFINITION OF COSTING

Costing may be defined as collecting, recording, classifying, and allocating expenditure, to ascertain the cost of products or services for planning and control purposes by indicating points where corrective action is required.

MAIN OBJECTS OF COSTING

1. To provide promptly the cost of each item of expense.

2. To summarise and apportion costs, thus giving the total cost of each product or service.

3. To provide budgets and standards for control.

4. To advise management on costing aspects which affect the selling price and economic production.

Costing Systems

The main systems (or techniques) for recording costs and dealing with costing problems are described below, followed by a survey of the methods of costing (finding actual costs based upon the type of production), which may be grafted upon any of the main costing systems.

1. Historical costing

This system records actual costs when or after the expense occurs. The basic costing methods associated with historical costing are *job costing* and *process costing* (see below); both methods provide essential information, but fail to give economic indications of the expected performance level of each cost. In other words, a yardstick is not provided to measure efficiency.

2. Standard costing

Standard costing provides a carefully planned estimate, based upon previous experience and expectation of each cost, which is compared with the actual cost of each item. Where variances occur, the cause is ascertained and action is taken to rectify the situation. Effective control occurs when costs are quickly provided and appropriate action steers them back to the standards.

3. Budgetary control

Budgetary control involves planning a financial estimate of income and expenditure for each department, assigning to departmental managers the responsibility for taking corrective action when variances occur, and the appointment of a budget committee which co-ordinates and controls all the departments by assessing comparative statements and summaries.

4. Marginal costing

This technique isolates fixed costs (those tending *not* to vary with changes in output) from variable, or marginal, costs, charges the fixed costs as a whole against sales revenue, and apportions the marginal costs to cost centres (e.g. a department) or cost units (e.g. a product, an employee). The result of segregating fixed costs shows more clearly the effects of fluctuations on the unit cost of products when output rises or falls, thus indicating the effectiveness of production capacity.

Methods of Costing

The two main methods are job costing and process costing. Various other methods are derived from these two. A description of each method is given below.

1. Job costing

This is the method of costing those jobs which have to be kept separate during production. These non-standard jobs include "one-off" products such as a large transformer, a bridge, a ship, or an office block. Each job is given a number and all costs connected with it are booked by allocating them to that number. All labour charges are allocated from job clock cards, materials from stores requisitions, and a proportion of production overheads. A proportion of selling, distribution, administration, and research and development expenses is allocated to give the total cost of the job *when* added to the production cost consisting of total labour, material, and overhead costs. These details are shown in the job cost summary, as in Figure 69.

2. Process costing

This method is suitable where products are manufactured by set processes which are not isolated to individual jobs as in job costing; e.g. where materials for processes are derived from earlier processes, where a number of products go through the same process, but cannot be distinguished until further processes alter the standard form. Such industries as chemicals, foods, paints, and textiles are, by nature, ideal for process costing.

Control of costs is achieved by ensuring that all charges associated with each process are allocated correctly. These charges include

---

JOB COST SUMMARY

Job Number................   Drawing Numbers.........

Product.....................

Date	Code	Description	Labour £ p	Material £ p	Overhead £ p

		£ p			£ p
Total Labour Cost	=		Total Factory Cost	=	
Total Material Cost	=		+ Selling	=	
Overhead	=		+ Administration	=	
Total Factory Cost	=		+ Distribution	=	
			Total Cost	=	
Job Started	=				
Job Finished	=		Selling Price	=	
			Total Cost	=	
			Profit/Loss	=	

Fig. 69.—*Job Cost Summary*.

"One-off" products are costed separately. The card shows that the total job cost is made up of the production cost (labour, materials and overheads) *plus* an allocated proportion of selling, distribution and administration expenses. Research and development may be recorded separately or may be covered by "administration".

PROCESS COST SHEET

Product					Date	

Date	Code	Description	Labour £ p	Material £ p	Overhead £ p	Cost Centre

Summary Cost Centre 1	£ p	Cost Centre 2	£ p
Labour =		Labour =	
Materials =		Materials =	
Overhead =		Overhead =	
Total =		Total =	

£ p

Transfer Cost 1 =

„ „ 2 =

Quantity Produced = ... yards

Total Cost—Centres 1 and 2 = £ p

Cost per Yard = £ p

Fig. 70.—*Process Cost Sheet*.

Process costing is used when a product passes in sequence through several distinct processes. All charges associated with each process must be allocated correctly. Notice that the *transfer cost* (from the previous process) is separated, giving a clear indication of the present process cost. The cost per yard is in fact the *average* cost per yard for the period covered.

labour, materials, and overheads, but the transfer cost (the cost from the previous process) is separated in the process cost sheet, thus giving a clear indication of the present process cost. Figure 70 shows a typical layout of a process cost sheet.

3. Other Methods

These are generally based on job and process costing methods.

(a) *Terminal and contract costing.* These methods are a form of job costing used in the building and construction industries.

(b) *Batch costing.* Where a number of jobs can be processed together, each batch is costed and the total cost is divided by the number of units in the batch, thus providing an average cost per unit.

(c) *Unit costing.* This method is suitable if manufacturing is continuous and the units of output are the same. Industries such as mining and brewing are examples.

(d) *Multiple costing.* A number of methods are combined to cost a range of manufactured products which are assembled both from components manufactured within the concern and from subcontracted parts. The car industry comes under this category.

(e) *Operation costing.* Large-scale production and repetitive work is suitable for operation costing. The method is based upon locating a unit cost for each operation and assessing the effect of waste at each stage of production.

(f) *Operating costing.* A form of unit costing to locate the cost of a service such as various types of transport, gas, electricity and water supplies.

Elements of Cost

The total cost is divided into a number of elements which may be grouped together to form suitable areas of expense for control purposes.

These elements are based both upon the main factors of production, e.g. (a) *labour* to change the form of (b) *materials* by (c) utilising premises, machines and equipment (*factory overheads*); and upon the non-manufacturing factors (overheads) e.g. (a) administration, (b) selling, (c) distribution, (d) research and development.

The area of production consists of two groups of elements known as *prime cost* and *factory overheads*, which together form the *factory cost*. The non-manufacturing overheads are added to the factory cost to form the total cost. The difference between total cost and selling price will provide the profit or loss figure. The diagram in Figure 71 illustrates the elements of cost and method grouping to arrive at the profit and selling price.

Each element of cost is now explained under its particular group.

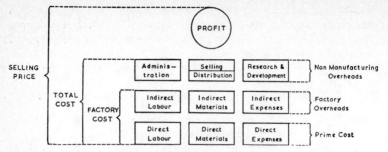

Fig. 71.—*Elements of Cost.*

These elements are based on production factors (factory cost) and non-manufacturing overheads. The relationship between this total cost and the selling price determines the profit or loss.

1. Prime costs of production

Where expenditure can be directly allocated to a product or cost centre (a particular or isolated point of production), instead of being apportioned or shared, it is called a direct cost.

The three elements of direct costs are:

(*a*) direct labour;
(*b*) direct materials;
(*c*) direct expenses.

(*a*) *Direct labour.* Those employees who directly work upon the manufacture of the product come under this element. The wages must be justified in allocating them direct to the product or unit and, in this connection, chargehands and foremen could be included as direct labour although generally they are classed as indirect labour.

(*b*) *Direct materials.* Those materials that are allocated to the product are called direct materials. They include raw materials, partly finished or finished components, and sub-assemblies, i.e. all material that becomes part of the product.

(*c*) *Direct expenses.* All expenses, other than labour and materials, which are directly employed on a product or unit, are charged as direct expenses. Such costs as tools and drawings would be included, provided the whole charge is absorbed in the processing of that particular product.

2. Factory overheads

All indirect expenses attributed to manufacturing are known as factory overheads and are divided into three elements:

(*a*) indirect labour;
(*b*) indirect materials;
(*c*) indirect expenses.

(a) *Indirect labour.* This element covers all labour indirectly connected with production and includes employees in service departments such as quality control and inspection, production control, tooling shops, internal transportation of materials, components and products, stores, the works dining room, maintenance, and welfare.

(b) *Indirect materials.* All consumables, such as oil, grease, cotton waste, sawdust, cleaning fluids, and small items such as nuts, bolts, and screws, are included where they cannot be traced back directly to the product.

(c) *Indirect expenses.* The remaining costs are running expenses, such as electricity, gas, water, rent, rates, and insurance.

3. Non-manufacturing overheads

All overheads other than factory overheads are included in this category and are divided into four elements:

(a) administration;
(b) selling;
(c) distribution;
(d) research and development.

(a) *Administration.* This element absorbs all management expenses not covered under selling, distribution, and production. The expenses of directing and controlling, and of the administration of functions such as finance, accounting, auditing, and secretarial and legal activities, are included.

(b) *Selling.* All expenses incurred to maintain and develop sales such as sales promotion, advertising, the sales general office, and the sales force of representatives, come under this element.

(c) *Distribution.* This overhead includes all expenses connected with external transport, storage, and warehousing.

(d) *Research and development.* All costs associated with improving or developing the product are termed research costs. When the results of research are applied and create some practical benefit to the product, these expenses are called development costs. If a new product is involved, development costs apply until the prototype is completed.

Allocation and Apportionment

Allocating and apportioning costs to products varies according to particular circumstances and the number of different products manufactured in the concern. The methods are discussed under the following headings.

(a) Direct costs—allocated direct to the product by using the most suitable method.

(b) Factory overhead costs—generally recovered in two stages: firstly, allocating (charging) them to departments (or cost centres); and secondly, recovering (apportioning) to each product.

(c) Non-manufacturing overhead costs—recovered in a variety of ways dependent upon circumstances.

Each heading is now discussed.

DIRECT COSTS

The methods used to record and allocate direct costs vary considerably, according to particular circumstances in an industry. The principal requirements, however, may be outlined, as follows.

Labour control

Any method of allocating labour costs usually includes the following activities. Responsibility generally rests with the individual, or department, mentioned in brackets.

(a) Engagement of employees: application form, records details, wage rate, and any revisions (Personnel Department).

(b) Record of attendance: clock card, or job card, records hours attended daily (Time Office).

(c) Direct hours worked on each product or cost centre: job card, or time sheet, records job numbers and hours (supervisor and employee).

(d) Calculation of direct labour cost for each product or cost centre: total costs calculated and entered on job cost summaries (Cost Department).

(e) Weekly wages calculated: total hours attended and bonus calculated from clock card, job cards, or time sheets (Wages Department).

Material control

A typical procedure for controlling materials is outlined below.

	Activity	Form	Responsibility
1.	Establish stock levels	Authorisation Sheet	Accountant, Purchasing Officer & Production Manager.
2.	Cost pricing method	Authorisation Sheet	Cost Accountant.
3.	Replenishing stocks	Purchase Requisition	Storekeeper.
4.	Ordering goods	Official Order	Purchasing Officer.
5.	Receiving goods	Goods Received Note	Storekeeper.
6.	Accepting goods	Inspection Note	Inspector.
7.	Payment for goods	Purchase Invoice	Accountant.
8.	Issuing materials	Materials Requisition	Storekeeper.
9.	Returning materials	Materials Returned Note	Supervisor.

Activity	*Form*	*Responsibility*
10. Transfers	Materials Transfer Note	Storekeeper.
11. Recording stock	Bin Cards Material Control Cards	Storekeeper and Stores Clerk.
12. Charging materials to product or cost centre	Materials Requisition Materials Returned Notes Job Cost Summaries.	Cost Clerk.
13. Checking stock	Stock Check Sheets	Stock Checker or Internal Auditor.

FACTORY OVERHEAD COSTS

The first stage is to decide upon a fair allocation of factory overhead costs to each production department or cost centre. A cost centre is a point or area where cost control may be applied; it could be a section, a group of machines, an individual or a group of individuals. A supervisor or a manager is responsible for each cost centre.

Bases of apportioning factory overhead costs

The main bases are detailed below.

(a) *Employees' wages.* Such overheads as national insurance contributions and employers' liability insurance may be charged under this method.

(b) *Number of employees.* Some items which may be fairly apportioned under this method are dining-room costs, wages department expenses, welfare costs, and costing expenses.

(c) *Floor area or cubic capacity.* Some examples which apply here are lighting, heating, rent, fire insurance and general upkeep.

(d) *Technical measurement.* Where actual measurement of the overhead is possible within the cost centre this method provides a fair means of apportioning the charge. Examples are: lighting, by assessing the number of bulbs, or kilowatts consumed; heating, by the number of radiators; electric power and water consumed by metering.

(e) *Value of buildings and plant.* The values of plant and buildings may be used as a basis for such items as depreciation, insurance, rates, and repairs.

(f) *Direct charges.* In some cases a direct charge is possible, when employees are engaged within a cost centre for such purposes as supervising and machinery maintenance.

Recovery and allocation

The second stage is to recover (or apportion) the factory overhead costs already allocated to each department or cost centre.

Recovery is straightforward when only one type of product is manufactured. The total factory overhead cost is divided by the number of products manufactured during the period, thus providing a uniform recovery rate for each product. When a range of products is manufactured, the allocation of a fair charge is more difficult. Job costing and many process costing systems have the same problems. Some of the methods used to allocate factory overheads in these circumstances are listed below.

(a) *Prime cost percentage.* The factory overhead for the period is divided by the prime cost and expressed as a percentage. In many cases expenses are omitted from the prime cost. The formula and an example are given below:

$$Percentage\ of\ Prime\ Cost = \frac{Factory\ Overhead}{Prime\ Cost} \times \frac{100}{1}$$

EXAMPLE

Period: July 19–2
Factory overhead = £2000
Direct labour   = £3000
Direct Material = £2000

$$\frac{2000}{5000} \times \frac{100}{1} = 40\%$$

Thus, a job with a prime cost of £100 would be charged £40 for factory overhead cost.

(b) *Direct wages percentage.* This simple method is generally inaccurate, but when such factors as wage rates, machines, and work content are of a similar nature for all the products manufactured, a higher degree of accuracy is attained. The formula and an example are given below:

$$Percentage\ of\ Direct\ Wages = \frac{Factory\ Overhead}{Direct\ Wages} \times \frac{100}{1}$$

EXAMPLE

Period: July 19–2
Factory overhead = £2000
Direct wages   = £3000

$$\frac{2000}{3000} \times \frac{100}{1} = 66.66\%$$

In this case a job with a direct wages cost of £100 would be charged with £66.66 for factory overhead cost.

(c) *Direct material percentage.* Generally this method is unsuitable where various materials—within a wide price range—are employed in the manufacture of products.

$$Direct\ Material\ Percentage = \frac{Factory\ Overhead}{Direct\ Material} \times \frac{100}{1}$$

EXAMPLE

Period: July 19–2
Factory overhead = £2000
Direct material   = £2000

$$\frac{2000}{2000} \times \frac{100}{1} = 100\%$$

(d) *Labour hour rate.* Where the operators' time is a very important aspect of the work, this method is useful because the calculation is based upon the number of direct labour hours for the job.

$$Direct\ Labour\ Hour\ Rate = \frac{Factory\ Overhead}{Direct\ Labour\ Hours}$$

EXAMPLE

Period: July 19–2
Factory overhead = £2000
Direct labour hours = 8000

$$\frac{£2000}{8000} = 25p.\ hr.$$

If a job takes twenty hours to complete, the factory overhead cost would be £5.

(e) *Machine hour rate.* Where the operating hours of machines are a dominant feature of production this method will be more accurate.

$$Machine\ Hour\ Rate = \frac{Factory\ Overhead}{Machine\ Hours}$$

EXAMPLE

Period: July 19–2
Factory overhead = £2000
Machine hours = 4000

$$\frac{£2000}{4000} = 50p.\ hr.$$

If twenty machine hours were taken to complete a job the factory overhead would be £10.

NON-MANUFACTURING OVERHEAD COSTS

The method of recovering these overheads again depends upon circumstances.

Administration costs may be written off as a general expense in the Profit and Loss Account, or apportioned between Work-in-Progress and Cost of Sales, or averaged out among all products. Selling and distribution costs are generally written off to Cost of Sales Account. Finally, research and development costs may be written off over a period of years (similar to fixed assets) and attached to factory overheads, or treated as a direct charge to the particular product, or written off as a general expense in the Profit and Loss Account.

Estimating

In many respects estimating is similar to production planning and, of course, costing plays an essential part in both these activities. The need for estimates arises in job production, as outlined in Chapter XXV. A customer's inquiry which involves particular requirements cannot be met by a standard product; therefore, an estimate or quotation must be calculated for the manufacture of the specific item required.

A reliable estimate must start at an earlier stage than production planning. The expense involved in research, design, drawings, and specification preparation can be very costly. Reference to past records of cost in these overheads is essential, but the future always contains the unknown factors which demand an intelligent guess by the specialists concerned with forecasting.

The actual cost of estimating must also be taken into consideration. The responsibility for an estimate is a heavy burden, as an error may involve the concern in a considerable loss which cannot be claimed from the customer in normal circumstances.

The estimator must have a clear idea of the customer's requirements, and be able to couple these with cost records. Although it is possible to build up an estimate by calculating the direct labour, material, and expenses involved, this tedious, lengthy process can be sidetracked by concentrating on the total cost of sub-assemblies or components which may be common to a number of jobs, thus building up a quotation in this form. Naturally some parts will require the full treatment of prime cost establishment and, where variable components are involved, it is possible for the estimator to build up a library of information by using statistical methods to cover a range of costs for a variable. The use of standard costs, if they are available, helps considerably in assessing the cost of components.

The problem of loading the total cost with a suitable profit margin rests with top management. The estimator may be given a percentage to work with, but on some occasions the loading varies with circumstances, e.g. the need to win a particular contract for prestige purposes or for lack of other work; or the desire to discourage the customer because of an over-full order book.

NOTE: The importance of the delivery date is often overlooked by companies. Delay can be costly to the customer and it is not unusual for penalty clauses to be included in contracts to overcome this problem. Such clauses operate on a set sum to be paid by the supplier for every day or week that delivery is overdue.

QUESTIONS

1. Define costing and outline its main objects.
2. Briefly describe the main costing systems.
3. Write an account of job costing and process costing.
4. Draw a diagram illustrating the main elements of cost and describe each element briefly.
5. How would you draw up an estimate?
6. Outline a typical procedure for controlling materials.
7. Describe the various ways of apportioning factory overheads.
8. Discuss the difference between historical costing and standard costing.
9. Describe a typical material control procedure.

CHAPTER XXIX

COSTING SYSTEMS

THE four main costing systems were mentioned briefly in the previous chapter. Standard costing, budgetary control, and marginal costing are now described more fully.

Standard Costing

DEFINITION

Standard costing is a method of cost accounting which estimates or predetermines the costs of each element; compares them with the actual costs; calculates the variances; and presents management with reports on those items requiring some action to stop the trend away from the standard.

THE SPHERE OF STANDARD COSTING

Standard costing can be used in most concerns regardless of size or type, although it is easier to apply in some industries where the product is standardised and long production runs are used.

Standards are based upon prevailing conditions and a particular output level; if these factors change then the standard costs are distorted and must be revised.

ESTABLISHING STANDARD COSTS

The most usual methods of establishing standard costs are described below.

1. Direct labour

Setting reasonable standards for labour costs demands the services of work study engineers, who can assess the work content and establish suitable times for each operation. Wage rates can now be applied and standard costs calculated. These costs should remain stable until there are alterations in the operation content or changes in rates of pay.

2. Direct materials

The quantity of material required for an operation is found by compiling a standard material specification. This is based upon drawings and on experience of the particular operation, which may include average scrap and waste through cutting. The standard quantity can now be priced by reference to the purchasing officer or a price manual, and an allowance should be made for forecasted changes in price for the period in mind.

3. Overheads

Normally the overhead expenses for each department are found by reference to a budget, calculated on such factors as machine hours, direct labour hours, or on prime cost. These factors are based upon the capacity of the particular department, the costs being divided into fixed and variable. Fixed costs tend not to fluctuate with the rate of production, whereas variable costs tend to alter in sympathy with the production rate.

The capacity of a department is open to a number of interpretations and a choice must be made, to ensure standard treatment of all overheads allocated to departments. The supervisor should understand clearly which definition of capacity is used, otherwise he will not be able to assess the variances accurately and take appropriate action.

If an assumption is made that the department runs without any loss of time, this is known as the *maximum theoretical capacity*; when normal time losses such as setting up times, idle time and breakdowns are deducted from the maximum theoretical capacity, the capacity is called *normal capacity to manufacture*; a further reduction for recessions in trade, especially seasonal sales, reduces the capacity to the definition of *normal capacity to manufacture and sell*; finally, when each year's sales capacity is used as a guide, it is known as *short period capacity to sell*.

SOME ASPECTS OF STANDARD COSTING

1. The essence of standard costing is to provide management with vital information for effective control. Whether effective control is achieved depends upon two main factors; *firstly*, the ability of management to take the correct actions and, *secondly*, the ability of the cost accountant to provide the information on time. Time is most important, and delays are expensive when costs are moving sharply away from standards. The supervisor must appreciate the importance of time and ensure that cost returns are made promptly.

2. The use of standards provides a measurement for comparison with actual costs which is superior to any other form of comparison. For instance, comparing the actual costs of one period with those of another period can be misleading. It gives no positive indication which is the more efficient cost or, if the costs are similar, no indication is given that they are at an effective level.

3. Variances from the standard are easily seen by using the *principle of exceptions*, i.e. presenting management with those costs which are deviating from the standard and omitting or excepting those that are conforming to the plan. Much time is saved in the avoidance of sorting through pages of costs, and more time can be spent on thinking out the correct action to be taken.

4. Clerical operation of this system is more economic because only information which is actually used is recorded, as against other

systems where masses of data are produced with no specific purpose in mind.

5. The effects of changes, e.g. different types of material, revised wage rates, bonus schemes, varying output, and new tools or machines, can be easily seen by "before and after" comparison.

6. The inherent process of maintaining a constant watch on standards and revising where necessary, encourages management and supervision to become cost conscious and aware of those costs which tend to deviate continually.

7. A reliable indication of the effectiveness of managers and supervisors is provided for top management. Reports on variances, the action taken and the results next period, clearly show the weak spots in the organisation. These, in turn, demand action from top management and the results of such action provide a guide to the effectiveness of this level also.

8. The system should not always be condemned if it does not work properly. The supervisor must appreciate that "standard costing" is sound. It should be clear from preceding paragraphs that much of its effectiveness depends upon individuals. Operators must record details accurately, and appropriate decisions are necessary throughout the various levels up to the Board of Directors.

Budgetary Control

Budgetary control is a system which establishes departmental budgets by pre-planning all the activities within the concern to form a master budget, through which co-ordination and control may be achieved.

Each budget is determined by the policy planned for the forthcoming period and the expectations of expense, based upon previous experience and estimated changes.

Co-ordinating all the budgets to maximise profit and maintain a stable business is one of the main problems of budgetary control. The system has the advantage, however, of setting clear targets for each department, all aligned in the same direction.

SIMILARITY BETWEEN BUDGETARY CONTROL AND STANDARD COSTING

Certain fundamentals are common to budgetary control and standard costing. These are:

1. a pre-planned standard for each item of expense;
2. measurement of actual costs;
3. comparison of actual with standard costs;
4. discovery of reasons for the variances;
5. recommended courses of action to correct the variances.

The practice has developed of relating standard costing to production activities alone, whereas budgetary control is a system applied to all activities in the concern including sales, production, stock, plant and buildings, and finance. Although budgetary control and standard costing are interrelated, some industries may have difficulty in introducing standard costing, but would be able to operate budgetary control effectively.

CONTROL

Effective control depends upon allocating responsibility to competent managers and supervisors for each activity or function; providing them with operating statements on time, with details of the standard, actual expense, and the variances, together with recommendations for action.

The time factor is important. Although the budget may be drawn up for a year, control is too remote over such a long period. Short periods of say, four weeks, allow frequent comparisons thus providing a firmer basis for control, if reports are made promptly.

ADVANTAGES OF BUDGETARY CONTROL

1. All the functions of the concern are co-ordinated and controlled, indicating clearly to each supervisor in the organisation his responsibility for a particular section of the master budget and the over-all importance of achieving the objective stated.

2. The continuing process of budgetary control gives more accurate indications of trends and eases the problems of forecasting. Signs of change become evident much earlier and management has the opportunity to take full advantage of the situation in its planning.

3. The risks connected with operating and financing the concern are reduced, as close control of working capital, including cash in hand, is assured through the budget statements. Similarly, all income and expenditure is both forecasted and checked as results become available, thus enabling any deviation to be brought under control quickly.

4. An effective system of budgetary control is a means of convincing prospective investors of the concern's stability, when more capital is required for expansion programmes.

BUDGETARY CONTROL PROCEDURE

Co-ordination and control of the budgets may be carried out by a budget controller or budget committee. When studying operating results, the controller would meet with the managing director and senior executives to discuss the circumstances, the current position, and possible courses of action. Changes in policy may then be decided upon at such meetings.

Actual forecasting of budgets follows the policy which governs sales targets, production of new lines and financial activities. Subsidiary budgets are forecast at this stage and they would include the following:

Sales Budget	Research & Development Budget
Production Budget	Capital Expenditure Budget
Plant Utilisation Budget	Personnel Budget
Stock Budget	Purchasing Budget
Production Cost Budget	Cash Budget
Selling Cost Budget	Profit & Loss Forecast
Distribution Cost Budget	Balance Sheet Forecast
Administration Cost Budget	

After the completion of forecasts, meetings are held to finalise the budgets by considering various plans submitted. The master budget is drawn up and issued. When period statements are circulated, the executives—who are responsible for the budgets—take appropriate action. The statements and reports from executives are fed back to the controller for discussion under the three aspects of policy-making, forecasting, and budget preparation, thus completing the control cycle.

Marginal Costing

DEFINITION

The technique of marginal costing was briefly described in the previous chapter. Marginal cost has been defined as the direct costs of labour and material plus variable overhead expenses, or as the additional cost of producing one more unit or product. The procedure of marginal costing is best shown in tabular form, as in Figure 72.

Explanations of the terms used are given below, before discussing the theory on which marginal costing is based.

(a) *Variable costs:* Those costs that tend to vary in relation to output. They include direct labour, material, and expenses (i.e. prime cost), variable overheads for the factory and, under some systems, the variable element of selling, distribution, and administration cost.

(b) *Fixed costs:* All costs that tend to remain constant for a period of time, and within a specified range of output. Typical examples are management and supervision costs, depreciation of fixed assets, rates, rent, heating, lighting, power, insurance, and subscriptions.

(c) *Sales revenue:* The actual amounts received from selling the products.

(d) *Contribution:* The sales revenue less the total variable costs (the marginal costs) for a product.

(e) *The fund:* The total sum of the contributions.

The total fixed costs are finally deducted from the fund to give the net profit.

A comparison between the conventional systems of costing and marginal costing is shown in Figure 72.

Conventional Costing

| Sales Revenue | less | Prime Cost | = | Gross Profit | less | Factory and Administration Overheads | = | Net Profit |

Marginal Costing

| Sales Revenue | less | Marginal Costs | = | Contribution (Fund) | less | Fixed Costs | = | Net Profit |

Conventional Costing

Products	£000's				
	Sales	Prime Costs	Gross Profit	Factory and Administration Overheads	Net Profit
W	10	— 4	6	— 6	0
X	14	— 5	9	— 8	1
Y	12	— 4	8	— 7	1
Z	8	— 2	6	— 5	1
Totals	44	— 15	29	— 26	3

Marginal Costing

Products	Sales	Marginal Costs	Contribution Fund	Fixed Costs	Net Profit
W	10	— 7	3 ⎫	⎫	⎫
X	14	— 10	4 ⎬ 10	⎬ —7	⎬ 3
Y	12	— 10	2 ⎪	⎪	⎪
Z	8	— 7	1 ⎭	⎭	⎭
Totals	44	— 34	10	—7	3

Fig. 72.—*Conventional Costing and Marginal Costing Compared.*
This illustrates the distortion factor met in conventional costing when attempting to apportion fixed overheads to cost centres fairly. The marginal costing technique eliminates this factor.

THE THEORY OF MARGINAL COSTING

Provided fixed costs tend to remain static, an increase in production should normally result in a reduced cost per unit. If production is decreased, an increase in cost per unit should be expected.

This theory is based on the assumption that all fixed costs are segregated and not affected by fluctuations in output, therefore, as output rises, the spread of fixed costs is greater and a smaller amount will be attached to each unit. As output falls, the load attached to each unit will be larger. (The term attached does *not* mean apportioned; it is used here to indicate the portion of fixed costs which will appear when calculating the average cost per unit.)

The term marginal cost—in accordance with this theory—will represent the change in variable costs when one unit more, or one unit less, is produced. This amount of change will be the difference between the two total costs when output changes by one unit.

MAIN ASPECTS

Variable and fixed costs

The supervisor may assume that variable costs will be constant per unit regardless of fluctuations in output. He should remember, however, that possible changes may occur through price alterations for raw materials and components and, if production is increased to a point where overtime is incurred, the rates of pay will be affected and variable costs will rise.

In practice, fixed costs also tend to vary over long periods of time as policy decisions involve additional capital expenditure on new factories or extensions of existing premises. Such costs are known as semi-fixed or semi-variable.

This aspect does not nullify marginal costing, as many decisions are based upon short-term runs of periods up to a year.

The important factor connected with fixed costs is that irrespective of production level they remain the same. Even when production ceases completely, the fact remains that fixed costs continue. This outlook, when the significance of this factor is appreciated, indicates the critical role played by those who control variable costs. The effectiveness of controlling these variable or marginal costs decides the amount of contribution, which governs the profit margin.

Contribution and new products

The importance of the contribution may now be extended to consider its effect on decisions involving new products. The question of whether to introduce a new line, or to decrease the range of products and increase production on particular lines, becomes easier to solve.

A simple example should clarify the issue involved:

Proposed New Line—Product B		*Proposed Product B*	
Product A			
	£		£
Sales	= 27,000	Sales	= 3,000
Less Marginal Cost	= 20,000	*Less* Marginal Cost	= 2,500
Contribution	= 7,000	Contribution	= 500
Less Fixed Costs	= 6,000	*Less* Fixed Costs	= 600
		(apportioned on total sales)	
Profit	= 1,000	Loss	= 100

The above calculations for a proposed new product B are based upon apportioning the load of fixed costs according to the sales value of each product. This calculation is misleading because it attempts to split fixed costs among the products and, therefore, distorts the situation. In reality the new product will contribute another £500 towards fixed costs and profit; thus in this case, as the contribution from product A already covers fixed costs, the contribution from the new product B directly increases the profit by £500, i.e. by 50 per cent.

The calculation using the marginal costing technique is shown below:

Product	Contribution	Fund	Fixed Costs	Profit
A	= £7,000 ⎫			
B	= £ 500 ⎭	£7,500	− £6,000	= £1,500

A further example, which may be of interest to the supervisor, involves a concern which manufactures three products. Under certain marketing conditions the company may need to investigate the possibility of reducing its range of products and determine the effect on profitability. The current situation is given first, followed by the effect of the proposal to abandon product A and divide the surplus capacity equally among the remaining products, B and C.

Existing Lines

	A	B	C	(£000s)
Sales	10	10	10	
Less Marginal Costs	7	6	5	
Contribution	3	4	5	
Fund				= 12
Less Fixed Costs				= 11
Profit				= 1

Proposed Change

	A	B	C	
Sales	Abandoned	15	15	
Less Marginal Cost		9	7½	(increased
Contribution		6	7½	proportionately)
Fund				= 13½
Less Fixed Costs				= 11
Profit				= 2½

Provided market conditions prompted such a change, the proposal stated above would show a substantial increase in profitability.

Unfortunately, the proposed change of product range indicated above is often not straightforward because of certain limiting factors. These factors, such as availability of trained labour, shortage of raw materials, production capacity available, limited cash resources, and the state of the market, must be considered in order to identify those products which will make best use of available resources.

Break-even techniques

An essential part of marginal costing is the break-even technique which includes calculations to indicate the change in profitability when output is altered or the product range is revised.

Break-even analysis is a technique which locates the level of production where sales revenue equals all the costs. It also indicates the relationship between sales revenue, variable costs, fixed costs, and profit or loss, at various levels of output. The *break-even point* is self-explanatory, it simply means the level of output where neither a profit nor a loss is incurred. The importance of this calculation and break-even analysis generally, lies in its ability to indicate such aspects as the amount of sales necessary to cover the degree of profit required for various purposes; the revision of selling prices to provide sufficient sales revenue to cover estimated profit and establish a particular break-even point; and the variable cost per unit.

The break-even point may be calculated by formula or plotted on a break-even chart. The formula is given below:

$$\text{Break-even Point} = \frac{\text{Fixed Costs}}{1 - (\text{Variable Costs} \div \text{Sales Revenue})}$$

EXAMPLE:

Sales revenue £10,000; Variable costs £6,000; Fixed costs £2,000.

$$\therefore \text{Break-even point} = £\frac{2,000}{1 - \frac{6,000}{10,000}} = £\frac{2,000}{1 - \frac{3}{5}}$$

$$= £\frac{2,000}{\frac{2}{5}} = £\frac{2,000 \times 5}{2}$$

$$= \underline{\underline{£5,000}}$$

The break-even chart

Construction of a break-even chart is based upon the choice of information required.

The X axis is used to show output or sales, whether it may be desired to indicate the volume of sales in units, or as a percentage, the output in value or units, or the capacity of the plant. The Y axis indicates the cost. An example is shown in Figure 73.

The main features to note are the fixed costs line which remains static at £30,000; and the variable costs line which is the total costs less the fixed costs, amounting to £20,000. The chart indicates the break-even point where the variable costs line cuts the sales line. The vertical line—from the break-even point to the X axis—intersects the point where output will provide sufficient funds to break-even, at 50,000 units.

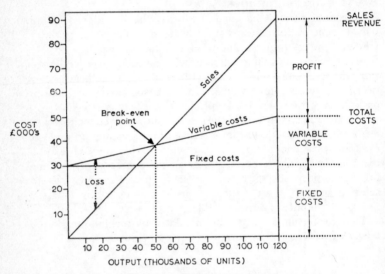

Fig. 73.—*Break-even Chart*.

Here the X axis shows output and the Y axis the cost. The X axis may be required to show the output in value, sales in units or as a percentage, or to show plant capacity. The dotted line indicates the point in output where sales exactly cover costs; neither profit nor loss is made.

The fact that costs do not behave in such a simple manner as drawn on the break-even chart has already been stressed. Costs do not always fit conveniently into fixed or variable groups; they vary for other reasons besides fluctuations in output. The supervisor will know by experience that when attempts are made to increase production, invariably extra costs appear—such as overtime and bonus—which explain the concept that maximum production does not necessarily match with maximum profit. On the marketing side, it is quite common to make price reductions when the concern decides to increase sales.

Whatever its disadvantages, the break-even chart clearly shows the relationships between fixed costs, variable costs, and sales revenue.

Within the relatively narrow limits of production fluctuations the errors inherent in straight line graphs are practically eliminated. Thus marginal costing and its techniques can help considerably in solving problems related to levels of production, range of products, pricing of products, and subcontracting.

There are many variations of the break-even chart which can be used for other purposes than analysing company output. For instance, in Figure 74 the technique is used by the consumer to find the break-even point between two tariffs offered for gas. If the consumption in a house is below 53 therms, Scheme A will be cheaper; if consumption is over 53 therms the break-even point is exceeded, therefore Scheme B will be cheaper so long as the consumption does not fall below that point each quarter.

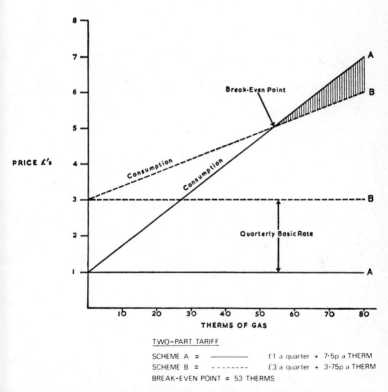

TWO–PART TARIFF

SCHEME A =	————————	£1 a quarter + 7·5p a THERM
SCHEME B =	– – – – – – –	£3 a quarter + 3·75p a THERM
BREAK-EVEN POINT = 53 THERMS		

Fig. 74.—*Form of Break-even Chart for Domestic Use.*

In this illustration the break-even technique enables the consumer to determine which tariff of gas to adopt. If the consumption is below the break-even point of 53 therms, Scheme A will be the cheaper. If consumption is higher Scheme B should be adopted.

QUESTIONS

1. Write an essay on standard costing.
2. What is the purpose and advantages of budgetary control?
3. Describe a simple system of marginal costing.
4. Describe the theory of marginal costing.
5. What is meant by the break-even technique? Illustrate your answer with a diagram.
6. How can costing help the supervisor?
7. When would it be worth while to accept an order at less than total cost?
8. Describe the most usual ways of establishing standard costs for labour, materials, and overheads.
9. Explain the use of the principle of exceptions in connection with standard costing.
10. Discuss any similarities between budgetary control and standard costing.

CHAPTER XXX

COST REDUCTION

Introduction

THE previous chapters on costing outlined the different methods of controlling costs by establishing standards and taking action when variances occur. This form of cost control has a natural tendency to keep costs within the established standards which, in fact, become objectives. This outlook towards costs is not sound when it exists in isolation: individuals are inclined to accept without question standards which are based on past and present conditions, and their vision tends to be limited to standard costs.

A healthier outlook is to regard cost control as an essential part of an over-all control system operated by effective management, who demand realism by incorporating cost reduction as a continuing process in the scheme. Probably it would be wiser to refer to the system as cost reduction and control, thus making it an integral part of control.

Cost reduction programmes must generate a questioning attitude towards standards which are really guides, begging to be reduced to achieve higher productivity and greater economy. Even more important is the need to broaden and raise the level of vision to those areas where standards do not exist. The supervisor will then possess the correct depth of understanding for appreciating the field of cost reduction. A good starting-point is to examine the question of waste.

Waste

On a national level, any form of waste drags a country down to a slightly lower standard of living. When all waste is coupled together the economic loss can be considerable. Waste is a complete loss of all the resources needed to produce that proportion which is discarded or misused.

Probably most people in the community are guilty of improper use of some service or product. Small incidents such as throwing away milk from a nearly empty bottle, discarding small quantities of food, leaving lights on, and dripping taps, are examples of useless consumption. The immediate retaliation from some individuals might be that they have the right to do as they please; they pay for the privilege of burning a light in an empty room; there is democratic freedom to buy an article and destroy it if we wish. Whether the same people would be prepared to hand out pound notes to strangers as they pass by would be doubtful, as they may think it is ridiculous to throw money away after it has been earned.

A more subtle sense of responsibility and understanding of economic life is needed before the same reply is forthcoming when pointless destruction of goods or services is committed. Shallow thinking and dilatory attitudes are often fostered by mistaken beliefs about freedom and what it really means. Freedom does not mean that individuals should be free to destroy and misuse the creations and efforts of individuals, although those individuals have been paid for their work.

Most people who pay income tax react sharply when they hear of waste connected with Government expenditure, as the connection is clear. Thinking out how people indirectly pay for waste is very involved and difficult to understand.

Within a company similar problems connected with the identification of individuals and waste exists. Attitudes are indicated by such remarks as "It is not my business"; "The company can stand it"; "They will not miss these few nuts and bolts"; "Plenty more where those came from"; "Why worry? There's another one in the stores"; and so on.

THE SUPERVISOR'S PART

The supervisor must appreciate the problem of attitude towards waste. He is responsible for reducing waste to a minimum which involves continually probing all forms of expenditure—in its broadest sense—to see whether cost reduction is possible.

Cost reduction may be defined as being able to reduce—on a long-term basis—any item of expense, without interfering with the effectiveness of the service rendered. The breadth of cost reduction—under this definition—includes some costs outside the direct control of the supervisor. The main areas generally associated with cost reduction are production, design, marketing and finance. Within the field of production the supervisor is concerned with labour, materials, plant and machinery, and other factors of expense. Possible improvements in design can often be seen from shop-floor level which may escape designers at a more remote point.

The supervisor ought to develop a searching attitude towards costs, which means something more than inquiring into the possibility of reducing the cost by direct means. Some examples are the use of a time switch to control lighting and heating; buying a more expensive tool which is cheaper in the long run; applying one coat of expensive covering instead of three coats of cheaper covering; replacing an unsuitable machine by a new one which will produce savings eventually. Such changes require expenditure first, while the savings come later. More direct ways should not be ignored such as cutting out shapes from metal sheet in a more economical way by altering the position of the pattern, or using a cheaper grade of material which does not impair the efficiency of the product.

CONTROL FACTORS

Some of the factors the supervisor may consider when planning a method of operating cost reduction as a continuing process, would be the following:

1. The time factor

Does the item vary in cost on a regular occurring or an intermittent basis? Waste may occur through an employee regularly having half a day off each week, or there will be cases of epidemics such as influenza or enteritis. An intermittent example may be absences to attend a race meeting or a football match.

2. Classes of items

These may be divided into labour, materials, machines, equipment, tools, and services.

3. Significance

The item may be measurable or estimated from the aspect of amount of waste. From this aspect it may be decided that the item is controllable, partly controllable, or uncontrollable.

4. Recording

The various factors mentioned above should be recorded together with a description of the item or type of waste. The question of responsibility is also involved; and timeliness of information is important so that action may be taken early.

Cost Reduction Check-Lists

A guide to each class of item is now given in the form of a check-list which indicates the main points, but is not intended to be a comprehensive summary. The supervisor should write out a list for use from his own knowledge and experience. The causes of waste vary with circumstances.

LABOUR CHECK-LIST

1. Skilled operators must be on skilled work, semi-skilled operators on semi-skilled work, and so on.

2. The wage should be appropriate to the job. It is wasteful to pay a high wage to a person and place him on low wage tasks. The importance of "servicing" (providing assistance to) highly paid employees is obvious, but often neglected.

3. Use the knowledge, skill and experience of employees. Unfortunately, the problem of rising and declining industries makes this task extremely difficult at times.

4. Avoid time wasted by employees through walking about; examine the possibilities of cutting down this factor. For example, it is cheaper for a storeman to bring materials to the skilled operator.

5. Aim to cut out idle time completely. Aim high, question the schedules, check the work flow, and try to close the gaps.

6. Reduce frustration of the operator through poor product design. Ferret out the ideas and make a fuss about the proposed improvement. Get something done!

7. Poor training produces poor operators. Try to improve training schemes.

8. Unsound incentives speak for themselves. Ensure that financial and non-financial incentive schemes are suitable, and are operating properly.

9. Inability to motivate employees. Learn more about motivation. Practise and experiment until better results are achieved. Motivating is an art which takes years to perfect unless you are one of the fortunate few.

10. Poor management attitude. You must make the best of a bad job; the managers cannot help—they do not know any better, but you do! Make excuses, point out to operators how busy managers are, the heavy burden they carry, the tremendous weight of responsibility, the shortage of time, which makes them easily misunderstood. Deep down they mean well and tolerance is essential. There is no logical alternative because unless you align yourself with managers and attempt to excuse their conduct, you will naturally side with your subordinates which is obviously unsound and widens the gulf between management and operators.

11. Using inexperienced labour. The danger of accidents, excessive scrap, and the effect on other employees, is apparent. Such causes as poor selection and lack of suitable labour are outside the supervisor's scope. He should complain and try to train the unfortunate individual as soon as possible.

12. Carelessness, laziness, accidents, and absenteeism, are four examples where the supervisor must take positive action after adequate investigation by personnel counselling.

13. Quality being neglected for quantity. An appraisal of the financial incentive scheme and attitudes is essential.

14. Working conditions below standard.

15. Unsuitable tools, machines, equipment, and materials.

16. Poor maintenance, resulting in breakdowns and frustration.

17. Inadequate instructions.

18. Inadequate induction schemes.

19. Avoidable overtime. Often employees and supervisors get into the habit of working overtime unnecessarily.

20. Low morale and high labour turnover. Better supervision and selection procedures, training schemes, and closer control, should improve this situation.

MATERIALS CHECK-LIST

1. Cheapest for the purpose. The important factor is that the quality of the finished article is not impaired.

2. Not requisitioning sufficient supplies. (Orders too small.)

3. Inadequate supplies available at the stores.

4. Damaged material through negligence.

5. Salvage. In some cases savings are possible by salvaging scrap and selling it already sorted to concerns.

6. Poor storage facilities; some materials are easily soiled and become shop worn if they are not properly stored at the work place.

7. Inadequate materials handling. Damaged materials and delays may be overcome by paying more attention to this factor.

8. Faulty materials. This problem should be investigated and reports sent to the Purchasing Officer, or executive responsible for supplies.

9. Excessive consumption of consumable materials. Such items as sandpaper, solder, emery, paint, files, and twist drills, tend to be treated carelessly and are subject to pilfering. Costs may rise considerably unless these items are strictly controlled.

10. Careless use of small parts or components. Small parts tend to be mixed together and waste can develop unless provision is made to separate them by placing in individual boxes.

MACHINES CHECK-LIST

1. Replacement of obsolescent machines by more efficient models.

2. Maintenance programmes to minimise breakdowns, and prompt attention when they occur.

3. Most effective layout of machinery and equipment.

4. Remove redundant machines.

5. Ensure economic operation of machinery by scheduling to reduce idle time.

6. Use the correct type of model for each operation.

7. Ensure that attachments which save time are fitted and used.

GENERAL CHECK-LIST

1. Application of Work Study to simplify, standardise, and generally improve methods, and to measure the work content.

2. Work planning and scheduling.

3. Correct use of jigs and tools.

4. Tolerances should be opened to limits which do not affect the quality of the product.

5. Check on housekeeping. Slackness leads to more accidents, increased cleaning costs, and loss of materials.

6. Excessive use of services such as lighting, heating, compressed air, water and power.

Maintenance

Unless a programme of maintenance is conducted on sound principles of control, the amount of waste can be considerable through breakdowns and the employment of an excessive number of maintenance staff. Although many executives recognise the problem of maintenance, there appears to be considerable reluctance to plan and control it. Some individuals insist that maintenance work cannot be measured, yet others have actually measured and successfully set standards by using the technique known as analytical estimating, which is explained in Chapter XXIII.

There is no doubt that maintenance problems will increase as machines are driven faster and higher precision is required. Automated equipment still needs attention, and higher purchase prices will inevitably demand more output from machines which, in turn, place a heavier cost load when breakdowns occur.

To achieve the object of maintaining the efficiency of buildings, plant, and equipment, maintenance must be arranged so that production is not interrupted and the safety of employees is assured. A planned maintenance programme is a typical example where expenditure is essential to achieve savings in the long run.

PLANNED OR SCHEDULED MAINTENANCE

This form of maintenance is designed to reduce the number of sudden breakdowns of machinery and equipment. The scheme aims to keep plant running continuously during production time by adopting a programme of continuous maintenance which reduces emergency maintenance to a minimum. Careful keeping of maintenance records and control procedures helps to reduce maintenance costs by making the best use of maintenance staff.

The two methods of planned maintenance are called Preventive Maintenance and Long Term Maintenance.

1. Preventive maintenance

This programme specifies periodic cleaning, servicing, inspection, and replacement of parts prone to breakdown. The scheme includes duplication of vital parts which are built in to the machines (where practicable) such as two valves, or two motors, which can be quickly switched from one to the other in the event of a breakdown. Where this system is not possible, provision is made for spares to be immediately available for replacement. Schedules are set for servicing time so that maintenance may be conducted without interrupting production.

Within this scheme, vital parts are replaced after a specified number of hours running time; they are then serviced and ready for replacement next time the change is due. The advantage is that the changeover time can be arranged in preference to a sudden breakdown which always seems to occur at the busiest period.

Preventive maintenance must be justified on a cost reduction basis. Records of previous waste through breakdowns compared with the new scheme will show the economies. Unfortunately plant still breaks down at inconvenient times in spite of preventive maintenance. A balance of savings must therefore be kept otherwise the tendency for the programme to grow and grow, in an attempt to stop breakdowns completely, would be uneconomic and practically impossible to achieve.

2. Long-term maintenance

More sophisticated forms of maintenance come under the heading of long-term maintenance. Briefly they include "built-in" maintenance devices which automatically compensate, or provide facilities for switching to duplicated sections, when breakdowns occur. Lubrication is a typical example where automatic or semi-automatic devices lubricate moving parts.

The use of protective covers and guards ensures that certain parts of the machine which are susceptible to dust and corrosion are safely sealed. Where practicable, permanently sealed units within a machine are built in. These units are stringently tested for endurance and are replaced at the end of their recommended life.

THE SUPERVISOR'S PART

In circumstances where the supervisor can call upon a Maintenance Department, his assistance in helping the department to plan the work may be invaluable. Much depends upon the attitude of the maintenance or plant manager and the programme of maintenance, if any. The supervisor should press for planned programmes if they do not exist, as invariably the cost of maintenance is more than offset by increased output.

If maintenance is largely the responsibility of the supervisor, the time spent on planning will be rewarding in the long run. Each item should receive a periodic overhaul and records should be kept for control purposes. A procedure for reporting and dealing with emergency breakdowns should be in operation.

From the human aspect, the supervisor must convince operators of the importance of treating machines and equipment with care. Any carelessness or deliberate negligence is a serious offence; the supervisor should investigate the circumstances and interview the employee to find out the basic cause of the act. The loss may be considerable through someone's lack of responsibility towards plant, and the case must not be treated lightly.

Conclusion

Responsibility for developing a cost-conscious outlook among employees rests largely with the supervisor who can assess the general attitude towards equipment and materials, and impress upon employees the important role they play in keeping costs down.

Eliminating waste is a vital part of the supervisory function. The supervisor must wholeheartedly support the use of various techniques which attempt to improve a generally poor situation. Value Analysis is a typical example where the supervisor can play an important part. This technique is described in Chapter XXIII. The success of such a scheme relies upon contributions from *all* employees. Supervisors must appreciate the significance of this fact and stress its importance to subordinates.

Similarly, the use of committees to control costs is becoming more popular as a means of creating enthusiasm among employees to be cost-conscious. A carefully-run suggestion scheme is a further method which is described in Chapter X. Some suggestion schemes have been very successful, and this technique is still undeveloped in many companies. Finally, the supervisor can make great improvements by attending to the many causes of waste which have already been described.

QUESTIONS

1. Discuss the problem of attitudes towards waste in the factory.
2. Outline the main sources of waste in a factory and state how you would attempt to reduce them.
3. There are two main ways of reducing costs which are termed direct methods and indirect methods. Explain how the supervisor can use both methods effectively.
4. As a supervisor, how would you conduct a cost reduction programme?
5. Discuss the ways in which labour costs could be reduced.
6. What methods would you employ for a survey of materials costs in your section?
7. In what ways could you develop a cost-conscious outlook among your subordinates?
8. What arguments would you use to convince an employee that cost reduction is very important?
9. How would you deal with an employee who has carelessly broken a tool if he says, "I can't see that it matters; there are plenty more in the stores and the firm can afford it"?
10. What measures can a supervisor take to cut down waste?
11. Describe ways of improving plant efficiency.
12. Outline a plan for an initial survey of the effectiveness of your department.

PART III: SUGGESTED PROJECTS

1. Conduct a small work study project in your establishment. Outline the procedure to be adopted; record your findings and any resistance by subordinates; give an account of the installation of the new method; and follow-up. Keep a detailed record of your study and include your personal observations.

2. Revise the layout of your workshop. Draw up diagrams to show the existing layout and the proposed layout. Include a detailed account of the reasons for your proposals and the probable snags you would expect to encounter during the changeover period.

3. Choose two assembly operations and carry out a thorough study of the methods in use. Revise the operations using the principles of method study and motion economy.

Write a detailed report on the existing operations and the proposed changes.

4. Conduct a survey of the existing production control system in your establishment. Analyse the system and the requirements; re-design a new system utilising Gantt charts if they are not already employed.

5. Study labour and machine utilisation in your concern. Draw up the existing scheme and re-design or design a scheme if one is not already in existence.

6. Study the production system in your concern and plan or revise a system of progressing. Illustrate your method with suitable diagrams and explanations.

7. Investigate the inspection activities in your establishment and devise a suitable system of quality control.

Make an account of the existing arrangements and justify your proposed scheme.

TERMS USED AT MEETINGS

Acclamation. A form of voting, in which those present at a meeting indicate their approval of the motion in no uncertain manner by loud cheering or the clapping of hands, etc. It does not necessarily mean unanimity, but the small minority of dissenting voices (if any) are obviously overwhelmed.

Ad hoc. This term means "arranged for a particular purpose". An *ad hoc* committee may be appointed to investigate or carry out work which is outside the constitution of the committee.

Addendum. An amendment to a motion by adding words. The original wording of the motion is not altered.

Addressing the Chair. Any member who wishes to speak should address the chair by saying: "Mr. Chairman" or "Madam Chairman". The speech should be addressed to the chair, as discussions between members are not normally allowed.

Adjournment. If the constitution allows, the chairman may adjourn a meeting, with the consent of members, because of shortage of time or to postpone further discussion.

Agenda. A list of the items for discussion in correct sequence is circulated to members in advance of the meeting, to give them the opportunity to consider the topics and to gather any information.

Amendment. An amendment to a motion actually amends the original wording by adding or removing words. If members agree to the amendment it becomes part of the motion which is then subject to further amendment if so desired.

Ballot. A method of voting employed when secrecy is desired, e.g. in parliamentary and other elections.

Casting vote. Normally the chairman is allowed a second vote, if there is an equal number of votes for and against a motion.

Closure. If a member has grounds for wishing the discussion on an item to stop he may submit a motion for closure.

Constitution. The rules and regulations drawn up which govern the way the committee should conduct proceedings.

Co-option. An individual may be co-opted, or asked to join the committee, although he has not been elected. This procedure is designed to allow a person who can offer advice to be present at the meeting, or to fill a vacancy which occurs between election times.

Delegate. A representative of others. He attends the meeting but his powers are limited compared with those of a member.

Dropped motion. A term applied to a motion which, with the consent of the meeting, has been withdrawn, abandoned or allowed to lapse by the original mover. The term is also used to describe a motion which failed to find a seconder, i.e. where the rules require a seconder.

Ex officio. A person who is appointed to a committee by virtue of the office he holds. He is not appointed as an individual and therefore if he changes his office the new holder automatically assumes his membership of the committee.

Formal motion. A motion intended to alter the procedure of a meeting, e.g. to curtail discussion, to adjourn the meeting, etc., and not requiring any previous notice. If misused, it is referred to as a "dilatory" motion.

Going into committee. If an unrestricted discussion is thought to be necessary, a motion may be moved to "go into committee". When sufficient time has passed, a further motion to "resume the meeting" is moved.

Majority. The number required to carry a motion is provided in the constitution. This number is known as the majority.

Minutes. A record of the proceedings at a meeting. The amount of detail is regulated by the constitution.

Motion. A proposal which is submitted by a member for discussion and approval, or rejection by vote. The motion may be submitted in writing before the meeting or submitted during the meeting verbally. A seconder is required where it is the practice of the meeting.

Point of order. At any meeting, a member may, at any time and without notice, interrupt debate by raising a "point of order", i.e. by drawing the chairman's attention to some irregularity in the proceedings, such as the use of offensive language, irrelevancy, breach of the rules, etc.

Proxy. Literally, one acting for another, or a document giving authority to one person to act for another. Thus, it may refer to a person appointed to attend a meeting (or meetings) on behalf of the appointor and to vote on his behalf—or to the proxy form on which such authority is given.

Quorum. The minimum number of members who must be present before the meeting may commence. The quorum is given in the constitution.

Requisition. As used in relation to a requisitioned meeting, the action of calling for the convening of a meeting, e.g. a right is sometimes given in the rules entitling a certain specified minority of members to requisition the convening body to call a meeting. The word "requisition" is also used to describe the document in which the written demand is made.

Rescission. The rescission of a resolution is usually regarded as sufficiently important to merit special treatment; thus, the rules may provide that it cannot be rescinded until a certain time has elapsed and, even then, an extended period of notice may be required for the meeting at which it is proposed to effect the rescission.

Resolution. A formal decision reached by the submission of a motion which is seconded and carried by the majority.

Right of reply. The proposer has the right of reply when the motion has been fully discussed. After the reply the motion is put to the meeting.

Special business. All business other than that which, according to the rules, constitutes "ordinary business". Meetings convened for the purpose of transacting special business often require longer than the usual period of notice. The notice convening the meeting should be explicit, and draw attention to the fact that special business is to be transacted.

Standing orders. The name given to the rules regulating the conduct and procedure of certain deliberative and legislative bodies, such as the permanent standing orders of local authorities.

Ultra vires. Beyond the legal power or authority of (say) a company; for example, a company may act "ultra vires" if it exceeds the authority it derives from the "objects" clause of its Memorandum of Association.

BIBLIOGRAPHY

Anson, C. J., *Quality Control as a Tool for Production (Seminar)*, British Productivity Council

Argyris, C., *On Organisations of the Future*, Sage, 1974

Batty, J., *Management Accountancy*, Macdonald & Evans, 1975

Beer, S., *Cybernetics and Management*, English Universities Press, 1968

British Institute of Management, *Production Control in the Small Factory*

British Standards Institution, *Anthropometric Recommendations for Dimensions of Office Machines, Operators' Chairs, and Desks*, No. BS 3404
Glossary of Terms in Work Study

Brown, J. A. C., *The Social Psychology of Industry*, Penguin, 1973

Cuming, M. W., *The Theory and Practice of Personnel Management*, Heinemann, 1975

Currie, R. M., *Work Study*, Pitman, 1977

Dunette, M. D., *Handbook of Industrial and Organizational Psychology*, Rand McNally, 1976

Fayol, H., *General and Industrial Management*, Pitman, 1967

Follett, M. P., *Dynamic Administration*, Pitman, 1973

Frank, W. F., *The Legal Aspects of Industry and Commerce*, Harrap, 1975

Gellerman, S. W., *Management by Motivation*, American Management Association, 1968

Graham, H. T., *Human Resources Management*, Macdonald & Evans, 1978

Gregory, D. & Ward, H., *Statistics for Business Studies*, McGraw-Hill, 1974

Hanson, J. L., *A Textbook of Economics*, Macdonald & Evans, 1977

Her Majesty's Stationery Office, *Industrial Training Act 1964*
Employment Protection (Consolidation) Act 1978
Health and Safety at Work etc. Act 1974
A Short Guide to the Factories Act 1961
Noise and the Worker (Safety, Health and Welfare, New Series No. 25)

Herzberg, F., *The Motivation to Work*, Wiley, 1972
Work and the Nature of Man, Crosby Lockwood, 1975

Houlden, B. T., *Some Techniques of Operational Research*, English Universities Press 1969

Illuminating Engineering Society, *I.E.S. Code for Lighting in Buildings*

International Labour Office, *Accident Prevention*

Likert, R. & Likert, J. G., *New Ways of Managing Conflict*, McGraw-Hill, 1976

McClelland, D. C., *The Achieving Society*, Free Press, 1967

McGregor, D., *The Human Side of Enterprise*, McGraw-Hill, 1960

Munro Fraser, J., *Employment Interviewing*, Macdonald & Evans, 1978

Murrell, K. F. H., *Ergonomics*, Chapman & Hall, 1965

Parker, Brown, Child & Smith, *The Sociology of Industry*, Allen & Unwin, 1977

Taylor, F. W., *Scientific Management*, Greenwood, 1972

Urwick, L. F., *Elements of Administration*, Pitman, 1974

Whitmore, D. A., *Work Study and Related Management Services*, Heinemann, 1968

Wood, F. & Hellings, J., *Accounting and Finance*, Longman, 1975

Works of Reference

Whitaker's Almanack. Contains a wide range of information on world affairs and the United Kingdom. Statistical information, banking, trade unions, etc.

Pears Cyclopædia. A variety of subjects including events, gazetteer, office compendium, personalities, ready reckoner, and legal data.

Government Reports. Official reports of proceedings in Parliament are called *Hansard.* The report is given verbatim (word for word).

Year Books. These give full details of an organisation in diary form. A county council, for example, generally prepares a year book which gives meetings, council members, standing orders, and any further information which will be of interest to the public.

Stock Exchange Official Year Book. A comprehensive guide to companies quoted on the Stock Exchange.

Technical Dictionaries. There are a number of technical dictionaries available on most subjects.

Encyclopædia Britannica. A comprehensive survey of universal general knowledge.

Keesing's Contemporary Archives. A weekly diary of world events with an index continually kept up to date.

INDEX

Technical jargon, 175
Technical skill, 16
Temperament, 125
Temperamental person, 129
Temperature and humidity, 314
Terminal and contract costing, 425
Terminal loop, control of, 323
Terminations, 231
Terms used at meetings, 454
T-group training, 153
Theories X and Y, 152
Theory of probability, 404
Therblig, 338
Timekeeping, 243
Time scale charts, 339
Time study, 350
Total cost, 425
Trade Union and Labour Relations Act
 1974, 267, 283, 313
Trades Union Congress, 275
Trade unions, 4, 134, 274
 forms of organisation, 274
 objects, 274
 structure, 274
Trading profit, 414
Training, 102, 217, 247, 305
 analytical method, 251
 environment, 251
 existing employees, 263
 importance of, 247
 scope of, 248
 supervisors, 19
 traditional method, 251
 within industry, 22, 23
Training methods
 planned programme, 249
 trial and error, 249
Training programme
 available facilities, 255, 256
 choice of methods, 255, 257
 plan, 255, 259
 results, 264
Transfers, 230, 231
Transient loop, control of, 323
Trend charts, 362
Tribunal, the, 226, 236
Tribunal hearing, 237
Truck Acts 1831/37/96 and 1940, 308
T.U.C., 67, 247
 delegates to Congress, 275
 General Council, 276
 objects, 275
Two-handed process chart, 338

Unconscious level, 124

Unit costing, 425
Unit expediting, 393
Unofficial benefits, 317
Urwick, L., 92, 94
Use of machines and equipment, 335

Value analysis, 337, 356
Value judgments, 107
Variable costs, 437, 439
Variable element time study, 352
Variables
 assignable, 403
 chance, 403
Varifactor synthesis, 351
VeFAC programming, 351
Vicarious liability, 290

Wages, 37, 75, 332
Wages Councils Act 1959, 308
Wages regulation order, 308
Washrooms, 316
Waste, 445
Weighted mean, 370
Weiner, N., 353
Welfare, 218, 307
 legal requirements, 307
Whitley Committee, 270
Whitley, J. H., 270
Whitmore, D. A., 352
WOFAC Corporation of America,
 351
Work factor (P.M.T.S.), 339
Work flow, 334
Work measurement, 310, 349
 application, 349
 techniques, 350
Work rate and fatigue, 303
Working area, 346
Working capital, 410
Working conditions, 135, 314
Working plan, organisation, 45
Works of reference, 456
Workshop layout, 334
Workshop schedule, 398
Work study, 101, 328
 aims, 329
 ancillary techniques, 349
 and the individual, 330
 definition, 328
 practitioner, 330
 scope, 329
 techniques, 337

Z charts, 364